Concord in Discourse

Approaches to Semiotics
125

Editorial Committee

Thomas A. Sebeok
Roland Posner
Alain Rey

Mouton de Gruyter
Berlin · New York

Concord in Discourse

Harmonics and Semiotics
in Late Classical and Early Medieval Platonism

by
Stephen Gersh

Mouton de Gruyter
Berlin · New York   1996

Mouton de Gruyter (formerly Mouton, The Hague) is a Division of Walter de Gruyter & Co., Berlin.

㉾ Printed on acid-free paper which falls within the guidelines of the ANSI to ensure permanence and durability.

Library of Congress Cataloging-in-Publication-Data

> Gersh, Stephen.
> Concord in discourse : harmonics and semiotics in late classical and early medieval Platonism / by Stephen Gersh.
> p. cm. − (Approaches to semiotics ; 125)
> Includes bibliographical references and index.
> ISBN 3-11-014684-3 (cloth ; alk. paper)
> 1. Semiotics. 2. Discourse analysis. 3. Language and languages − Philosophy. 4. Order (Philosophy) 5. Harmony (Philosophy) 6. Neoplatonism. I. Title. II. Series.
> P99.G47 1996
> 302.2−dc20 96-10922
> CIP

Die Deutsche Bibliothek − Cataloging-in-Publication-Data

> **Gersh, Stephen:**
> Concord in discourse : harmonics and semiotics in late classical and early medieval Platonism / by Stephen Gersh. − Berlin ; New York : Mouton de Gruyter, 1996
> (Approaches to semiotics ; 125)
> ISBN 3-11-014684-3
> NE: GT

© Copyright 1996 by Walter de Gruyter & Co., D-10785 Berlin
All rights reserved, including those of translation into foreign languages. No part of this book may be reproduced or transmitted in any form or by any means, electronic or mechanical, including photocopy, recording or any information storage and retrieval system, without permission in writing from the publisher.
Disc conversion: Fotosatz-Service Köhler OHG. − Printing: Gerike GmbH. − Binding: Lüderitz & Bauer, Berlin.
Printed in Germany.

A. G. G. in memoriam

Acknowledgements

Sections of this text were originally presented as lectures to the following organizations in Europe and North America: the Centre National de la Recherche Scientifique, U. P. R. 76 — Histoire des doctrines de la fin de l'Antiquité et du haut Moyen Âge, Paris; the Centre d'Information et de Documentation „Recherche Musicale", Paris; the Département de Philosophie, Université de Paris XII — Val de Marne; the Warburg Institute, University of London; the Center for Medieval and Renaissance Studies, University of California at Los Angeles; and the Department of Romance Languages, University of Washington at Seattle. I should like to thank participants in those meetings for suggestions incorporated into the final version. In addition, the following individuals allowed me to benefit from their knowledge by providing textual references, transcriptions of manuscripts, and miscellaneous information: M. Allen, W. Beierwaltes, C. Bower, C. Burnett, M. Dixsaut, P. Dronke, H. Dufourt, É. Jeauneau, F. Lochner, D. O'Brien, B. Panciera, and E. Vance.

Miramar, Puerto Rico,
December, 1992   *Stephen Gersh*

Table of Contents

Conventions of translation and transliteration xii

Introduction 1
0.1 Modern notions of structure and signification 1

Part I: Concord 11
Chapter 1: Concord in general 13

1.1 Harmony, signification, and the structure of semantic fields . . 13
1.2 The schemata of writing and reading 17
1.3 Augustine's understanding of order and concord 21
1.4 Eriugena's understanding of order and harmony 28
1.5 Musical paradigms in Augustine and Boethius 34
1.6 The concept of relation in ancient and modern philosophy 45
Excursus to Chapter 1 56
Excursus to section 1.3 56
Excursus to section 1.5 58

Part II: The logical 67
Chapter 2: Components of concord — Binary relations
 (ontological) 69

2.1 Eriugena and the square of opposition 69
2.2 Relation in ps.-Augustine: *Categoriae decem* 73
2.3 Eriugena's theory of relation 77
2.4 Ratio in Boethius' *De institutione arithmetica* 86
2.5 Eriugena's theory of ratio 89
2.6 Extensions of the Eriugenian theory of ratio 97
Excursus to Chapter 2 104
Excursus to section 2.2 104
Excursus to section 2.4 107
Excursus to section 2.6 111

x   Table of Contents

Part III: The harmonic 113
Chapter 3: Components of concord — Ternary relations
      (ontological) 115

3.1 Trinitarian concord in Thierry of Chartres and his sources 115
3.2 The resolution of oppositions according to Augustine 121
3.3 Mediation in the cosmology and psychology of Calcidius 128
3.4 Ancient and medieval antecedents of the "semiotic square" ... 139
3.5 Mediation in the cosmology and angelology of Eriugena 141
3.6 The Eriugenian transcendent harmony 156
Excursus to Chapter 3 167
Excursus 1 to section 3.4 167
Excursus 2 to section 3.4 170
Excursus 3 to section 3.4 172

Part IV: The semiotic 179
Chapter 4: Components of concord — Ternary relations
      (semantic) 181

4.1 Eriugena and the triad of signifier, signified, and signification 181
4.2 Signification in Martianus Capella: *De nuptiis Philologiae et Mercurii* 188
4.3 Eriugena's theory of signification 191
4.4 Symbolism in ps.-Dionysius' *De caelesti hierarchia* 199
4.5 Eriugena's theory of symbolism 201
4.6 Extensions of the Eriugenian theory of symbolism 216
Excursus to Chapter 4 221
Excursus to section 4.2 221
Excursus to section 4.4 224
Excursus to section 4.6 227

Part V: Translations and commentary 229
Chapter 5: The notion of concord in ancient and medieval
      philosophy 231

5.1 Concord among angels and saints 233
5.2 Concord in the spiritual world 236
5.3 Concord in the world soul 240
5.4 Concord of the elements in the world 248
5.5 Concord among planets and stars 255
5.6 Concord in the celestial world 265

5.7 Concord in the human soul 268
5.8 Concord of the elements in man 271

Notes 274

Bibliographies 341
Addenda to bibliography (1995) 379

Index 380

Conventions of translation and transliteration

1. *Latin citation*. Phrases and sentences translated from Latin are occasionally introduced by the symbol †. This indicates that the syntactic context if not the basic meaning of the original has been altered in order to facilitate rapid citation.

2. *Concordia/harmonia, proportio*. Translation shifts from "concord" to "harmony" and back reflecting changes between *concordia* and *harmonia* in the original sources. Augustine uses the first term primarily, Eriugena the second term primarily, and Boethius both terms equally. However, these and other writers treat them as broad equivalents within the metaphysical context. Translation also shifts between "ratio" and "proportion". When the Latin *proportio* occurs on its own in the sources and signifies a 2-term numerical relation, "ratio" is the more natural English rendering. But when the term occurs in the sources together with *proportionalitas* [proportionality] which signifies a 3-term numerical relation, "proportion" more accurately reflects the original usage.

3. *Greek transliteration*. Phrases and sentences quoted in Greek have normally been transliterated according to a standard modern practice. However, in cases where such terminology comes not from an original Greek text but via a Latin intermediary, some degree of variation has been permitted.

Introduction

0.1 Modern notions of structure and signification

A Tandem Fama nuntiante cognoscunt quod Phoebo gaudet Parnasia rupes. Licet inde quoque ad Indici montis secretum obumbratumque scopulum nube perpetua posterius migrasse perhibebant, tamen Cirrhaeos tunc recessus et sacrati specus loquacia antra conveniunt. Illic autem circumstabat in ordinem quicquid imminet saeculorum, Fortunae urbium nationumque, omnium regum ac totius populi. Videbantur aliae transacti cursus emensa fugientes; consistebant aliae sub conspectu, adveniebantque quamplures, atque ita nonnullis eminus vanescebat disparata prolixitas, ut velut fumidae caligationis incredibilis haberetur aura. Inter haec mira spectacula Fortunarumque cursus motus nemorum etiam susurrantibus flabris canora modulatio melico quodam crepitabat appulsu. Nam eminentiora prolixarum arborum culmina perindeque distenta acuto sonitu resultabant; quicquid vero terrae confine ac propinquum ramis acclinibus fuerat, gravitas rauca quatiebat. At media ratis per annexa succentibus duplis ac sesqualteris nec non etiam sesquitertiis, sesquioctavis etiam sine discretione iuncturis, licet intervenirent limmata, concinebant. Ita fiebat, ut nemus illud harmoniam totam superumque carmen modulationum congruentia personaret. Quod quidem exponente Cyllenio Virtus edidicit etiam in caelo orbes parili ratione aut concentus edere aut succentibus convenire. Nec mirum quod Apollinis silva ita rata modificatione congrueret, cum caeli quoque orbes idem Delius moduletur in Sole, hincque esse quod illic Phoebus et hic vocitetur Auricomus; nam Solis augustum caput radiis perfusum circumactumque flammantibus velut auratam caesariem rutili verticis imitatur; hinc quoque Sagittarius, hinc quoque Vulnificus, quod possit radiorum iaculis icta penetrare.

[Thanks to Rumour's report, they eventually learn that the rock of Parnassus is graced by the presence of Phoebus. Although one also heard that he had since departed for the peak of an Indian mountain hidden and shaded by perpetual cloud, they nevertheless repair to his Cirrhaean abode and the talkative recesses of his sacred cave. All around there stood in due order the events which time will bring to pass: the fortunes of cities and nations, of all kings and every people. Some of these appeared to flee on completing their measured course; others stood in full view; many were approaching. Some vanished afar, with so great a distance between them that a mysterious gust of dark vapour seemed to seize them. Amid these wondrous sights and the vicissitudes of Fortune, a sweet harmony arose from the movement of the trees as the breezes whispered through them with a certain melodious effect. For the crests of the largest trees, being more elevated and therefore extended, resonated with the highest pitch. The roughness of the lowest pitch shook whatever was close or near to the ground in drooping boughs. But the crests of the median trees in the fixed intervals of their mutual accompaniments sounded duple (2:1), sesquialter (3:2), sesquiterce (4:3), and even indivisible sesquioctave (9:8) intervals not without intervening limmata. So it happened that this grove resounded with the whole of harmony and the divine song in the consonance of its modulation. As the Cyllenian explained these things, Virtue also learned that the heavenly spheres emit melodies or contribute to their accompaniments in a similar manner. And it is not surprising that Apollo's grove is concordant in such a fixed harmony, since the same Delian god in the shape of the sun also modulates the heavenly spheres. So it happens that in one place he is called Phoebus and in another Auricomus — because the august head of the sun filled and encircled by flaming rays is akin to a shining head of golden hair. For this reason, he is also called Sagittarius and also Vulnificus, since he can penetrate what he strikes in casting his rays]. Martianus Capella: *De nuptiis Philologiae et Mercurii* I. 11–13.

B Mais il suffit d'écouter la poésie, ce qui sans doute était le cas de F. de Saussure, pour que s'y fasse entendre une polyphonie et que tout discours s'avère s'aligner sur les plusieurs portées d'une partition. Nulle chaîne signifiante en effet qui ne soutienne comme appendu à la ponctuation de chacune de ses unités tout ce qui s'articule de contextes attestés, à la verticale, si l'on peut dire, de ce point. C'est ainsi que pour reprendre notre mot: arbre, non plus dans son isolation nominale, mais au terme d'une de ces ponctuations, nous verrons que ce n'est pas seulement à la faveur du fait que le mot barre est son anagramme, qu'il franchit celle de l'algorithme saussurien. Car décomposé dans le double spectre de ses voyelles et de ses consonnes, il appelle avec le robre et le platane les significations dont il se charge sous notre flore, de force et de majesté. Drainant tous les contextes symboliques où il est pris dans l'hébreu de la Bible, il dresse sur une butte sans frondaison l'ombre de la croix. Puis se réduit à l'Y majuscule du signe de la dichotomie qui, sans l'image historiant l'armorial, ne devrait rien à l'arbre, tout généalogique qu'il se dise. Arbre circulatoire, arbre de vie du cervelet, arbre de Saturne ou de Diane, cristaux précipités en un arbre conducteur de la foudre, est-ce votre figure qui trace notre destin dans l'écaille passée au feu de la tortue, ou votre éclair qui fait surgir d'une innombrable nuit cette lente mutation de l'être dans l'*hen panta* du langage:

> *Non! dit l'Arbre, il dit: Non! dans l'étincellement*
> *De sa tête superbe*

vers que nous tenons pour aussi légitimes à être entendus dans les harmoniques de l'arbre que leur revers:

> *Que la tempête traite universellement*
> *Comme elle fait une herbe.*

Car cette strophe moderne s'ordonne selon la même loi du parallélisme du signifiant, dont le concert régit la primitive geste slave et la poésie chinoise la plus raffinée. Comme il se voit dans le commun mode de l'étant où sont choisis l'arbre et l'herbe, pour qu'y adviennent les signes de contradiction du: dire "Non!" et du: traiter comme, et qu'à travers le contraste catégorique du particularisme de la *superbe* à l'*universellement* de sa réduction, s'achève dans la condensation de la tête et de la tempête l'indiscernable étincellement de l'instant éternel.

[But it is enough to listen to poetry — as was undoubtedly the case with F. de Saussure — for a polyphony to make itself heard and for all discourse to appear laid out along the various staves of a musical score. In fact, there is no signifying chain which does not subtend, as though attached to the punctuation of each of its units, all the relevant contexts articulated vertically, so to speak, in respect of this point. In such a manner, we shall see by citing our word "tree" once again — this time not as an isolated noun but at the boundary-point of one of these punctuations — that it crosses the bar of the Saussurian algorithm not only through the fact that the word "bar" is its anagram (barre → arbre). For broken down into the twofold spectrum of its vowels and consonants, it recalls along with the rubber and the plane tree the significations of strength and majesty which it possesses according to our flora. Tapping all the symbolic contexts where it occurs in the Hebrew of the Bible, it sets up on a leafless mound the shadow of the cross. Then it is reduced to the capital Y of the sign of dichotomy which, were it not for the image adorning a book of heraldry, would owe nothing to a tree however genealogical it is said to be. Circulatory tree, tree of life in the cerebellum, tree of Saturn or of Diana, crystals precipitated in a tree conducting lightning, is it your countenance which traces our destiny in the tortoise-shell heated by a fire, or your irradiation which gives rise to that slow mutation of being from the unnameable night in the *hen panta* of language?

> *No! says the Tree. It says: No! in the sparking*
> *Of its proud head*

lines which we consider as legitimately understandable in terms of the tree's harmonics as are their continuation:

> *Which the storm treats as universally*
> *As it does the grass.*

This modern verse is arranged according to the same law of the signifier's parallelism which harmoniously governs both the primitive Slavic epic and the most refined Chinese poetry. This is apparent from the selection of the tree and the grass from a common mode of existence so that the signs of contradiction — saying "No!" and treating as — may occur there, and that through the categorical contrast of the particularity of *proud* with the *universally* of its reduction may be accomplished in the condensation of the head (*tête*) and the storm (*tempête*) the indiscernible sparkling of the eternal instant].
Lacan: 1966: 503–504.

A satisfactory understanding of these two passages is perhaps to be realized only after completion of the analysis which they demand, though even before it the reader may detect with what ingenuity they interconnect the topics of harmony and signification. This interconnection represented in ancient times and still represents in the modern era a certain profound intuition. So it easily justifies its own exploitation in a discussion which is both historical and speculative. But since one could argue that what is interconnected with signification is nowadays structure rather than harmony, some observations on this further topic are worth inserting as preface to any commentary arising from the two passages themselves.

The notion of "structure"[1] can be interpreted ontologically or semantically — that is, with the structured terms corresponding to existent things or to semantic properties[2] — and in modern times it is the second viewpoint which has predominated.[3] Why? Undoubtedly because structure itself is seen to be significant and signification itself to be structured.

Considering it initially from a pre-semiotic angle[4], we can say that the modern account of structure has a minimalist component. Structure is here understood as a relation between 2 terms such that each exists through or is known through the other[5], this relation — since there are only 2 terms involved — being best characterized as "opposition"[6]. The modern account of structure can also be said to have a maximalist element. Here, structure is conceived as a relation between n terms such that each exists through or is known through all the others[7], this relation — since there are now n terms involved — being best characterized as "difference".[8] That both varieties of structure involve relations between terms such that each exists through or is known through the other(s) is the reason why structure in general can be said to depend more on its relation than on its related terms.[9]

Yet structure is often viewed as equivalent to signification, because its underlying relation, seen primarily in the form of difference-in-sameness, is itself identified with the significant. In fact, signification can only arise from the relation of difference-in-sameness. For example, where two terms differ as the presence and absence of some determination, the difference is significant on one condition: that both the presence and absence of that determination are combined with the presence of a further determination. Conversely, signification cannot arise from the relation of difference alone. The apparent suggestion of Derrida that this is possible depends on certain further assumptions: i. that the two terms differing as presence and absence of a determination can be treated as a single term in violation of the law of contradiction — the difference therefore providing its own sameness — and ii. that the two terms differing as presence and absence of a determination can be combined with a third term which is left unexpressed, such assumptions being integrated easily into the polysemous discourse of "différance".[10] In short, since the underlying relation, seen primarily in the form of difference-in-sameness, can be identified with signification, structure itself may be viewed as equivalent to the significant.

But Eco has criticized the linguist Jakobson for describing two different things as "structures": a set of differential elements which are not meaningful in themselves — viz. the phonemic units —, and a set of differential elements correlated with another set of differential elements and becoming meaningful through that correlation — viz. the phonemic units correlated with semantic components — ; whereas Eco himself prefers to call the former a "structure" and the latter a "code".[11] Such criticism which implies the possibility of dissociating structure and signification conceals a complex sequence of premisses. 1. Relation is difference while correlation is difference-in-sameness; 2. Only correlation produces meaning; 3. Structure is relation while code is correlation; and 4. Only code involves meaning. Now it is perhaps justifiable to argue that structure implies relation or difference (= 3) and that meaning implies correlation or difference-in-sameness (= 2). Yet it does not follow that structure can be non-meaningful. Two things differ in possessing-not possessing some property with respect to their simultaneous possession of a further property: e.g. /b/ and /p/ differ in being voiced-unvoiced with respect to their simultaneous status as bilabially plosive. In other words, this relation is itself *co*-relative in nature.

Considering it from a post-semiotic angle,[12] we can therefore say that the modern analysis of structure has as its minimalist component: a *sig-*

nifying relation between 2 terms such that each exists through or is known through the other, this relation — given that there are only 2 terms involved — being describable as "signifying opposition". The modern analysis of structure can also be said to have as its maximalist element: a *signifying* relation between n terms such that each exists through or is known through all the others, this relation — given that there are now n terms involved being describable as "signifying difference".

However, if there is a functional equivalence between structure and signification, one should not assume a similar equivalence between structure and sign. This is especially the case when the latter is understood from the orthodox Saussurian viewpoint as that union between acoustic image = signifier and concept = signified on which oral language is founded.[13] In fact, the non-equivalence between structure and sign in this sense was demonstrated by some of the best critical writing of the 1970s.

An illustration of this tendency is provided by an argument of Kristeva:

1. She argues initially for replacement of the unity of sign by the plurality of "network".[14] Whereas signs or single vertical relations between terms have been the object of conventional semiotics[15] — especially those linking the Saussurian signifiers and signifieds — networks or pluralities of vertical-horizontal relations between terms must be the object of its regenerate counterpart.[16] In accordance with Saussure's own teaching about anagrams,[17] these networks of vertical-horizontal relations must not only be studied but also produced[18] as models of vertical-horizontal relations.

2. The models or "paragrams"[19] constitute formalizations of relations[20] arising within texts, between texts, or within and between texts.[21] Within texts, they may contain varying numbers of relations: a comparatively large number, a comparatively moderate number, or a comparatively small number.[22] Between texts, the paragrams may exhibit various types of relation: linking writer to reader, linking writer to anterior text, linking reader to anterior text, or linking writer to reader and to anterior text.[23] Within and between texts, they may embody other types of relation: linking phonemic or phonemic to non-phonemic units, linking semantic or semantic to non-semantic units, or linking syntactic or syntactic to non-syntactic units.[24]

3. These quasi-mathematical[25] models are also to be understood as dynamic in contrast to the staticity of traditional notions of "form",[26] and infinite in contrast to the finitude of traditional ideas of "system".[27] How-

ever, the presence of these two characteristics is particularly associated with a further refinement of the theory.

4. The models or paragrams constituting formalizations of relations arising within, between, or within and between what are now styled "phano-texts" exist in relation to another level of linguistic functioning now labelled "geno-text".[28] Geno-text can be contrasted with phano-text as productive to communicative,[29] as signifier to signified,[30] and — in a spatial analogy — as depth to surface.[31] Corresponding to an apparatus of signifying practices in general,[32] the geno-text may also be defined negatively as neither transcendent object[33] nor transcendent thought[34] and positively as both plurality[35] and totality.[36] Corresponding to any individual printed text,[37] a phano-text may also be described as that object of structural semantics[38] whose fundamental unit is the signifying ensemble.[39] Geno-text has a relation to phano-text which is materially implicative,[40] activated in the process of reading,[41] and forming a point of intersection — another spatial image[42] — called the "signifying differential".

5. Kristeva argues ultimately for replacement of the unity of sign by the plurality of a "signifying differential"[43] although aspects of the unity of sign are preserved.[44] This signifying differential — which underlies all the vertical-horizontal relations between terms:[45] that is, in their dynamic extension from the word-sign to the infinite signifier,[46] all the semic articulations of homonymy, synonymy,[47] etc. — is the object of a regenerate semiotics.[48] The signifying differential owes something to the notion of distinctive features in Prague linguistic theory[49] and to that of the signifying chain in Lacanian psychoanalysis,[50] although dispensing with the former's assumption of fixed opposition and with the latter's of fundamental units.

According to this argument, although there may be a functional equivalence between structure and signification — in the sense of signifying differential[51] — one should not assume a similar equivalence between structure and sign. The same conclusion emerges when the latter is considered not just from the Saussurian viewpoint as the union between acoustic image and concept[52] but in the variety of its traditional philosophical guises. In fact, the non-equivalence between structure and sign in general is the only assumption which makes this historical variation intelligible.

A typology of earlier theories might be sketched in the following way:

The minimalist post-semiotic structure discussed earlier[53] provides the starting-point. This structure is analyzable into a. referent, b. relation, and

c. relatum[54] or else — with caution against misinterpretation in Saussurian terms — into a. signifier, b. signification, and c. signified[55] or else — using language less redolent of Saussure — into a. significatory referent, b. significatory relation, and c. significatory relatum. It is easy to demonstrate that most philosophical theories of the sign have operated with this underlying signifying structure, such accounts differing among themselves only 1. according to their mode of realizing the units a, b, and c; and 2. according to their selection among the units a, b, and c to be realized. In case 1, the units may be treated as ontological, conceptual, or linguistic.[56] For example, Peirce's representamen[57] is an ontological realization of a; the Saussurian signifier and Hjelmslev's "substance of expression"[58] its conceptual realization. Hjelmslev's "form of expression"[59] is a linguistic realization of a. The Hjemslevian sign-function[60] is a linguistic realization of b. Frege's referent[61] is an ontological realization of c; the Saussurian signified and Hjelmslev's "substance of content"[62] its conceptual realization. Hjelmslev's "form of content"[63] is a linguistic realization of c. In case 2, such units may be combined in dyads or triads.[64] For example, Saussure combines signifier and signified in a dyad of conceptually realized a + conceptually realized c; Hjelmslev substance of expression and substance of content in a dyad of conceptually realized a + conceptually realized c.[65] Peirce combines representamen, object, and interpretant in a triad of conceptually realized a + ontologically realized c + conceptually realized c.[66] Since all these philosophical theories of the sign have operated with different modes of realizing the structural units and different selections among the structural units to be realized,[67] it is obvious that the sign corresponds to a particular manifestation of the general signifying structure rather than to that signifying structure itself.

Two further aspects of this signifying structure should be stressed. First, the minimal structure is always expandable since each of its terms is itself a relation between two further terms and each of those further terms itself another relation, etc. — hence arises the maximal structure mentioned earlier.[68] Secondly, the maximal structure is always contractible since any of its relations is itself one term of a further relation and any of those further relations itself another term, etc. Such infinite expansion and contraction through the reciprocal convertibility of relation and term is easy to visualize when the units are linguistic, more difficult when they are conceptual, and most difficult when they are ontological in nature.[69]

This understanding of a signifying structure has been criticized perhaps most articulately by Eco.[70] However, his main arguments that, since a presence is always a non-relational element, a signifying structure opposing a presence to an absence cannot be constituted by relation alone; and that, since a signifying structure by definition opposes a signifier to a signified, the idea of such a structure as consisting of signifiers alone is incoherent, fail to convince. To the first criticism one can reply that only a presence with respect to the given signifying structure is required; with respect to another structure that same presence is reducible to a relation. Furthermore, relation cannot be treated simply as a binary opposition like 0/1. The second criticism can be countered by saying that only a signified with respect to that specific signifying structure is necessary; with respect to another structure that same signified is conceivable as a signifier.[71] Moreover, a signified in the narrow sense of concept prior to language can certainly be ruled out.

As originally suggested, the notion of "structure" can be interpreted ontologically or semantically — where the structured terms correspond to existent things or to semantic properties.[72] Although in modern times it is the second approach which has been dominant, in the ancient and medieval worlds the two approaches were pursued concurrently with the second dependent on the first.[73] Our project is therefore to employ the modern semantic notion of structure to interpret both the ancient ontological and the ancient semantic notions of structure in an intertextual reading.[74] But since the corresponding term *structura* is unknown or rare in the relevant passages, we must begin the detailed analysis with its primary surrogate.[75]

Part I: Concord

Chapter 1

Concord in general

1.1 Harmony, signification, and the structure of semantic fields

Semiotic literature has been marked by a tendency to privilege the "harmonic".[76] This fact strikes any reader of such material who is not entirely satisfied by following the interplay of diversities but also willing to entertain that *homoion theōrein* [contemplation of similarity] described by Aristotle as the mark of superior intelligence.[77] The privileging of harmonic elements is illustrated by one modern phonologist's analogy between the interrelation of phonemes and the articulate sounds representing them and that of values contained in a musical score and their realizations.[78] In his study of native American mythology, another theorist compares the relations between components of mythical narratives and those between the mythical narratives themselves to an elaborate musical structure.[79] This is no passing metaphor but an isomorphism systematically developed, since mythology and music are both conceived as linguistic in character. In fact, a threefold comparison is proposed between articulate speech at one extreme and musical language at the other with mythical expression occupying an intermediate position. But in noting all these tendencies it is important not to reinvent the wheel. That ideas emerging at a particular point in time correspond with others prevalent during earlier periods of human history can easily be obscured through modifications of the conceptual contexts in which these ideas are presented. We must not forget such similar privilegings of harmonic elements as the medieval theologian's analogy between the interrelation of musical sounds and the silences punctuating them and that of substances comprising the created order and their privations.[80]

An attempt follows to explore something diffused through a major segment of literary history which has previously eluded interpretation: the appearance of the lexeme "harmony" and the activation of certain of its semes in conjunction with the lexeme "signification" and the activation of some of its semes in medieval philosophical texts.[81] Given that they are not logical universals capable of abstraction from some particularity, the semantic objects "harmony" and "signification" together with their unfolded properties cannot be comprehended before the textual reading. On the other hand, since they may be treated as *pseudo*-universals for certain limited purposes, these semantic objects and their unfolded properties can perhaps be *pseudo*-summarized in advance of that reading.[82]

It is generally understood that the significant is a species of relative. For example, dictionary definitions[83] of "signification" suggest a relation of something present to something absent leading to communication, where the present element is a conventional token or more specifically a linguistic item:[84] ideas reappearing in that technical definition of "sign" — which has been debated in linguistic and semiotic literature from Saussure onwards[85] — as containing the three aspects of signifier, signified, and signification.[86] It is also obvious, though less frequently discussed, that the harmonic is a species of relative. Thus, dictionary definitions[87] of "harmony" suggest a relation of some quantity to another quantity leading to pleasure, where the two quantities are parts of a whole or more specifically musical pitches in a chord.[88]

That the significant and the harmonic are different species of relative is a statement to which one may quickly agree, and there is abundant testimony in medieval philosophical texts to the drawing of this conclusion. That the significant and the harmonic are a *single* species of relative is a more contentious matter, although evidence for the drawing of this further conclusion by medieval writers is no less abundant.

What seems to have occurred was the transformation of a logical into a semiotic principle. The latter assumes that if two semantic objects contain a sufficient number of properties in common, they may be treated as identical, notwithstanding their actual positions within the logical hierarchy of genus and species.[89] For the significant and the harmonic this sufficiency was achieved through their common properties of relativity and ternarity.

In many texts, harmony is treated as a ternary relation describable as equality, inequality, and harmony itself. This complex relation can arise through 1. the addition of components, 2. the complementarity of relations, 3. the constancy of ratios, or 4. the substitution of properties, examples of the first being provided by A. the theory of versification and of the second by B. the reconciliation of good and evil in the providential order. In as many texts, signification is handled as a ternary relation describable as sameness, difference, and harmony itself. This complex relation can occur between 5. signifier, signified, and signification,

6. mediated signified, unmediated signified, and signification, or 7. signified, signifier, and interpreter, examples of the first being supplied by C. the reconciliation of negative and affirmative in the divine naming and of the second by D. the theory of symbols. Finally, in a few texts the connection between harmony and signification is strengthened by a singular property of harmony as such: a self-contradiction which generates and is sustained by a semantic shift.[90]

So the significant and the harmonic are treated as identical, irrespective of their actual positions within an *Arbor Porphyriana*, because of their common semantic properties of relativity and ternarity. It is important not to forget that a logical principle has been replaced by a semiotic one.[91] Otherwise, many aspects of the broader complex of semes associated with the two primary lexemes will not be understood.

As seems likely, the broader complex of semes[92] conferring an implicit structure on the "harmony-signification" discussion of the medieval period includes the following items: "absolute-relative", "binary-ternary", "simple-complex", "existent-understood", and "dialectical-mathematical". Eventually more discussion will be needed on the reasons for isolating precisely these.[93] For the present, we should merely note: first, the list comprises items ultimately structured in a semantic field rather than an ontological hierarchy; secondly, their interrelation follows not a single but a variety of patterns; third, the list comprises items entirely structured according to textual use rather than abstract reflection.

1. The status of "absolute", "relative", etc. as elements[94] structured in a semantic field will be underlined by our handling of them neither as concepts referring to things, nor as words referring to things, nor as concepts referring to other concepts, but as words referring to other words. This constitutes a purely intensional semantics[95] dealing with the interrelation of semantic objects through the presence of common semantic properties. Yet in the primary texts, the semantic elements distinguished by our analysis will sometimes be treated as concepts or things and sometimes not so treated by the authors themselves. So the purely intensional semantics operates as a sort of zero-degree in comparison with which the departures of medieval writers into psychology or ontology[96] can be measured.

2. The variety of patterns governing the interrelation of items in the list is best explained by considering some of those models for the organization of semantic fields currently under discussion.[97]

A first model is based on what are termed "family resemblances".[98] As applied to the present context, this envisages within a given lexeme an interrelation of sememes through the possession of common semes so that, by beginning with a sememe S_1 containing the semes s_1, s_2, s_3, s_4 and passing through a series including the sememe S_3 which contains as semes s_3, s_4, s_5, s_6, we reach a sememe S_5 containing the semes s_5, s_6, s_7, s_8.[99] The series contains sameness between sememes S_1 and S_2 through the presence of semes s_2, s_3, s_4 in both S_1 and S_2, mediation between sememes S_1 and S_5 through sememe S_3's possession of semes s_4 and s_5, and difference between sememes S_4 and S_5 through the presence of seme s_4 in S_4 and seme s_8 in S_5, and so forth.[100]

The triad of sign, object (or ground), and interpretant in Peirce's semiotics provides a second model.[101] Here the "sign" is something which stands to somebody for something.[102] It produces in the mind of that person an equivalent or more developed sign called the "interpretant" of the first sign.[103] The sign stands for something which is its "object".[104] Yet it stands for that object not in all respects but in reference to an idea called the "ground" of the sign.[105] Furthermore, the interpretant must have a second triadic relation. In this, the sign's relation to its object becomes the interpretant's object and produces another interpretant to this relation. Likewise, the second interpretant will have a third triadic relation. In this, the interpretant's relation to its object becomes the second interpretant's object and produces yet another interpretant to this relation.[106] According to Peirce's theory, the process of interpreting signs continues indefinitely.

For present purposes, it is especially the nature of the interpretant which needs clarification. This emerges not as something physical and perhaps not even as something psychic, but rather as a set of semantic properties.[107] Assuming the single triad as described, a second group of semantic properties will function as the interpretant of a first set by selecting from these first properties. Assuming the multiplication of such triads, a third group of semantic properties will function as the interpretant of the second set by selecting from these second properties, and so on.[108] In both these cases, selection may occur in accordance with sameness or difference of properties. Sameness between two groups of semantic properties means that these properties are named by the same interpretant. Difference between two sets of semantic properties means that the properties are named by different interpretants.[109]

A third model consists of what is termed the "semiotic square".[110] According to this, a semantic element should be viewed as possessing a special type of relationality which permits it to be analyzed into the semes s_1 and s_2 of a first, the semes s_2 and $\bar{s}_1$ of a second, the semes $\bar{s}_1$ and $\bar{s}_2$ of a third, and the semes $\bar{s}_2$ and s_1 of a fourth semantic axis.[111] In addition, each of the four semes resulting from this process may be combinable with each of the four semes resulting from analysis of another semantic element.[112] The relations emerging between different pairs of semes are now defined more precisely as contrariety on the axes between s_1 and s_2 and between $\bar{s}_2$ and $\bar{s}_1$; as contradiction on the axes between s_1 and $\bar{s}_1$ and between s_2 and $\bar{s}_2$; and as implication on the axes between $\bar{s}_2$ and s_1 and between $\bar{s}_1$ and s_2.[113] In theory, similar relations emerge between the further pairs of semes which interact through criteria like compatibility or incompatibility with the relations between the original pairs.[114]

These three models for the organization of semantic fields can be applied to the list of items distinguished earlier in various ways. Some items may be understood as properties entering into a family-resemblance structure of overlapping samenesses and differences or divided into such a structure, some as constituting pairs of terms whose relation is comprehended through a third term[115] or as constituted by such terms, and some as properties entering into a square pattern of contrary, contradictory, and implicated[116] or divided into such a pattern. In certain situations two or three of these models can be applied simultaneously or in overlap to a given semantic phenomenon.[117]

3. The status of "absolute", "relative", etc. as elements structured according to textual use[118] will be revealed through the complex interdependence between the language of the primary sources and our metalanguage relative to the latter. But at this point, some new factors must be introduced into the discussion.

1.2 The schemata of writing and reading

If it is true that the approach to the history of philosophy in any period called "deconstruction" is a meditation on writing,[119] it is equally true that an approach to the history of philosophy during the Middle Ages of any description is such a meditation. This is because philosophical activity was understood to be primarily exegetical in character during the medieval period, and for medievals and moderns alike exegetical activity focusses attention on the nature of writing as such.

18   *Concord in general*

One justification for the role of interpretation in philosophical method might nowadays run as follows: if philosophy involves an expansion rather than a reduction in language's everyday semantic functions, this expansion is promoted most readily by a system of durable signs.[120] Moreover, if philosophy is expressed more fully through discourse in written than through that in oral form, this written form is comprehended most fully by a systematic method of exegesis. In the Middle Ages, certainly, the role of interpretation in philosophical method was justified along different lines: i.e. that since the written text of the Bible was the ultimate source of philosophical truth, likewise other written texts — themselves interpreting the Bible — were secondary sources of that truth. Nevertheless, this reasoning led in turn to a provocative conception of the exegetical situation itself where the individual who writes is also the reader of an anterior text, that individual reading in the process of writing and writing in the process of reading.[121] Another justification for the role of interpretation in philosophical method today might therefore take the same form: we can write a philosophical text and also be readers of its earlier counterparts, reading those texts in the process of writing and writing that philosophy in the process of reading.[122]

Given that our project constitutes such a reciprocal interaction of interpreting text and interpreted texts, certain features of its presentation are appropriate. For example, the structure of the ensuing discussion as a whole will mirror that of certain primary sources; partial schemata used in that discussion will parallel other patterns arising in the original sources. Such intellectual categories are neither simply established by medieval writing, nor simply projected from modern reading,[123] but generated through the indissoluble combination of the two.

Forming the structure of the entire discussion is a threefold division of topics into "logical", "harmonic", and "semiotic".[124] The triadicity as such subsists in reciprocal dependence with triadicities underlying the narrative structures of many primary sources, although the nature of the triadicity depends reciprocally on a more convoluted semantic structure detectable in those sources. Its topography can be summarized as follows:

i. The lexemes "harmony" and "signification" both contain the semes "relative" and "ternary".
ii. The lexeme "relation" contains the semes "binary" and "ternary" as well as other semes coordinate with the latter, while the semes

"binary" and "ternary" are contained by the lexeme "relation" as well as by other lexemes coordinate with the latter.[125]
iii. The lexemes "harmony" and "signification" both contain the seme "relative" but no other seme coordinate with the latter, while the seme "relative" is contained by both the lexemes "harmony" and "signification" as well as by other lexemes coordinate with the latter.
iv. The lexemes "harmony" and "signification" are semiotically identical with one another.

Inspection of this complex semantic structure furnished by the sources reveals three unfolded lexemes to be analytically useful — a. Relation (L) + binary (s), b. Harmony (L) + relative (s) + ternary (s), c. Signification (L) + relative (s) + ternary (s) — which we shall henceforth call "logical", "harmonic", and "semiotic" respectively.[126]

Regarding the partial schemata used in our discussion, some more extended preliminary remarks are necessary.

Most prominent among these is the schema of opposition. The enormous proliferation of oppositional schemata during the last thirty years in semiotic literature need not be described here. It is enough to note that different types of opposition formulated in phonological research[127] — for example, the privative (where two terms have an identical element and one term has an element missing in the other),[128] the equipollent (where two terms have an identical element and each term has an element missing in the other),[129] the bilateral (where two terms have an identical element which is not found in other terms),[130] and the multilateral (where two terms have an identical element which is found in other terms)[131] — can be discovered in medieval texts and/or applied to their interpretation.[132] The difficulties of transferring phonological oppositions to the semantic sphere are well known, and are paralleled by those of translating phonological oppositions into the philosophical domain. Nevertheless, it will be useful to think in terms of certain semantic oppositions: especially those of "simple-complex", "existent-understood", and "dialectical-mathematical", when reading the primary sources.

Another prominent schema, or rather type of schema, is the geometrical analogy. It is nowadays common to describe linguistic and semiotic phenomena by using geometrical images, as when the "syntagmatic" plane of language (sequential combination of linguistic items in utterances) and the contrasting "paradigmatic" plane (associative simultaneity of linguistic items in memory) are depicted as horizontal and vertical axes respectively.[133] It is equally viable to treat logical and metaphysical ideas in this manner, although such applications have the peculiarity of increasing both ambiguity and reification. For example, from the simultaneity of certain spatial relations in the diagram:

Figure 1. Reciprocity of relations

one assumes without hesitation the reciprocity of those relations which it depicts.[134] And given the presence of certain graphic relations in the schema:

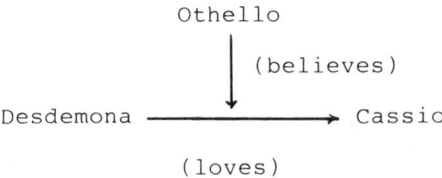

Figure 2. Existence of relations

one assumes with no less hesitation the existence of the relations which are depicted.[135] Nevertheless, since medieval writers found such images a natural mode of expression, we shall follow that practice in our interpretation of their texts.

Another prominent schema is the square of oppositions already mentioned.[136] Detailed analysis of its application in semiotic literature of recent years is best deferred until the relevant section of chapter three. For the present, it should merely be noted that a version of that square involving two generations of terms — where each of the four terms taken in sequence is superimposed on the previous term in the sequence (a_1 on $\bar{a}_2$, a_2 on a_1, $\bar{a}_1$ on a_2, and $\bar{a}_2$ on $\bar{a}_1$) to produce four new combined terms (b_1, b_2, $\bar{b}_1$, and $\bar{b}_2$);[137] and where combinations of earlier contrary and complementary pairs produce the new contrary pairs, of earlier contradictory pairs the new contradictory pairs, and of earlier complementary and contrary pairs the new complementary pairs — can be discerned in medieval texts and/or applied to their interpretation.[138] It is only to be expected that a combination of oppositions can be utilized less frequently and should be employed with greater caution than any individual opposition in philosophical contexts. However, there will be compelling reasons for articulating the set of semantic elements: creating (a_1), created (a_2), not creating ($\bar{a}_1$), and not created ($\bar{a}_2$) together with some of its analogues in reading the primary sources.

If this project indeed constitutes a reciprocal interaction of interpreting text and interpreted texts, one final consequence of importance may perhaps be noted. That the presence of three or more levels of discourse in such a literary phenomenon somewhat reduces the difficulty — which has long bedevilled attempts at formulating a cogent theory of exegesis — of determining precisely how to partition the text under discussion into minimal significant units for purposes of interpretative equation, comparison, or contrast.[139] When the text being analyzed is not exegetical in character, the segmentation will depend entirely on its interpreter's choice. But when the text itself takes exegetical form, the points at which it passes either between direct quotation and mere paraphrase or between the exegetical and non-exegetical modes themselves will be determinable, provided also that the previous materials are extant. These principles are applied in the interpretations of Augustine and Eriugena which now follow.

1.3 Augustine's understanding of order and concord

Within the tradition of European metaphysics, the work of Augustine of Hippo (A.D. 354–430) is rightly seen as a landmark. During the earlier years of his career, Augustine was occupied with the task of assimilating teachings of the pagan Platonic philosophical tradition — represented primarily by Plotinus — and of distancing himself from the influential but deviant Manichaean sect. In pursuing both these aims, it was necessary for him to come to grips with a mathematically-based view of reality to which concepts drawn from harmonics made a significant contribution. This fact is documented by the composition of his first literary work entitled *De pulchro et apto*. The book is no longer extant, although we can gain some impression of its content from remarks in Augustine's later autobiographical *Confessiones* and from the employment of the terms *pulchrum* [beautiful] and *aptum* [fitting] elsewhere in his writings. That the second term is etymologically connected with the Latin word *apere* indicating the joining of two things is important. This verb performs a linguistic function analogous to that of the Greek verb *harmozein*. The latter in its turn is etymologically linked with the word *harmonia* which signifies the joining of sounds in music. There is no doubt that Augustine was aware of this bilingual constellation of meanings since he exploits it quite systematically in his earlier works.[140] Considering the nature of his Neopythagorean and Neoplatonic philosophical education, it would have been more surprising had he avoided it.

Nevertheless, when looking for evidence of harmonic language in Augustinian philosophy, we cannot be restricted to the occurrence of *harmonia* and its cognates. Employed here is an intimidating multitude of terms whose overlapping meanings can only be comprehended by painstaking study of the different contexts. Within this network, the relation between *ordo* [order] and *concordia* [concord] provides the starting-point most convenient from the methodological angle.

In his early work *De moribus Ecclesiae Catholicae et de moribus Manichaeorum*, Augustine distinguishes between the views of the two religious groups especially by criticizing the Manichaeans' negative attitude to the contents of the sensible or corporeal world. Sensing the conflict with the book of *Genesis'* explicit teaching that the created world is good, he underlines the positive features of physical objects:

> Haec vero quae tendunt esse, ad ordinem tendunt: quem cum fuerint consecuta, ipsum esse consequuntur, quantum id creatura consequi potest. Ordo enim ad convenientiam quamdam quod ordinat redigit. Nihil est autem esse, quam unum esse. Itaque in quantum quidque unitatem adipiscitur, in tantum est. Unitatis est enim operatio, convenientia et concordia, qua sunt in quantum sunt, ea quae composita sunt: nam simplicia per se sunt, quia una sunt; quae autem non sunt simplicia, concordia partium imitantur unitatem, et in tantum sunt in quantum assequuntur.
>
> [Those things which tend towards being, tend towards order. When they have achieved it, they achieve being itself, so far as a creature can achieve it. For order reduces that which it orders to a kind of agreement. But being is nothing other than unity. Therefore, to the extent that each thing obtains unity, it also exists. The operation of unity consists in the agreement and concord through which composite things exist in so far as they exist. Simple things exist through themselves because they are unified. But things which are not simple imitate unity through the concord of their parts. They exist to the extent that they achieve it].[141]

A text such as this presents many difficulties to a conceptually innocent reader, although its meaning becomes tolerably clear when read against the historical background of Greek Neoplatonism. Augustine adapts a classical ontology in envisaging on one side, a metaphysically transcendent (non-spatial and atemporal) creator God and on the other, a created world characterized primarily by its dynamic tendency towards the creator. In marking out this structure, a number of terms — being, unity, order, concord — are connected with one another through various meanings which they share. An obvious difficulty for the reader lies in deciding whether these terms apply to the creator God, the creature, or both. This can be allayed by noting that in early Augustinism such terms apply simultaneously in all these senses not through any conceptual imprecision but in order to capture the peculiar nature of the relation between creative and created being. However, in the present passage being and unity seem to refer primarily to the creator and in a derivative sense to his creation: they are properties which he somehow transmits. The status of order seems more ambivalent in the scheme. By contrast, concord is applied specifically to the creature in the text, since it results from a certain limitation in its tendency towards divinity. We can perhaps summarize the argument now by saying that the created world strives towards being and unity, that being is equivalent to unity, and that both terms characterize the divine cause. Created things also have tendencies towards order and concord, order somehow being the precondition of concord, although both arise in the course of the creature's striving. Finally, the relation between the two pairs of goals is made explicit in the depiction of the creative process itself. The creator God, as unity, creates by imparting of himself in a kind of downward projection of divine power. Created things strive upwards towards that unity, but can only capture it so far as their composite status permits: that is as concord of their parts.

This compressed but elaborate theory, which recalls the Plotinian and Porphyrian teaching about the *proodos* [procession] and *epistrophē* [reversion] of reality, is important for us in several ways. In the first place, it shows how concord lies at the heart of created being itself and secondly, it signals the association of concord and order. In the writings of Augustine from the earliest period until the end of his life, there is a continuous preoccupation with the philosophical notion of "order" — he even devoted a dialogue explicitly to this question (*De ordine*). Although the topic has been much discussed by modern scholars, we should briefly review the evidence for it in other Augustinian texts.[142]

In a general sense, order signifies that multiplicity of the created world which corresponds to the unfolding of divine providence. The implications of this notion of multiplicity are worked out with some care by Augustine who in different contexts shows how created things are characterized by equality, difference, and opposition to one another. The dramatic conclusion of *De musica* is that God's providence distributes numbers through all creation. Numbers begin from unity, are beautiful through *aequalitas* [equality] or similarity, and are connected by order. Created things likewise desire unity, strive to achieve the greatest similarity to themselves, and seek salvation in a definite spatial or temporal order. Furthermore, all things must be made by a unitary principle, through a form *aequalis* [equal] and similar to its goodness, and through the goodness by which the two are connected. This intricate analogy between the number series, the created world, and the trinitarian God links the notions of order and equality in all three cases.[143] The association between the concepts of difference and order emerges from the passage in *De civitate Dei* where various senses in which peace can be found among created things are explained: that is in the parts of the physical body or the faculties of the soul, among the dwellers in an earthly community or the saints who comprise the celestial city, and so forth. In all these instances, we see that order *parium dispariumque rerum sua cuique loca tribuens* [which assigns appropriate positions to equal and unequal things].[144] The notions of order and opposition are linked in a section of the anti-Manichaean polemic of *Contra Faustum*. Against the thesis that the presence of *contraria* [opposites] like white and black, hot and cold, sweet and bitter in the visible world reveals the operation of antagonistic primary causes: God and Hyle, another viewpoint is urged. Since a sensory quality repellent to one creature may be attractive to another, it is rather the power of order which is apparent. Even the members of the race of darkness envisaged by Manichaean mythology find that nourishment which sustains them sweet, although both they and their food are products of the negative principle of Hyle in the universe.[145] These three texts drawn from both earlier and later phases in Augustine's career provide the materials necessary to understand his conception of order. Clearly it represents the multiplicity of creation in which each thing has a specific status determined by equality, difference, and opposition to others.

However, the Augustinian notion of order implies not only that the world is structured but that its structure has a positive ethical value. This aspect is underlined by the role played by order within interpretations of the Scriptural text: *Wisdom* 11. 21. That God created the world in *mensura* [measure], *numerus* [number], and *pondus* [weight] is an idea which forms the starting-point of extended philosophical discussions.[146] Given that the Scriptural teaching itself originated in the context of Hellenistic Pythagoreanism, the exploration of what might be termed the quasi-mathematical connotations of divine providence was not inappropriate.[147] The clearest evidence of such development occurs in passages where order appears in a grouping of terms the first two members of which correspond to those in the Scriptural triad.[148] This pattern is mirrored in cases where the same notion occurs inside a triadic grouping in juxtaposition with the first member only of the Scriptural set.[149] Similar thinking is revealed in passages where order occurs in a grouping of terms of which none is identical with the members of the Scriptural triad.[150] The importance of the superimposition of these patterns in Augustine's works is considerable, since their combined effect is to remind us of two major themes of his philosophical reflection from the earliest years: one pagan and one Christian.[151] The pagan element is the Neoplatonic triad of first principles with whose implications he was wrestling at the time of his conversion. He could have known from reading Plotinus' and Porphyry's writings that the third principle — Universal Soul — was constructed mathematically according to the teaching of the Platonic *Timaeus*. The other element is the Christian Trinity whose third Person was at the same period in his career the most difficult to conceive. Yet he knew that the Holy Spirit was somehow responsible for the unfolding of divine providence in created things.

It would be unnecessary and perhaps tedious to describe in detail the repetition of triadic motifs in the writings of Augustine. Suffice it to say that the frequent appearance of order as the third term in such configurations points to the importance of the notion as a synonym for the unfolding of divine providence. However, something should be said about the association between triadic schemata and the notion of concord. This link has emerged *en passant* in several of the texts already considered, yet there is at least one in which the issue is brought into the centre of focus.

Augustine's *De musica* concludes with an account of the operation of the Trinity in creation where the numerical theories developed earlier in the treatise are put to extensive use. That this divine power extends even to the lowest reaches of the visible world is shown by considering the element of earth:

> Quae primo generalem speciem corporis habet, in qua unitas quaedam et numeri et ordo esse convincitur. Namque ab aliqua impertili nota in longitudinem necesse est porrigatur quaelibet eius quantumvis parva

particula, tertiam latitudinem sumat, et quartam altitudinem qua corpus impletur. Unde ergo iste a primo usque ad quartum progressionis modus? Unde et aequalitas quoque partium, quae in longitudine et latitudine et altitudine reperitur? Unde corrationalitas quaedam (ita enim malui analogiam vocare), ut quam rationem habet longitudo ad impertilem notam, eamdem latitudo ad longitudinem, et latitudinem habeat altitudo? Unde, quaeso, ista, nisi ab illo summo atque aeterno principatu numerorum et similitudinis et aequalitatis et ordinis veniunt? Atqui haec si terrae ademeris, nihil erit. Quocirca omnipotens Deus terram fecit, et de nihilo terra facta est. Quid porro? Ipsa species qua item a ceteris elementis terra discernitur, nonne et unum aliquid quantum accepit ostentat, et nulla pars eius a toto est dissimilis, et earumdem partium connexione atque concordia suo genere saluberrimam sedem infimam tenet?

[For this primarily possesses the general form of body in which is proven to be a certain unity, numbers, and order. Each particle of this, however small it may be, must be extended from a partless point into a length. It must assume in third place a width, and in fourth place a height by which the body is completed. Whence comes this mode of progression from the first to the fourth? Whence also the equality of parts which is found in length, width, and height? Whence that certain correlation — for this is my preferred rendering of "analogy" — according to which the proportion between the length and the partless point corresponds to that between width and length, and to that between height and width? Whence, I ask, do these arise except from that supreme and eternal principle of numbers, similarity, equality, and order? If you take these properties away from earth, it will be nothing. So the omnipotent God has made earth, and earth is made from nothing. But one can go further by considering the form itself by which that same earth is distinguished from other elements. Does it not show how much it has received a certain unity? Is it not true that none of its parts is dissimilar to the whole? Does it not hold that lowest position which is salutary for its kind through those same parts' connection and concord?][152]

The meaning of the text becomes clear when read in conjunction with the passage cited at the beginning of this section. The background of Neoplatonic ontology is the same — the contrast between the metaphysically transcendent God and spatio-temporal created things — although the present passage gives less and more information on different points. The framework is less elaborate in that the created world in general is replaced by the physical element of earth, and that the created is no longer characterized as dynamically tending towards its creator. Conversely, greater elaboration is shown in the clear demarcation between creative and created being, in the more extensive selection of terminology applied to the creature: unity, number, equality, similarity, order, and concord, and in the precise geometrical analysis of the creature's concord of parts. However, most important of all is the explicit trinitarian motif which emerges in the final lines. The creative principle confers form on the physical element in a threefold manner reflecting the trinity of its own essence, the conferring of concord being the third moment in this creative act.

Having benefitted from this first encounter with the primary sources, we may perhaps return to the more external perspective for a moment. This allows us to perceive in the frequent substitution of the notion of order for that of concord by these texts a semiotic identification between the two lexemes. Moreover, the corresponding substitution of the notion of concord for that of order within the treatment of the triadic principle allows us to approach the semiotic identification from the other direction. Yet the situation is also complicated by other factors. Association of the concept of order with those of equality, difference, and opposition can be understood as the actualization of three primary semes within the lexeme "order". Association of concord with the concepts of equality and proportion can be understood as the actualization of two primary semes within the lexeme "concord".

Two points should be made about these groupings of terms which I shall for convenience henceforth call the "isotopies of order and concord".[153] In the first place, there is not identity between the meanings of concord and order but merely overlap. It is undeniable that, for Augustine, the term "concord" has certain senses not parallel to those of the term "order". Yet there is certainly a range of meanings within which the two lexemes may be treated as identical. The second point is that in studying the interrelation between concord and order one can begin equally well with the former as with the latter. Augustine does not state that "concord" is the fundamental term in comparison with which the meaning of "order" should be assessed nor the reverse. Furthermore, his practice in employing the terms gives no suggestion of such an arrangement of priorities.

The perspective sketched above is perhaps adequate for viewing the interrelations between the notions of concord, order, equality, difference, proportion, and opposition. But in reading the primary sources it has already become obvious that the meanings of these concepts can only be grasped fully within an even wider range of philosophical terms. Thus, further notions like creating and created without reference to which concord, order, and the rest make little sense must be introduced as secondary semes actualized within the various lexemes. There should be no attempt to catalogue these additional factors exhaustively, since the possibilities of semiotic implication are immense or even infinite. However, the importance of the division into creating and created being and the subdivision of the latter into proceeding and returning — part of what I shall term the "isotopy of creation" — needs to be underlined. Likewise the division into atemporal + non-spatial and temporal + spatial being and the mediation of the two by non-spatial + temporal being — part of what will be termed the "isotopy of time-space" — cannot be overlooked. Naturally when exploring such further ramifications of terminology, the principles stated earlier concerning identity, overlap, and reciprocity of meanings must be kept in mind.

1.4 Eriugena's understanding of order and harmony

Almost five centuries separate the creative activities of Augustine and Iohannes Scottus Eriugena (fl. 850–870). Yet there is a considerable degree of similarity between their respective methods and intentions. Eriugena, unlike his predecessor, stood in the presence of a well-established tradition of Christian theological speculation in Latin. His philosophy was uniquely influenced by those Greek patristic writers: Gregory of Nyssa, pseudo-Dionysius the Areopagite, and Maximus the Confessor, to whose translation he must have devoted the labour of many years. Unlike Augustine, the later writer remained most of his life a practising teacher of the secular liberal arts. But despite these differences, the indebtedness of Eriugena towards the greatest philosopher of the early western church is apparent on every page of his writings. Especially, we see him looking back over his shoulder to Augustine's earlier works: the anti-Manichaean treatises and the dialogues most influenced by Greek Neoplatonism. All this makes it reasonable to approach Eriugena using the framework suggested by the previous analysis of texts.

The topic of order is perhaps less frequently emphasized by the ninth-century writer, although it remains interwoven in the texture of his thought. This is true from the time of his early polemical *De praedestinatione* (850–851), through the period of his masterpiece *Periphyseon* (or *De divisione naturae*), down to that of the *Expositiones in Ierarchiam caelestem* (probably 865–870). Something of a shift of interest is clearly visible between earlier and later works, since the notion of order is expressed increasingly in the languages of mathematics and harmonics.

This is almost the mirror-image of the development which took place during Augustine's career.

For Eriugena also, order signifies the multiplicity of the created world corresponding to the extension of divine providence. In the *Periphyseon*, he explains how the traditional arrangement of the primordial causes — a Christian counterpart of the transcendent Platonic Forms — in terms of more generic and more specific must be understood. This does not signify that the causes were created in the divine essence in some temporal sequence, but that they were brought forth by providence in a certain ineffable and incomprehensible *ordo* [order].[154] Later in the same work comes a remarkable interpretation of creation from nothing in which "nothing" signifies the divine essence as it contains the primordial causes in their state transcending space and time, and "from nothing" the unfolding of the divinity through the emanation of the primordial causes into the realm of multiplicity. According to this view, every *ordo* [order] of natures from the celestial beings to the lowest level of the physical world constitutes a manifestation of the divine, brighter or darker depending on its proximity to the utterly transcendent source of all illumination.[155]

So far, Eriugena's argument follows closely along the Augustinian track. Yet in an important passage explaining the classical Platonic theory of participation between different levels of being he moves more resolutely into the region of harmonic imagery.

> Omne quod est aut participans aut participatum aut participatio est aut participatum simul et participans. Participatum solummodo est quod nullum superius se participat, quod de summo ac solo omnium principio quod deus est recte intelligitur. Ipsum siquidem omnia quae ab eo sunt participant... Participans vero solummodo est quod supra se naturaliter constitutum participat, a nullo vero infra se posito participatur quoniam infra se nullus ordo naturalis invenitur, sicut sunt corpora quorum participatione nulla rerum subsistit... Cetera vero quaecunque ab uno omnium principio per naturales descensiones gradusque divina sapientia ordinatos usque ad extremitatem totius naturae qua corpora continentur in medio sunt constituta et participantia et participata sunt et vocantur.

> [Everything which exists is either participant, or participated, or participation, or simultaneously participated and participant. That which is only participated is that which does not participate in anything above itself. This is understood rightly of the supreme and sole principle of all things, namely God. For all things which derive from him participate in him... That which is only participant is that which participates in something placed naturally

above it but is not participated by anything situated below, since no natural order below it is found. Bodies are such things, and nothing subsists through participation in them... But all other things, placed in the middle according to the natural descents and gradations arranged by the divine wisdom, between the one principle of all and that extremity of all nature in which bodies are contained, are and are called participant and participated].[156]

In this relatively straightforward presentation of the different levels within the multiplicity of nature, three categories are postulated. Their basis is provided by dualities of active and passive, and of affirmative and negative within the notion of participation itself. The passage continues the discussion of the category of participant and participated by focussing on the notion of order:

Excellentissima namque inter quae et summum bonum superius nulla creatura interposita est immediate deum participant et sunt principia omnium rerum, hoc est primordiales causae circa et post unum principium universale constitutae... Videsne quemadmodum primus ordo universitatis conditae et particeps est unius omnium principii et participatus ex subsequentibus se creaturis? Simili ratione de ceteris ordinibus intelligendum. Omnis enim ordo a summo usque deorsum in medio constitutus, hoc est a deo usque ad corpora visibilia, et superiorem se ordinem participat et ab inferiori se participatur ac per hoc et participans est et participatus.

[For the most excellent things, between which and the supreme good above them no creature is interposed, participate in God non-mediately. These are the principles of all things: that is, the primordial causes constituted around and subsequently to the one universal principle... Do you see how the first order of the created universe is both participant in the one principle of all and participated by the creatures which follow it? The same argument applies to the other orders. For every order placed in the middle between the highest and the lowest: that is, between God and visible bodies, both participates in the order above it and is participated by the one below. Therefore it is both participant and participated].

The inherent duality of participation which was described in the first segment of the text continues to be assumed here. However, this duality is now expanded into a more complex structure indicated by the occurrence of terminology like "first order", "other orders", "every order" within an account of the category of participant and participated. Eriugena continues by drawing upon the conceptual resources of mathematical sciences.

Participatio vero in omnibus intelligitur. Ut enim inter numerorum terminos, hoc est inter ipsos numeros sub una ratione constitutos, similes proportiones, ita inter omnes ordines naturales a summo usque deorsum participationes similes sunt quibus iunguntur; et quemadmodum in proportionibus numerorum proportionalitates sunt, hoc est proportionum similes rationes, eodem modo in naturalium ordinationum participationibus mirabiles atque ineffabiles armonias constituit creatrix omnium sapientia quibus omnia in unam quandam concordiam seu amicitiam seu pacem seu amorem seu quocunque modo rerum omnium adunatio significari possit conveniunt. Sicut enim numerorum concordia proportionis, proportionum vero collatio proportionalitatis, sic ordinum naturalium distributio participationis nomen, distributionum vero copulatio amoris generalis accepit, qui omnia ineffabili quadam amicitia in unum colligit.

[And participation is understood in all things. For as between the terms of numbers: that is, among the numbers themselves when arranged according to a single rule, the proportions are similar, so between all the natural orders from the highest to the lowest, the participations by which they are connected are similar. And as between the proportions of numbers there are proportionalities: that is, similar rules of proportion, in like manner the wisdom which is creator of all things has established between the participations of the natural orders marvellous and ineffable harmonies through which all things come together into a kind of single concord, amity, peace, love, or whatever other name can signify the unification of all things. For as the concord of numbers has received the name of proportion, the combining of proportions that of proportionality, so the distribution of natural orders has obtained the name of participation, the connection of the distributions that of universal love which brings all things into unity in a sort of ineffable amity].

Despite the opening reference to participation in general, the topic is still the complexity and order within the category of participant and participated. However, the argument of the second segment of the text is extended by illustrating that complexity with analogies between single participations and proportions and multiple participations and proportionalities respectively. At this point, the straightforward presentation of the levels of nature takes on further implications whose discussion must be postponed.

An argument like that just considered depends on numerous assumptions typical of classical ontology. As in the case of Augustine, the essential background is a contrast between a metaphysically transcendent (non-spatial and atemporal) creator God and a created world which proceeds from and reverts to that creator. But Eriugena's argument centres upon the behaviour of those principles called primordial causes. Their nature is explained at great length in the pages of *Periphyseon* from which a pronounced dynamic or evolutionary line of thought emerges. The primordial causes pre-exist in the divine essence in a non-spatial and atemporal state, they emerge from that essence into the diversity and multiplicity of the spatio-temporal world, and they strive to return to the transcendent state beyond space and time. This scheme constitutes an analysis both of the processes of creation and salvation in general and of individual creative and salvific acts by the divinity. It can also be expressed as a dynamic process in which the divine principle exists as a container of non-spatial and atemporal primordial causes, as an expansion through which these causes are distributed among the diversity and multiplicity of spatio-temporal things, and as a contraction into which they are elevated to recapture the transcendence of space and time. One may conclude even from this brief description that Eriugena's primordial causes correspond both to Platonic and to Aristotelian Forms. This is because the causes may be considered as having a transcendent and an immanent phase in their evolution. In addition, the state in which the primordial causes have emerged into spatio-temporal multiplicity through the expansion of the divine essence parallels the Augustinian notion of created being.

A comparison between the Augustinian and Eriugenian concepts of the order or harmony of creation reveals striking agreements in method. Like his great predecessor, Eriugena draws out the implications of created multiplicity by stressing its features of equality, difference, and opposition. The final segment of the *Periphyseon* passage recalls Augustine in citing the analogy between the number series and created things. Just as there may be similar proportions within a given sequence of numbers — here he is presumably thinking of the series based on arithmetical, geometrical, or harmonic progressions described in Boethius[157] — so between levels of being there are *participationes similes* [similar participations]. Although Augustine's argument is peculiar in being embedded in a trinitarian reflection, the earlier and later writers agree in seeing an all-pervasive similarity as a primary characteristic of created being. The connection between the order or harmony of creation and the notion of difference is also common to Augustine and Eriugena. A passage from the latter's *Expositiones in Ierarchiam caelestem* explicitly discusses the relation between order and harmony and gives a formal definition which perhaps verbally echoes Augustine's earlier one in *De civitate*

Dei: *est enim harmonia dissimilium inaequaliumque rerum adunatio* [harmony is the unification of dissimilar and unequal things].[158] The two writers further agree in seeing the notion of opposition as a third fundamental characteristic of created being, although Eriugena's thinking is no longer the offspring of anti-Manichaean polemic. A few pages beyond the passage from *Periphyseon* quoted above, the topic of the multiplicity of created being is again taken up. This multiplicity must consist not only of things which are similar but of those which are dissimilar and even *opposita* [opposite] — the references to opposites apparently added by Eriugena himself to the second recension of his text.[159]

The most obvious point of methodological disagreement between Augustine and Eriugena in describing the order and harmony of creation lies in trinitarian theory. The ninth-century writer reveals nothing like the preoccupation with finding triadic motifs in creation characteristic of the church father. No doubt this is connected with the predominant fourfold structure of creating and not created, created and creating, created and not creating, and not creating and not created which informs his *Periphyseon*. Yet even though triadic thinking is a less typical element on the surface of Eriugena's text, it reasserts itself periodically as an undercurrent. That God has created everything in measure, number, and weight according to *Wisdom* 11. 21 is stated in a context similar to those in which Augustine used the passage. The three terms are linked with the notion of harmony and to the third is appended the gloss: *pondere, id est, ordine* [weight, that is, order].[160] The triad is intimated in another passage dealing with creation but this time with substitution of its first two terms in the Augustinian manner. Each created thing is seen to have an analogy through which it is determinate, a number through which it coheres, and a *pondus* [weight] through which it finds its appropriate *ordo* [order] in the universe.[161] The trinitarian implications of such texts if not already obvious are underlined by Eriugena's other descriptions of the order and harmony of creation. In the part of *Periphyseon* where this line of thought is most actively pursued, it is the Holy Spirit to which has been allotted the function of determining each creature's position in the total scheme of things.

The comparison between Augustinian and Eriugenian approaches to this particular set of philosophical problems must take account of a terminological shift. Although both writers employ the term *ordo* [order] in similar contexts, there is perhaps a contrast between Augustine's emphasis on the associated notion of *concordia* [concord] and Eriugena's preference for the corresponding term *harmonia* [harmony]. Inspection of the lexica available for studying the two authors does not reveal any serious philosophical intent governing the different selection of terminology. Augustine speaks predominantly of concord — using it in both a metaphysical and a socio-political sense — but seemingly avoids the more technical term harmony.[162] Eriugena employs both concord and harmony, but prefers the latter and emphasizes metaphysical connotations. If he sees a difference of meaning between the two terms, it would be that concord represents the wider concept within which harmony falls. This is indicated in passages where he particularly associates concord with the state of nature or the universe as a whole.[163] In fact, the different selection of terminology made by these authors probably results from their respective sources: Cicero's writings on physics and politics in the case of Augustine,[164] and technical writers on the liberal arts like Calcidius, Macrobius, Martianus Capella, and Boethius in that of Eriugena.[165] Standing at the end of centuries of evolution in Latin terminology, it is naturally Eriugena whose language is more striking.

The association between ideas of concord, order, equality, difference, and proportion in Augustine's thought has already been treated as a semiotic identification between two lexemes within which various primary semes are actualized. These isotopies of order and concord occur also in Eriugena. The only modification to the picture demanded here is the adding of proportionality to the list of primary semes and the replacement of the lexeme "concord" by the lexeme "harmony". In Eriugena similarly the isotopies of creation and time-space must be understood. But here the inclusion of participation and other notions among the secondary semes adds considerably to the complexity of the whole theory.

1.5 Musical paradigms in Augustine and Boethius

The argument must now be interrupted by a return to Augustinian material. Our justification is a remarkable development of the basic equation of order and concord found in Augustine's writings between *De Genesi contra Manichaeos* (A.D. 388–389) and *Contra adversarium Legis et Prophetarum* (A.D. 420). This takes the form of a musical simile sometimes in conjunction with quotation of the sapiential triad. Since the material has scarcely received the attention from modern interpreters which it deserves, a fresh analysis should perhaps start with presentation of Augustine's very words. Proceeding in chronological order, we find the following:

A Universum autem ab unitate nomen accepit. Quod si Manichaei considerarent, laudarent universitatis auctorem et conditorem deum; et quod eos propter conditionem nostrae mortalitatis in parte offendit, redigerent ad universi pulchritudinem, et viderent quemadmodum Deus fecerit omnia non solum bona, sed etiam bona valde. Quia etiam in sermone aliquo ornato atque composito si consideremus singulas syllabas, vel etiam singulas litteras, quae cum sonuerint statim transeunt, non in eis invenimus quid delectet atque laudandum sit. Totus enim ille sermo non de singulis syllabis aut litteris, sed de omnibus pulcher est.

[The universe has taken its name from unity. And if the Manichaeans saw this, they would praise God the author and creator of the universe. That which offends them in the part thanks to the condition of our mortality, they would relate to the beauty of the universe, and they would see how God has not only made all things as good but as extremely good. Indeed, as with some ornate and structured speech, if we consider individual syllables or even individual letters which immediately pass away when they have sounded, we do not find anything in them delightful or praiseworthy. For that whole speech is not beautiful because of its individual syllables or letters but because of their totality].[166]

B ... quas ab eo tamen ordinatas intellegimus, cum dicitur: *et divisit deus inter lucem et tenebras,* ne vel ipsae privationes non haberent ordinem suum deo cuncta regente atque administrante, sicut in cantando interpositiones silentiorum certis moderatisque intervallis, quamvis vocum privationes sint, bene tamen ordinantur ab his, qui cantare sciunt et suavitate universae cantilenae aliquid conferunt...

[However, we must understand these privations to have been ordered by him, when it is stated "And God separated the light from the darkness." This was lest the privations themselves might be without their own order under God's universal rule and governance. As in singing, the silences interposed at definite and measured intervals — although they are privations of sound — are yet well ordered by those who know how to sing and can contribute something in sweetness to the whole song].[167]

C Cur ergo, inquis, quod naturae deus dedit, tollit corruptio? Non tollit, nisi ubi permittit deus; ibi autem permittit, ubi ordinatissimum et iustissimum iudicat pro rerum gradibus et pro meritis animarum. Nam et species vocis emissae praeterit et silentio perimitur; et tamen sermo noster et praetereuntium verborum decessione ac successione peragitur et moderatis silentiorum intervallis decenter suaviterque distinguitur. Ita sese habet etiam temporalium naturarum infima pulchritudo, ut rerum transitu peragatur et distinguatur morte nascentium.

[Why then, you ask, does corruption destroy what God has given to nature? It only destroys where God so permits, and he permits it only where he judges such a thing most ordered and most just: that is, according to the levels of reality and the merits of souls. For the form of the voice once pronounced, passes away, and is effaced in silence. Yet our speech consists of the departure and succession of words which pass, and is marked sweetly and becomingly by measured intervals of silence. The same applies even to the lowest beauty of temporal natures which consists of the passing of things and is marked by the death of what has been born].[168]

D Sicut enim sermo peragitur quasi morientibus atque orientibus syllabis, quae per morarum certa intervalla tenduntur ct spatiis suis inpletis ordinata consequentium successione decedunt, donec ad suum finem tota perducatur oratio, nec in ipsis decurrentibus sonis, sed in loquentis moderatione positum est, quantum producatur corripiaturve syllaba, vel qua specie litterarum singulae suorum locorum momenta custodiant, cum ars ipsa, quae sermonem facit, nec sonis perstrepat nec pervolvatur varieturque temporibus: sic ortu et occasu, decessu atque successu rerum temporalium certis ac definitis tractibus, donec recurrat ad terminum praestitutum, temporalis pulchritudo contexitur.

[A speech consists of syllables which arise and decay, so to speak, are extended through definite intervals of time, and fall away before the ordered succession of what follows — having filled their own spaces — until the whole discourse is brought to its end. And it is not on the sounds which pass but on the speaker's sense of measure that the length or brevity of a syllable depends or the manner in which each letter maintains the importance of its position. For the art which produces the speech does not itself ring with sound nor unfold through temporal changes. In the same way, the temporal beauty is woven from the birth and death and the departure and succession of temporal things in precise and definite intervals until it reaches its predetermined goal].[169]

E Fit autem decedentibus et succedentibus rebus temporalis quaedam in suo genere pulchritudo, ut nec ipsa, quae moriuntur vel quod erant esse desinunt, turpent ac turbent modum et speciem et ordinem universae creaturae: sicut sermo bene compositus utique pulcher est, quamvis in eo syllabae atque omnes soni tamquam nascendo et moriendo transcurrant.

[There arises a certain temporal beauty in things which depart and those which succeed them: a beauty of its own kind, whereby neither the things themselves perishing nor those altering their former nature damage or disturb the measure, form, and order of the created universe. In the same way, a speech well composed is especially beautiful, even though the syllables contained and all its sounds pass by as if in birth and death].[170]

F Quae tamen etiam privationes rerum sic in universitate naturae ordinantur, ut sapienter considerantibus non indecenter vices suas habeant. Nam et deus certa loca et tempora non inluminando tenebras fecit tam decenter quam dies. Si enim nos continendo vocem decenter interponimus in loquendo silentium: quanto magis ille quarundam rerum privationes decenter facit sicut rerum omnium perfectus artifex? Unde et in hymno trium puerorum etiam lux et tenebrae laudant deum...

[But even privations of things are so ordered in the universe of nature that their alterations are not unbecoming when wisely observed. For God has made certain places and times without illumination, and darkness as fittingly as light. And if we, by holding back the voice, interpose a becoming silence in our speech, how much more fittingly has he — the perfect artificer of the universe — made privations of certain things? Whence in the hymn of the three boys, even light and darkness praise God].[171]

G Non enim frustra per prophetam, qui haec divinitus inspirata didicerat, dictum est de deo: *Qui profert numerose saeculum.* Unde musica, id est scientia sensusve modulandi ad admonitionem magnae rei etiam mortalibus rationales habentibus animas dei largitate concessa est. Unde si homo faciendi artifex carminis novit, quas quibus moras vocibus tribuat, ut illud, quod canitur, decedentibus ac succedentibus sonis pulcherrime currat et transeat, quanto magis deus, cuius sapientia, per quam fecit omnia, longe omnibus artibus praeferenda est, nulla in naturis nascentibus et occidentibus temporum spatia, quae tamquam syllabae ac verba ad particulas huius saeculi pertinent, in hoc labentium rerum tamquam mirabili cantico vel brevius vel productius, quam modulatio praecognita et praefinita deposcit, praeterire permittit.

[For it is not vainly stated of God through the prophet: "Who brings forth the world in number", but learned through divine inspiration. Hence music, that is the knowledge or sense of modulation has been granted through God's bounty even to mortal beings with rational souls to remind them of something great. A man concerned with the making of song knows which durations should be assigned to certain words, so that what is sung with departing and succeeding sounds should run and pass most beautifully. But God's wisdom, through which he has made everything, is by far preferable to any art. So how much more does he ensure that every space of time through which natures are born and decay is neither shorter nor longer than the pre-conceived and pre-defined modulation demands. In this wonderful song, so to speak, of passing things, syllables and words correspond to periods within this world].[172]

H Fides tamen illa, quae deo suo dicit: *Omnia in mensura et numero et pondere constituisti,* quamvis amore vivendi conditionem mortis exhorreat, creatorem tamen omnium bonorum etiam de bonis mortalibus laudat. Nam iste ipse, qui reprehendit nec deum esse credit, cuius terrena opera videt esse mortalia, eundem sermonem suum, qui usque adeo illi placuit, ut eum litteris memoriaeque mandaret, nisi vocibus ad sua quaeque verba pertinentibus et incipientibus tamen et deficientibus implere non posset, ita pulchritudinem disputationis, qua vult persuadere quidquid oritur et moritur bonum esse non posse, nisi orientibus et morientibus syllabis non potuit explicare.

[For that faith which says to its God: "You have established all things in measure, number, and weight," although it fears the condition of death through love of living, praises the creator of all goods even in respect of mortal goods. For that very person who attacks this and does not believe him to be God whose earthly works he perceives as mortal could not complete his own speech using sounds which relate to specific words but begin and pass away — yet he thought enough of this speech to commit it to writing and memory. This man was not able to unfold the beauty of that discourse by which he wishes to persuade that whatever arises and perishes cannot be good without recourse to syllables which arises and perish].[173]

In juxtaposing all these materials as a kind of supertext, it is easier to grasp the impact of this elaborate musical simile on Augustine's mind. Such a method of textual coagulation — the reverse of the atomizing process used in the earlier part of this chapter — is not alien to the spirit of late antique *florilegia*. It also reflects the fact that Augustine's entire literary output is in a sense a single "text", and indeed the tradition of commentary upon that output merely its extension. The importance of the musical simile is underlined not only by its reiteration in passage after passage but by the Biblical quotations associated with it: *Isaiah* and the addition to *Daniel* together with *Wisdom* 11. 21. It is not diminished as far as Augustine is concerned by any suspicion that these quotations might be apocryphal or mistranslated.

The texts here under consideration involve the sets of metaphysical assumptions previously labelled the "isotopies of order and concord". So no further commentary is required on these points. However, the extraordinary complexity of the musical simile which becomes apparent on closer inspection demands a brief analysis. This is perhaps best done by approaching the texts in various groupings.

In all cases, the fundamental assumption is that the relation between the composer of a song and his materials is analogous to that between God and the things created by him. There are three features of the hypothetical song which attract Augustine's attention: the question of lengthening or shortening of syllables, the insertion of silences, and the relation between syllables and the entire composition.[174] In addition, the selected feature can be exploited by the analogy in two ways: in indicating the duration of a created thing's existence, or its level within the universe as such. Looking at these possibilities separately, we find the question of lengthening or shortening syllables as the central feature of the song described in texts *D* and *G*. In both cases, the variation of duration takes place within limits determined by an atemporal numbering source: the musician's art or, by analogy, God's wisdom. In text *G*, the relation between the atemporal number in the divine mind and the unfolding numerosity of the cosmos is derived from *Isaiah* 40. 26 in the LXX translation: *ho ekpherōn kat'arithmon ton kosmon autou*. The two passages agree in applying the simile of lengthening or shortening syllables to the durations between birth and death of various mortal creatures. Regarding insertion of silences as the salient feature of the musical piece, it is texts *B*, *C*, and *F* which are most instructive. Here, Augustine wishes to emphasize that silence of the voice is a privation — the negative counterpart of form in the Aristotelian and Neoplatonic traditions — but an essential component in the musician's performance. Similarly, the privations which occur in the physical cosmos are a necessary ingredient within the unfolding providence of the creator. In text *B*, these privations are understood from the reference to God's separation of darkness from light in *Genesis*; in text *F*, it is the addition to *Daniel* which furnishes the necessary allusion to the dark: the latter source being particularly well selected given that light and darkness are there said to sing the praises of the creator.[175] In the application of this simile of silence within a musical piece, a certain variation is detectable between the three passages. Text *C* treats silence as a symbol of that physical privation which supervenes at the end of mortal existence. On the other hand, texts *B* and *F* view it as symbolizing the already inherent physical privation which determines the level of something's being. Turning to the final feature of Augustine's hypothetical song, we find the relation between syllables and the entire composition described in texts *A*, *B*, *E*, and *H*. In each case, imperfection can be admitted in the parts without marring the perfection of the whole: the totality of syllables or its analogue the history of the world. Text *H* argues for the interdependence of partial and total within the life of the universe on the basis of *Wisdom* 11. 21 where it is the meaning of the last member of the triad *mensura, numerus, pondus* which is most significant. The four passages coincide in relating the contrast between syllables and the entire composition to the disparity between the life-spans of individual creatures and the whole world, although some ambiguity is detectable in text *B*.

A little probing of these apparently straightforward texts has revealed an inner richness which is still not exhausted. In particular, three further points should be made. First, the passages suggest a clearer relation to the isotopy of time-space which emerged in association with the isotopies of order and concord. The discussion of syllabic length especially contains a definite reference to the dimension of time.[176] But in the passages studied earlier in this chapter, it was normally left unclear whether the concord under discussion was spatial or temporal in character. Secondly, Augustine indicates in several of the texts that the process of musical composition is directly patterned on the divine creative activity and that mankind can achieve knowledge of the latter through examination of the former.[177] This interpretation of the isotopy of creation carries the further suggestion that there are different manifestations of concord which are ontologically and epistemologically linked with one another. Finally, the super-text reveals that a deeper understanding of Augustinian thought on these subjects must take account of its self-reflective character. The argument proving that the Manichaean's discourse itself contains the beauty which he denies to created things is a case in point.[178] According to this, one cannot describe concord without recourse to a linguistic or semantic structure which is itself concordant.

Development of the equation of order and concord into this impressive musical simile is not copied by many later "Augustinians". However, its essential features are absorbed within the well-known doctrine of the three musics formulated by Boethius (ca. A.D. 480–524). This writer was a self-declared follower of Augustine's teaching on theological matters, and a connoisseur of the Greek arts and sciences by general agreement of his contemporaries. Among numerous works produced in the scientific field is his *De institutione musica*, dated by modern scholars to around A.D. 502–507, which is apparently a translation of Greek treatises by Nicomachus of Gerasa and Ptolemy. That this book aroused much attention during the Middle Ages is indicated by the careful glosses assembled around the text. In addition, many philosophical writings and technical treatises on music echo its teachings.[179]

Near the beginning of *De institutione musica*, Boethius states his doctrine of the threefold music:

> Sunt autem tria. Et prima quidem mundana est, secunda vero humana, tertia, quae in quibusdam constituta est instrumentis... Et primum ea, quae est mundana, in his maxime perspicienda est, qua in ipso caelo vel compage elementorum vel temporum varietate visuntur. Qui enim fieri potest, ut tam velox caeli machina tacito silentique cursu moveatur?... Unde non potest ab hac caelesti vertigine ratus ordo modulationis absistere. Iam vero quattuor elementorum diversitates contrariasque potentias nisi quaedam armonia coniungeret, qui fieri posset, ut in unum corpus ac machinam convenirent? Sed haec omnis diversitas ita et temporum varietatem parit et fructuum, ut tamen unum anni corpus efficiat... Humanam vero musicam quisquis in sese ipsum descendit intellegit. Quid est enim quod illam incorpoream rationis vivacitatem corpori misceat, nisi quaedam coaptatio et veluti gravium leviumque vocum quasi unam consonantiam efficiens temperatio? Quid est aliud quod ipsius inter se partes animae coniungat, quae, ut Aristoteli placet, ex rationabili inrationabilique coniuncta est? Quid vero, quod corporis elementa permiscet, aut partes sibimet rata coaptatione contineat?... Tertia est musica, quae in quibusdam consistere dicitur instrumentis. Haec vero administratur aut intentione ut nervis, aut spiritu ut tibiis, vel his, quae ad aquam moventur, aut percussione quadam...

> [There are three types. The first is cosmic, the second human, and the third produced by certain instruments... Now the first type, the cosmic, is particularly evident in those things which are observed in heaven itself, or in the combining of elements, or in the variation of seasons. For how can it happen that so swift a heavenly machine can move with a noiseless and silent course?... Hence, a fixed order of modulation cannot be absent from this celestial rotation. And if a certain harmony did not join the diversities and contrary powers of the four elements, how could it happen that they should come together into a single body and mechanism? But all this diversity produces a variety of both seasons and fruits which nonetheless results in a unifie system of the year... Whoever descends into his own self understands human music. For what blends that incorporeal vigour of reason with the body except a certain adjustment and, so to speak, tuning of low and high pitches as though producing one consonance? What else connects to one another the parts of the soul itself which, as Aristotle maintains, is composed of rational and irrational? What indeed mingles the

elements of the body or holds its parts together in a fixed adjustment?...
The third type of music is said to be produced by certain instruments. This
is governed either by tension as in strings, or by breath as in pipes or water-
activated devices, or by a certain percussion...][180]

Of immediate significance is the emphasis upon the term *musica*
[music] in the passage, since this seems divergent from the usages to
which we have grown accustomed. Yet any doubt that the terrain is familiar is removed by closer inspection of Boethius' words. For example, in
connection with the first kind of cosmic music, he speaks of the *ordo
modulationis* [order of modulation] among the planetary orbits, and when
discussing the second type, he refers to *quaedam harmonia* [a certain
harmony] between the elemental powers. In fact, the change of vocabulary
probably indicates a different perspective towards subject-matter the same
as before. Whereas the notion of harmony reveals something about the
structure of the external world, that of music rather suggests the approach
to that structure through an act of knowledge.[181]

Although it is tempting to begin immediate discussion of the various
musics — a project to which Boethius himself points in explanatory foot-
notes on the celestial and seasonal kinds — some introductory remarks are
necessary concerning the format of this actually ninefold analysis. Looking at the historical context, it is not far-fetched to suggest that juxtaposition of the types of music was more important than their individual
depiction. Medieval readers of the passage certainly started from this
assumption and, given an inbuilt bias towards encyclopaedism typical of
that period, even attempted to raise the structure to higher levels of com-
prehensiveness. We shall therefore treat the Boethian ninefold theory as a
conceptual mould in which various answers to the question what types of
music there are could be cast.

Later students of *De institutione musica* tend to one of three possible
responses. Either they adopt the theory of the musics without significant
modification, or they replace it with an alternative scheme more suitable
to their needs, or they employ it as a foundation for new developments.
The first response occasionally yields interesting results especially when
the different subdivisions of the scheme are depicted with a literary
flair.[182] Likewise the second, in which the conflict between the obviously
theoretical depiction of the nine types and the demand for a practical classification of music comes to the forefront.[183] However, the third response
is most interesting from our viewpoint since the basic scheme can be sub-

jected to a variety of developments. These are difficult to categorize exhaustively although a rough distinction may be ventured. On one hand, the ninefold classification is preserved intact whereas the nature of the original subdivisions is described with greater exactitude than in Boethius' own presentation. On the other, the subdivisions are delineated in a manner reflecting the original while the classification is expanded through the insertion of additional terms. The history of medieval responses to the theory of the musics has already been mapped to an extent making one hesitant to add to the literature.[184] However, studies of the question have generally been confined to enumerating mere repetitions of the scheme in order to determine something about its increase or decrease in popularity during the course of time. These studies have also been directed towards problems resulting from its encounter with the divergent aims of some practical music maker. Fresh remarks may therefore be justified concerning responses to the theory which develop or extend its various features. This is especially so when such observations take a form scarcely concealing that indwelling tendency to systematic proliferation present from the beginning.

Boethius' first type of music is cosmic. Of the three subdivisions within this — celestial, elemental, and seasonal — it was the first which puzzled later commentators. Although the original passage contains enough detail for its readers to imagine a cosmos in which the planetary bodies encircling the earth are correlated with a scale of musical pitches, there is doubt regarding the nature of that correlation. In particular, do the rotating planets actually produce sounds through their friction against the static air which correspond to specific pitches in a scale? Or is it the ratios between the dimensions of their orbits which correlate with the ratios in string-length underlying such a scale? This is the fundamental ambiguity immediately confronting any attempt to elaborate on Boethius' sketchy presentation. It was evident in the ancient philosophical tradition — perhaps going back to the earliest Pythagorean origins of the theory. It continued to plague the medieval commentators.[185] These normally inclined to one or other solution depending on the teaching of whatever additional sources were invoked in support.[186]

That the first type of music has a tripartite division is important. By about the beginning of the twelfth century, the availability of technical knowledge in the sciences had increased to the extent that division of physical reality into planets, elements, and seasons was no longer adequate. Further subdivisions were therefore made within the original categories.[187]

That these usually took a similar triadic form shows the tendency to self-proliferation inherent in conceptual systems of this kind. It also suggests that the method by which the nine types of music were presented was as important to medieval readers as the content of any individual kind.[188]

Boethius' second type of music is the human one. Of its three subdivisions — relation between soul and body, between the soul's parts, and between the body's parts — it was again the first which confused later commentators. The original passage obviously indicates that incorporeal and corporeal things are somehow connected, yet the precise nature of this connection is not specified. For example, does the relation between soul and body consist of some general affinity in structure which encourages their combination? Or is it something more specific like the process whereby the soul's silent inner thoughts achieve external expression in sound? On the basis of Boethius' text alone there are real difficulties in deciding between these alternatives. Philosophically educated readers of the ancient period would have chosen the former — given their knowledge of the Platonic psychological theory which was implied. However, medieval commentators had no such guidance.[189] For them the other solution was more appealing since it permitted them to accommodate the later emphasis upon vocal music with traditional ideas.[190]

The tripartite division of the second type of music is also significant. From the early twelfth century onwards, the wider availability of philosophical sources provided a clearer understanding of the psychology on which the division was based. This permitted the original analysis into relations between soul and body, between the soul's parts, and between the body's parts to be reappropriated. Further subdivision along triadic lines within each of these categories then became an option which was occasionally carried into practice.[191]

This ninefold classification of music represents an interesting complement to Augustine in the similar conviction regarding the power of harmonic language which it reveals. Yet there is both similarity and difference relative to his predecessor's use of the great musical simile. A point of agreement is provided by the one passage later in *De institutione musica* which returns to the doctrine of cosmic music. Here, Boethius explains how the scale on a lyre's strings is *quoddam ordinis distinctionisque caelestis exemplar* [a kind of transcript of the celestial order and distinction].[192] Clearly the establishment of a paradigmatic relation between cosmic and instrumental music adds an important new element to our conception of the ninefold scheme. It also mirrors the metaphysical relation between divine and human musics described by Augustine within the physical context.[193] A second point of agreement lies in the self-reflective character of the Boethian theory as a whole. Since music consists of the arrangement of proportions, while the nine musics are in proportional relation to one another, then music defines the relations between the nine musics. As with Augustine's Manichaean who could not reject art without using it, the Boethian music is contained in the circularity of its own language.[194] Finally, there is a point of difference indicated by the explanatory notes accompanying the original presentation of cosmic music. In this passage, Boethius describes how the *in gravibus chordis...vocis modus...in acutis* [measure of pitch in low or high strings] which parallels the balance of seasonal forces must be maintained at a moderate level.[195] That pitch is the aspect of instrumental music used to illustrate a corresponding feature in the cosmic domain contrasts with Augustine's exclusive reliance upon rhythmic imagery. However, *De institutione musica* is not too distant from its forerunner given the widespread belief of ancient theorists in a precise analogy between pitch and rhythm.

1.6 The concept of relation in ancient and modern philosophy

Before looking at further medieval texts, something should be said about the interpretation of the "relative" during the period concerned. Given that the significant and the harmonic are different species of relative and also — from a semiotic viewpoint — a single species of relative,[196] the prerequisite of grasping the true nature of the relative itself for an understanding of these terms needs no further argument. Our purpose will best be served by treating relation as a lexeme within which certain semes are activated for the duration of a discourse or — stressing the interpreter's role — as the centre of a semantic field through which paths run in various directions. Moreover, the unfolding of this lexeme will be most strikingly displayed in contrast with its unfolding in another discourse of comparable yet different motivation.[197]

Analysis of relation by a twentieth-century logician might begin by distinguishing as fundamental elements the "referent" or term from which the relation goes, the "relatum" or term to which it goes, and the "sense" or direction in which it goes.[198] For example, in the relation "husband" where x and y are husband and wife, x is the referent, y the relatum, and x

and *y* the sense. It might continue — treating the binary as the basic type — by classifying relations into i. "symmetrical": those which, when they hold between *x* and *y*, *must* also hold between *y* and *x*; "non-symmetrical": those which, when they hold between *x* and *y*, *may* also hold between *y* and *x*; and "asymmetrical": those which, when they hold between *x* and *y*, *cannot* also hold between *y* and *x*;[199] and into ii. "one-many": those where, if *x* has the relation in question to *y*, there is no other term x^1 which also has the relation to *y*; and "one-one": those where, if *x* has the relation in question to *y*, no other term x^1 has the same relation to *y*, and *x* does not have the same relation to any term y^1 other than *y*.[200] In accordance with this classification, the analysis might also distinguish as fundamental features of relation the "domain" or class of all possible referents to a given relation, the "converse domain" or class of all possible relata to a given relation, and the "field" or classes of referents and relata taken together.[201] In the example of relation mentioned above all husbands are the domain, all wives the converse domain, and all husbands and wives together the field.

The hypothetical treatment of relation might continue — extending its viewpoint beyond the binary sphere — by classifying relations into iii. "transitive": those which, when they hold between *x* and *y* and between *y* and *x*, *must* also hold between *x* and *z*; "non-transitive": those which, when they hold between *x* and *y* and between *y* and *z*, *may* also hold between *x* and *z*; and "intransitive": those which, when they hold between *x* and *y* and between *y* and *z*, *cannot* also hold between *x* and *z*.[202] In accordance with this and the earlier classification, it might also define a relation giving rise to order as one belonging to the classes of asymmetrical, transitive, and connected;[203] a relation similar to another as one belonging to the same classes as that other,[204] and so forth.

By contrast, that the analysis of relation in our medieval sources assumes a different articulation of the semantic field can be demonstrated easily enough. First, the distinction between referent and relatum is understood albeit without a special terminology. However, although these sources frequently describe symmetrical relations — e.g. same, different, equal, unequal, similar, dissimilar[205] — as well as asymmetrical ones — e.g. greater, lesser, before, after, higher, lower[206] — they do not assign separate logical properties to the two classes. Similarly, although they occasionally mention one-many relations — e.g. father[207] — as also one-one relations — e.g. ratios[208] — they do not distinguish the logical properties of the respective groups. The distinction between domain and

Table 1. Aristotle's category of relation[1]

A. [Simple classification][2]
   1. [binarity][3]
   2. contrariety[4]
   3. gradualness[5]
B. [Complex classification][6]
   I. [Strict sense][7]
      a. Its relation to another[8]
         1. Numerical exceeder to exceeded[9]
            α. Indefinite[10]
            β. Definite[11]
         2. Active to passive[12]
            α. [Without temporal reference][13]
            β. With temporal reference[14]
         3. Involving privation of potency[15]
      b. Another's relation to it[16]
         [Object to subject][17]
   II. [Loose sense][18]
      α. Through class membership[19]
      β. Through an [essential] property[20]
      γ. Through an accidental property[21]

Notes

1. Items in square brackets are implied but not stated in the text. The ancient commentators make various attempts at a *diairesis* [division] of this category: i.e. a systematic inventory of its types based on enumeration of characteristics. Ammonius: *iACa.* 67. 16–26 lists relatives i. by homonymy e.g. similar to similar, ii. by heteronymy e.g. right to left, iii. by container and contained e.g. double to half, iv. by ruler and ruled e.g. master to slave, v. by judger and judged e.g. sensation to sensible, vi. by participant and participated e.g. knowledge to knowable, vii. by cause and caused e.g. father to son, viii. by active and passive e.g. striker and struck, ix. by spatial difference e.g. left to right. Other divisions are made by Iamblichus and Simplicius: see Simplicius: *iACa.* 161. 12–162. 11.
2. Set out in Aristotle: *Ca.* 7. 6^a 36–8^b 24.
3. See p. 69 ff. In addition to those mentioned in nn. 4–5, the following examples occur in the course of the chapter: greater to lesser, master to slave, knowledge [to…], habit [to…], sensation [to…].
4. *enantiotēs/to enantion.* The examples are virtue to vice, knowledge to ignorance.
5. i.e. admitting *to mallon kai to hētton* [more and less]. The examples are similar, dissimilar, equal, unequal.
6. Set out in Aristotle: *Me.* Δ. 15. $1020^b26 - 1021^b11$.

Table 1 (continued)

7. Aristotle contrasts this implicitly with division II at *Me. Δ.* 15. 1021ᵇ3.
8. *tōi hoper estin allou legesthai auto ho estin.*
9. *hyperechon pros hyperechomenon.* Or alternatively: *pollaplasion pros pollostēmorion* [numerical container to contained] depending on subdivision α or β below.
10. *haplōs.* The examples are multiple to one, $\frac{n+1}{n}$ to n.
11. *hōrismenōs.* The examples are double to half, triple to third.
12. *poiētikon pros to pathētikon.* According to Aristotle's metaphysical theory, this also implies a relation of passive to active *potency*. The examples are heater to heated, cutter to cut.
13. No examples are given. This active to passive relation can be defined by comparison with β below.
14. *kata chronous ēdē.* The example is father to son. The idea seems to be that the active to passive relation subsisted in the past.
15. *kata sterēsin dynameōs.* The examples are incapable [to capable], invisible [to visible].
16. *tōi allo pros ekeino.*
17. The examples are measurable to measure, knowable to knowledge, sensible to sensation.
18. See n. 7.
19. For example, medicine is relative because knowledge is.
20. For example, equality and similarity are relative because equal and similar are.
21. For example, man is relative because he is double something.

converse domain is also understood if not specified in terminology. However, although medieval sources often mention transitive relations — e.g. equal, before, after[209] — as well as intransitive ones — e.g. one unit larger[210] — they again do not assign separate logical properties to the two classes. Finally, the precise definition of relations which give rise to order or are similar to others is totally lacking.

But what precisely is meant by "a different articulation of the semantic field"? On the one hand, it implies that certain semes within the lexeme "Relation" activated by the modern theory were not activated formerly, especially the ones guaranteeing distinctions between symmetry and asymmetry, between transitivity and intransitivity, and so forth.[211] This non-activation partly reflects a limited interest in the logical possibilities of relation invested in propositional functions and the like,[212] but also contextual pressures from the ontological determination of relation in a philosophical "encyclopaedia".[213] On the other hand, the phrase "a different articulation of the semantic field" implies that certain semes within the lexeme "Relation" not activated nowadays were activated by the older speculation, and primarily those reinforcing coherence between the lexeme and others to which that discourse assigned a prominence.[214] It is not difficult to discover the identity of these others.

The different articulation of the semantic field assumed by medieval treatments of relation could be imagined as stages in a process of deviation whereby three premisses are successively inserted into the argument above: 1. that two terms must be present; 2. that relation somehow "exists"; and 3. that the two terms must be fused into one. Underlying the insertion of these premisses is an irresistible desire to find metaphysical unity behind the variegated structure of the Aristotelian category of *pros ti* [relation]. This structure was found primarily in two passages — *Categories* 7 and *Metaphysics* Δ. 15 — of which only the first became known to early medieval writers in Latin translation.

Aristotle had described the category of relation by gradually enumerating the characteristics of what is called "the relative" (table 1).

A certain plurality is detectable in the category owing to Aristotle's references to pairs of terms rather than single terms — one must speak of "relatives" in the plural,[216] and by his enumeration of overlapping rather than universal properties — one makes of relatives but a *hoion* [quasi] definition.[217] Since the search for unity is a fundamental motivation of Neoplatonic thought in general, this plurality of relation arouses circumventing responses in many Greek commentators.[218] On the one hand, Plotinus argues that the category is inapplicable to the intelligible world — which is characterized instead by the Platonic genus of *heteron* [difference] — and of limited application even among sensible things;[219] on the other, Simplicius maintains that the category is applicable metaphorically to the intelligibles — which are therefore characterized by a *logos tēs scheseōs* [reason of relation] — but has normal application within the sensible sphere.[220] According to some Greek commentators, the redefinition of relation in the latter part of *Categories* 7 shows implicit substitution of an intelligible for a sensible perspective.[221]

The first stage in our construction of the ancient theory of relation is the premiss that two terms must be present. This underlies Aristotle's earlier definition of relatives: "whatever are described as being 'of others' or in some way in respect of another"[222] as also his later definition: "those having their essence identical with their relatedness in some way"[223] in the *Categories*. The primarily grammatical expression of binarity in the earlier definition is developed by Porphyry who observes that the relational structure may be expressed by a genitive, a dative, or a prepositional phrase.[224] A more elaborate development along the same lines occurs in the commentary on Aristotle's treatise by Simplicius.[225]

The second phase in our construction of the ancient theory is the premiss that relations somehow "exist". Plotinus approaches this question by distinguishing relations which imply an activity and therefore the production of an existent — e.g. sensation/sensible and measure/measured — from relations which imply no activity and consequent production of an existent — e.g. similar/similar and equal/equal.[226] For Plotinus, the former type of relation implies participation in a reason or form indirectly through the mediating activity, but the latter type participation in a reason or form directly and without a mediator.[227] Moreover, although the second type of relation is said initially to arise in the process whereby the mind compares two terms,[228] his theory ultimately traces all relations back to *logoi* [reasons] pre-existing in the transcendent realm. Simplicius tackled the same problem by distinguishing a meta-relation in particulars which corresponds to the relative and which participates from a relation-in-a-reason which corresponds to the reason of relation and which is participated.[229] For Simplicius, neither the relation totally immanent in the particulars nor that totally transcending them but only that simultaneously immanent and transcendent can explain the status of this category.[230]

The third stage in our construction of the ancient theory of relation is the premiss that the two terms must be fused into one. This underlies Aristotle's later definition of relatives: "those having their essence identical with their relatedness in some way" in the *Categories*.[231] The primarily ontological conception of binarity in this definition is developed by Porphyry who argues that, although the terms of a relation produce a mediator of some kind, the latter is not something other than the contact between them.[232] This co-existence of relatives was more elaborately contrasted with the existence of non-relatives in the lost commentary on Aristotle's treatise by Iamblichus according to later testimony.[233]

The doctrine of categories in Aristotle and his Greek commentators therefore discloses an articulation of the semantic field surrounding the lexeme "Relation" quite different from that presented by our hypothetical twentieth-century logician. As suggested previously, the phrase "a different articulation of the semantic field" implies both that certain semes within the lexeme activated by the modern theory were not activated formerly: especially the ones guaranteeing distinctions between symmetry and asymmetry and between transitivity and intransitivity; and also that various semes within the lexeme not activated nowadays were activated by the older speculation.[234] These necessarily brief remarks on the categorical doctrine of Aristotle and his Neoplatonic commentators have perhaps been sufficient to reveal that the semes concerned here are those of binarity, existence, and fusion.

But it would clearly be a mistake to assume that differences between articulations of the semantic field surrounding the lexeme "Relation" in modern and ancient theories preclude an effective philosophical dialogue between the two. In fact, the most important metaphysical debate concerning relation in the twentieth century — that between Russell and the British Hegelians[235] — could just as easily be viewed as a response to the Neoplatonic tradition. It may be useful to summarize the main issues of this debate which centers on the roles of internal and external relations and on the monistic and pluralistic ontologies associated with these. Given Russell's own position as principal architect of the modern logical theory of relation discussed earlier,[236] his presentation and criticism of Hegelian doctrine can be placed as a fitting conclusion to this chapter.

Among various possible interpretations of relation, at one extreme is that termed "internal".[237] Logically speaking, this perspective implies that a proposition asserting a relation is always reducible to a subject-predicate proposition concerning the whole composed of the relation's terms.[238] In a more ontological sense, the interpretation holds that any relation of two terms corresponds to a property of the terms and of the whole which they compose,[239] is therefore *in* rather than *between* the said terms,[240] and cannot be altered without affecting the natures of the terms and of the whole which they constitute.[241] Epistemologically speaking, this viewpoint implies that knowledge of any part automatically produces knowledge of the whole and of every other part.[242] Of course, the interpretation of relation at the other extreme termed "external" is based on the converses of all these statements.[243]

In several of his earlier works, Russell was concerned with combatting the theory of internal relations and monistic ontology advocated by Bradley and with establishing his own doctrine of external relations and pluralistic ontology called "logical atomism".[244] At that time, his most telling argument against the internal theory was that, although monadic relations can always be reduced to dyadic ones — as when the Platonic doctrine of Forms explains a particular's possession of the property x by its participation in the Form of x —, dyadic relations can only be reduced to monadic ones in certain cases.[245] Thus, if the relation is the symmetrical one expressed by the proposition "A is equal to B," one may speak of A and B as having a common predicate; whereas if the relation is the asymmetrical one expressed by the proposition "A is greater than B," one cannot speak of A and B as having a common predicate.[246] Given that reduction of dyadic to monadic relations was the fundamental feature of the internal theory, the latter could only be deemed valid in connection with a small and perhaps atypical group of relations.[247] In later years, Russell came to reject both the doctrine of internal relations and the doctrine of external relations in their extreme forms, on the grounds that these theories are equally inconsistent with what he termed "the theory of types".[248] According to this viewpoint, the meanings of words are of various logical types, and it is inadmissible to substitute words having meanings of one type for words having meanings of another: for instance, one cannot enunciate a meaningful proposition in which an attribute or a relation occupies the position appropriate to a substance.[249] As Russell explains, "the proper symbol for 'yellow' is not the single word 'yellow' but the propositional function 'x is yellow'...similarly the relation 'precedes' must not be represented by this one word but by the symbol 'x precedes y'."[250] The consequence of all this for the doctrines of internal and external relations in their radical forms is that neither can be expressed in a manner which is logically true as long as *verbal* language unable to maintain the difference of type between a relation and its terms is employed.[251]

The Greek Aristotelian commentators also describe what amount to internal and external relations but without exploring their philosophical implications. For them, the intelligible world is differentiated by a primal relation which involves neither presence in a substratum nor binarity of substrata — this relation, corresponding to difference, represents the internal mode.[252] For them, the sensible world is differentiated by secondary relations which are either inherent in substrata and altered together with them or separate from substrata and altered independently of them — such relations, illustrated by right/left in bodily organs and spatial motion respectively, represent the contrast of internal and external modes.[253] Nevertheless, the occurrences of asymmetrical relations which were understood metaphysically as fusions of a relation's two senses were not permitted to undermine the preeminence of internality.[254]

Note

To find something comparable to the theory of internal relation criticized by Russell, one should turn to the Hegelian *Wissenschaft der Logik* and trace the fortunes of the German terms *Beziehung, Verhältnis*, and so forth. It would be impossible and unnecessary to do justice to Hegel's theory of relation at this point. However, a brief sketch of its main tendencies may be useful in order to clarify not only the Russellian theory to which it is opposed but also the Neoplatonic doctrine with which it agrees.

The importance of relational thinking in Hegel is indicated not only by those passages where the corresponding Aristotelian and Kantian theories are subjected to the usual dialectical re-evaluation. A more striking testimony is the occurrence of the language of relation in numerous contexts exhibiting the dialectical process itself from abstract beginnings in the realm of Being to fulfilment in the Absolute Idea. Towards the end of the dialectic (Hegel 1934, 2: 235), Hegel explains that Being and Essence — the first two primary spheres of the logic — are contained within the Notion — the last primary sphere — in a special sense. The Notion does not differentiate itself into these determinations, but constitutes the *substantielles Verhältnis* [substantial relation] where being and essence achieve their determination through one another. Near the beginning of the same dialectic (Hegel 1934, 1: 54), Hegel declares that Being is immediate — as the starting-point of logic — and mediate — as the culmination of Phenomenology — at the same time. This situation is possible given that immediacy itself *bezieht sich auf* [contains a relation to] its distinction from what is mediated. The Hegelian dialectical process therefore begins and ends its characteristically triadic development in relational terms. Any conceptual category to which dialectic is applied acquires its deeper significance through the transformation of discrete into continuous by means of the relative.

There is also an illuminating presentation of the contrast between internal and external relations in the *Logik*. The second "remark" appended to the discussion of Quantum concerns the expression of philosophical notions through numerical determinations, and amounts to nothing less than a confrontation between Hegelian thought and aspects of the Pythagorean and Neopythagorean traditions (Hegel 1934, 1: 207–212). Hegel is usually at his best within the various *Anmerkungen* which besprinkle his text, since there he writes liberated from the self-inflicted constraint of triadically unfolding terms. The second remark about Quantum is a good example of the genre and therefore deserves to be studied with care.

Hegel first considers Pythagoras (Hegel 1934, 1: 207–208). It was typical of his method to depict *Vernunftverhältnisse* [rational relations] in numbers on the assumption — shared by some modern theorists — that numerical operations are those where mind reveals its most characteristic relations and in general the *Grundverhältnisse des Wesens* [fundamental relations of essence]. Yet this exalted function should not be given to arithmetic, since its objects are devoid of *innere Verhältnisse an sich* [inner and intrinsic relations]. They do not contain the Notion but are rather the antithesis of it. In handling the objects of arithmetic, the thought process has as its subject-matter *Äusserlichkeit* [externality] itself. Hegel next turns to Moderatus as quoted by Porphyry (Hegel 1934, 1: 208 - 212). According to this more profound version of the theory, numbers do not reveal rational relations but function as their *Bezeichnung* [designation] for instructional purposes: for example, different numbers express the categories of like, unlike, limit, infinity, and so forth.

For Hegel there are on one hand, true thoughts *nur im Beziehen begriffen* [comprehended only in relation] and on the other, the element of *Aussersichsein* [self-externality] in numbers. The richer in determinations and therefore in relation things become, the more confused it is to interpret them in numerical terms. To take numbers as mere symbols of something else is not necessarily misleading, although this language contributes nothing to the intelligibility of the objects concerned. Philosophy should therefore find its resources not in the *äusserlicher, gedankenloser Unterschied* [external and thoughtless differentiation] of the logical element manifested in the form of number, but in that very logic which alone guarantees the significance of the numerical.

In this interesting "remark", Hegel has neatly distinguished between internal and external relations (cf. Hegel 1934 1: 181, 2: 221, 258). The former occurs especially in the speculative logic which his treatise strives to depict, while the latter is associated with certain types of mathematical operation. Two further clarifications of what Hegel has juxtaposed here in terms of internal and external relation should certainly be made: first, that the logic here contrasted with mathematics is not the formal Aristotelian type which in fact manifests a similar degree of externality (see Hegel 1934, 2: 253–259); secondly, that the mathematics here contrasted with logic is not the arithmology of the Neopythagoreans which was actually more speculative than he is prepared to admit. Still, one must commend the perspicacity with which these extreme cases of relationality have been identified.

Of course, Hegel's theory of relation does not consist entirely of depicting pure internal and external varieties without any mediate terms. In particular, the discussion of mathematical ratio provides a sense in which number is beginning to acquire a more decidedly "notional" character. This is apparent from the layout of the logical sphere itself since, within the division of Being, Quality is opposed by Quantity, and their opposition overcome in Measure; and within the subdivision of Quantity, Quantity is opposed to Quantum, and their opposition overcome in Quantitative Ratio. So the category of Quantitative Ratio (Hegel 1934, 1: 322–324) represents a higher truth than Quantum since the terms involved are no longer *als äusserliche Quanta aufeinander bezogen* [related to one another as external quanta] but each acquires its determinateness *in dieser Beziehung auf das Andere* [in this relation to the other]. More specifically, the category constitutes a higher truth since the quanta involved are beginning to acquire the qualitative character which points towards the eventual overcoming of Quantity within Measure. For example (Hegel 1934, 1: 245 ff.), in the ratio 2:7 the numbers retain their original *quantitative Bestimmtheit* [quantitative determination] but *als eine in sich seiende qualitative* [as one which is in itself qualitative] owing to their presence in a ratio. Because of the determinateness possessed by the ratio, the numbers could be replaced by 4 and 14, 6 and 21, and so forth to infinity without altering the value of the fraction. What emerges from discussions like these is a conviction that, within the realm of mathematics, the manipulation of ratios is a higher form of thinking than operations like addition and subtraction. In other words, the criticism levelled against mathematical thought is directed only against its most external manifestations.

Some of Hegel's discussion here represents an interesting commentary on the mathematical relation conceived by Eriugena. See chapter two, p. 89 ff.

Excursus to Chapter 1

Excursus to section 1.3

Texts:

A. Alan of Lille: *Anticlaudianus* II. 209+212+242−258.
B. Alan of Lille: *Anticlaudianus* VII. 56−73.
C. Alan of Lille: *De planctu Naturae*, pr. 3, 13+44−50.
D. Alan of Lille: *De planctu Naturae*, pr. 4, 208−216.

In passage *A* and *B*, *Concordia* is personified — clearly under the influence of Prudentius: *Psychomachia* 823 ff. — and depicted as a creative principle. In *A*, she establishes specific harmonies among the elements, among the planets, and between soul and body; in *B*, she constitutes the harmony between soul and body in particular. In the latter text, Concord's association with both arithmetic and music is emphasized. Passages *C* and *D* depict the assignment of concord as an abstract property to created things by Nature and by God respectively. *C* explores the presence of this property in both macrocosm and microcosm, and *D* the association of the property with dialectical and rhetorical notions of relation, genus-species, and *loci* [places]. Both texts also stress the nature of concord as a combination of opposites.

A

Concord…holds forth as follows: "…If I had not bound the elements with a stable tie, a harmonious covenant, perpetual peace, and my alternations, a clangour within would still be shaking the dissonant foundations of things and internecine warfare arousing them. The elements would lie removed from their tasks, ignorant of motion, rusted from inactivity, confused in position, confounded in shape, and agitated in a random manner. And if the stars of heaven, the alternations of the sky, and the seven planets were not willingly submissive to my laws and joined by order, peace, trust, number, and bond, they would all rush heedlessly to a fortuitous destruction. If my joining had not bound souls to bodies, the spirit would come forth and return to its own origins, disdaining to inhabit the shacks and workhouses of the flesh. Reason proves, states, argues, teaches, insists, and demonstrates that nothing is preserved in existence which refuses to obey my laws and edicts."

B

As soon as Nature's right hand has blessed the matter with human features, Concord allies soul with flesh and connects dissonant things with a stable tie. She fits the simple to the complex and the refined to the crass with a delicate connection and subtle adhesives, binds them in an agreeable treaty, and marries the divine to flesh. Thus she joins day to night and aether to earth; thus diverse things maintain peace; thus dissonant things set aside their normal enmity. Flesh no longer threatens war, but yields to spirit — not without considerable grumbling. And spirit no longer shrinks back in horror from the corporeal garment, but is gladdened by such a shelter and shade. So that Concord may better complete her work, the maiden who pledges to us the lore of numbers and the one who shows us the binding of voices and the linking of sounds assist the process in hand. They strengthen the marriage of the two, bind them with numbers, and unite them in a reliable compact, so that the substance of heaven may wed the flesh.

C

And Nature said: "...I am the one who has modelled human nature after the archetypal paradigm of the world's mechanism, so that the nature of the world itself might appear inscribed in him as though in a mirror. For just as the concordant discord, the unitary plurality, the dissonant consonance, and the inharmonious harmony of the four elements produce the structure of the world's palace; so also the disparate parity, the unequal equality, the unlike likeness, and the differentiated sameness of the four blendings establish the fabric of the human body..."

D

So God assigned various species of things to the palace of the world and, although they were separated by the conflict of differing genera, he moderated them with the harmony of legitimate order, imposed laws on them, and bound them with decrees. Thus with the relational embrace of a certain reciprocal condition, he allied things representing contraries in the opposition of their genera and segregated into places opposite to one another, and turned the strife of contradiction into the peace of friendship. So when all things were concordant in the subtle links of an invisible chain, multiplicity ran back to unity, difference to identity, dissonance to consonance, and discord to concord in a peaceful unification.

58   *Excursus to Chapter 1*

Excursus to section 1.5

Texts:

A. Aurelian of Réôme: *Musica disciplina* 3, pp. 64–66.
B. Hrotsvitha: *Pafnutius* 1, 4–7 + 9–17.
C. Adelard of Bath: *De eodem et diverso* p. 26, 34–27. 19.
D. Hugh of St. Victor: *Didascalicon* II. 12, 756B–757A.
E. Bernard Silvestris: *In Martianum* 3, 4–6 + 19–23 + 36–63.
F. Alan of Lille: *Anticlaudianus* III. 410–441.

All these texts are developments in some form of Boethius: *De institutione musica* I. 2, 187. 20 ff. on the classification of musics. Passage *A* is a direct quotation of the original together with some additional elements: citations of Scripture and Gregory the Great (cf. *D*), the notion of a relation between macrocosm and microcosm (cf. *B, E, F*), and a redefinition of the second type of human music as that within parts of the soul *and* of the body. Hrotsvitha's text (*B*) prefaces the Boethian classification of musics with discussions of the macrocosm to microcosm relation, of the contrariety underlying concord — it is here argued that the contrariety between body and soul is greater than that between the elements and that there is nothing contrary to substance —, and of the sameness and difference underlying concord (cf. *F*). Boethius' classification is then presented with both selection and expansion: the three main types of music are related to one another, the cosmic music is identified with the celestial music manifested in both spatial intervals and audible notes, the three types of music are related to the various consonances (cf. *F*), and the human music is divided into that uniting body and soul, that involving high and low pitches, and that contained in periodic natural processes. Passage *C* establishes an intertextual relation between the Boethian material and Plato's *Timaeus*, arguing that the various musics are produced by the world-soul. It also elaborates the theory of consonance from an epistemological perspective (cf. *E*). In passage *D*, Hugh of St. Victor develops Boethius' classification of musics by extending it with further triadic subdivisions:

Figure 3. Hugh of St. Victor's classification of musics

and by reinforcing the theory with scriptural citation. Passage *E* explores an intertextual relation between the Boethian material and Martianus Capella's *De nuptiis*, placing the various musics under the administration of Hymenaeus. The classification of musics is presented clearly in its original form, although there are certain additions to that argument: the idea of macrocosm and microcosm, and an epistemological perspective — different musics are judged with different psychic faculties and therefore to be studied in a definite order. Alan of Lille's text (*F*) again explores an intertextual relation between the Boethian material and Martianus Capella's *De nuptiis*, finding visual depictions of the various musics on the robe of a personified Musica. These are selected from the original classification of musics, although there are also additions to that discussion: the idea of macrocosm and microcosm, the notion of contrariety underlying concord, the description of consonances, and the problem of bisecting the tone.

Texts *A* to *F* were probably written with knowledge of the glosses on Boethius' *De institutione musica* then in circulation. Among those which are extent, the glosses in the MSS. *Paris, Bibliothèque nationale, latin 7200 and London, British Library, Arundel 77* contain developments along philosophical lines similar to those in Hrotsvitha's text (*B*) in particular.

A

There are known to be three kinds of music: the first cosmic, the second human, and the third produced by certain instruments. The cosmic is particularly evident in those things which are observed in heaven itself or in earth, and in the variation of elements or seasons, for philosophers say that the heaven rotates. And how can it happen that so swift a heavenly machine can move with a noiseless and silent course? If indeed that sound does not reach our ears, still we know that a certain harmony of modulation is present in this heaven, particularly since the Lord says in Job: "Or who has put to sleep the symphony of heaven?" And if a certain harmony did not join the diversities of the four elements: that is, winter, spring, summer, and autumn, how could it happen that they should come together into a single body and matter?... Human music is most fully present in the microcosm — that is, that "lesser world" which the philosophers call man since "mikros" in Greek corresponds to "minor" in Latin and "kosmos" in Greek to "mundus" in Latin. Hence, man is called a lesser world and the Lord says: "Preach the Gospel to every creature" meaning to man alone as the blessed Gregory has explained more than sufficiently. For what blends that incorporeal vigour of reason with the body except a certain adjustment and, so to speak, tuning of low and high pitches as though producing one consonance? What else connects to one another the parts of the soul and body in man himself who, as Aristotle maintains, is composed of rational and irrational: that is, in receiving spirit from the sun and body from the moon? What is there besides this which mingles the elements of the body or holds its parts together in a fixed adjustment? The third type of music is produced by certain instruments, for example organs, citharas, lyres, and much else...

B

Pafnutius. Just as the greater world is made up of four elements which are contrary yet concordant according to a harmonic regulation at the creator's behest, so man also is fitted together not only from these same elements but also from parts which are more contrary.

Disciples. And what is more contrary than the elements?

P. Body and soul. This is because the elements, although contrary, are however corporeal. But the soul is not mortal like the body, nor the body spiritual like the soul.

D. That is true.

P. But if we follow the dialecticians, we do not admit even these to be contraries.

D. Who could deny it?

P. Someone who knows how to argue dialectically, since nothing is contrary to substance although she is the recipient of contraries.

D. But what is the meaning of your phrase "according to a harmonic regulation"?

P. It means that, just as lower and higher pitches when joined harmonically produce something musical, so dissonant elements when coming fittingly into concord complete a single world.

D. It is strange how dissonant things can be described as concordant and concordant things as dissonant.

P. This is because nothing seems to be composed of similar things or of things joined by no principle of ratio and distinct from one another in their entire substance and nature.

D. What is music?

P. One of the disciplines in the quadrivium of philosophy…

D. What is its task?…

P. It discusses sounds.

D. Is there one music or several?

P. There are said to be three kinds. However, each is joined to another by such a principle of ratio that whatever properly belongs to one is not absent from the other.

D. And what differences are there between the three?

P. The first is called cosmic or celestial, the second human, and the third that which is performed on instruments.

D. Where does the celestial occur?

P. In the seven planets and the celestial sphere.
D. How does it occur?
P. In the same manner as does that using instruments, since as many spatial intervals, corresponding pitches, and the same consonances are found there as in strings.
D. What are these spatial intervals?
P. Distances measured either between planets or between strings.
D. What are pitches?
P. The same thing as tones.
D. We are ignorant of those also.
P. A tone arises from two sounds and has the ratio of the "epogdoos" number or 9:8.
D. The more quickly we attempt to pass over the topic of discussion, the more difficult for us are the things which you keep bringing up.
P. A discussion of this kind requires it.
D. Give us some kind of summary regarding consonances, so that we may at least understand the term's meaning.
P. A consonance is said to be a blending in modulation.
D. Why is that so?
P. Because it is achieved sometimes with four, sometimes five, and sometimes eight notes.
D. Since we know that the consonances are three, we would like to distinguish their individual names.
P. The first is called "diatessaron" as though from four notes, and possesses the "epitritus" ratio or 4:3. The second is called "diapente" and arises from five notes: it is in the "hemiolius" ratio or 3:2. The third is called "diapason", being in the ratio of 2:1 and completed in eight notes.
D. Do the sphere and planets emit a sound so that they merit comparison with strings?
P. A very loud one.
D. Why is it not heard?
P. This is explained in various ways. Some contend that it cannot be heard because it is continuous, others because the air is too dense. However, some argue that such a volume of sound cannot enter the narrow passages of our ears. There are even those who maintain that the sphere emits so pleasant and so sweet a sound that, if it were heard, all men alike would become unconscious of themselves and disregard

D. It is better for it not to be heard.
P. This was foreseen by the creator.
D. May that suffice on the topic. Continue regarding the human music.
P. What about it?
D. In what is it perceived?
P. Not only, as I have said, in the conjunction of body and soul, and in the emission of voice now low and now high, but also in the pulsing of veins and in the measurement of certain limbs like the joints of fingers. By measuring, we find here the same ratios mentioned above in connection with consonances, since music is said to be the agreement not only of sounds but also of other dissimilar things.

C

So the same philosopher mentioned earlier said that a world soul was established with harmonies of this kind, not because he understood it simplistically in such a manner but suggesting as an inner meaning that, while the soul has many powers, one of its most important is the power whereby, being concordant with itself, it loves to impart that same property to bodies and that, inasmuch as it perceives the bodies' parts as harmonious, it exercises its own powers in them. So it also happens that soul does not cease to animate one body, while leaving another body inanimate for some time. And Pythagoras did not overlook this fact when investigating the soul's distinctions with a concern far from superficial and, lest posterity might be ignorant on this topic, committed it to writing. He taught first that there is one music which is cosmic, another which is human, and another which is instrumental — for qualities of elements, weights, and periods of time are not removed from this concord. Next he argued that those sounds which among the innumerable multitude are to be assigned the dignity of consonance — reducing them to a small and definite number on the grounds that anything valuable is rare — are to be analyzed not by sensory discernment incapable of grasping any subtlety but by rational judgement. For he himself had only understood the science of music when led by a rational deduction from the sound of hammers, and reasoned mathematically from that sound to the other kinds of instrument.

D

There are three types of music: cosmic, human, and instrumental. Of the cosmic, one kind is in the elements, another in the planets, another in the seasons; of the elemental, one kind is in weight, another in number, another in measure; of the planetary, one kind is in their position, another in their motion, another in their nature; of the seasonal, one kind is in days — in the alternation of day and night —, another in months — in the waxing and waning of the moon —, another in years — in the changing of spring, summer, autumn, and winter. Of the human music, one kind is in the body, another in the soul, another in the connection of the two; of the bodily, one kind is in the vital power by which it grows — belonging to all creatures brought to birth —, another in the humours through whose blending the human body subsists — which is common to all sensing things —, another in the activities belonging specifically to rational creatures — among which the mechanical is preeminent... Of the soul's music, one kind is in its virtues — for example justice, piety, and temperance —, another in its faculties — for example reason, anger, concupiscence. The music between body and soul is that natural amity whereby the soul is connected to the body not by corporeal bonds but by certain affections in order to impart motion or sensation to that body. In accordance with this amity, "no man has hated his own flesh." This music implies that the flesh should be loved but the spirit more, and that the body should be cherished and virtue not destroyed. Of instrumental music, one kind is in striking — as occurs with drums and strings —, another in blowing — as with pipes and organ —, another in the voice — as with songs and chants...

E

Being about to discuss the conjunction of speech and reason, the philosopher begins with the cause of conjunction: namely the beneficial concord which unites natures, even dissonant ones, into a single essence... So let Hymenaeus who presides over marriage represent concord, the cause of all conjunction, since the meaning of the Greek word Hymenaeus is "alliance". This universal music has many powers which we understand as the functions of this god... But music is divided into cosmic, human, and instrumental. The cosmic music is in elements, seasons, and planets; the human in the humours of the body, the powers of the soul, and the conjunction of the soul and the body; the instrumental in metres, rhythms, and songs. So there are three functions of Hymenaeus. It should also be noted that, since there are three modes of judging in the soul, there are also three parts of music. Instrumental music has as its adjudicator partly sense and partly reason, for hearing perceives the low and high pitches but reason the interval, ratio, and number. The adjudicator of the cosmic is reason, and of the human reason to the extent that body and intelligence to the extent that soul is involved. Since sense is more familiar to man than reason, and also reason more familiar than intelligence — which belongs only to God and very few outstanding men — the instrumental is first to be taught and apprehended, the cosmic second, and the human last. Just as man is greater than the world which was made for his benefit, so the human is greater than the cosmic music. But that superiority is determined in respect of the soul, for man is called microcosm in respect of the body… It was taking account of the aforesaid order that Boethius, when he undertook the task of describing the whole of music, began with the instrumental, intending to speak next of the cosmic and finally of the human. Teaching chooses the order of apprehension rather than that of nature in dealing with things. Hence a discussion of creatures always precedes a discussion of the creator; hence Plato also set a treatment of the body before that of the world soul. In observing the same order, Martianus first indicates the power of the instrumental by saying: "You, whom as harpist…" etc.; then the cosmic with these words: "Who the seeds with arcane…" etc.; and finally the power of the human…

F

Attired in a striking gown, the maiden shows herself to be the foster-child of peace and no seeker of war's lightning-bolts. On it is sported the smiling playfulness of a picture revealing in various designs what music can accomplish: what are its bonds, with what ties it fits all things together; what are the species of the art; which music connects the hours, distinguishes the months, arranges the seasons of the year, limits their excesses, binds the elements, and joins the planets; which music moves the stars, connects their various alternations, and arranges the parts of the human body and the lesser world — honouring him with the image of a better world as a pygmy might deserve to be the little brother of giants and the lesser to be depicted in the image of the greater; which music unites the parts of the soul, allies it to the flesh, and strengthens this compact; which music distinguishes notes, and varies the intervals between them with numbers; what is the reason that not one note but their combination produces every song and sweet-sounding melody — its sound being dissimilar and similar, different and identical, unitary and simple, double, diverse, and other; in what manner music changes herself when the melody is changed, interweaving laughter with tears and serious with playful — now to resound in the enharmonic, now lamenting her depiction of sad events in a diatonic refrain, and now revelling in the chromatic; which note has duple ratio to another or which melody sounds at the octave; which sound has sesquialter ratio to it or sounds as its concord at the fifth; which coupling of notes produces a fourth with one sounding note contending or rather playing with three others; what is the reason that one part of a tone always overflows in transgression the other part so that the whole tone cannot be divided into equal portions...

Part II: The logical

Chapter 2

Components of concord — Binary relations (ontological)

2.1 Eriugena and the square of opposition

As outlined in the previous chapter,[255] our project is to examine the appearance of the lexeme "harmony" and the actualization of certain of its semes in conjunction with the lexeme "signification" and the actualization of some of its semes in medieval philosophical texts. Of the three unfolded lexemes determined to be analytically useful — a. Relation (L) + binary (s), b. Harmony (L) + relative (s) + ternary (s), and c. Signification (L) + relative (s) + ternary (s) — it is natural to begin with the first. During the interpretative process, it will be necessary to activate various further semes which are discovered by a method not explicitly proposed in the texts but correlated according to principles officially formulated there. Although the unfolded lexemes are technically speaking the Latin *relatio (referre), habitus (habere)*, etc. rather than the English "Relation" to which they correspond, in analyzing their primary semes there is no compelling reason to adopt a Latin in preference to an English meta-language.[256]

To study the actualization of semes is to elaborate that strategy which produces any coherent reading of texts but is perhaps not formally definable. It may be useful to think in terms of "isotopies" or sets of semantic categories permitting the uniform reading of a narrative: the isotopy comprising an amalgamation of recurrent semes within various lexemes,[257] the further isotopy constituting an amalgamation of recurrent semantic categories derived from those semes, and so forth.[258] In our discussion of binary relation, the actualized semes would enter into an amalgamation of the second type. It may also be convenient to think in terms of "topics" or mental processes inferring causes from effects and rules by abduction: one could therefore distinguish a topic promoting the amalgamation of recurrent semes[259] within various lexemes, and another topic producing the amalgamation of recurrent semantic categories derived from those semes. Nevertheless, these remain crude attempts to characterize a

70   *Components of concord — Binary relations (ontological)*

strategy which is really as variegated as the semes with whose actualization it deals.

In the identification of semes, the first stage is to isolate semantic features [260] which the chosen texts display most frequently. A listing of the terms "cognitive", "complex", "dialectical", "existent", "mathematical", and "simple" implies an alphabetical arrangement which would dissociate such features from a hidden set of priorities — appropriately enough during the initial moments of an investigation. However, the selection of terms like "cognitive", "complex", and "dialectical" to begin with suggests a hierarchical assumption whereby the features are derived from a pre-existing encyclopaedic competence of some description. [261]

The second stage in the identification of semes is to isolate semantic features which recur with the greatest frequency in pairs. This is because the primary question is how semantic elements operate in combination, and the minimal combinatory unit is a pair of such elements. From the purely theoretical viewpoint the following groups could occur: 1. "cognitive" + 2. "complex"; 1. "cognitive" + 3. "dialectical"; 1. "cognitive" + 4. "existent"; 1. "cognitive" + 5. "mathematical"; 1. "cognitive" + 6. "simple"; 2. "complex" + 3. "dialectical"; 2. "complex" + 4. "existent"; 2. "complex" + 5. "mathematical"; 2. "complex" + 6. "simple"; 3. "dialectical" + 4. "existent"; 3. "dialectical" + 5. "mathematical"; 3. "dialectical" + 6. "simple"; 4. "existent" + 5. "mathematical"; 4. "existent" + 6. "simple"; and 5. "mathematical" + 6. "simple". In such cases, the relations within pairs of semantic features could be assumed as those of synonymity, difference, or antonymity conformable to everyday linguistic usage. [262] Nevertheless, from the strictly empirical viewpoint the following groups occur predominantly: 1. "cognitive" + 4. "existent", 2. "complex" + 6. "simple", and 3. "dialectical" + 5. "mathematical". Here, the relations within pairs of semantic features are definitely revealed as being "equivalence", "continuity", and "pseudo-hierarchy" according to certain technical definitions. Semantic relations [263] like these can perhaps most fittingly be visualized in terms of geometrical axes. Moreover, given that they have been determined to be three in number, such relations are peculiarly comparable with height, width, and depth respectively. [264]

In speaking of the identification of semes, it has already been necessary to mention relations between semantic elements. This shift of emphasis is not unpremeditated, given that some medieval writers understood linguistic content as a network of oppositional terms where the relations between units are the determining factor, thereby anticipating modern structural semantics.²⁶⁵ But this question can be pursued further using certain arguments supplied by Eriugena's *Periphyseon*.

According to Eriugena, the organizing principle not only of nature itself but also of the text disclosing nature is a square of opposition. The first passage outlining this schema utilizes essentially semantic terms of reference by describing as the sphere of possible discourse:²⁶⁶ a single *vocabulum* [word] — that is, a lexeme — *physis/natura* [nature];²⁶⁷ and by finding within it four *differentiae* [differences] — that is, semes — : *quae creat* [creating] (a_1), *quae non creatur* [not created] ($\bar{a}_2$), *quae creatur* [created] (a_2), and *quae non creat* [not creating] ($\bar{a}_1$)²⁶⁸ these combining to form four *species* [species] — that is, sememes — : *quae creat et non creatur* [creating and not created] ($b_1 = a_1 + \bar{a}_2$), *quae et creatur et creat* [both created and creating] ($b_2 = a_2 + a_1$), *quae creatur et non creat* [created and not creating] ($\bar{b}_1 = a_2 + \bar{a}_1$), and *quae nec creat nec creatur* [neither creating nor created] ($\bar{b}_2 = \bar{a}_1 + \bar{a}_2$).²⁶⁹ The semantic framework is retained when Eriugena further explains the interrelation of sememes as *oppositio/e contrario/contradicere* [opposition/ contrariety/contradiction] between $\bar{b}_1$ and b_1 and between $\bar{b}_2$ and b_2.²⁷⁰

The second passage outlining the square of opposition combines semantic and ontological terms of reference: in other words, isotopies of existence, transcendence of spatio-temporality, etc. activate additional semes.²⁷¹ For example, — after some introductory remarks which, by contrasting the relation of sememes to lexeme with those of species to genus and of parts to whole, show a true appreciation of semantic complexity — Eriugena interprets the four sememes as an ontological and processive-revertive or as an epistemological and divisive-collective schema.²⁷² From the processive and divisive viewpoint, he describes the interrelation of the sememes $\bar{b}_1$ and b_1 and of the sememes b_2 and $\bar{b}_2$ as *veluti quodam diametro ad se invicem e regione opponi* [direct opposition to one another as though along some diameter];²⁷³ that of the semes a_1 and a_1 in the sememes b_2 and b_1, of the semes a_2 and a_2 in the sememes $\bar{b}_1$ and b_2, of the semes $\bar{a}_1$ and $\bar{a}_1$ in the sememes $\bar{b}_1$ and $\bar{b}_2$, and of the semes $\bar{a}_2$ and $\bar{a}_2$ in the sememes $\bar{b}_2$ and b_1 as †*similis/ similitudo* [similarity]; and that of the semes a_2 and $\bar{a}_2$ in the sememes b_2 and b_1, of the semes $\bar{a}_1$ and a_1 in the sememes $\bar{b}_1$ and b_2, of the semes a_2 and $\bar{a}_2$ in the sememes $\bar{b}_1$ and $\bar{b}_2$, and of the semes $\bar{a}_1$ and a_1 in the sememes $\bar{b}_2$ and b_1 as †*distare/differre/ dissimilis* [difference/dissimilarity], largely retaining the semantic framework. But from the revertive and collective viewpoint things become more complicated. Although he admits the interrelation of the semes a_2 and a_2

72 *Components of concord — Binary relations (ontological)*

in the sememes b_2 and $\bar{b}_1$ to be similarity but that of the sememes b_2 and $\bar{b}_1$ themselves to be difference — the similarity and the difference being existent as well as perceived relations —, he declares the interrelation of the semes $\bar{a}_2$ and $\bar{a}_2$ in the sememes b_1 and $\bar{b}_2$ and that of the sememes b_1 and $\bar{b}_2$ themselves to be similarity — the similarity being a fully existent but the difference a merely perceived relation. This is possible because the four sememes are now articulated ontologically as God the beginning ($= b_1$), primordial causes ($= b_2$), spatio-temporal effects ($= \bar{b}_1$), and God the end ($= \bar{b}_2$) respectively.

It is obvious that relations between semantic elements in general can be delineated using these arguments supplied by Eriugena.[274] Given that he himself employs them in different contexts — to mention only the treatment of relations between oppositional terms like participating/participated,[275] understood/named,[276] and spiritual/corporeal[277] elsewhere in his writing —, it could be said that he actively endorses such general application. But in order to pursue the question further, we must return to certain conclusions already reached.[278]

In the correlation of semes, the first stage is to apply the square of opposition to pairs of semantic features which the selected texts display most frequently. From the purely theoretical viewpoint the following groups could occur: X. "existent" + "not cognitive" ($b_1 = A_1 + B_0$), "cognitive" + "existent" ($b_2 = B_1 + A_1$), "cognitive" + "not existent" ($\bar{b}_1 = B_1 + A_0$), and "not existent + not cognitive" ($\bar{b}_2 = A_0 + B_0$); Y. "dialectical" + "not mathematical" ($b_1 = A_1 + B_0$), "mathematical" + "dialectical" ($b_2 = B_1 + A_1$), "mathematical" + "not dialectical" ($\bar{b}_1 = B_1 + A_0$), and "not dialectical" + "not mathematical" ($\bar{b}_2 = A_0 + B_0$); Z. "complex" + "not simple" ($b_1 = A_1 + B_0$), "simple" + "complex" ($b_2 = B_1 + A_1$), "simple" + "not complex" ($\bar{b}_1 = B_1 + A_0$), and "not complex" + "not simple" ($\bar{b}_2 = A_0 + B_0$).[279] Of course, the semantic features should be discovered rather than invented, and the influence of certain encyclopaedic predispositions cannot be discounted.[280] So from the strictly empirical viewpoint the following groups are excluded: 1. "existent" + "not cognitive" ($b_1 = A_1 + B_0$) and "cognitive" + "not existent" ($\bar{b}_1 = B_1 + A_0$); 2. "dialectical" + "not mathematical" ($b_1 = A_1 + B_0$). We shall henceforth characterize the axis discerned in the existent and the cognitive, where b_2 and $\bar{b}_2$ are present but b_1 and $\bar{b}_1$ absent: i.e. where neither constituent term is present affirmatively with the negative of the other, as that of equivalence.[281] Its arrangement results from an encyclopaedic predisposition which might be called "idealism". The axis discerned in the dialectical and the mathematical, where b_2, $\bar{b}_1$, and $\bar{b}_2$ are present but b_1 absent: i.e. where one component is present affirmatively and negatively with the other but not vice versa, will be that of pseudo-hierarchy.[282] This arrangement stems from an encyclopaedia which could be termed "Neopythagoreanism". We shall henceforth characterize the axis discerned in the complex and the simple, where b_1, b_2, $\bar{b}_1$, and $\bar{b}_2$ are present: i.e. where each constituent term is present affirmatively with the negative of the other, that of continuity.[283] Its arrangement results from an encyclopaedic predisposition which might be called "emanationism".

The second stage in the correlation of semes is to apply the square of opposition to pairs of semantic features which recur with the greatest frequency in clusters. This is because the primary task is to ascertain how semantic elements operate in combination, and clusters of such elements are the most typical combinatory units. Of the 24 clusters available,[284] $X(b_2) + Y(b_2) + Z(b_1)$, $X(b_2) + Y(b_2) + Z(\bar{b}_1)$, $X(\bar{b}_2) + Y(\bar{b}_1) + Z(\bar{b}_1)$, and $X(\bar{b}_2) + Y(\bar{b}_2) + Z(b_2)$ are particularly common — corresponding to the spatio-temporal, primordial causes, the monad, and God respectively. It is extremely useful to visualize the semantic relations implied here by recalling the geometrical image. Given that they can be interpreted as three different axes, such relations exhibit a close analogy with the dimensions of physical space.

In addition to those paired on axes, it is necessary to apply a further isotopy without which a coherent reading of our texts will not be possible. This could be called the "isotopy of internal relation". In fact, the assumption that all relations are internal[285] underlies the presentation of the axes of equivalence, pseudo-hierarchy, and continuity, explaining that the affirmations and negations establishing those axes overlap rather than cancel one another in the logical sense. The philosophical history of the isotopy of internal relation has been discussed in the first chapter. At this point it should merely be added that a geometrical analogy is particularly fitted to capture such an isotopy on account of its obviously continuous rather than discrete character.[286]

2.2 Relation in ps.-Augustine: *Categoriae decem*

The earliest period of creative philosophical activity during the Middle Ages ran from the eighth to ninth centuries. In this so-called "Carolingian" era, a number of treatises dealing with logic and derived ultimately from the Aristotelian *Organon* were available: Boethius' translation of Porphyry's *Isagoge*, the same writer's commentary on Aristotle's *Categories*, and the pseudo-Augustinian *Categoriae decem*.[287] Although perhaps least well known to modern scholars of the history of logic, it was the treatise falsely attributed to Augustine which obviously impressed the Carolingians, since they included it in all their logical manuscripts and glossed it profusely. From this text it was possible to extract not only Aristotle's original classification of logical terms under ten headings — substance, quantity, relation, quality, action, passion, situation, place, time, condition — but also some non-Aristotelian elaboration. In fact, the latter rather than the former was often the primary source of inspiration.

The ps.-Augustinian *Categoriae decem* can be divided into an introductory section and the section on the categories proper. The introductory section is explicitly structured as two overlapping parts dealing with words — which *significant* [signify] — and with things — which *significantur* [are signified] — respectively.[288] Our anonymous author goes on to cite his contemporary Themistius by way of explanation: Aristotle's interest lay primarily in things, but he could not avoid discussing thoughts — *sēmainomena sive phantasias, imagines rerum insidentes animo* [signifieds or phantasies, images of things residing in the mind] — and words,[289] since thoughts are arising from things and communicated by words. However, this explanation seemingly demands a threefold rather than the twofold structure actually presented.

The part of the introduction dealing with words begins by explaining the unique importance of substantives and verbs: the linguistic items which indicate something with a word.[290] It continues by distinguishing A. where many things are named with one word, and B. where one thing is named by many words; within A, 1. homonyms which are united in the term but separate in its interpretation, 2. synonyms which are united both in the term and in its interpretation, and 3. paronyms having the name of homonyms but the function of synonyms; within B, 1. polyonyms where the diversity of names has no rational explanation, and 2. heteronyms where it has a rational explanation; within A 1, a. homonyms arising accidentally, and b. homonyms established deliberately; and within A 1, b. homonyms established deliberately α. through similarity, β. by analogy, γ. from unity, and δ. to unity.[291] The verbal part of the introduction concludes by stressing the special relevance of uncombined words: those not producing complete utterances capable of being true or false.[292]

The part of the introduction dealing with things is for its author the more important. It establishes a context for understanding Aristotle's ten categories by explaining the distinction between substance and accident — four classes are articulated: 1. †*de subiecto significantur et in subiecto non sunt* [things signified of a subject but not existing in a subject] i.e. universal substances; 2. †*nec in subiecto sunt nec de subiecto significantur* [things neither existing in a subject nor signified of a subject] i.e. individual substances; 3. †*quae et in subiecto sint et de subiecto significentur* [things both existing in a subject and signified of a subject] i.e. universal accidents; and 4. †*in subiecto quidem sunt sed de subiecto minime significantur* [things existing in a subject but not signified of a subject] i.e. individual accidents — and by showing that the first category is a substance and the other nine accidents.[293] This context is reinforced by explaining the distinction between genus, differentia, and species — of these three a. genus is that which in many different things is signified *quid sit specie* [as to substance by form]; b. differentia that which likewise is signified *quale sit specie* [as to quality by form]; and c. species that which likewise is signified *quid sit numero* [as to substance by number] — and by showing that the categories are genera.[294]

The whole introductory section of the ps.-Augustinian treatise ends by classifying the ten categories. Of those contrasted with substance, the three categories of quality, quantity, and situation are described as inside substance, the three categories of place, time, and condition as outside substance, and the three categories of relation, action, and passion as both inside and outside substance.[295] After this comes the main section of the treatise with successive discussions of substance, quantity, relation, quality, action-passion, situation, time-place, and condition; and supplementary notes on opposition, priority, simultaneity, and motion.

The section of *Categoriae decem* dealing with the term *ad aliquid = pros ti* [relation] is one of the longer. It begins by defining this category as *quae id quod est dicitur ex altero sine cuius societate esse non possit* [whatever is declared to be what it is through another without whose association it could not exist].[296] Examples are given of double to single, greater to lesser, and similar to similar. Pseudo-Augustine points out that other terms connected with the category like *habitus* [condition] or *disciplina/scientia* [knowledge] are so defined — a condition is always the condition of something — and that such relational notions also approximate to the category of quality.[297] There is a difference given that knowledge may be of the knowable and therefore in relation or of a man and thereby a quality. Nevertheless, relation *in omnes enim videtur incurrere* [seems to arise in all the categories].[298]

The text now essays a second definition in postulating relation *cum sub uno ortu atque occasu et id quod iungitur et id cui iungitur invenitur* [when that which is connected and that to which it is connected are discovered with a single beginning and end].[299] Further illustrations are provided of master to slave and double to single. Pseudo-Augustine observes that this category is only rightly understood when *singulare ad singulare refertur* [an individual is related to an individual].[300] He also rejects the opinion of those who discover it in situations apparently lacking simultaneity of beginning and end. For example, in the relation between knowable thing and someone's knowledge of it, the knowable object and the *potentia* = *dynamis* [potentiality] of someone's knowledge do nevertheless begin and end together.[301]

The author next rephrases his second definition with greater confidence. Things related are †*semper ea simul vel extingui vel nasci* [those which are invariably either destroyed or born at the same time].[302] The earlier illustrations of master to slave and double to single are repeated this time with comments on the Latin grammatical cases involved. Ps.-Augustine notes that with this category *inter coniuncta duo, quae ex se pendeant, sit alterna conversio*, [there should be a reciprocal convertibility between the two connected terms depending on one another].[303] By so doing he resolves a confusion in the minds of some between the relation of one term to another and the possession of an attribute by a substance. For example, "the wing of the winged thing" represents the latter only since it cannot be converted into the form "the winged thing of the wing".[304]

The section on relation concludes with some further observations. In particular, it is important to distinguish this category from *opposita* = *antikeimena* [opposition] although the two notions often seem alike. Thus, *calidum non frigidi calidum sed frigido oppositum… iustum non iniusti iustum sed iniusto contrarium* [hot is not the hot of cold but opposed to cold, and just not the just of unjust but contrary to unjust].[305] Another point is that relation sometimes exhibits the possibility of *magis et minus* [more and less] and sometimes not. Indeed, similar can become more similar to the similar although father cannot become more father to his son.[306]

2.3 Eriugena's theory of relation

Among philosophical writers of the Carolingian era who respond constructively to the ps.-Augustinian teaching, a pre-eminent status must clearly be assigned to Iohannes Scottus Eriugena.[307] His discussion of dialectical relation constitutes a lengthy section of *Periphyseon* book I. Since this is embedded within a particularly complex account of all ten Aristotelian categories,[308] it may be useful to preface our interpretation of it with a summary of that wider context. A pseudo-logical structure for the latter can be constructed as follows:[309]

Table 2. Eriugena's account of the categories

1.	List of the categories
2.	Application of categories to God
2.1.	Substance, quantity, quality applied to God
2.2.	The problem of relation
2.3.	Situation applied to God
2.4.	The problem of condition
2.5.	Other categories applied to God
3.	List of the categories
4.	Interpretation of categories in terms of motion and rest
4.1.1.1.	Are condition and relation at rest?
4.1.1.2.	Condition and relation are in motion
4.1.2.	"In a subject" means in motion, "not in a subject" means at rest
4.1.3.1.	Are quantity, situation, and place in motion?
4.1.3.2.	Quantity, situation, and place are at rest
4.1.4.	Are quantity, situation, and place substances or accidents?
4.2.1.	Aristotle's fourfold classification and the meaning of "in a subject"
4.2.2.	Gregory of Nyssa's twofold scheme and the meaning of "in a substance"
4.2.2.1.	Substance, quantity, quality and this scheme
4.2.2.2.	Relation
4.2.2.3.	Condition
4.2.2.4.	Other categories
5.	Interdependence of the categories
6.1.	Properties of substance, quantity, quality
6.2.	Properties of relation
6.3.	Properties of situation
6.4.	Properties of condition
6.5.	Properties of other categories

78   *Components of concord — Binary relations (ontological)*

This summary has been constructed to reveal the function within the wider context not only of the category of relation but also of that of condition.[310] Each of these is discussed four times: in the account of the categories' application to God, in connection with motion and rest, in connection with the notion: "in a subject", and in the analysis of the categories' own properties.[311] That we must take account not of one category but a pair follows from certain ambiguities in the traditional presentation of these doctrines and in Eriugena's highly original development of the latter.

The relevant parts of Periphyseon I can now be quoted in full:[312]

> *A.* ...atque ideo cum summa diligentia investigandum esse video utrum proprie in summa ac sancta trinitate trium maximarum substantiarum pater relative ad filium dicitur, similiter filius ad patrem, spiritus quoque sanctus ad patrem et filium quia spiritus amborum est — haec enim nomina habitudinem esse sanctus Gregorius theologus indubitanter asserit... *N.* categoria relationis... Restat igitur ut intelligamus hanc etiam categoriam sicut et ceteras translative de deo praedicari, vera siquidem ratiocinatio ad hoc invitat atque coartat ne ea quae praedicta sunt incipiant vacillare. Quid enim? Numquid veris ratiocinationibus obsistit si dicamus patrem et filium ipsius habitudinis quae dicitur ad aliquid nomina esse et plus quam habitudinis?... Non enim est ulla categoria fere in qua habitus quidam inveniri non possit. Nam et essentiae seu substantiae habitu quodam ad se invicem respiciunt. Dicimus enim rationabilis essentia irrationabilisque qua proportione, id est quo habitu, ad se invicem respiciunt (non enim irrationabilis diceretur nisi ab habitu absentiae rationis, quomodo non aliunde rationabilis vocatur nisi habitu praesentiae rationis). Omnis enim proportio habitus est, quamvis non omnis habitus proportio. Proprie namque proportio non minus quam in duobus potest inveniri, habitus vero etiam in singulis rebus inspicitur. Verbi gratia: habitus rationabilis animae virtus est. Est igitur proportio species quaedam habitudinis. Si autem exemplo vis declarari quomodo habitus proportionalis in essentia invenitur, ex numeris elige exemplar. Numeri enim, ut aestimo, essentialiter in omnibus intelliguntur. In numeris namque omnium rerum subsistit essentia. Vides igitur qualis proportio est in duobus et tribus? *A.* Video plane. Sesqualteram esse arbitror; et hoc uno exemplo aliorum omnium substantialium numerorum inter se invicem collatorum varias proportionis species possum cognoscere. *N.* Intende itaque ad reliqua... *A.* In quantitatibus magna et parva et media inter se comparata multa pollent habitudine. Item in quantitatibus numerorum linearum temporum aliorumque similium habitudines proportionum perspicue reperies. Similiter in qualitate. Verbi gratia, in coloribus album et nigrum mediusque qualiscunque sit color

habitu sibimet iunguntur. Album siquidem et nigrum quia extremos colorum locos obtinent, habitu contrarietatis ad se invicem respiciunt. Color autem ad extrema sui, album dico nigrumque, habitu medietatis respicit. In ea quoque categoria quae dicitur *pros ti*, id est ad aliquid, clare apparet, qualis habitus patris ad filium seu filii ad patrem, amici amico, dupli ad simplum ceteraque huius modi. De situ quoque facile patet quomodo stare et iacere habitudinem quandam inter se invicem possideant. Haec enim ex diametro sibi invicem respondent: nequaquam enim intellectum standi absolutum ab intellectu iacendi cogitabis sed semper simul tibi occurrunt, quamvis in re aliqua non simul appareant. Quid dicendum est de loco quando superiora inferiora et media considerantur? Nunquid habitudine carent? *N*. Nullo modo. Non enim haec nomina ex natura rerum proveniunt sed ex respectu quodam intuentis eas per partes. Sursum siquidem et deorsum in universo non est atque ideo neque superiora neque inferiora neque media in universo sunt, nam universitatis consideratio haec respuit, partium vero introducit intentio. Eadem ratio est de maiori et minori. Nullum enim in suo genere parvum aut magnum esse potest, ex cogitatione tamen comparantium diversas quantitates talia inventa sunt, ideoque locorum seu partium contemplatio habitum in talibus gignit. Nulla enim natura maior aut minor alia natura sit, sicut neque superior neque inferior, cum una omnium subsistat natura ex uno deo condita. *A*. Quid de tempore? Nonne in ipsis dum inter se invicem conferuntur luculenter habitus arridet?... *A*. Quid in diversis agendi et patiendi motibus? Nonne habitus ubique relucet?... *N*. Ratane itaque tibi videtur haec divisio categoriarum in motu atque statu, id est quattuor in statu, sex in motu? *A*. Rata quidem. Sed adhuc de duabus non satis mihi patet, de habitu dico et relatione. Hae nanque duae categoriae magis mihi videntur esse in statu quam in motu... *N*. Fortassis non magnopere haesitasses si diligentius intuereris quia omne quod non simul connaturaliter perfecte inest creaturae sed per incrementa quaedam ad inseparabilem incommutabilemque perfectionem procedit in motu esse necesse est. Omnis autem habitus motu quodam ad perfectionem ascendit in eo cuius habitus est... De relatione item miror cur dubitas cum videas eam in uno eodemque esse non posse, in duobus nanque semper videtur. Duorum autem ad se invicem appetitus motu quodam fieri quis dubitarit?... Categoriarum igitur quaedam circa ousian praedicantur... Quaedam vero in ipsa sunt... item relatio extra ousian : pater ad filium filius ad patrem. Non enim sunt ex natura sed accidenti corporum corruptibili generatione. Siquidem pater non naturae filii pater est neque filius naturae patris filius est; unius enim eiusdemque naturae sunt pater et filius. Nulla autem natura se ipsam gignit aut a se ipsa gignitur. In ipsa vero ousiai relatio est cum genus ad speciem refertur et species ad genus. Genus enim speciei est genus et species generis est species. Habitus quoque et extra ousian et intra reperitur, ut armatum indutum secundum corpus dicimus.

Habitus vero ousiai generis aut speciei virtus ipsa immobilis per quam genus dum per species dividitur in se ipso semper unum individuumque permanet et totum in speciebus singulis et singulae species in ipso unum sunt. Eadem virtus et in specie percipitur quae dum per numeros dividatur suae individuae unitatis inexhaustam vim custodit, omnesque numeri in quos dividi videtur in infinitum in ipsa finiti unumque individuum sunt... *N*. Num et ea quae a Graecis dicitur *pros ti*, a nobis vero ad aliquid vel relatio, alium locum proprie in natura rerum possidet nisi in proportionibus rerum seu numerorum inque reciprocis eorum quae ad se invicem respiciunt conversionibus inseparabilibus ita ut quod unum dicitur non a se ipso sed ab altero quod ei opponitur accipere intelligatur? Cuius inconcussae amicitiae inseparabilisque copulae exempla sunt multiplices numeri inter se invicem copulati, dupli tripli quadrupli ceterique id genus in infinitum, item particulares, ut sunt sesqualteri sesquitertii sesquiquarti ceterique huius modi... *N*. Habitus restat, ut aestimo, qui apertissime in virtutum seu vitiorum certis possessionibus inspicitur. Omnis enim disciplina, hoc est omnis rationabilis animi motus aut irrationabilis, dum ad certum statum pervenerit ita ut nullo modo ab eo ulla occasione moveri possit sed semper animo adhaeret ut unum idipsumque ei esse videatur habitus dicitur, ac per hoc omnis perfecta virtus animo inseparabiliter adhaerens vere ac proprie habitus appellatur. Proinde in corporibus, in quibus nil stabile videtur esse, aut vix aut nunquam proprie habitus invenitur. Quod enim semper non habetur quamvis ad tempus haberi videatur abusive habitus nominabitur.

[(2.2) *A*. I therefore see that we must investigate with the greatest diligence whether in the highest and holy Trinity of three supreme substances Father is properly said in relation to Son, and similarly Son to Father, and also Holy Spirit to Father and Son being the Spirit of both — for Saint Gregory the Theologian indubitably asserts that these names represent a condition... *N*. the category of relation... So it remains that we should understand also this category like the others as predicated metaphorically of God. Indeed, true reasoning invites and compels us to this lest our earlier conclusions should begin to waver. For surely it does not oppose sound reasoning if we say that Father and Son are names of that condition which is called relation and more than condition... (2.4) And there is almost no category in which some condition cannot be found. Even essences or substances stand to one another in a certain condition. For we say in what proportion or condition rational and irrational essence stand to one another. Essence could not be called irrational except through the condition of absence of reason, nor named as rational otherwise than through the condition of presence of reason. For every proportion is a condition although not every condition is a proportion. In the proper sense, proportion is discoverable where there are at least two things, but condition is observed even in single things. For example, the condition of a rational soul is virtue. So proportion is a certain species of condition. But if you desire it shown by example how proportional condition is found in essence, take the case of numbers. For numbers, I think, are understood essentially in all things since the essence of all things subsists in numbers. Do you see then what proportion there is between 2 and 3? *A*. Yes indeed. I think that it is the proportion of 2:3. And by this one example I can understand the various species of proportion of all the other substantial numbers compared among themselves. *N*. Then pay attention to the other categories... *A*. In quantities, the great, small, and median compared among themselves abundantly reveal condition. Likewise, in quantities of numbers, lines, times, and other such things, you will clearly find conditions of proportions. The same applies to quality. For example, among colours white, black, and whatever the mediate colour is are joined to one another by condition. Indeed, white and black by holding the extreme positions in colour stand to one another in the condition of contrariety. Yet colour to its own extremes, that is white and black, stands in the condition of mediateness. In that category which is called *pros ti* or relation, it is clearly apparent what condition there is of father to son or son to father, of friend to friend, of 2:1, together with other such things. In situation also it is easily seen how standing and sitting possess a certain condition among themselves, for they are diametrically opposed to one another. You will certainly not acquire a notion of standing separate from the notion of lying, these always coming to you simultaneously even though they do not appear simultaneously in some object. What should be said about place when higher, lower, and median are considered? Do these lack condition? *N*. Certainly not. For these names do not arise from the nature of things but from a certain viewpoint of someone observing them partially. In the universe there is no up or down and so neither higher, lower, nor mediate in the universe. Consideration of the totality rejects such things, although attention to its parts introduces them. The same argument applies to greater and lesser. For nothing is small or large in its own kind, such ideas having been formed rather from the thinking of those who compare different quantities. Thus, contemplation of places or parts generates the condition in such things. *A*. What about time? Is not condition clearly manifest in times when these are compared among themselves?... *A*. What about different motions of action and passion? Surely condition is everywhere apparent?... (4.111) *N*. So does this division of the categories according to motion and rest — that is four at rest and six in motion — seem correct to you? *A*. It does. Yet it is still not sufficiently clear to me regarding two of them: I refer to condition and relation. For these two categories seem to me more at rest than in motion... (4.112) *N*. Perhaps you would not have hesitated much if you had observed more carefully that everything which does not simultaneously, naturally, and perfectly inhere in a creature but by certain increases proceeds towards inseparable and unchangeable perfection must necessarily be in motion. However, every condition ascends by a certain motion to perfection in that of which it is the condition...I am likewise amazed that you are doubtful about relation when you see that it cannot exist in one and the same thing, but always appears in two. And who would doubt that the attraction of two things to one another takes place with a certain motion?... (4.222) Of the categories therefore, some are predicated around substance...some are within it...Relation is outside substance as with father to son and son to father. For these relations are not in their nature but in a corruptible generation accidental to their bodies. Indeed, the father is not father of the son's nature, nor the son son of the father's nature. For father and son are of one and the same nature, and no nature begets itself or is begotten by itself. But relation is even within substance when genus is related to species and species to genus. For a genus is the genus of a species and species the species of a genus. (4.223) Condition also is found both outside and within substance. We say that someone is armed or clothed according to his body. Yet the condition of substance is that unchangeable power itself of genus or species through which the genus remains in itself always one and indivisible while it is divided among its species. It is a whole in its individual species, while the individual species are a unity in it. The same power is also perceived in the species which always maintains the inexhaustible power of its indivisible unity while it is divided among individuals. All the individuals into which it seems to be divided infinitely are in it finite and an indivisible unity... (6.2) *N*. And surely that which is called *pros ti* by the Greeks and relation by us does not properly occupy any place in the nature of things except among the proportions of things or numbers and the reciprocal convertibilities in which they stand to one another, so inseparable that when one thing is mentioned it is understood as determined not by itself but by something else opposed to it? Examples of this indestructible amity and inseparable bond are the multiple numbers linked among themselves, such as 2:1, 3:1, 4:1 and others of this kind up to infinity; and the particulars, such as 3:2, 4:3, 5:4 and others of the type...(6.4) *N*. Condition remains, I believe, which is seen most clearly in the certain possessions of virtues or vices. For every science, that is, every motion of the rational or irrational mind, when it reaches a definite state from which it cannot be dislodged by any means or at any time but which always adheres to the mind in seeming unity with it, is called a condition. Thus, every perfected virtue inseparably adhering to the mind is truly and properly called a condition. By the same token, in bodies where nothing stable is seen to be, condition is hardly found and never in the strict sense. For that which is not possessed permanently although seemingly possessed for a time, will incorrectly be named a condition].

Having passed Eriugena's discussion of the categories through a kind of textual sieve, we are left with an informative account of dialectical relation.[313] Although on the level of mere definitions and examples, there is little deviation from the earlier teaching of the pseudo-Augustinian *Categoriae decem*, the philosophical developments from these modest beginnings are in a style characteristic of Eriugena. These developments clearly originate in his desire to assimilate certain theological uses of relation into the logical framework: for example, as God's procession through created things in pseudo-Dionysius,[314] and as the reciprocity of Christ's divine and human natures in Maximus the Confessor.[315] It is with reference to such broader questions that the three-dimensional geometrical image described earlier can perform a useful function.

One must admit from the outset that the English lexeme "Relation" which the geometrical image is primarily intended to explain has a very complicated association with the Latin text.[316] In fact, the interpreter must pass from this original lexeme to certain Latin lexemes and back to further English lexemes through a system of overlaps whose only consistent element is the semantic property of opposition.[317] Within the original lexeme are the sememes a. "substance-substance", b. "opposition", c. "genus-species", d. "ratio", and e. "substance-accident" — which exhibit a special connection with axis Y.[318] The Eriugenian text itself employs three principal Latin lexemes: 1. *relatio*, 2. *habitus*, and 3. *proportio*, to be identified with three further English lexemes: 1. "relation", 2. "condition", and 3. "proportion" — which reveal a special connection with axis Z.[319] Finally, lexeme 1 contains sememes a, c, and d, lexeme 2 contains sememes b, c, d, and e, and lexeme 3 contains sememe d from the original lexeme.[320] That one should apply the geometrical image to the English lexeme "Relation" rather than any Latin lexeme from the start follows from the metalinguistic role of the former language here.[321] In reality, an interpreter could move as easily from an English lexeme to various Latin lexemes and back to further English lexemes as from a Latin lexeme to certain English lexemes and back to further Latin lexemes provided that the procedure is consistently maintained.[322]

Eriugena's discussion of the categories clearly does not establish the full equivalent, continuous, and pseudo-hierarchical configuration of the three-dimensional geometrical image applied to Relation.[323] One must therefore distinguish a "local" and a "global" actualization of semes — actualization in a given extract and in a complete text respectively — and be content to begin with the former. A minimal oppositional configuration for each successive dimension can be assumed in comparison with which the fuller structures are indicated as far as textual details permit.[324] Within those reduced perspectives the local actualizations will then be completed through a kind of zigzag movement from one side of the semantic field to the other.

That dialectical Relation can be shifted along the axis of existent and cognitive emerges from a comparison of passages where Eriugena speaks of Relation as an existent principle and those in which that existence corresponds to a mental category.[325] Since condition seems to be the only relational term employed in the second context, interaction between a lexical selection and the axis of existent and cognitive itself does not become significant.

Throughout the extract of *Periphyseon* I, Eriugena treats Relation as an attribute of the real world although in section 2.4 — where the appearance of opposites in various categories is discussed — he describes it as implying perception. This interpretation is particularly applied to the category of situation. Since one cannot acquire a notion of standing separately from one of lying — opposition within the category of situation — the Relation between these opposites depends upon the observer. The same insight is also applied to categories like place and quantity. Nothing is really higher or lower in the universe — opposition within the category of place — nor greater or smaller in an absolute sense — opposition within the category of quantity — because the Relations between these opposites are formed in the thinking of an observer who compares positions or quantities.

To contrast the existent Relation and the cognitive Relation in the manner outlined is to compare local rather than global actualizations of semes within the lexeme "Relation". However, since the axis of existent and cognitive itself is characterized by equivalence, there is no point at which the global actualization could reveal a different configuration of semantic elements.[326]

A shift between complex and simple senses of dialectical Relation is revealed by inspection of other passages. In these, complexity is associated with the binary and simplicity with the unitary — both of which are interpreted in a metaphysical rather than a mathematical sense — so that their axis implies the possible reduction of dyadic to monadic relations.[327] Modern logicians would allow this procedure in cases where the relation is symmetrical but not in those where it is asymmetrical.

Given that binarity is the seme primarily actualized within the Latin lexeme *relatio*, an interaction between lexical selection and the axis of complex and simple can be detected. For example, relation alone is said to require the presence of two things in 2.4 and 4.1.1.2, and relation alone is illustrated by the dualities of father and son and of friend and friend in 2.2, 2.4, and 4.2.2.2. That binarity is particularly associated with relation is the reason why Eriugena, in his discussions of the Trinity,[328] suggests that the names of Father, Son, and Spirit can only be applied to the divinity in a metaphorical sense. It is likewise the reason why the writer, in his references to substance,[329] suggests that relations such as that between father and son are external to the substances concerned.

Since unicity is the seme primarily actualized within the Latin lexeme *habitus*, the interaction between lexical selection and the axis of complex and simple is again detectable. Thus, condition alone is said to occur in single things according to 2.4, and condition alone is illustrated by the unities of virtuous soul and of clothed body in 2.4, 4.2.2.3, and 6.4. That unicity is particularly associated with condition is the reason why Eriugena, in the same discussions of the Trinity,[330] suggests that the names of the three Persons can be applied to the godhead in a proper sense. It is similarly the reason why the author, in his references to substance,[331] suggests that conditions such as that between genus and species are internal to the substances concerned.

The interaction between lexical selection and the axis of complexity and simplicity seems to be undercut in a few places where Eriugena activates a seme of unicity also within the lexeme *relatio*. For example, his discussion of the Trinity indicates that Father, Son, and Spirit are names of conditions which may be called "relations",[332] and his references to substance that genus and species are linked by a condition or by a relation.[333] But in these instances the axis of complexity and simplicity is merely shown to be continuous, and therefore to support the existence of mediating terms which are simultaneously unitary and binary.

To contrast the binary and unitary Relations in this manner is to compare local actualizations of semes within the lexeme "Relation". Yet to mediate the binary and unitary Relations in addition is to extend the comparison from that of a local to that of a global actualization of semes. This is because the contrasting and mediating together produce the entire articulation of the semantic field involved.

That Relation can be shifted along the axis of dialectical and mathematical emerges from a comparison of passages where Eriugena speaks of

Relation as something existing between terms and those in which such terms correspond to numerical values.[334] Since condition, relation, and proportion are all employed in the second context, interaction between a lexical selection and the axis of dialectical and mathematical itself does not become significant.

Throughout the extract of *Periphyseon* I, Eriugena interprets Relation as a feature of logical structure although in section 6.2 — where a classification of proportions is outlined — he describes it as implying calculation. The analysis presented here contains two interesting elements. First, there is the assignment of proportions themselves to two classes: the multiple — 2:1, 3:1, 4:1 and others of this type until infinity — and the particular — 3:2, 4:3, 5:4 and others of this type until infinity. Secondly, there is the statement that such proportions display a characteristic of Relation in general: a reciprocal convertibility where each term is determined not by itself but by an opposing one.

To contrast the dialectical Relation and the mathematical Relation in the manner described is again to compare local rather than global actualizations of semes within the lexeme "Relation". Since the axis of dialectical and mathematical itself is characterized by pseudo-hierarchy, the global actualization will ultimately reveal a different configuration of semantic elements.[335]

2.4 Ratio in Boethius' *De institutione arithmetica*

The Carolingian era is remarkable for its assimilation not only of ancient logic but also of ancient mathematical sciences. At this period, two basic types of material derived from the Neopythagorean tradition of late antiquity re-emerged onto the scene: Latin encyclopaedic treatises which included Greek mathematical texts among their sources, and Latin translations of the Greek mathematical treatises themselves. Within the first category, works like Martianus Capella's *De nuptiis Philologiae et Mercurii* attracted the attention of Carolingian scholars and within the second, Boethius' translations of Nicomachus of Gerasa and Ptolemy.[336] The Boethian translation known as *De institutione arithmetica* had entered into the mathematical curriculum by the middle of the ninth century. This work faithfully transmitted Nicomachus' doctrine concerning the nature of number — divided into applications within arithmetical, harmonic, and geometrical contexts — to writers on theology and the liberal arts. It also laid the foundations of a Latin technical vocabulary which would not change for three centuries.

After some introductory remarks on the nature of mathematics, Boethius' treatise turns to arithmetic proper. This is studied first by explaining the distinction between even and odd numbers in book I, chapter 3, and then by surveying the even numbers in chapters 8–12 — whose main varieties are the evenly even, evenly odd, and oddly even — and the odd numbers in chapters 13–20 — their main types being the incomposite and composite, and the perfect, imperfect, and more-than-perfect. After a section applying harmonics to arithmetic where relative numbers or ratios are considered, Boethius' treatise turns to geometrical arithmetic. This is studied first by explaining the difference between plane and solid numbers in book II, chapter 4, and then by examining the plane numbers in chapters 6–19 — whose main variety is the triangular — and the solid numbers in chapters 20–39 — their main type being the pyramidal. A final section is devoted to the three means: arithmetical, geometrical, and harmonic.

The opening section of *De institutione arithmetica* provides more information about the term *ad aliquid* [relation]. Here, Boethius explains that wisdom is concerned with things whose substance is immutable and incorporeal but in which the participation is mutable and corporeal: for example, qualities, quantities, forms, magnitudes, smallnesses, equalities, conditions, acts, dispositions, places, and times.[337] Such essences are classified more precisely into magnitudes which are continuous and not divided by internal boundaries, and multitudes which are discontinuous and internally divisible.[338] In their turn, the multitudes are classified into those which †*sunt per se ... ut sit nullo indiget* [are in themselves and need no other in order to be] like 3 and 4, and those which †*ad quiddam aliud referuntur...nisi relatum sit ad aliud, ipsum esse non possit* [are referred to some other and, unless referred to another, could not themselves exist] like 2:1, 1:2, 3:4.[339] The magnitudes are then classified into those which are immobile, and those which are subject to temporal change.[340] Since wisdom consists in the knowledge of these four kinds of object, a separate science belonging to each can be envisaged: arithmetic to multitude in itself, music to multitude in relation, geometry to immobile magnitude, and astronomy to mobile magnitude.[341] Together these constitute the *quadrivium* [four ways] by which the human intellect ascends to contemplation of truth.

After some remarks about the infinite addition of multitudes and the infinite division of magnitudes, Boethius explains the hierarchy of sciences.[342] In particular, arithmetic takes precedence over music because *illa natura priora sunt, quae per se constant, quam illa, quae ad aliquid referuntur* [those things which exist in themselves are prior in nature to those which are referred to another].[343] This is because of the general principle that when two things are compared in the order of reality, that which may continue to exist when the other is destroyed is prior to that which cannot thus continue, and the obvious fact that things existing in themselves fall into the former class while those referred to another fall into the latter. Arithmetic also takes precedence over music because intervals like the *diapente* (= perfect fifth), *diatessaron* (= perfect fourth), and *diapason* (= octave) are understood by means of *antecedentis numeri nomina* [the names of the preceding number] as $3:2$, $4:3$, and $2:1$.[344] Using similar arguments, Boethius shows that arithmetic is prior to geometry, music prior to astronomy, and geometry prior to astronomy in the hierarchy of their objects.

The actual description of ratios in *De institutione arithmetica* is complicated from the mathematical viewpoint and also dependent on philosophical assumptions. It fills the last eleven chapters of book I and the first of book II, the discussion corresponding roughly to the section of the treatise where arithmetic is applied to harmonics.

Boethius begins his discussion of quantity in relation — presumably a synonym for the earlier multitude in relation[345] — with a mathematical presentation. Whatever is measured by comparison with another may be i. either *aequale* [equal] or *inaequale* [unequal].[346] In the former case, the two terms possess the same names: equal to equal is like friend to friend or neighbour to neighbour. Furthermore, there is no subdivision of the equal. In the latter case, the two terms have different names: unequal to unequal is like teacher to student or attacker to victim. Whatever inequality there is between two things may be ii. either *maius* [greater] or *minus* [lesser].[347] There are five subdivisions of the greater: a. *multiplex* [multiple] when a number compared with another contains the latter more than once — for example 2.1, $3:1$, $4:1$;[348] b. *superparticularis* [superparticular] when a number compared with another contains the latter entirely together with some one factor of it — for example $3:2$, $4:3$, $5:4$;[349] c. *superpartiens* [superpartient] when a number compared with another contains the latter entirely together with more than one factor of it — for example $5:3$, $7:4$, $9:5$;[350] d. *multiplex superparticularis* [multiple superparticular] when a number compared with another contains the latter more than once together with some one factor of it — for example $5:2$,

7:3, 9:4;³⁵¹. e. *multiplex superpartiens* [multiple superpartient] when a number compared with another contains the latter more than once together with more than one factor of it — for example 8:3, 11:4, 12:5.³⁵² There are five corresponding subdivisions of the lesser: a. *submultiplex* [submultiple] when a number compared with a larger is contained by the latter more than once — for example 1:2, 1:3, 1:4, and so forth.³⁵³

Boethius then turns to philosophical questions. All types of inequality proceed from equality and return to equality, the inequalities themselves being termed *formae, species, substantia* [forms, species, substance].³⁵⁴ That the context is thoroughly ontological is indicated by two illustrations of this mathematical derivation at work. First, in the nature of things is juxtaposed goodness which is limited and stable with evil which is unlimited and unstable. More precisely, the former produces, limits, and restrains the latter.³⁵⁵ Secondly, within the human soul intelligence which is associated with goodness and cupidity which is associated with inequality are contrasted. Here, the former is said to restrain the latter.³⁵⁶ In both these cases, the relation between higher and lower terms reformulates the double process of mathematical derivation. Finally, Boethius notes that, just as unity is the *principium* [cause] of quantity in itself, so is equality the *mater* [mother] of quantity in relation.³⁵⁷

2.5. Eriugena's theory of ratio

Among philosophical writers of the Carolingian period who develop the implications of Boethius' teaching, once again Iohannes Scottus Eriugena comes to the forefront.³⁵⁸ His discussion of mathematical relation is scattered through a number of texts in *Periphyseon* III - V and elsewhere. Although on the level of mere definitions and examples there are few departures from the earlier teaching of Boethius' *De institutione arithmetica*, the philosophical elaborations on these rudimentary bases are in a style typical of Eriugena. These elaborations clearly stem from his eagerness to incorporate various metaphysical uses of relation into the numerical framework: for instance, as the periodicity of spiritual numbers in Augustine,³⁵⁹ and as God's procession through created things in pseudo-Dionysius.³⁶⁰ It is in connection with such broader issues that the three-dimensional geometrical image described earlier can serve a useful purpose. So here also the axes of existent and cognitive, of dialectical and mathematical, and of simple and complex articulate the conceptual structure.

One must enter this discussion with the realization that the English lexeme "Ratio" which the geometrical image is primarily intended to clarify has a very complicated association with the Latin text.[361] In effect, the interpreter must pass from this original lexeme to certain Latin lexemes and back to further English lexemes through a network of overlaps in which not even the semantic properties of greater and lesser are a consistent element.[362] Starting from the sememe "ratio", a first pair of analytical motions discloses that the sememe "ratio" is contained in four Latin lexemes: 1. *inaequalitas*, 2. *proportio*, 3. *habitus*, and 4. *numerus*; and that lexeme 1 contains the sememe a. "ratio", lexemes 2 and 3 the sememes a. "ratio" and b. "relation", and lexeme 4 the sememes a. "ratio", b. "relation", and c. "number" — this double motion being variously activated on axes X, Y, and Z.[363] But starting from the sememe "ratio", a second pair of analytical motions reveals that "ratio" and "number" are both contained in the Latin lexeme 4. *numerus* as denotative sememes; and that the sememes "ratio" and "number" both contain d. "unfolded reason" as a connotative sememe — this double motion becoming gradually more pronounced from axis X to Y to Z.[364] It is obvious that the process is unusually complicated because it takes place not only between lexemes and sememes but between lexemes and sememes and other sememes.[365] For this reason, it would theoretically be preferable for the interpreter to pass from a Latin lexeme to certain English lexemes and back to further Latin lexemes in a direction contrary to the one already described.[366]

That mathematical Ratio can be shifted along the axis of existent and cognitive emerges from a comparison of passages where Eriugena speaks of Ratio as an existent principle and those in which that existence corresponds to a mental category.[367] Since these texts exploit the twofold denotation of *numerus* as "number" and "ratio" throughout, there is a prominent interaction between lexical criteria and the functioning of the axis.

Although the majority of Eriugena's arguments assign to number a non-cognitive status, we need only cite those rarer but significant texts assigning a cognitive status — where it is explicitly characterized as "intellectual"[368] — in order to underline the shift described. Many passages also express the paradigmatic status of number in cognitive terms. One explains how things like quantities, equalities, and conditions exist primarily as concepts created in the human intellect by God;[369] another that inequalities result from a refraction through creaturely perception of that divine light which is emitted from its source as equality alone.[370]

An argument where Eriugena develops the Pythagorean teaching on the generation of number from the monad is especially revealing.[371] Here, he argues not simply for a generation of numbers in reality itself, nor for a cognitive production in the mind which contemplates, but oscillates between the two viewpoints in the course of several paragraphs. The discussion begins by explaining the meaning of four terms — "force", "power", "act", "operation"[372] — corresponding to stages in the emergence of number. The first represents the state where numbers subsist eternally and immutably in the monad, and the second the possibility of their being multiplied into quantities, proportions, and proportionalities. The third term signifies their actual multiplication into various genera and species in the mind's operation alone, and the fourth this multiplication in the mind's operation together with lower faculties like memory, imagination, and sense. After this the oscillation between generation and cognitive production of number becomes apparent when Eriugena adds some further notes to clarify the fourfold process.

Initially, the non-cognitive viewpoint is stressed by saying that numbers are not multiplied or created by the perceiving intellect but by the multiplier and creator of all things: otherwise there would be no harmony of their reasons. But then the shifting to cognitivity begins.[373]

> Proinde non ideo intellectus intellectuales numeros creare putandus est quia in se ipsos contemplatur — ab uno autem creatore omnium in intellectibus sive humanis sive angelicis fieri credendum est, a quo etiam in monade aeternaliter substituti sunt — per intellectus vero in notionem descendunt...
>
> [Therefore, one should not think that intellect creates the intellectual numbers because it contemplates them in itself — one should, however, believe that they arise through that single creator of all things in either human or angelic intellects through whom also they were eternally established in the monad. Yet they descend into thought[374] through intellects].

The final phrase implies an element of cognitivity in linking the numbers' descent somehow with the intellective process, although the non-cognitive presentation remains to the fore. The text continues by depicting a primal status — presumably within the monad — of mathematical objects where they are undivided according to quantity, space, time, and so forth. After this, Eriugena describes numbers as analogous with scientific objects in general while shifting to the cognitive viewpoint in a more pronounced manner:[375]

> non enim intellectus naturalium artium factor est sed inventor, non tamen extra se sed intra se eas invenit...
>
> [For intellect is not the maker but the discoverer of the natural arts. Yet it discovers them not outside but inside itself].[376]

But despite this blatantly ambivalent sentence in which the cognitive implication of linking the numbers' descent with intellection is both denied and affirmed, the non-cognitive presentation is still not totally abandoned. In fact, a secondary stage in the derivation of mathematical entities is described — outside the monad — where their previously hidden divisions are revealed. But then Eriugena repeats the analogy between numbers and scientific objects in general while moving finally and decisively to the cognitive position.[377]

> et haec processio prima artis ab ipsa scientia in qua primitus subsistit per intellectum in rationem ipsius intellectus actu perficitur: omne siquidem quod ex secretis naturae in rationem provenit per intellectus actionem accedit...
>
> [And this initial procession of the art from the knowledge in which it originally subsists through intellect into reason is accomplished by the act of intellect itself.[378] For everything which emerges into reason from the hidden places of nature does so through the action of intellect].

By this point the shifting to cognitivity is complete. The argument continues by distinguishing further stages in the human intellect's handling of the multiplied numbers: their transmission from reason to memory and imagination, and from memory and imagination to corporeal sense.[379]

To contrast the existent Ratio and the cognitive Ratio in the manner described is to compare local rather than global actualizations of semes within the lexeme "Ratio".[380] Nevertheless, since the axis of existent and cognitive itself is characterized by equivalence, there is no point at which the global actualization could disclose another arrangement of semantic features.[381]

A shift between dialectical and mathematical sense of Ratio is revealed by inspection of other passages.[382] Given that these exploit the twofold denotation of *numerus* as "number" and "ratio" throughout, there is a prominent interaction between lexical criteria and the functioning of the axis. With the appearance of the connotation "unfolded reason", the beginnings of a further interaction are detectable.

In the first place, Eriugena shows a tendency to employ logical language in the description of numerical objects and numerical language in the description of dialectical ones. Examples of this are his references to the numbers which unfold from the arithmetical monad as genera and species or forms [383] — he is thinking of the odds, evens, evenly odds, and evenly evens described in Boethian arithmetic — and to the individuals contrasted with logical genera and species as numbers. [384] One may perhaps be thought too ingenious in detecting a conflation of logical and numerical senses in such terminological usages. However, resolution of the two methods of thinking is expressed more definitely in his employment of the notoriously difficult term "reason". [385] It is a doctrine frequently asserted by Eriugena that differences between the primordial causes proceeding from the first principle result from the different reasons of those primordial causes pre-existing in the first principle. It is also repeatedly stated that differences between numbers unfolded from the monad follow on a similar diversity of their reasons pre-existing in the monad. An obvious conclusion is that the contents of both logical and numerical thinking depend on underlying principles whose nature transcends this dichotomy. But Eriugena also maintains that the multiplicity of primordial causes or numbers outside their respective originating principles is inseparable from their multiplicity within those principles. Thus, transcendence of the dichotomy must somehow characterize both logical and numerical objects even as they unfold into the multiplicity of nature.

One text in particular [386] exhibits this interplay of logical and numerical thought achieved through the peculiar function of reason. Eriugena begins with logic by explaining that individuals are present in species, species in genera, and genera in primal essence in such a way that every posterior term maintains its reasons distinct from the reasons of its coordinate terms in the prior. He continues:

> Nonne omnes numeri... in monade unum subsistunt? Et quidem in ipsa nulla numerorum compositio, vel confusio, vel mixtura numerorum est: singuli autem suas singulares rationes in ea vi et potestate custodiunt. Quis enim recte disputantium dixerit, binarium numerum vel ternarium in monade compositos esse, ita ut binarius in ea bis singulis, et ternarius ter singulis subsistat? Si enim hoc fieret, non esset monas, sed multarum diversitatum et partium exaggeratio, et discrepantium numerorum

cumulus. Est autem monas, in qua omnium numerorum mirabili quadam adunatione fons unus manat. In ipsa enim binarius et ternarius unum sunt, et proprias rationes custodiunt, qua sibi invicem conveniunt... Non aliter, sed eadem ratione de omnibus numeris a monade progredientibus, et in eandem resolutis intelligendum.

[Surely all the numbers...subsist as unity in the monad? But there is no composition of number there, nor confusion, nor mixture of number, since each preserves its own peculiar reasons [387] there in force and power. For who would say in valid argument that the numbers 2 and 3 are so compounded in the monad that the 2 in it subsists as 2×1 and the 3 as 3×1? If that were so, it would not be a monad but an aggregate of many diversities and parts and an accumulation of different numbers. Yet the monad is that in which the unitary fount of all numbers flows with a certain amazing unification. For in that unification through which they harmonize with one another, 2 and 3 are equivalent to 1 and maintain their proper reasons [388] ... One should understand not otherwise but in the same manner regarding all the numbers proceeding from the monad and resolved back into it].

The argument concludes with geometry by describing how lines constituting figures are present in the point with a similar combination of unification and distinctness.

To contrast the dialectical and mathematical Ratios in this manner is to compare local actualizations of semes within the lexeme "Ratio". But since the axis itself is characterized by pseudo-hierarchy, local and global articulations will reveal different arrangements of semantic features. To compare global actualizations of semes within that lexeme is to juxtapose the dialectical and mathematical in another way. This necessitates the placing of mathematical monad before dialectical essence in accordance with certain texts already examined.[389]

That mathematical Ratio can be shifted along the axis of unitary and binary emerges from a comparison of passages where Eriugena speaks of Ratio as a single principle and those in which that principle is unfolded into duality.[390] Since these texts exploit the respective denotations of *numerus* as "number" and of *proportio* as "ratio" throughout, there is a prominent interaction between lexical criteria and the functioning of the axis. Since they also exploit the shared connotation of "number" and "ratio" as "unfolded reason", there is a further interaction of equal prominence.

Although the majority of Eriugena's arguments speak of the numbers' procession from and return to the monad, we need only cite those rarer but significant texts dealing with the ratios' production — where inequality is derived from and called back to equality[391] — in order to underline the shift described. Some passages also refer both to the derivation of numbers and to the derivation of ratios but without explaining their interconnection. One describes that multiplication of numbers into different quantities, ratios, and proportions which is sustained by indissoluble equality and consonance;[392] another cites Boethius for the theory that numbers possess causes of their individual diversities pre-existing in the monad, that multiple ratios have similar causes lying behind the 2, 3, 4… which begin each series, and that the same is true regarding superparticulars, superpartients, and so forth.[393] However, some passages refer both to the derivation of numbers and to the derivation of ratios which they mediate through the notion of "reason".

The argument is best illustrated with a juxtaposition of three texts. These present a coherent group of features — the element of number, the element of ratio, mathematical properties of the number 12, mathematical properties of the number 6, the principle of unity, and the principle of reason — although no single text includes all of them.

The first text is from Eriugena's *Commentarius in Evangelium Iohannis* and runs:[394]

> Item duodenarius intra se totius musicae harmonias continet: habet enim diatessaron in quaternario cum ternario collato, habet diapente in ternario et binario, habet diapason inter seipsum et senarium,… habet tonum inter novenarium et octonarium. Qui omnes numeri intra terminos duodenarii continentur.
>
> [Besides, the number 12 contains within itself the harmonies of all music. For it has the perfect fourth in the comparison of 4:3, the perfect fifth in that of 3:2, the octave in that of 12:6…the tone in that of 9:8. All these numbers are contained within the limits[395] of the number 12].

Here, he explains the symbolic meaning of 12 by breaking it down into the implied series 12, 9, 8, 6 which constitutes the geometrical harmony of Boethius' *De arithmetica*.[396] Between these numbers arise all the ratios needed to construct a diatonic musical scale. Thus, 4:3 occurs between 12 and 9 and between 8 and 6; 3:2 between 12 and 8 and between 9 and 6; 2:1 between 12 and 6; and 9:8 between 9 and 8.

The second passage comes once again from the *Periphyseon*.[397] Eriugena's context is a demonstration that the monad was never without the numbers and the numbers never without the monad. During this he argues that each number together with its amount (6,7,8…) has a unitary nature (as one 6, one 7...). Furthermore, it is in combining these two features that the numbers can be described as participating in the monad. The demonstration is performed using the number 6 as example:

> Si autem quis dixerit et unitatem numerorum et ipsos numeros simul esse inseparabiliter... non negandum... senarius numerus ab unitate et multiplicatione aliorum numerorum non secluditur... Suis nanque partibus perficitur, sexta videlicet et tertia et dimidia... perfectus iste numerus, senarius videlicet, in unitate numerorum constituitur...

> [If anybody should say that both the unity of numbers and the numbers themselves are simultaneous and inseparable...this should not be denied...the number 6 is not excluded from the unity and multiplication of other numbers...for it is perfected in its parts, namely the sixth, the third, and the half...that perfect number, namely 6, is constituted in the unity of numbers].[398]

The connection between statements about the unity of various numbers and about the number 6's perfection resulting from addition of its factors is not immediately obvious. However, a closer reading suggests Eriugena's desire to explain this unity — with illustration of the factorizing process — by contrasting it with the possible division of each number.

The final text is from Eriugena's *Expositiones in Ierarchiam caelestem*.[399] Here, he explains the mathematical structure of the spiritual world by combining the Boethian geometrical harmony of the numbers 12, 9, 8, 6 with the pseudo-Dionysian angelic harmony of 3×3 terms.[400] As before, all the ratios needed to construct a diatonic musical scale are discovered among these numbers. However, a new feature is the idea that ratios derived by a mathematical operation have pre-existing reasons in the original numbers from which they are derived. He writes:

> ... nihil aliud esse celestes essentias, nisi... theophanias in perfectissimis senarii numeri rationibus substitutas... duodenarius siquidem senarii numeri duplus est. Intra quos terminos omnes musicas symphonias diligens rationis inquisitio proportionaliter colligit: intra octonarium quippe et senarium sesquitertia proportio, quae est diatessaron symphonia, inter novennarium et senarium sesquialtera, quae est diapente, inter differentiam duodenarii numeri ad octonarium, et octonarii differentiam ad senarium, dupla, quae est diapason, copulatur. Novem et octo toni obtinent rationem.

> [The celestial essences are nothing other than...theophanies established in the most perfect reasons of the number 6^{401}...12 is the double of the number 6. Within its limits, the diligent inquiry of reason proportionally

finds all the musical consonances. For between 8 and 6 is the ratio of 4:3 which is the consonance of the perfect fourth, between 9 and 6 that of 3:2 which is the perfect fifth, between the difference of the number 12 to 8 and of the number 8 to 6 that of 2:1 is joined. 9 and 8 possess the reason of the tone...]

The respective conclusions of these three passages might be summarized as follows: 1. that ratios are derived from number, 2. that unified numbers are derived from the monad, and 3. that reasons in number produce ratios.

To contrast the unitary Ratio and the binary Ratio in the manner described is to compare local rather than global actualizations of semes within the lexeme "Ratio". Yet to mediate the unitary Ratio and the binary Ratio in addition is to extend the comparison from that of a local to that of a global actualization of semes. This is because the contrasting and mediating together produce the entire articulation of the semantic field involved.

2.6 Extensions of the Eriugenian theory of ratio

It is possible to pursue the mathematical aspect a little further in Eriugena's philosophical writing, although this requires us to abandon the purely "atemporal" relations discussed throughout this chapter. That temporal ratios are founded on atemporal ones and connected to the latter through a series of quasi-temporal levels[402] — a hierarchical conception arising partly from the presence of the two sememes "ratio" and "number" within the Latin lexeme *numerus*,[403] and partly from the Neoplatonic understanding of being as an emanative continuum[404] — was one of Augustine's most difficult theses. Eriugena expands this in a section of *Periphyseon* III where the mechanisms of the five senses and especially of sight and hearing are described in considerable detail.[405]

In all these cases, when *corporales numeri* [corporeal numbers] are formed in sensible things, the soul is potentially present to the resulting phantasies or images formed in its sensory instruments. Moreover the soul successively receives those phantasies through *occursores* [encountering] numbers, introduces them through *progressores* [progressive] numbers, commends them to memory through *recordabiles* [recalling] numbers, arranges them through *rationabiles* [rational] numbers, and approves or rejects them through *intellectuales* [intellectual] numbers. This last process is in accordance with rules of *divini numeri* [divine numbers] and consists of judging all the numbers involved in the earlier phases.[406] That Eriugena is here concerned with numbers in the sense of mathematical ratios or as the metaphysical basis of such ratios is indicated by the authorities cited — Augustine's *De musica* and *Confessiones* and Gregory of Nyssa's *De imagine*[407] — since these patristic writers were either arguing in the context of or drawing illustrations from musical theory when referring to numbers. In fact, six of the eight varieties of number occur in the final book of Augustine's treatise on music where they constitute a kind of metaphysical hierarchy underlying those ratios aurally perceptible in rhythm.[408] The relation between soul and body is that outlined in several chapters of Gregory's anthropological text where the soul's employment of body for perception and communication is compared to a musician's performance on his instrument.[409]

The continuation of this argument supplies more precise information about the eight orders of numbers first, by specifying the relation between each one and the soul itself. Thus, the numbers occurring in sensible bodies and in the sensory organs are described as below the soul, the five orders of numbers called encountering, progressive, recalling, rational, and intellectual as within the soul, and the divine numbers according to which the other numbers are judged as above the soul.[410] One should not assume that Eriugena has imposed three rigidly distinguishable ontological categories on the system of numbers, since the soul is clearly viewed as present to the numbers in the sensory organs and to the numbers of the transcendent realm even though it does not contain them as it does the five intermediate orders. Nevertheless, by introducing the ontological categories of below, within, and above the soul, he adds to the Augustinian theory an unmistakable element of schematic thinking absent from the original.[411]

The continuation of the argument furnishes more information about the eight orders of numbers secondly, by invoking a vivid analogy between the soul and a city. Here, Eriugena illustrates the function of the numbers inside the soul with respect to incoming phantasies by comparing the encountering numbers to those persons who go to meet certain visitors, the progressive to those who guide them to the citadel of memory, the recalling to those who introduce them there, the rational to those who distribute them within the citadel of memory, and the intellectual to those who plan this distribution.[412] Given that Gregory of Nyssa had used this analogy to explain how the mind combines impressions entering each of the senses and then distributes the reconstituted impressions to parts of the memory, Eriugena has significantly transformed its application by emphasizing the strictly numerical aspects of the different phases within the process. However, Gregory's immediately preceding comparison of the sensory process itself with musical performance confers some legitimacy on the transformation.[413]

The doctrine that there are grades of number corresponding to mathematical ratios or to the metaphysical bases of such ratios recurs in two other passages of *Periphyseon*. These more directly address the ontological issues raised by the theory: especially concerning the numbers' status in connection with space and time. In Augustine's view, the lowest numbers are both spatial and temporal, the intermediate numbers temporal but not spatial, and the highest numbers neither spatial nor temporal.[414] The Eriugenian revision of this viewpoint would perhaps have been more subtle had it been elaborated beyond the preliminary stages.

During the discussion of man's nature, Alumnus is permitted to respond at length — by quoting and paraphrasing Gregory of Nyssa — to a difficult question. Given that man has been fashioned from a body comprising matter and form and from a soul consisting of vital motion, sense, reason, and intellect, is he the image of God throughout these parts or only in respect of the higher?[415] He loses no time in replying that the human soul wherein the divine image resides consists of a whole not distinct from its parts but present in each of its parts. Moreover, this soul receives *tota* [as a whole] the phantasies of sensible things; is present as a whole in the encountering numbers which first receive the phantasies of sensible things, in the progressive numbers which introduce those phantasies, and in the recalling numbers which commend the phantasies to memory; and exists as a whole in the whole memory and above the whole memory. All this is possible because the human soul is a diversity not of parts but of motions and because *motus quippe eius partes eius sunt... quos etiam numeros animales vocant* [its motions are its parts...those motions which they also call psychic numbers]. Thus, one psychic motion or number through which the soul contemplates God in a manner transcending understanding is called intellect, another through which it investigates the causes of nature is called reason, another through which it distinguishes those causes of nature is called interior sense, and another through which it receives the phantasies of sensible things through bodily organs is called exterior sense.[416]

The passage is important for showing that the sensory numbers in the original list correspond to the soul's faculty of exterior sense, the encountering, progressive, and recalling numbers to its faculty of interior sense, the rational numbers to its faculty of reason, and the intellectual numbers to its faculty of intellect. Although there are certain inconsistencies with the account of the varieties of number earlier in *Periphyseon* — perhaps inserted deliberately to reveal that Alumnus has not grasped all the details of Nutritor's theory[417] — the basic ontological position stated here is one which Eriugena might endorse. This would entail that most varieties of number are not divisible spatially or even temporally since the metaphysical principle present in each of them is a whole not distinct from its parts. The sensory numbers could, however, be so divisible given that the exterior sense to which they correspond is elsewhere treated as outside the image of God strictly speaking.[418]

It is during his discussion of the notion of place included among the ten Augustinian — or more correctly ps.-Augustinian — categories that Nutritor comes closest to expressing this ontological position.[419] Here, as support for the conclusion that place and time are not simply characteristics of created things but also principles prior to them, the authority of Augustine's sixth book concerning music is explicitly quoted.[420] This states that the *numerus...locorum et temporum* [number of places and times] precedes all things because the measure of created things logically precedes their creation and the place of all things corresponds to this measure. Of course, this does not imply that place and time are not *in numero* [in the number] of created things, but merely that they have ontological precedence over everything else in the universe created by God.[421]

Despite his predilection for word-play which is strikingly manifested at this point, Eriugena's philosophical view is fairly explicit: namely, that number is prior to space and time in the normal senses of those terms. He does not state whether this conclusion applies only to the highest numbers or also to one or more of the psychic grades. But if we read these latest remarks in conjunction with those made earlier regarding the presence of soul as a whole in its encountering, progressive, recalling, rational, and intellectual numbers, the notion that the strictly psychic numbers[422] are prior to normal spatio-temporality becomes quite acceptable.

Since Eriugena does not himself develop these ideas further, the modern reader is left wondering about many aspects of his theory. The *Periphyseon* certainly borrows other doctrines from the Augustinian musical treatise: for example, that the sensory faculties of vision and hearing operate using tenuous bodies derived from fire and air respectively.[423]

From the same source comes an argument that there are two kinds of phantasies: one the *phantasia* [phantasy] proper acquired from bodies by the exterior sense and involving the experience of an external object, the other the *phantasma* [phantasm] derived either from the memory or from a phantasy and not implying the experience of any external object [424] — this climaxes his account of the unfolding of numbers, proportions, and proportionalities based on Boethius [425] and therefore shows Eriugena interpreting Augustine's teachings with reference to writers other than Gregory of Nyssa. Also from the Augustinian musical treatise comes the notion that the human soul is separated from its creator not by spatial distance but by mental affection when it sins. [426] The *Annotationes in Martianum* borrow one technical detail from the same source: the translation of *analogia* as *corrationabilitas* to signify the notion of mathematical proportionality [427] — since *analogia* had previously been employed by ps.-Dionysius in describing the interrelation of his nine angelic hierarchies, [428] Eriugena misses few opportunities of repeating Augustine's and his own Latin translation in the *Expositiones in Ierarchiam caelestem*. [429] Nevertheless, despite so much evidence of general literary dependence, further development of the theory about eight orders of numbers is lacking.

The situation changes if one takes into account the glosses on Augustine's *De musica* in MS. *Bamberg Staatsbibliothek, Class. 36* datable to the eleventh century. [430] These contain enough doctrinal peculiarities to reveal their nature as a reworking of material ultimately stemming from Eriugena's own teaching or that of an immediate disciple. The glosses on Augustine's sixth book are particularly remarkable for their willingness to tackle fundamental metaphysical questions raised by that section of the treatise.

During most of his discussion, the glossator operates with five varieties of number called *sonantes* [sounding], *occursores* [encountering] *progressores* [progressive], *recordabiles* [recalling], and *iudiciales* [judging] as in Augustine's text. [431] However, in order to follow the original argument that progressive numbers occur in pronunciation, he also reduces the grades of number to four by combining the sounding and the progressive into a single auditory class. [432] In order to follow Augustine's argument that judging numbers have both a reactive and an analytic aspect, he also expands the varieties of number to six by distinguishing two classes within the judging. [433] This whole arrangement obviously differs from that presented in *Periphyseon* by making no distinction between numbers in corporeal things and in sensory phantasies,[434] by treating the progressive numbers as occurring in pronunciation,[435] and by making no reference to numbers in the divine realm.[436] There is seeming agreement with Eriugena in postulating a triad of intellect, reason, and interior sense within the human soul,[437] and in speaking of certain varieties of number as either intellectual or rational.[438] There is even an "Eriugenian" argument where the progressive numbers are associated with the category of *facere* [making], three other grades with one of *fieri* [made], and the judging numbers with one of *nec fieri nec facere* [neither made nor making].[439] But in the former case, the triad of intellect, reason, and interior sense is neither equated with the intellectual, rational, and lower numbers nor with the five normal varieties of number. In the latter, the association of the sounding, intermediate, and judging numbers with the three categories is embedded in a text reworked by somebody unaware of their idiomatic usage.

Ontological issues associated with the doctrine that there are grades of number corresponding to mathematical ratios or to the metaphysical bases of such ratios are tackled in other glosses. In particular, the numbers' priority to space and time in the normal senses of these terms is indicated when the commentator contrasts numbers themselves as incorporeal and only considered by intellect and traces of numbers occurring externally in bodies, places, or times.[440] That numbers — other than the sounding and the progressive — are prior to time is also revealed by his discussion of the judging numbers. The commentator at first seems to endorse Augustine's statement that judging and by implication lower numbers are temporal in arguing that, since each individual body has its own proportionality in relation to universal space and each individual sense a similar proportionality in relation to universal time, then the judging aspect of sense can only comprehend certain lengths of time appropriate to it.[441] Later, however, he makes his own and perhaps also Augustine's position clear by arguing that judging numbers are temporal not in themselves but to the extent that they judge temporal things.[442] That numbers — at least the higher grades among them — are not temporal was concluded by Alumnus' lengthy discussion of the divine image in *Periphyseon* IV.[443]

The same ontological issues are tackled elsewhere in the glosses: for example, when considering the association between sinfulness and certain numbers. According to the commentator, if the natural human body had not been converted from spirituality to corruptibility by original sin, corporeal numbers would not have affected it. There would have been no image impressed on the sense, no recalling of images in the memory, and no need for active numbers — we may paraphrase: there would have been no encountering, no recalling, and no progressive numbers.[444] Similarly, if human nature had not been diverted from contemplation to curiosity by the sinful superaddition, it would not have laboured among the various numbers.[445] However, the obviously non-Eriugenian implication of such glosses that the varieties of number are inextricably linked with acquired corruptibility — and therefore with the normal spatio-temporal features of that state — is elsewhere counteracted in a spirit more akin to the author of *Periphyseon*. Here, the commentator interprets that transmission of form from God through soul described in Augustine as referring to the general soul,[446] and that joining of souls by number also described in Augustine as referring to the joining at the Return.[447] This permits him to exemplify the Augustinian thesis that it is not the various numbers themselves but the love of those numbers which constitutes sin[448] by depicting grades of number continuing to obtain among souls unified at resurrection. Such souls will have inner encountering numbers whereby they accept or reject other souls, inner progressive numbers in which they employ each other as substrata, inner recalling numbers whereby they enter into each others' memories, and inner judging numbers in which they evaluate other souls.[449] There can be little doubt that these grades of inner number will enjoy a special ontological status: namely, freedom from corruptibility and the normal spatio-temporal aspects of the latter.

Excursus to Chapter 2

Excursus to section 2.2

Texts: A. Boethius: *De Trinitate* 5, 1–29 + 6, 14–19.
         B. Boethius: *In Categorias Aristotelis* II. 235C –236C.

Passages *A* and *B* are extracted from the two most important analyses of relation known during the early Middle Ages. They supplemented the discussion of ps.-Augustine: *Categoriae decem* although passage *B* was not extensively used until after the Carolingian period.

Passage *A* begins with the question: are relatives predicated through themselves/in the status of substance? The immediately preceding discussion explains that such predication arises when a property and its bearer constitute a unity and when modification of the property consequently entails modification of the bearer. Boethius now defines and illustrates relatives. According to him, these are terms subsisting through another e.g. master and slave and/or terms understood by comparison with another e.g. right and left — where the related terms are different — or equal and equal, similar and similar, and same and same — where the related terms are identical — the crucial feature being their duality. From this account an answer to the original question emerges. Since a relatum and its referent constitute a duality and since modification of the relatum therefore does not entail modification of the referent, the predication described earlier does not arise in the case of relatives. So these are not predicated through themselves/in the status of substance.

Passage *B* limits the definition of relatives in passage *A*. Relatives are terms whose essence involves a relation to something, while something is relative not because of the way it is described but because of the way it exists. To paraphrase: relatives are terms which subsist through another, while something is relative not by being understood through another but by subsisting through that other. The non-relative is then contrasted with the relative in mathematical illustrations: 4 is 4 in its nature and in itself but a double in its relation and in comparison with 2; 2 is 2 in its nature and in itself but a half in its relation and in comparison with 4. Passage *B* also reiterates a characteristic of relatives mentioned in passage *A*: that relations arise without any mutation of the things which are related. In other words, modification of a relatum does not entail that of its referent nor modification of a referent that of its relatum.

A

Let us now investigate relatives — we have directed everything said towards that discussion — for those things clearly perceived to subsist through the presence of another are by no means seen to generate a "predication through themselves". Given that master and slave are relative, let us see whether either can form the basis of a "predication through itself" or not. If you remove slave, you will also remove master; whereas if you remove whiteness, you will not also remove the white thing — although since whiteness is a property of the white thing, when the whiteness is suppressed, the thing certainly perishes as white. With master, if you remove slave, the term through which it is called master perishes. Yet master is not a property of slave as whiteness is a property of a white thing, but denotes a certain power by which a slave is controlled. And since this power is destroyed when the slave is removed, it clearly does not determine the master "through itself" but somehow externally through his acquisition of slaves. Therefore, one cannot assert that a relative predication adds, diminishes, or changes "through itself" any aspect of the thing to which it is applied. This whole predication exists not in the status of a substance but in that of a comparison of some kind, and in that of a comparison not always with the different but frequently with the same. For suppose that somebody is standing. If I approach him on my right, he will be left compared with me, not because he is left in himself but because I have approached on my right. Again, if I approach him on my left, he likewise becomes right in relation to me, not because he is right in himself — as he might be white or long in himself — but because he becomes right through my approaching him. What he is is through me and from me and in no way from himself... One must understand that a relative predication is not always such that it is predicated of the different as in the case of master and slave where the terms are different. For every equal is the equal to an equal, every similar the similar to a similar, and every same the same to a same...

B

For Aristotle applies the term "relative" to those things whose very essence involves a relation to something in some manner. It is as though he were saying: those things are relative which are related to something in some manner. But to those who consider the matter more precisely and more acutely, the import of his full definition will appear more readily and more truly. For we do not consider something as relative from the way it is described but from the way it exists: indeed, they are relative which we consider by a certain comparison and relational condition. Thus, the number 4 is this itself which it is described as — namely, 4 — and something else — that is, double — if compared with the number 2. But in speaking of 4, that it is 4 involves a relation to the nature of the number 4 itself; but that is is double is not in relation to the number 4 but to the number 2 of which it is described as double and exists as double through its own relation. Also, the number 2 is both 2 and a half: 2 according to its own nature and half according to its relation to the number 4. On these grounds, we consider those things which are relative thus by a certain comparison or condition: for the number 4 is not described as relative to the extent that it is 4, but it is relative to the extent that is is double the number 2: that is to say, compared with 2. Likewise, the number 2 is not related to something to the extent that it is 2, but to the extent that it is half: that is to say, compared with the number 4. Consequently, 4 requires not the number 2 but the relation "half" in order to be double and the 2 requires not the number 4 but the relation "double" in order to be a half. Do you not see that by a certain condition and comparison things having one property in their natures are something else in their relations? And they obtain this status not through their own but through their relational nature, for a number is a double through the relation "half" and a number is a half through the relation "double". Moreover, this accrues externally to the things which are relative, while the relations themselves arise without any passivity or mutation of the things which are related. For the number 4 undergoes no mutation if, as a double, it is related to the number 2; and the number 2 undergoes no change if, as a half, it is related to the number 4. So the essence — that is, the nature and substance — of relatives is to have an existence involving relation to something: that is, they are not only described as relating but also do relate. This is why he says that relatives are those things whose very essence involves a relation to something in some manner. It is as though he were saying: they are relatives whose substance consists of relating to something else, and which are in such a manner that their very existences are related to another, and whose essence consists of relating to something else. Yet not all things described as relating to another also derive existence from the other.

Excursus to section 2.4

Texts: A. Martianus Capella: *De nuptiis* VII. 758–762.
B. William of Aubérive: *Regulae* 15, pp. 112–114.

Of these two passages dealing with ratio theory the first is a late antique discussion independent of Boethius. Clearly the writer had direct access to Greek mathematical writings. However, he seems not to have fully comprehended his sources since the mathematical definitions in general are imprecise and the examples of the last two kinds of ratio incorrect. The second passage is a twelfth-century paraphrase of the Boethian discussion itself. Excerpts from the original text are joined together with occasional glosses. The resulting argument is mathematically correct, although the elliptical mode of citation leads to conceptual confusion at ** and to several grammatical inconsistencies which I have corrected silently.

The following table shows the terminology employed for the five kinds of ratio and the examples of ratios given in the respective texts:

Table 3. The five kinds of ratio

Boethius	Martianus
equal (3:3, 10:10)	equality (2:2, 3:3)
unequal	greater and... smaller
1 multiple (2:1, 3:1, 4:1)	multiplication (6:3, 8:4)
sub-multiple (1:2, 1:3, 1:4)	– (3:6, 4:8)
2 superparticular (3:2, 4:3, 5:4)	of members (3:2, 4:3, 5:4, 9:6)
sub-superparticular (2:3, 3:4, 4:5)	– (6:9)
3 superpartient (5:3, 7:4)	of parts (7:4)
sub-superpartient (3:5, 4:7)	– (4:7)
4 multiple superparticular	multiplication/of members (8:3!)
sub-multiple superparticular	– (3:8!)
5 multiple superpartient (8:3, 16:6)	multiplication/of parts (5:2!)
sub-multiple superpartient	– (2:5!)

A

Since this is so, a number has a relation of equality — which the Greeks call "isotes" — to the same number: for example, 2 to 2, 3 to 3. This is also the relation of a perfect number to its parts, so that such a number is considered superior to others. For what can be better than equality? But where one number is greater and another smaller, there is immediately a difference between them — as occurs with all numbers which exceed or are exceeded in a ratio of members or of parts. Therefore, these numbers are inferior for which there will be some difference between themselves and their parts. Yet while the difference between two numbers which are greater and smaller is the same, the ratio between those same numbers is nonetheless contrary. For there is the same difference between 3 and 4 as between 4 and 3, although the ratio between each pair of numbers is different — taking a form to be revealed below. I have stated that the primary ratios are in multiplication: the number 6 has a ratio of multiplication to 3, and 8 to 4. Conversely, 3 has a ratio of division to 6, and 4 to 8. That number surpasses in a ratio of members if it exceeds by a solid member or members: for example, 9 in respect of 6 since it surpasses by 3 which is found twice in the number 6. Conversely, 6 is surpassed by 9 according to a ratio of members. However, a number surpasses in a ratio of parts if it contains within itself both the smaller number and some part or parts of the latter: for example, when 7 is compared to 4, 4 and 3 parts of the 4 are contained in the 7. Conversely, 4 is surpassed by 7 according to a ratio of parts. One and the same number exceeds both by multiplication and in a ratio of members if, for example, 8 and 3 are connected. For 8 contains 3 twice and has a member in 2 besides. However, it is both by multiplication and in a ratio of parts that 5 surpasses on comparison with 2. For in 5 there are twice 2 and one part of the 2 besides. Conversely, among these numbers the smaller are surpassed by the larger at the same time through division and according to either a ratio of members or a ratio of parts. But just as these are the classes of ratios among numbers, so also there exist several types within each class. Thus — to come to the multiplication and division first — between these numbers is either a duple or a triple or a quadruple ratio, the multiplication being able to proceed also beyond this… But when there is a ratio of members between larger and smaller numbers, the larger surpasses either by a half, or a third, or a fourth — the "superdimidius", "supertertius", and "superquartus" ratios called "hemiolios", "epitritos", and "epitetartos" in Greek — this ratio proceeding to the "superquintus", "supersextus", and beyond... The ratio of parts is in certain cases closest to the "supertertius", in others to the "superquartus", the ratio being able to proceed beyond these. It is like the "supertertius" where the larger number includes the smaller number itself and several third parts of it, and like the "superquartus" where it includes that smaller number and fourth parts of it...

B

The first division of relative quantity is twofold, for whatever is measured by comparison with something else is either equal or unequal. The equal is that which, when compared with something, neither falls short of it as a lesser amount nor surpasses it as a greater amount: for example, 10 compared with 10, 3 with 3, a cubit with a cubit, a foot with a foot, and so forth. This part of relative quantity is naturally undivided. There is, however, a twofold division of unequal quantity: namely, into the greater and the lesser. Of the greater inequality there are five parts, for one is that which is called multiple, another superparticular, another superpartient, the fourth multiple superparticular, and the fifth multiple superpartient. To these five parts of greater inequality are opposed five parts of lesser inequality, just as the greater itself is always opposed to the lesser. They are given the same names — distinguished only by a prefix — since they are termed submultiple, subsuperparticular, subsuperpartient, submultiple superparticular, and submultiple superpartient. So a multiple number is that which, when compared with another or a second number, contains the latter more than once. This will occur first in the sequence of natural numbers, and to 1, 2 will therefore be duple, 3 triple, and 4 quadruple. Thus, by proceeding in order they weave all the multiple quantities. Set in contrast to this is the number called submultiple which, when brought into comparison with another, measures the larger amount more than once. If the lesser only measures the larger number twice, it will be called subduple, if three times subtriple, if four times subquadruple... So 1 is described as the subduple of 2, the subtriple of 3, the subquadruple of 4, and so forth. The superparticular number is that which, when compared with another, contains the whole of the smaller number together with some part of the latter. If it has its half, it is called "sesquialter", if its third part "sesquitertius", if its fourth "sesquiquartus", the form of the superparticular also proceeding to infinity with the infinite extension of such names. Of the subsuperparticular numbers — those which are contained as a whole together with some part of themselves —, one type is called "subsesquialter", another "subsesquitertius", another "subsesquiquartus"... *There is also an infinite multitude of such types, since the types of the same number are involved in an infinite progression. Greater numbers are called leaders and lesser ones followers.* The superpartient number is that which, when compared with another, contains the whole of the latter together with certain parts of it: that is, as many as the comparison itself discloses. For example, 5 contains the whole of 3 together with two of its parts, 7 the whole of 4 together with three of its parts. There are innumerable types of this number: superbipartient, supertripartient, and so forth. This relation begins with two times a third part. Subsuperpartient numbers are those which are contained as a whole together with several parts of themselves: for example, 3 in 5 and 4 in 7. The multiple superparticular is a number which, when compared with another, contains the latter more than once together with some part of the latter... So for example, one which contains some number twice together with the latter's half is called a "duplex sesquialter", one which does this together with the latter's third a "duplex sesquitertius", one which does this together with the latter's fourth a "duplex sesquiquartus". But if it contained that number three times together with the latter's half, third, or fourth part, it would be called "triplex sesquialter", "triplex sesquitertius", "triplex sesquiquartus". And similarly elsewhere, each thing is called by the name which is appropriate. The multiple superpartient is a number which, when compared with a number, contains the whole of the latter more than once together with the latter's two, three, or however many parts according to the form of the superpartient number. One should take care, in this case as in that of the superpartient, that there are not two halves, or two fourths, or two sixths in respect of the whole number with which comparison is made but two thirds, or two fifths, or two sevenths. Otherwise the number will not be superpartient or multiple superpartient but in a completely different relation for, where two halves occur the duple relation will arise, where two fourths the "sesquialter", and where two sixths the "sesquitertius". Indeed two fourths are a half and again two sixths a third. Because of illustrations given earlier, it is not difficult to find such numbers in addition to our own examples. These will be called, according to their own parts, duple superbipartient, or duple supertripartient, or triple superquadripartient, and so forth. Thus, 8 compared with 3 makes a duple superbipartient, and 16 compared with 6, and all numbers which start from 8 and surpass one another by 8 when compared with those numbers which start from 3 and exceed one another by 3. It will not be difficult for those who are diligent to find other parts of the number in the aforesaid manner. And we should remember here that the lesser numbers or followers are not named without the prefix "sub-": for example, subduple superbipartient, subduple supertripartient, subtriple suprtripartient, subtriple superquadripartient.

Excursus to section 2.6

Text: A. Censorinus: *De die natali* 7.1 + 9.1 + 9.3 + 11. 1–6.

Aside from Augustine's *De musica*, this passage contains the most detailed application of temporal ratios to cosmology known in the early Middle Ages. It is also notable for its reference to a traditional Pythagorean tetractys: 6, 8, 9, 12. This group of four numbers embraces all the ratios forming the primary consonances and the tone.

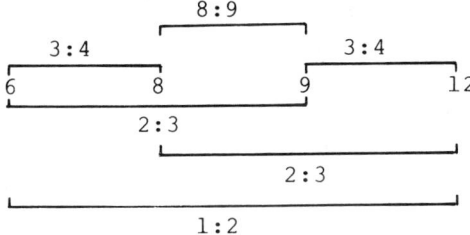

Figure 4. Ratios within the tetractys

A

It remains to speak of the times at which foetus are usually ready for birth. I must handle this topic with much greater care, since it is necessary to touch upon certain aspects of astrology, music, and arithmetic... Having explained this doctrine of the Chaldaeans, I pass on to the Pythagorean viewpoint discussed by Varro in his book called "Tubero" and subtitled "On the Origin of Man"... Yet Pythagoras, with greater probability, said that there are two kinds of foetus: one of seven months and the other of ten, but that these acquire shape in different numbers of days in the former and latter cases respectively. In fact, the numbers producing some transformation in every foetus — when semen is converted into blood or blood into flesh or flesh into human form — have in comparison with one another that same proportionality which is possessed by the notes called "symphonoi" in music… I return to my subject in order to explain what Pythagoras believed concerning the number of days pertaining to foetus. First, as I have indicated in a general manner above, he said that there are essentially two kinds of foetus: the lesser which they call "seven-month" and which emerges from the uterus on the two hundred and tenth day after conception; and the greater or "ten-month" which is brought forth on the two hundred and seventy-fourth day. The first or lesser foetus is particularly sustained by the number 6. For that which is conceived from the semen is, according to Pythagoras, a milky liquid for the first six days and then a bloody one for the next eight. When the eight are combined with the first six, they make the first consonance: the "diatessaron". A third stage is represented by nine further days which now produce the flesh and, when these are compared with the first six, produce the ratio of 3:2 in the second consonance: the "diapente". During the twelve days following in succession after this the body now formed appears, a comparison of these twelve also with the same number six producing the third consonance: the "diapason" based on the ratio of 2:1. These four numbers 6, 8, 9, and 12 added together make 35 days. And the number 6 is not undeservedly the foundation of generation — the Greeks call it "teleion" and we "complete" — since its parts: the sixth, the third, and the half or alternatively: 1, 2, and 3 complete the number itself. But just as the initial state of the semen, that milky principle of conception, is originally completed in this number; so also the initial state of the formed human being and, so to speak, second principle of maturation — being 35 days multiplied by 6 — is brought forth in its maturity on the 210th day. However, that second foetus which is greater is sustained by a larger number: namely 7…

Part III: The harmonic

Chapter 3

Components of concord — Ternary relations (ontological)

3.1 Trinitarian concord in Thierry of Chartres and his sources

Among ternary relations, that of concord possesses a status which is certainly unique. The philosophical theory of the Trinity disseminated in various commentaries on Boethius' *Opuscula sacra* by students of Thierry of Chartres dramatically exploits this notion. So it is fitting to introduce the topic of ternary relations with a discussion of Trinitarian concord.[450]

Contemporary evidence reveals Thierry as the leading teacher of the liberal arts in Northern France from about 1130–1150.[451] Since these were taught through an exegesis of textbooks produced in the late ancient philosophical milieu, he automatically became the principal exponent of Platonic wisdom.[452] Although only one or two extant works can be assigned to his direct authorship, the glosses forming the basis of his oral teaching were apparently transcribed on various occasions, these transcriptions themselves being multiplied by further copying.[453] The result is a collection of materials which were not written by Thierry of Chartres but clearly embody his thoughts, and which intersect through doctrinal and textual affinities in a manner too complex to permit classification into primary and derivative. It was natural that glosses produced in connection with Boethius' *Opuscula sacra* would be primarily theological in style. But following a method well established since at least the Carolingian period, these were developed with extensive reference to the teachings of both *trivium* and *quadrivium*.

Understanding the theory of concord in these commentaries seemingly demands that sequential engagement with primary texts practised in the foregoing pages. Yet one can benefit from the repetitive and overlapping character of the material by adopting another strategy: that of beginning with a summary of the entire theory from which the important elements are retained for subsequent discussion. This is not unlike listening to some percussive sound whose component frequencies are activated simultaneously but resonate for differing lengths of time.

It is a quite general notion of concord which is exploited in Thierry's Trinitarian doctrine. Here, he accepts the normal medieval premiss that any valid discussion of the Trinity — aside from purely dogmatic statements — is confined to analysis of its reflection in created things, concluding that the mystery of three Persons is particularly revealed in the mathematical properties of unity, equality, and connection/concord of unity and equality.[454] Most versions of his gloss cite Augustine as explicit source of this teaching.[455]

Thierry explores the triple created reflection at some length by associating further concepts yielded by philosophical analysis with the primary ones. These additional elements can best be summarized under five headings, although only three (a, c, e) represent things ontologically distinct within the created state.

a. Unity is associated with the being[456] of created things according to a bilingual etymology: *unitas* → onitas/entitas. Unity is the cause of matter[457] by descending into otherness, and the source of the number series.[458]

b. The relation of unity to equality is exemplified in the arithmetical operation $1 \times 1 = 1$. When the first of the two multiplications — of a number by itself and of a number by another — is applied to unity, an equality results.[459] This arithmetical analogy for Trinitarian generation is considered a hallmark of Thierry's teaching, although it had already occurred to Otloh of St. Emmeram.[460]

c. Equality is associated with the mind or providence[461] described as secondary principle by Neoplatonic writers like Calcidius and Macrobius.[462] It is also linked with truth[463] since a perceiving mind thereby achieves an equation with: that is, a state of being neither more nor less than, its object. Equality is the source of form[464] and measure[465] in created things, and the basis of mathematical ratios.[466]

d. The relations of both unity and equality to concord are intimated in the linguistic form of "equal to...".[467] Given that something is always equal to something also equal to it, the further notion of reciprocity is contained in that of equality. This linguistic analogy for Trinitarian double procession — found only in one later recension of the Boethian glosses — reads more like the work of some disciple of Thierry.[468]

e. Concord is associated with the world soul[469] described as tertiary principle by Calcidius and Macrobius,[470] the spirit[471] mentioned in Latin

Hermetic writings,[472] and the fate[473] viewed as the unfolding of providence by Calcidius and Boethius.[474] Concord is the cause of matter's unification with form[475] in producing physical elements, and the source of mathematical proportionalities.[476]

One feature of the triple created reflection which is absolutely essential to its function although liable to pass unnoticed concerns the relation between equality and inequality. Since Thierry has explicitly stated that equality is the origin of mathematical ratio,[477] and the traditional Boethian terminology for a ratio is an inequality,[478] then equality is the cause of its own contrary. Such a conclusion is logical from the viewpoint of that Neopythagorean tradition to which both writers belong, given that the monad or unity — corresponding to goodness, being, identity, and equality — was believed to generate by emanation the numbers — characterized by evil, non-being, otherness, and inequality — while the relation between the monad/its equivalents and the numbers/their equivalents was understood not as juxtaposition of discrete opposites but the unfolding of a continuum of values.[479] That Thierry believed equality to be the cause of inequality emerges from a number of his statements. In one passage he paraphrases the argument of Boethius' *De institutione musica* that equality is the beginning of multiplicity, that multiplicity involves the inequality of greater and lesser terms, and that equality is therefore the beginning of inequality.[480]

Since Thierry's mathematical image of the Trinity has a second term which corresponds to the relation of first to second, and a third term which represents the combination of the relations of first to second and second to first, it actually constitutes not three related things but three relations. Various further conclusions can be drawn from this. For example, the relations representing the created trinity must reflect those within the triune divinity itself in being internal rather than external in character.[481] This deduction is supported by combining statements elsewhere in the glosses that: 1. relations within the creative trinity should be indicated by the expression "construction of relations"[482] since they are relations in a certain sense only; and 2. one can equally maintain that the divinity is present in all created things and that all created things are present in the divinity.[483] In addition, these relations constituting the created trinity will reveal the ambivalence between unity and multiplicity characteristic of the modern notion of "structure" in a pronounced manner.

Thierry of Chartres' argument about the theological foundation of concord in the created realm is clearly indebted to Augustine and Boethius.[484]

So the contribution of these sources — the primary transmitters of Greek Neopythagorean harmonic theory to the west — is worth examining in detail. Something should especially be said concerning their views of the relations which subsist between equality, inequality, and concord.

Augustine's *De musica* envisages a concord arising in musical duration. In the course of five books, the treatise moves progressively from simpler elements — individual duration ratios constituting metrical feet — to more complex ones — sequences of those ratios forming complete verses. On both levels it advocates a combination of equality and inequality, in which the former is present to a greater and the latter to a lesser degree, and identifies this with concord.

Augustine seems particularly intrigued by the phenomenon of connection itself, and the verb *coniungere* and its synonyms occur frequently in the text. This explains why he studies the combination of equality and inequality primarily on the level of complete verses formed by the connection of duration ratios, speaking of the different numbers of half-feet in a verse's two segments as an inequality referred to a certain equality,[485] and of the relation between groups of 5 and 3 half-feet respectively as an inequality sustained by a certain law of equality.[486] On the other hand, the necessity that equality be present to a greater degree in the combination is explained both on the level of individual ratios or feet — those with parts in the ratios of 1:1 (dactyl), 1:2 (iamb), and 2:3 (bacchius) are preferred to those with parts in the ratio of 1:3 (amphibrach) in forming combinations[487] — and on that of connections.[488]

The necessity that inequality be present to a lesser degree in the combination is studied primarily on the level of complete verses formed by the connection of duration ratios, and he speaks of dividing a verse into two segments of different length which cannot be interchanged,[489] and of the superiority of a division into 7 and 5 half-feet respectively over one into 6 and 6.[490] On the other hand, he interprets the combination of equality and inequality as concord both on the level of individual ratios or feet[491] and on that of connections — unequal segments of 5 (2+3) and 3 (2+1) half-feet are equal by the addition of their respective first (2+2=4) and second (3+1=4) sub-segments.[492] In this case, the element of concord is heightened by its presence among units which are themselves already concordant.

Boethius' *De institutione musica* studies concord as manifested in musical pitch. In this massive exploration of the intervals and scales of Greek musical theory based on Nicomachus and Ptolemy are encountered numerous philosophical assumptions which parallel those in the Augustinian treatise. However, the later work differs in focussing on individual ratios, contrasting the specific notion of auditory consonance with the general idea of concord, expressing the components of concord in a wider range of terminology, and stressing ontological and epistemological questions.

That consonance results from the combination of equality and inequality is shown by Boethius' classification of pairs of sound-producing motions into equals, less unequals, moderately unequals, and greatly unequals[493] of which the third type represents consonance. According to his standard definition of consonance, the relevant pitch ratios are necessarily those in which unity is present to a greater degree than disunity;[494] and according to his presentation of the hierarchy among consonances, necessarily those in which similarity is present to a greater extent than dissimilarity.[495] That inequality must also be present to a lesser degree with equality is indicated by Boethius' classification of pairs of sound-producing motions,[496] and that dissimilarity must also be present to a lesser extent with similarity by his criticism of the Platonic teaching.[497] According to his standard definition of consonance, this combination of equality and inequality exemplifies the general principle of concord.[498]

In fact, Boethius argues that there exists among consonant ratios a double hierarchy. This is from one viewpoint ontological since some ratios precede others according to priority of value.[499] It is from another angle epistemological given that certain ratios surpass others in being easier to contemplate/more knowable/preceding in knowledge.[500] Although this twofold hierarchy is based on the degree to which unity or equality predominate over inequality in different ratios, theorists could not agree on the predominance sufficient to confer the title of "consonance" in the technical sense. Thus, Nicomachus believed that only the multiple ratios 2:1, 3:1, and 4:1 (yielding octave, octave-plus-fifth, and double octave) and the superparticulars 3:2 and 4:3 (yielding fifth and fourth) achieved a sufficient level of unity or equality.[501] Ptolemy, however, added the multiple superpartient 8:3 (yielding octave-plus-fourth) by arguing that ratios producing corresponding intervals below and above the octave must have similar character.[502]

At this stage, we are clearly confronted by a philosophically provocative notion of concord. Whereas the traditional definitions of this term advanced by Censorinus and Boethius[503] to be reiterated in Carolingian and twelfth-century discussions of music[504] suggest the presence of two unequal things linked by a binary relation of concord, the conception emerging from the Augustinian and Boethian passages collected above reveals something more interesting: the presence of two undetermined things linked by a ternary relation of equality, inequality and concord. This second formulation will occur as the true basis of much early medieval thought.

A few examples may illustrate its application in philosophical contexts to be investigated during the remainder of this chapter. In the first instance, the presence of unity, inequality, and concord may be compared in Augustine's description of the different (= unequal) verse-segments becoming equal through the addition of their components and thereby producing concord,[505] and the Augustinian account of the opposites (= unequals) in the providential order which achieve unity through the complementarity of their relation and likewise yield concord,[506] these formulations being virtual mirror-images of one another:

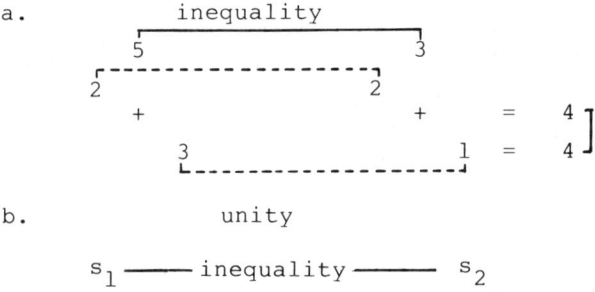

Figure 5. Concord in Augustine

In a second instance, the presence of equality, inequality, and concord may be compared in Calcidius' and Boethius' accounts of the terms (= unequals) in a mathematical progression becoming equal through the constancy of their ratio and thereby generating concord,[507] and the Calcidian and Eriugenian descriptions of the different (= unequal) physical elements which achieve continuity through the substitution of their properties and likewise produce concord,[508] these formulations again being virtual mirror-images of one another:

a.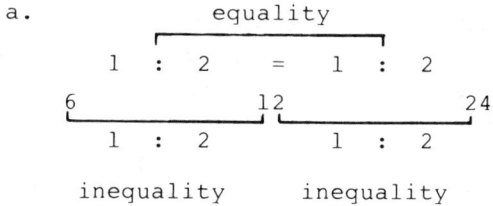

b.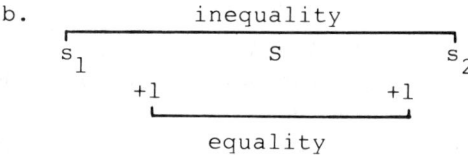

Figure 6. Concord in Calcidius, Boethius, and Eriugena

Such philosophical developments based on the discovery of equality, inequality, and concord among phenomena obviously differ among themselves.[509] In all probability, there is only a succession of intersecting likenesses — a family resemblance — to be discovered underlying the technical term "concord". Yet it would be a mistake to dismiss this association as the fantasy of an over-ingenious modern exegete, since the ancient writers were at least partially conscious of the true situation. One has merely to recall Augustine who explores the concordant element in verse, compares a verse to cosmic history, and treats cosmic history as the activity of the Holy Spirit. Given that Augustine's early conception of the Holy Spirit owed much to the Platonic theory of the world soul which forms the basis of physical concord, the movement of philosophical ideas joins its end to its beginning in a circle not only geometrical in nature.

3.2 The resolution of oppositions according to Augustine

To study the handling of ternary relations in a more general sense, one must turn to philosophical rather than musical texts yet once again to the writings of Augustine. Here, there are comparatively few discussions of such relations outside the specialized context of Trinitarian thought.[510] However, at least one topic recurring throughout the Augustinian corpus from the earliest to the latest works may be construed as a refashioning of the same problematic.

Beginning with the dialogues written at Cassiciacum and the first anti-Manichaean treatises of the 380s, Augustine explains the presence of evil — moral and natural — in the world by using an explicitly two-term and implicitly three-term conceptual scheme. The argument running through these texts is remarkable for showing how an author who reports his own mastery of Aristotle's *Categories*[511] can handle the concept of relation in a thoroughly non-Aristotelian manner. This approach presumably resulted from his openness to other influences during the same period: the teachings of Neoplatonists like Plotinus and Porphyry.

Accordingly to Aristotle, things included within the category of relation are characterized by interdependence with other things to which they are related,[512] this interdependence being either existent — the related begin and end simultaneously in reality[513] — or cognitive — the related begin and end simultaneously for perception.[514] Such features distinguish members of this category from at least two other types of thing: on the one hand contraries like good and evil or black and white[515] and on the other, parts and wholes like wing and bird or head and body.[516] If things included in the category of relation were assimilated to these other types, then the latter would acquire the characteristics of existent and cognitive interdependence attributed by Aristotle's teaching to the former.

It is precisely this assimilation of the concept of relation to those of contrariety and inclusion which occurs in many Augustinian texts. Its further consequences are a. that discussion of contraries can be blended with that of parts and whole through the shared implication of relationality, and b. that the mingling of these discussions yields the concept of a whole containing not simply parts but contrary parts. In fact, Augustinian texts reiterate three ideas in almost formulaic manner: i. a contrary relates to its contrary ($s_1 \rightarrow s_2$),[517] ii. a part relates to a whole ($s_1 \rightarrow S$), and iii. a contrary together with its contrary relates to a whole (($s_1 + s_2) \rightarrow S$).[518] At times, there is only one component but at others, two or three in operation within this triangular schema.

Undoubtedly the earliest traces of Augustine's interest in such matters occurred in his first literary endeavour called *De pulchro et apto*.[519] According to one later testimony, the fittingness concerned here was that which is judged *nec ex semet ipso sed ex eo cui conectitur* [not from itself but from that to which it is connected] and the beauty that which is esteemed *per se ipsum* [through itself][520] — a distinction clearly exploiting the notion of relationality. According to another report, the fittingness of the title concerned †*aliud...accommodari alicui, sicut pars corporis* [what is adapted to something like part of a body] and the beauty †*in ipsis corporibus aliud esse quasi totum* [what is as if a whole in bodies themselves].[521] It is significant that this earliest discussion of the relative and of part and whole occurred in a treatise clearly dealing with harmonics in the Neopythagorean sense.

Turning to Augustinian works still extant, we find similar ideas together with further developments. The easiest way to approach this material is perhaps by studying successively its presentation of the leading tenets i, ii, and iii mentioned above. In accordance with variations in the texts themselves, one may also distinguish treatments of the constituent relations as existent and cognitive respectively.[522]

To begin with, the relation between a contrary and its contrary[523] is implied in various accounts of the order of creation. Here, the contraries represent determining properties of different things like good angels, evil angels, and human souls which can be arranged in some order of prior and posterior. In *De libero arbitrio*, Augustine argues that one can assign blame or praise to each level of creation depending upon the manner in which it uses its autonomous will. However, since every creature becomes less good from a status where it was originally good, †*contra naturam esse omne vitium, etiam eius rei cuius est vitium* [every vice is contrary to the nature even of that thing of which it is the vice].[524] This argument postulating the simultaneous presence of contraries in a single subject — where the contraries are also relatives[525] — is mirrored in *De vera religione*. Here, Augustine explains how an observer may have clear or deceptive knowledge of each level of creation in accordance with the degree of unity which it possesses. Yet the deception arises not from its true unity *quod est* [which exists] but from its *falsa unitas* [false unity] which is non-being relative to the former.[526]

Other texts shift the focus from the relation between a contrary and its contrary within the order of creation to that between a part and the whole.[527] In the same argument of *De libero arbitrio*, the writer tackles the question why God has created both non-sinful and sinful souls rather than the non-sinful alone. The answer is given employing a simile between the hierarchies of physical and spiritual creation. If somebody asks why the creator has made both superior and inferior luminaries — the sun and moon — rather than the superior alone, one can point to the lunar light's special value for nocturnal purposes. Augustine concludes:[528]

...quem ad modum corporum differentias contemplando videns alia clariora iniuste petis auferri quae obscuriora conspexeris aut clarioribus adaequari, sed ad perfectionem universitatis referens omnia quanto magis minusve inter se clara sunt tanto magis cernis esse omnia... sic etiam differentias animarum cogites in quibus hoc quoque invenies, ut miseriam quam doles ad id quoque valere cognoscas, ut universitatis perfectioni nec illae desint animae quae miserae fieri debuerunt quia peccatrices esse voluerunt.

[As when, in observing the differences of bodies and noting that some are brighter, you unjustly seek to remove those which you perceive as darker or to make them equal to the brighter yet, by referring all things to the perfection of the universe, you more readily perceive all things to exist inasmuch as they are more or less bright among themselves... Similarly you should also view differences among souls, where the same situation is found, so as to recognize the wretchedness which you lament as contributing also to the same end: namely, that souls deserving of wretchedness because they desired to sin should not be lacking to the perfection of the universe].

That this argument is concerned with the relation between a part and the whole is indicated by its allusions to the contrast of created things with the *universitas* [universe] and to the connection between them accomplished by a †*referens* [referral].[529] The conclusion might perhaps be summarized as follows. Since something having a negative value considered as a part can also have a positive value considered as a part in relation to the whole, God has created things subject to negativity in both the physical and spiritual orders to complete the perfection of the universe.

The relation between a contrary together with its contrary and the whole[530] is shown in various other accounts of the order of creation. Here, the contraries continue to represent determining properties of good angels, evil angels, human souls and the like arranged in an order of priority. However, the spotlight is no longer on individual created things but on the manner of their contribution to the hierarchy of being. In *Contra Faustum*, the divine art is described as †*neque enim universum condit in singulis, sed ad universi conplexum condens singula* [not creating its universe in individual things but creating individual things in relation to the universe].[531] Created things are dissimilar among themselves but similar to God in a peculiar sense: namely, that through the combination of their specificities they produce a unity reflecting that higher unity of the creative principle.[532] The point about dissimilarities of created things together constituting the whole is taken up in *De civitate Dei*. Here, Augustine cites as parallel the rhetorician's use of antitheses to explain why God has created both non-sinful and sinful spiritual beings rather than the non-sinful alone. Just as beauty of language is achieved through the *contraria contrariis opposita* [opposition of contraries], so also — through a kind of rhetoric of things — is beauty of the world produced by the contrarieties manifested in its constituent beings.[533]

Before turning to another set of passages dealing with the same concepts but from a more explicitly cognitive viewpoint, one should try to determine something about the logical status of these contraries and relatives.[534]

As argued earlier, Augustine has taken an un-Aristotelian step in assimilating the relative to the contrary, this assimilation leading to an identification of properties which can be present simultaneously in a single subject with those which cannot be so present.[535] One text written late in Augustine's career shows clearly that he was aware of the direction in which his own arguments had pointed. Here, he explains that in speaking of good and evil in a created thing, the contrary properties are affirmed simultaneously of the substance. According to the dialecticians' rule †*nulli rei duo simul inesse contraria* [in no thing can two contraries be simultaneously present] or more precisely no thing can have *simul ubi...ibi* [at one time and in one place] contrary properties. This rule applies when the contraries are terms like dark and light, sweet and bitter, white and black, and ugly and beautiful, but not when they correspond to good and evil. In this case, the contraries *non solum simul esse possunt* [can not only be present] but often are present since, although good can exist without dependence on evil, evil cannot exist without dependence on good.[536] It might be argued that Augustine's denial of complete interdependence now precludes assimilation of the contrary to the relative. This argument would, however, leave no explanation of that daring conclusion which could only have resulted from such assimilation: his albeit temporary rejection of the law of contradiction.[537]

Augustine's assimilation of the relative to the contrary in these texts — a move showing the isotopy of internal relation in full operation — is once again the result of his doctrinal dependence on Plotinus.[538]

The anti-Manichaean treatise *De natura boni* contains probably the most sustained discussion of the relation between a contrary and its contrary[539] in the Augustinian corpus. One passage in particular repeats many of the arguments advanced in other texts — the notions that something is only defective in relation to its own goodness, and that even privations are included within the divine ordering of the universe — but adds an important rider linking contraries with cognitivity. According to Augustine, within the order of creation those things which are lesser *in maiorum comparatione contrariis nominibus appellantur* [are called by contrary names in comparison with the greater].[540] For example, the beauty of an ape's form is called ugliness in comparison with that of a man's.[541] After some remarks about the naming of evil by comparison with good, illustrations of such contraries are given: slow and fast, low pitch and high pitch, silence and sound, and darkness and light. Regarding the final pair, he emphasizes that *tamquam duo contraria dicuntur; habent tamen et obscura aliquid lucis* [these are spoken of as two contraries although even darkness possesses something of light].[542] In other words, the naming of one contrary through another implies some minimal ontological connection between them.[543] Finally, the conclusion of the analysis is introduced: that unformed matter cannot be called evil since, as capacity for form, it possesses something of its contrary's goodness. The central idea of this passage that the contraries manifested in the created world are to some extent dependent upon a process of naming recurs in *De Genesi ad litteram*. Here, Augustine considers why paradise contained a tree of good and evil before man had learned of evil by experience, and answers that knowledge concerning things of which one was previously ignorant is attainable from contrariety. In this way, nothingness is conceived from what exists, death from what is alive, and so forth.[544]

If the relation between a contrary and its contrary can be associated with cognitivity, it is not surprising to find a similar interpretation of the corresponding one between a part and the whole.[545] This emerges clearly from a passage in *De musica* where Augustine considers the position of man as subject to sin within the providential order established by the creator. He writes:[546]

> In quibus multa nobis videntur inordinata et perturbata, quia eorum ordini pro nostris meritis assuti sumus, nescientes quid de nobis divina providentia pulchrum gerat. Quoniam si quis, verbi gratia, in amplissimarum pulcherrimarumque aedium uno aliquo angulo tanquam statua collocetur, pulchritudinem illius fabricae sentire non poterit, cuius et ipse pars erit. Nec universi exercitus ordinem miles in acie valet intueri... Ita peccantem hominem ordinavit Deus turpem, non turpiter. Turpis enim factus est voluntate, universum amittendo quod Dei praeceptis obtemperans possidebat, et ordinatus in parte est, ut qui legem agere noluit, a lege agatur.

[Many of these things seem disordered and confused to us since we are linked to their order according to our merits, but ignorant of that beauty which divine providence accomplishes through us. For example, if someone were placed like a statue in one corner of a large and beautiful house, he would not perceive the beauty of that structure of which he was himself a part. Nor can a soldier at his post observe the disposition of the entire army...God has so ordered sinful man in his baseness though not in a base manner, since man has been rendered base through his will. He has lost the wholeness which he possessed when he obeyed God's commands and been ordered in a part. So that he who would not follow the law is led by the law].

This text is striking for the manner in which contrasts of a part with the whole and of ignorance with knowledge are interwoven in argument.[547] Within the divine plan, the sinning individual is described as *ordinatus in parte* [ordered in a part] or compared to a statue which is *pars* [part] of a building. As such, he †*nescire* [is ignorant of] or †*sentire non posse* [cannot perceive] the broader structure which contains him. In its turn, the encompassing divine providence is characterized as a *universum* [wholeness] or compared to a *universus exercitus* [entire army] in which he serves as a soldier. The conclusion of the argument is that the relation between a part and the whole is a cognitive one where the former acquires meaning through the latter.

The Augustinian Biblical commentary *De Genesi contra Manichaeos* presents another discussion of the relation between a contrary together with its contrary and the whole.[548] In this passage also many earlier arguments are reiterated — the notions that dissimilar parts together constitute the whole, and that this arrangement represents God's creation in measure, number, and weight — yet with greater emphasis upon the cognitivity linking contraries with the whole. Augustine points to the presence of both harmful and beneficial things within the order of creation, but adds that the former only *videantur adversa* [appear hostile] to us because of our ignorance and sinfulness.[549] Further, if one admits the distinction between sense and reason, the contrast between harmful and beneficial apparent to the lower faculty is resolved by the higher.[550] In a vivid analogy, understanding of divine providence's workings by a man blinded by sin can be compared with that of a forge's operations by someone ignorant of the blacksmith's craft. Such a man enters the smithy, burns himself on the molten metal which he touches, and concludes that the whole operation is productive of injury.[551] This argument, which clearly shifts the emphasis from existent contraries combined in the universe to contrary notions resolvable in some higher perception and therefore from existent to cognitive [552] recurs in *De civitate Dei*. Here, the writer describes the contrast among created things between good and evil elements/notions whose combination/resolution cannot be accomplished because of our mortality. Looking at the divine order from a sinful state is like standing in the middle of a tapestry and seeing only threads. [553]

Although the passages studied in this section do not individually make the meaning explicit, their cumulative effect is to develop further the notions of fittingness and beauty outlined in early Augustine. [554] This development is underlined by remarks suggesting that his discussions of contraries or of parts and wholes are really elements in a broader theory which might be characterized as "harmonic". One striking instance occurs in Augustine's demonstration that all created things exhibit goodness to different degrees and that this arrangement reveals how *caelestibus terrena concordent* [the earthly are concordant with the heavenly]. It concludes by citing his favourite analogy between the created order and a line of verse. [555] An only slightly less memorable example occurs in his argument that goodness is perceived both in the parts and in the whole of creation, but that partial goods are more pleasing when *in universum aliquid conveniunt atque concurrunt* [they come into some accord or agreement with the whole]. Again he follows this by citing the analogy between created things and the metrical line. [556] That Augustine considers his discussions of contraries or of parts and wholes to be elements in a general "harmonic" theory of providence would follow from his interpretation of the Holy Spirit. This principle under whose administration the entire life of the cosmos takes place has been invoked repeatedly under the name *concordia* [concord]. [557]

3.3 Mediation in the cosmology and psychology of Calcidius

Whereas the Augustinian passages studied in the previous section presented the ternary or concordant relation not in its original mathematical application but in a derivative application to metaphysics, [558] the passages of Calcidius to be examined in this section will present this relation both in its original mathematical application and in a twofold derivative application to physics and psychology. One could describe such transformations of meaning in more technical language as substitutions of one encyclopaedia for another — that of "physics" for that of "mathematics", etc.[559] — through the de-activation and activation of various groups of semes. Although it is naive to imagine that the ternary or concordant relation really has an original usage in one sphere and a derivative usage in another rather than several equally original and derivative usages in different spheres, we shall proceed as though Calcidius understood this relation as first mathematical, second physical, and third psychological for our own expository convenience.

The historical importance of Calcidius, a Christian writer who translated Plato's *Timaeus* into Latin and added a philosophical commentary during the later fourth century, is a fairly recent discovery. Well established by now is the extent to which twelfth-century writers like William of Conches, who extended many of its arguments in his own glosses on the dialogue, were influenced by this combined translation and commentary. It is not so widely known that Calcidius' work had already become a scientific handbook in the Carolingian schools inspired by Alcuin's pedagogy from which perhaps it filtered through to the circle of Iohannes Scottus Eriugena.[560] The latter used the translation and commentary explicitly when glossing Martianus Capella's philosophical material and without acknowledgement on several other occasions.

In two sections of the commentary on the *Timaeus* — explaining Plato's remarks about the structures of physical elements and of soul respectively — Calcidius develops an extensive theory of mediation. This forms the main component of a fundamentally harmonic conception of the cosmos.[561] Since mediation is a mathematical term which is here applied to physics and psychology, while the latter can be treated as subdivisions within the dialectical sphere, Calcidius' argument reveals a shift along the axis of mathematical and dialectical.[562]

The context for the first of Calcidius' discussions is provided by the Platonic account of the world's body. Because this body needed characteristics of visibility and tangibility, the divine artificer established the elements of fire and earth as its foundations. Yet these elements could not cohere indissolubly without the binding provided by congruent measure[563] where three terms are connected so that the relation between the lowest and the middle is identical with that between the middle and the highest. Given that the world's body also required depth together with height and width, the artificer established two middle terms to connect the lowest and the highest. Thus, the elements of air and water were interposed with the relation between fire and air identical with that between air and water,[564] and so forth. This construction produced an equilibrium in the world's body protecting it from dissolution save at the artificer's behest.[565]

Calcidius' commentary takes up two problems raised by this mixture of mathematical and physical ideas: first, what is the precise nature of the mathematical series?; and secondly, with what physical properties do the mathematical values correlate?

The first question is answered with reference to the numerical progression known in Greek as *analogia* and in Latin as *competens*.[566] Such progressions may be classified into two types: continuous, where are juxtaposed at least three terms among which the relation of the first to second is identical with that of the second to the third; and disjunct, where at least four terms are juxtaposed among which the relation of the first to second is identical with that of the third to the fourth. It is the continuous *analogia* which is used by the artificer in fashioning the cosmic body.

The second question is answered at greater length using words perhaps worth quoting in full:[567]

> ... memores nos esse debere eorum quibus Plato... Dixit enim, si meminimus, similitudinem non solum in formis et figuris sed etiam in potentiis et qualitatibus quaeri oportere... Quare si inter ignem et terram nulla est in specie et velut in vultu similitudo, quaerenda erit in naturis ac qualitatibus ipsorum elementorum iuxta quas faciunt aliquid aut patiuntur et in his proprietatibus ex quibus utriusque elementi vis et germanitas apprime designatur. Sunt igitur tam ignis quam terrae multae quidem et aliae proprietates, sed quae vel maxime vim earum proprietatemque declarent, nimirum hae: ignis quidem acumen, quod est acutus et penetrans, deinde quod est tener et delicata quadam subtilitate, tum quod est mobilis et semper in motus, terrae vero obtunsitas, quod est retunsa, quod corpulenta, quod semper immobilis. Hae vero naturae licet sint contrariae, habent tamen aliquam ex ipsa contrarietate parilitatem — tam enim similia similibus quam dissimilia dissimilibus comparantur — et haec est analogia, id est ratio continui competentis: quod enim est acumen adversum obtunsitatem, hoc subtilitas iuxta corpulentiam, et quod subtilitas iuxta corpulentiam, hoc mobilitas adversus immobilitatem; et si verteris, ut id quod medium est extimum fiat, quae vero sunt extima singillatim in medio locentur, servabitur analogiae norma. Quatenus igitur inter haec duo solida corpora, quorum est talis similitudo qualem demonstravimus, alia duo solida interiecta facient continuationem iuxta rationem continui competentis, docet arithmetica disciplina. Si enim vicinum igni elementum quod sit et ex quibus conflatum voluerimus inquirere, sumemus ignis quidem de proximo duas virtutes, subtilitatem et mobilitatem, unam vero terrae, id est obtunsitatem, et invenietur genitura secundi elementi quod est subter

ignem, id est aeris; est enim aer obtunsus subtilis mobilis. Rursumque si eius elementi quod est vicinum terrae, id est aquae, genituram consideremus, sumemus duas quidem terrae virtutes, id est obtunsitatem et corpulentiam, unam vero ignis, id est motum, et exorietur aquae substantia, quae est corpus obtunsum corpulentum mobile. Atque ita inter ignem et terram aer et aqua de extimorum concretione nascentur, ex quibus constat mundi continuatio. Conservatur autem hoc pacto analogia quoque geometrica iuxta rationem continui competentis; ut enim ignis adversum aera, sic aer adversum aquam et demum aqua iuxta terram, retrorsumque ut terra adversum aquam, sic aqua adversum aera et aer adversus ignem.

[We should remember those words of Plato... For he said, if we recall, that similarity should be sought not only in forms and shapes but also in powers and qualities.... So if there is no similarity between fire and earth in appearance and, so to speak, countenance, we should seek it in those natures and qualities of the elements themselves according to which they manifest some activity or passivity, and in those characteristics through which the essence and affinity of the two elements is primarily designated. Indeed, there are many other properties of both fire and earth, but those which especially declare their essences and characters are surely: of fire, acuity — since it is sharp and penetrating, rarefied in a certain delicate subtlety, and mobile in its eternal motion; but of earth, obtuseness — since it is blunt, corpulent, and eternally immobile. Although these natures are indeed contraries, they possess a certain equality through that very contrariety — for similars are compared to similars as much as dissimilars to dissimilars — and this is analogy or the principle of continuous progression. As acuity stands in respect of bluntness, so does subtlety in relation to corpulence; and as subtlety stands in relation to corpulence, so does mobility in respect of immobility. And if one inverts the terms so that the mediate becomes an extreme while the extremes are placed in mediation one after another, the pattern of analogy will be preserved. The arithmetical discipline teaches how two other solid bodies, interposed between the two solids whose similarity was demonstrated above, will produce a connection according to the principle of continuous progression. For if we wish to ascertain what is the adjacent element to fire and of what properties it consists, we shall take two powers of fire from the next position: subtlety and mobility, and one power of earth: bluntness. The generation of the second element which is below fire — that is, air — will be discovered since air is blunt, subtle, and mobile. Again, if we examine the generation of that element which is adjacent to earth — that is, water — we shall take two powers of earth: bluntness and corpulence, and one of fire: motion. The substance of water will arise, since this is a body which is blunt, corpulent, and mobile. In this way, between fire and earth through concretion from the extreme terms' properties will be born air and water, and in the latter the continuity of the world exists. A geometrical analogy also according to the principle of continuous progression is preserved by this arrangement. For as fire stands in respect of air, so does air in respect of water, and finally water in relation to earth. In the reverse order, as earth stands in respect of water, so does water in respect of air, and air in respect of fire].

In this passage, Calcidius' argument is deceptively simple. Following Plato's exposition in the *Timaeus,* the commentator begins with the two extreme elements of fire and earth and then proceeds to the intermediate elements of air and water. During the discussion of each pair of terms, Calcidius selects some physical properties, explains the mathematical principle of *analogia,* and describes the properties' interrelation using that principle. Regarding the selection of properties, it is obvious that the assignment of sharp, subtle, and mobile to fire; of blunt, subtle, and mobile to air; of blunt, corpulent, and mobile to water; and of blunt, corpulent, and immobile to earth is not the only one possible. Calcidius states this explicitly and himself illustrates alternative methods. For example, an earlier paragraph of the commentary describes the rudiments of a scheme where elements are classified according to degrees of brightness, hotness, and solidity.[568] Concerning the mathematical principle of *analogia,* detailed discussion should be postponed until later in this chapter. However, the commentary reveals at the outset its preference for a progression which is 1. continuous — involving three or more terms —, and 2. geometrical — with the same ratio between successive terms. Regarding the interrelation of properties, a striking fact is that Calcidius envisions two applications of the mathematical principle: one between individual properties within the groups characterizing opposing elements, and the other somehow between the groups themselves characterizing adjacent elements. The text is particularly imprecise regarding this second application since actual properties in the groups seem not at issue. Presumably Calcidius intends the mathematical principle to govern the repetition or substitution of properties as one element is compared with the adjacent in sequence. At all events, what the commentator means by the selection of physical properties, the mathematical principle of *analogia,* and the properties' interrelation in terms of that principle needs a more detailed investigation. This should focus separately on the two halves of the exposition distinguished for methodological convenience above.

In the first part of the passage — dealing with the extremes of fire and earth — Calcidius explains the application of continuous progression. Al-

Mediation in the cosmology and psychology of Calcidius 133

though the two natures are contraries,[569] he observes, they possess a certain equality through that very contrariety[570] given that similars are compared to similars and dissimilars to dissimilars. The most peculiar feature of this statement, offered as an actual illustration of continuous progression, is the notion of equality among contraries or dissimilars. Assuming that Calcidius does not intend to violate the law of contradiction, this equality must be not within a pair of contrary terms but between each term and a term potentially the member of a further pair of contrary terms: in other words, it arises from the fact that different pairs of terms are alike in being contraries. This interpretation is confirmed by the examples of physical properties which follow in the text, for acuity stands in respect of[571] bluntness as does subtlety in relation to[572] corpulence, while subtlety stands in relation to[573] corpulence as does mobility in respect of[574] immobility. It is crucial to the argument that one pair of terms — subtlety and corpulence — should appear twice, since otherwise the progression between successive pairs would not be continuous (see figure 7).

In the second part of the passage — dealing with the intermediates of air and water — Calcidius makes a further application of continuous progression. This relation is visible, he notes, for fire stands in respect of[575] air as does air in respect of[576] water and water in relation to[577] earth; while in reverse, earth stands in respect of[578] water as does water in respect of[579] air and air in respect of[580] fire. Obviously the progression here is between groups of physical properties — that is elements themselves — rather than individual properties as before. This is shown by Calcidius' description of the relation between fire and air earlier in the text stressing the two powers[581] which air shares with fire: subtlety and mobility, and the one power[582] not shared: bluntness; and in reverse order by the description

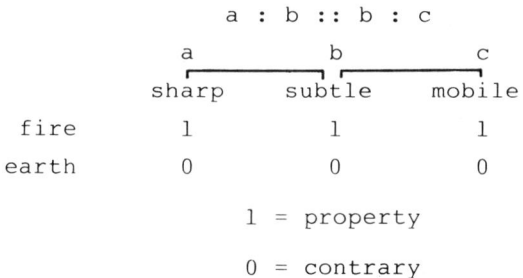

Figure 7. Application of continuous progression to the elements

of the relation between earth and water emphasizing the two powers[583] which water shares with earth: bluntness and corpulence, and the one power[584] not shared: mobility. But this still leaves the question precisely where the progression resides. Since it cannot be between the physical properties making up the groups but only between their formal characteristics, the number of physical properties which change between each element and the adjacent must be the deciding factor (see figure 8).

The context for the second of Calcidius' discussions is furnished by the *Timaeus'* account of the world's soul. After the initial blending process, the divine artificer divides the psychic substance into portions whose size is determined according to mathematical principles. The initial stage of this division involves the taking of a single portion of unspecified magnitude followed on one hand, by parts two times, four times, and eight times the original portion and on the other, by parts three times, nine times, and

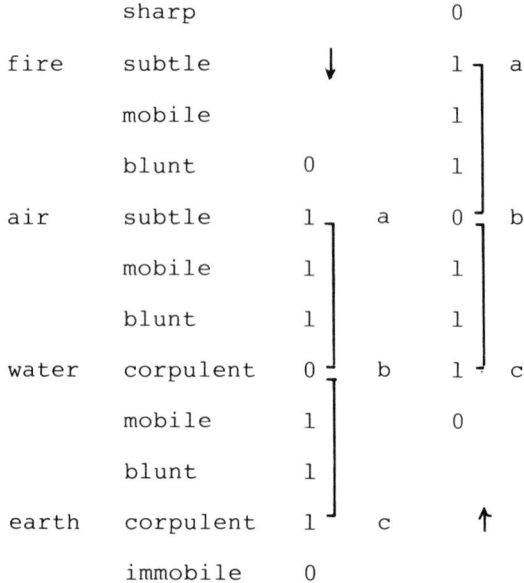

1 = retain property

0 = change to contrary

Figure 8. Further application of continuous progression to the elements

twenty-seven times the original. Division continues by selecting portions whose dimensions are those of the harmonic and arithmetical means [585] respectively between successive portions arranged in order of increasing magnitude within the two sequences. The next stage of the division includes the taking of further parts whose sizes possess the ratio 9:8 to the original portions and to those determined as their harmonic and arithmetical means. The artificer concludes by cutting the whole psychic substance thus apportioned into two strips, and by arranging these in the form of the Greek letter χ.[586]

Calcidius approaches this text by combining two kinds of comment: one dealing with the nature of the mathematical structures involved, and the other with the psychic correlates of these mathematical structures.

The commentator begins with the seven original portions of psychic substance which he has depicted graphically:[587]

> Ista ergo descriptio quae partium ex quibus anima constare dicitur genituram seu coagmentationem deliniat, ostendit rationem animae corporisque coniugii. Quippe corpus animalium, quod inspiratur animae vigore, habet certe superficiem, habet etiam soliditatem. Quae igitur cum vitali vigore penetratura erat tam superficiem quam soliditatem, similes soliditati, similes etiam superficiei vires habere debuit, siquidem paria paribus congregantur.

> [So this diagram, which sketches out the generation or combination of those parts in which soul is held to subsist, reveals the basis of soul's connection with body. For the body of a living thing which is animated by the force of soul certainly has surface and also solidity. Since soul was to permeate both surface and solidity with vital force, it had to possess powers similar to the solid and also to the surface, given that like collects with like].

The next paragraph explains how soul's internal structure is the necessary prototype of tri-dimensionality, by interpreting the two sequences of parts originally established as stages in the generation of solid objects. At the head of both sequences is the single portion corresponding to an indivisible geometrical point. Next come, in one sequence, the parts two times, four times, and eight times the original portion corresponding to a line which is two times the point,[588] a surface which is two times the line,[589] and a cube which is two times the surface.[590] After this, in the other sequence, come the parts three times, nine times and twenty-seven times the original corresponding in a similar fashion to line, surface, and cube. The end of the paragraph gives a second explanation of why soul's internal structure is the prototype of tri-dimensionality: namely, because the numbers involved exhibit a geometrical and therefore quasi-spatial character. On one side, eight stands in respect of four as does four in respect of two and two in respect of one while on the other, twenty-seven stands in respect of nine as does nine in respect of three and three in respect of one. Therefore, the sequences of portions originally established illustrate the principle of continuous progression of the geometrical type.[591]

Calcidius ends his commentary on this section of Plato's text with the parts of psychic substance correlating with the harmonic and arithmetical means.[592]

> Horum numerorum intervalla numeris aliis contexi volebat, ut esset in animae textu corporis similitudo. Itaque limitibus constitutis, uno sex, altero duodecim qui est duplex, duabus medietatibus, octo et novem sex et duodecim limitum intervallum continuavit epitrita, item sescuplari potentia, perindeque ut inter ignis limitem terraeque alterum limitem insertis aeris et aquae materiis mundi corpus continuatum est [ut] ita numerorum potentiis insertis <ut> tamquam elementis materiisque membra animae intellegibilia conecterentur essetque aliqua inter animam corpusque similitudo.

> [The artificer wished these numerical intervals to be interwoven with other numbers, so that there might be a likeness of body in the fabric of soul. He established as the limits six and twelve which is two times six together with the two means eight and nine. Thus, he connected the interval between the limits of six and twelve with the force of the ratios 4:3 and 3:2, after the same fashion in which the world's body has been connected through insertion of the elements air and water between the limits of fire and earth. This was so that intelligible divisions of soul could be joined by insertion of numerical potencies as if by elements and substances, and that there could be a likeness between soul and body].

The mathematical information presented in these texts is conventional and illustrated by readily available parallels in Nicomachus of Gerasa, Theo of Smyrna, and the fragmentary earlier traditions documented by such writers. Traditional elements are the presentation of the original division within psychic substance using what is termed the *labdōma* (a diagram in the form of the Greek letter Λ);[593] and the account of the three means: geometrical — among numbers corresponding to the original division —, harmonic and arithmetical — among additional numbers inserted into the original division.[594] The only point where Calcidius perhaps went beyond more ancient sources is in his employment of three distinct lambda diagrams. These are attached to chapters 32, 41, and 49 and represent the original series of numbers — corresponding to the portions of psychic substance first selected by the artificer — , the original numbers multiplied by 6 — permitting the insertion of the means into the series —, and the original numbers multiplied by 132 — allowing the insertion of smaller intervals into the series and the explanation of the irregular semitone.

It is in their application of mathematical ideas to other spheres of knowledge that these passages in Calcidius are more remarkable. He himself provides an excursus on the multiple meanings acquired by a number like seven when understood successively in the fields of chronology, anatomy, and physics,[595] and this explains the polysemous function of various mathematical terms when applied now to the psychic and now to the physical in the texts we have examined. That number can apply both to a division in soul and to a division among the elements also permits the division in soul to "apply" to the division among the elements through number. Thus, the original parts of psychic substance correlate with point, line, surface and solid in the sphere of physical bodies while — thanks to the doctrine of harmonic and arithmetical means — the original and supplementary parts of psychic substance correlate with extreme and intermediate elements in that sphere of physical bodies.

But something should be said regarding the correlation of the harmonic and arithmetical means[596] with the elements of air and water. According to the last paragraph studied, air represents the harmonic mean between fire and earth and water the arithmetical mean between fire and earth. If we assign the values 6 and 12 to fire and earth respectively as Calcidius indicates, the following ratios between adjacent elements result: fire to air = 3:4, air to water = 8:9, and water to earth = 3:4. Yet according to the earlier discussion of elements, air represents the geometrical mean between fire and water and water the geometrical mean between air and earth. To make this intelligible we must assign 6 and 48 to fire and earth respectively, yielding the following ratios between adjacent elements: fire to air = 1:2, air to water = 1:2, and water to earth = 1:2 (see figure 9).

This discrepancy does not suggest our interpretation of the passages concerned is mistaken or that Calcidius' entire methodology is flawed. Rather, it brings home the flexibility and creativeness with which mathematical elements are being transferred as conceptual tools to other departments of knowledge.

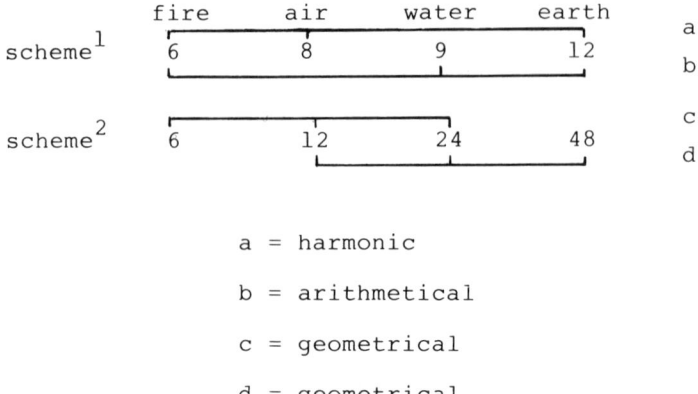

Figure 9. Correlation of means with the elements

It is obvious that these discussions in Calcidius imply a pattern of ideas different from the Augustinian one considered earlier in this chapter. To recapitulate, the latter included as components: i. the relation of contrary to contrary ($s_1 \rightarrow s_2$) and ii. the relation of both contraries to the whole (($s_1 \rightarrow S$) + ($s_2 \rightarrow S$)). Augustine generally interpreted these contraries as the elements of good and evil in created things, but also as dualities overlapping with these: being and non-being, beauty and ugliness, and so forth.[597] The Calcidian pattern, however, can be analyzed into the components: i. the relation of extreme to extreme ($s_1 \rightarrow s_2$) and ii. the relation of both extremes to the mediator (($s_1 \rightarrow S$) + ($s_2 \rightarrow S$)). Calcidius usually interprets these extremes as arithmetical values, as physical elements — fire, air, water, and earth — or selected properties thereof, and as constituents of psychic substance.

A comparison of the Augustinian and Calcidian schemes reveals two divergences in addition to the shift from contraries to extremes. First, the former involves only two real objects (s_1, s_2) whereas in the latter there are three (s_1, s_2, S). Secondly the former scheme is not susceptible to multiplication (consisting of s_1, s_2, S only) while the latter is susceptible (s_1, s_2, S can all become s_1... of another set).

3.4 Ancient and medieval antecedents of the "semiotic square"

That mathematics is so closely associated with dialectics that one may speak of an "axis of pseudo-hierarchy" between them is clearly demonstrated by Calcidius' application of the doctrine of extremities/mediation to both spheres. This mathematico-dialectical theory occurs frequently in Neopythagorean philosophical literature of late antiquity, yet makes its most dramatic appearance in the metaphysical treatise of Iohannes Scottus Eriugena entitled *Periphyseon*.

Its lengthy discussion of the categories refers several times to a type of relation combining the features of mathematical proportion and dialectical condition. For Eriugena, this *habitus proportionalis* [proportional condition][598] is most clearly revealed between the subaltern species of a genus and between extremes and mediator within certain categories. So in the former instance, he explains how irrational and rational being have a *proportio... habitus ad se invicem* [proportion or condition to one another] — irrational being also having a *habitus absentiae rationis* [condition of reason's absence] and rational being also a *habitus praesentiae rationis* [condition of reason's presence];[599] and in the latter, how within the category of quality white, black, and colour †*habitu sibimet iungi* [are joined to one another by condition] — white also having to black a *habitus contrarietatis* [condition of contrariety] and colour also to white and black a *habitus medietatis* [condition of mediateness].[600] Eriugena himself explains this theory using the metaphysical premiss that number is the essence of all things,[601] although it really represents a semiotic entanglement whose pivot is the lexical item "extremity". Inspection of the broader context shows that this lexeme actualizes semes representing the poles of two semantic axes: the mathematical-dialectical (Y) and the simple (= binary)-complex (= ternary) (Z).[602] Extremity can therefore have actualized within it the semes "mathematical" and "dialectical" on one axis and the semes "binary" and "ternary" on the other. Moreover, the lexeme can have simultaneously actualized within it the semes "mathematical" + "binary", or the semes "dialectical" + "binary", or the semes "mathematical" + "ternary", or the semes "dialectical" + "ternary"; the numerical ratio $3:5$, the differentiae irrational/rational, the numerical series $2-4-8$, and the qualities white/colour/black being examples of these four uses. Obviously the lexical item "extremity" will occur in conjunction with the lexeme "mediator" in some of these cases but not in others.[603]

140 *Components of concord — Ternary relations (ontological)*

The axis of pseudo-hierarchy between mathematical and dialectical underlies not only Eriugena's handling of extremities/mediation in general but also his treatment of the square of opposition. This becomes especially clear when the celebrated fourfold schema is analyzed into components whose functions are influenced by their historical provenance.[604]

Modern scholarship has associated the square of opposition with the Greek Neoplatonist Porphyry who utilized it for the purpose of classifying things in general.[605] From this source it enters the Latin tradition with Marius Victorinus who presents a schema based on four semes — existent (a_1), not truly ($\bar{a}_2$), truly (a_2), and not existent ($\bar{a}_1$) — which combine to form four sememes — not truly existent ($b_1 = a_1 + \bar{a}_2$), truly existent ($b_2 = a_2 + a_1$), truly not existent ($\bar{b}_1 = a_2 + \bar{a}_1$), and not truly not existent ($\bar{b}_2 = \bar{a}_1 + \bar{a}_2$)[606] — and with Boethius who describes one based on four semes — of a subject (a_1), not in a subject ($\bar{a}_2$), in a subject (a_2), and not of a subject ($\bar{a}_1$) — which combine to form four sememes — of a subject but not in a subject ($b_1 = a_1 + \bar{a}_2$), both in a subject and of a subject ($b_2 = a_2 + a_1$), in a subject but not of a subject ($\bar{b}_1 = a_2 + \bar{a}_1$), and neither of a subject nor in a subject ($\bar{b}_2 = \bar{a}_1 + \bar{a}_2$).[607] Modern scholars have also detected an earlier square of opposition in the Greek Neopythagoreans who employed it with the aim of classifying the numbers 1–10.[608] From this background it enters the Latin milieu with Macrobius and Martianus Capella who present a schema based on four semes — generating (a_1), not generated ($\bar{a}_2$), generated (a_2), and not generating ($\bar{a}_1$) — which combine to form four sememes — generating but not generated ($b_1 = a_1 + \bar{a}_2$), both generated and generating ($b_2 = a_2 + a_1$), generated but not generating ($\bar{b}_1 = a_2 + \bar{a}_1$), and neither generating nor generated ($\bar{b}_2 = \bar{a}_1 + \bar{a}_2$).[609] Incomplete examples of the square without the fourth position occur in Augustine and Claudianus Mamertus[610] possibly reflecting both Neoplatonic and Neopythagorean sources.

That Eriugena prefixes his fourfold schema to a discussion of things in general and comments on its arithmological antecedent in Martianus Capella suggests that he has learned from all these traditions.[611] Indeed, the historical provenance of the square of opposition would be sufficient to show him that the axis of pseudo-hierarchy between mathematical and dialectical underlies its construction.[612]

And Eriugena's own descriptions of the square of opposition clearly indicate that the schema is underpinned by that relation which combines the features of mathematical proportion and dialectical condition. He does not explicitly state that the fourfold division of nature contains proportional condition although he once refers allusively to this idea by saying that,[613] since there is nothing prior to God which has *ei principii vel causae proportio* [the proportion of a beginning or cause to him], he himself is — and we may clearly supply: "has the proportion of a" — beginning or cause to all things.[614] On the other hand he does, by describing all four terms as *species* [species],[615] imply that they have a condition of some property's presence or absence in respect of one another; and also, by characterizing the second and third terms together as a †*medietas/mediae* [mediator],[616] that these have a condition of mediateness to the first and fourth. All this suggests that the semiotic entanglement pivoting on the lexical item "extremity" which influenced the discussion of the categories also determines the presentation of the fourfold schema.

One final point should be noted. That the semantic axes of mathematical-dialectical (Y) and of simple (= binary)-complex (= ternary) (Z) can be used in explaining the Eriugenian square of opposition does not conflict in any problematic sense with the fact that the selfsame square was used in establishing these semantic axes in the first place. What occurs here is simply an illustration — and a particularly striking one — of the only stable truth in semiotic research: that processes of interpretation represent substitutions of signifiers for signifieds theoretically *ad infinitum*.[617]

3.5 Mediation in the cosmology and angelology of Eriugena

That Eriugena had knowledge of Plato's *Timaeus* is clearly indicated by references to both author and dialogue for the teaching concerning the world's soul[618] — combined with further testimony from Virgil and Pliny — and to author alone for the definition of angels or demons.[619] Since his early work the *Annotationes in Martianum* mentions Calcidius' exposition by name on several occasions,[620] it seems certain that he derived his knowledge of Plato's text from its fourth-century exegete. Nevertheless Eriugena's notion of dialectical mediation[621] is based neither on Plato alone nor on Plato together with Calcidius but on Plato and Calcidius together with various patristic sources: especially Gregory of Nyssa and pseudo-Dionysius the Areopagite.

The final point is reinforced by the discussions of *analogia* in Eriugena's late work *Expositiones in Ierarchiam caelestem* which show this application of mathematical terms to another sphere. In one place[622] the expositor describes how the originative principle has produced each thing according to its analogy: that is, a measure of its own createdness congruent with itself.[623] This definition of analogy fits in with remarks at the beginning of the text[624] where, glossing the ps.-Dionysian statement that all created things are somehow lights, Eriugena connects the same notion with a triadic configuration. Things are lights because various of their aspects may illuminate an onlooker's mind: he may perceive them through their analogy as good and beautiful, through their number as differentiated by genus and species, and through their weight[625] as tending to a position in the cosmic order. Of these two passages the first recalls Calcidius' definition of mathematical analogy as congruent measure,[626] and the second Augustine's Trinitarian analyses of created being by measure, number, and weight.[627]

Eriugena's notion of dialectical mediation is complicated not only because it reflects Platonic-Calcidian and patristic influences but because it is associated with a range of philosophical questions whose extent cannot be fully mapped here. These can however be reduced to the two primary topics — corresponding roughly to the physical and psychological analyses of Calcidius — of elemental and vital theory respectively. In the first, Eriugena blends Platonic-Calcidian teachings with those of Gregory of Nyssa and Ambrose in explaining the relations of fire, air, earth, and water among themselves; in the second, he mixes Plato-Calcidius with ps.-Dionysian doctrines in order to delineate a generic life shared by angels, men, and irrational creatures.

Among different versions of the elemental theory, one can be identified by its classification of physical bodies according to the pairs of qualities: lightness-heaviness and mobility-immobility. This is stated initially during an analysis of the distinction between place and body in *Periphyseon* I. Here, Eriugena begins by quoting Plato for his doctrine that the world is composed of soul and body, but then passes to the authority of Gregory of Nyssa's *De imagine* in his own Latin translation:[628]

>...conditorem universitatis hunc mundum visibilem inter duas sibi invicem contrarias extremitates constituisse, inter gravitatem dico atque levitatem, quae sibi omnino opponuntur, atque ideo quoniam in gravitate terra est constituta semper immobilis manet nam gravitas moveri nescit et est in medio mundi constituta extremumque ac medium obtinet terminum, aetheria vero spatia propterea ineffabili velocitate semper circa media volvuntur quoniam in natura levitatis constituta sunt quae stare ignorat et extremum mundi visibilis obtinent finem. Duo vero in medio elementa

constituta, aqua videlicet et aer, proportionali moderamine inter gravitatem et levitatem assidue moventur ita ut proximum sibi extremum terminum utraque magis sequantur quam ab eis longe remotum. Aqua nanque tardius movetur aere quoniam gravitati telluris adhaeret, aer vero velocius aqua concitatur quoniam aetheriae levitati coniungitur.

[The founder of the universe established this visible world between two extremes contrary to one another: I mean, between the heaviness and lightness which are totally opposed among themselves. Since earth, then, is established in heaviness, it remains always immobile. For heaviness knows no motion, is established in the centre of the world, and holds the extreme and central limit. The aetherial regions always revolve around the centre with undescribable velocity, since they are established in the nature of lightness. They are ignorant of rest and hold the extreme boundary of the visible world. But the two elements established in mediating position, namely water and air, move constantly in a proportional moderating between heaviness and lightness. In consequence, each follows the extreme limit which is nearer more closely than the one which is far removed. For water moves more slowly than air because it adheres to the heaviness of earth; air moves more rapidly than water since it is joined to the lightness of aether].

The same theory is recalled when Alumnus provides a footnote to the main discussion of physical bodies later in the text:[629]

Quamvis itaque qualitatum quaedam quidem in quibusdam corporibus plus, quaedam vero minus sensibus appareant, synodus tamen ipsorum catholicorum elementorum una eademque uniformiter commensurabilis in omnibus est. Mens siquidem divina examinationem totius mundani corporis inter duas extremitates sibi invicem e contrario oppositas aequali lance libravit, inter gravitatem dico et levitatem, inter quas omnis medietas visibilium corporum ponderata est. Proinde omnia corpora in quantum gravitatem participant in tantum terrenarum qualitatum capacia sunt, hoc est soliditatis et stabilitatis, in quantum vero ex levitate attrahunt in tantum qualitates caelestes participant, inanitatem dico et mutabilitatem, media autem, quae simili libramine extremitates attingunt, aequali participatione illarum qualitates possident. In omnibus autem quattuor elementorum universalium unus idemque motus est et status et capacitas et possessio.

[Thus, although some qualities appear to sensation more and others less in certain bodies, there is nevertheless in all things a single, self-identical, and uniformly commensurable gathering of the universal elements themselves. The divine mind balanced its weighing of the entire world's body in equipoise between two extremes opposed through contrariety to one another: I mean, heaviness and lightness between which all that is mediate in visible bodies is weighed out. Therefore, all bodies, to the extent that they participate in heaviness, are receptive of earthly qualities — that is, solidity and stability — but, to the extent that they acquire something of lightness, participate in celestial qualities — namely, subtlety and mutability. Mediate bodies, which touch the extremes in a similar balancing, possess the latters' qualities by participating in them equally. Yet there is a single and self-identical motion, rest, receptivity, and possession in all four universal elements].

Another version of the elemental theory can be identified by its classification of physical bodies according to the pairs of qualities: hotness-coldness and dryness-wetness. This predominates during the interpretation of the Biblical creation narrative in *Periphyseon* III. Here, Eriugena explains how the firmament and the lower waters — following suggestions in Ambrose's *Hexaemeron* — can be interpreted as elementary qualities' transcendent and immanent states respectively.[630]

> ... et in universalibus elementis quae Graeci catholica *stoicheia* vocant, eo quod sibi invicem conveniant et concinant — *stoicheiōsis* enim est *diatypōsis,* hoc est conformatio: illorum nanque concursu omnia corpora visibilia conficiuntur, ideoque Athenienses *stoicheia* litteras appellant quarum coitu articulata vox perficitur —, nec immerito. Dum enim viritim considerantur pura et a se invicem segregata videntur esse contraria — Frigus siquidem calori, humiditas siccitati contradicit —, dum vero in se invicem misceantur omnium rerum visibilium harmonia quadam mirabili atque ineffabili compositiones efficiunt — ... quattuor simplicium elementorum universitatem, quae dum per se purissima sint et incomprehensibilia omni corporeo sensu et ubique universaliter diffusa, invisibili suo meatu proportionalique coitu in se invicem omnia corpora sensibilia perficiunt, sive caelestia sint sive aeria sive aquatica sive terrena...

> [... and in the universal elements which the Greeks call the universal *stoicheia* because they agree and harmonize with one another — for *stoicheiōsis* corresponds to *diatypōsis*: that is, conformation — while all visible bodies are produced through their coming together. The Athenians also call the letters *stoicheia* because the articulated voice is completed through their combination. When the universal elements are considered singly and in their purety and distinction from one another, they appear to be contrary: for coldness contradicts hotness, and wetness dryness. But when they are blended with one another, they bring about the compositions of all visible things in a certain wonderful and ineffable harmony... The universality of the four simple elements which, although in themselves most pure and incomprehensible to every bodily sense in their omnipresent

Mediation in the cosmology and angelology of Eriugena 145

and universal diffusion, by their invisible motion and proportional concourse with one another complete all sensible bodies whether celestial, aerial, aquatic, or terrestrial...]

The same theory is restated with a more detailed account of the qualities' confluence during the next few paragraphs: [631]

> Ubi notandum quod non ex coitu substantialium elementorum, dum sint incorruptibilia et insolubilia, sed ex eorum qualitatibus sibi invicem proportionaliter copulatis corpora sensibilia conficiuntur. Qualitates autem quattuor elementorum notissimae sunt quattuor: caliditas humiditas frigiditas siccitas, ex quibus omnia corpora materialia adiectis formis componi physica perhibet theoria, quarum quidem activas esse duas philosophi dicunt caliditatem et frigiditatem, passivasque duas, humiditatem et ariditatem. Dum enim caliditas humiditati et frigiditas ariditati naturali quodam coitu miscentur, omnia quae in terra et mari nascuntur procreationem accipiunt... Hinc colligitur, ut duae qualitates activae sibi invicem contrariae, caliditatem dico et frigiditatem, duabus passivis sibimet oppositis, humiditati videlicet et ariditati, copulatae occasionem omnibus in terra et in aquis nascentibus praebeant generationis et incrementorum.

[And here it should be noted that sensible bodies are produced not from the concourse of substantial elements, since these are incorruptible and indissoluble, but from their qualities joined to one another proportionally. The most well-known qualities of the four elements are four in number: hotness, wetness, coldness, and dryness from which physical theory asserts that all material bodies are composed when forms are added. Philosophers say that two of these are active — hotness and coldness — and two passive — wetness and dryness. For when by a certain natural concourse hotness is blended with wetness and coldness with dryness, all things which are born in land and sea achieve their procreation... From this it follows that the two active qualities which are contrary to one another — I mean, hotness and coldness — when joined to the two passive qualities which are opposed among themselves — namely, wetness and dryness — provide the occasion of generation and growth to all things born in earth or water].

Eriugena's basic doctrine of the four physical elements can be extracted from these passages. It is formulated using a repertoire of traditional mathematical concepts among which those of extremes, mediation, balance, and proportionality are perhaps the most important. The first two passages describe how God arranges visible things between two extremes contrary to one another,[632] while all four refer to various pairs of physical qualities as contraries or opposites. Presence of extremes suggests the possibility of mediation, and Eriugena speaks several times of physical elements which occupy a mediating position.[633] The second passage reformulates this mediation between extremes more dynamically as an equipoise, balancing, weighing[634] among physical qualities which inclines them in neither direction, the first alluding to a similar moderating among visible things. Moreover, the combination of extremes and mediators is an instance of proportionality, and Eriugena speaks frequently of the proportional[635] concourse of physical qualities. However, the manner of applying these traditional mathematical ideas in another sphere testifies to an innovative tendency. This application is crucially affected by the dichotomy underlying most of these texts between transcendent and immanent states of the elements and their qualities.

Such a development has its roots in the Bible, for God is described at *Genesis* 1. 6–7 as making the firmament in the middle[636] of the waters, and dividing waters above the firmament from waters below it; and at *Proverbs* 8. 28 as establishing the heavens, and balancing[637] the sources of the waters. Since the cosmological tradition had associated mediation with the elements as a matter of course — although this procedure was applied to certain elements rather than to the group as a whole — Eriugena thought it logical to take the further step of connecting the elements with the firmament. In fact, he elaborates a far-reaching interpretation of the relevant Biblical passages in *Periphyseon* III, according to which the higher waters represent primordial causes, the firmament a transcendent state of the elements and their qualities, and the lower waters an immanent state of elemental qualities.[638]

These different states are characterized more precisely as follows: 1. Transcendence. In one version of Eriugena's theory of elements,[639] the determining pairs of qualities are lightness-heaviness and mobility-immobility. Since their single, self-identical, and uniformly commensurable gathering[640] is contrasted with their appearance to varying degrees in physical bodies, the transcendent elemental qualities — including those in mutual opposition — must be insusceptible to quantitative variation. Eriugena seems to construe these pairs of qualities as somewhat interdependent in that lightness always implies mobility and heaviness always implies immobility. A second version of his theory of elements[641] operates with the pairs of qualities: hotness-coldness and wetness-dryness. When viewed as transcendent, these pairs are described as contradictory[642] within themselves and therefore not liable to quantitative variation. For Eriugena, the pairs are independent since either hotness or coldness can join with either wetness or dryness. 2. Immanence. In the first version of Eriugena's theory of elements[643] where the determining pairs of qualities are lightness-heaviness and mobility-immobility an immanent state contrasts with the transcendent. Given that the intermediate physical bodies enjoy a proportional moderating between heaviness and lightness,[644] the immanent elemental qualities — including those in mutual opposition — must be susceptible to quantitative variation. Eriugena again interprets these pairs of qualities as partially interdependent in that lightness is always accompanied by mobility and heaviness always by immobility. The other version of his theory of elements[645] which operates with the pairs of qualities: hotness-coldness and wetness-dryness also presents an immanent state contrasting with the transcendent. When seen as immanent, the pairs are described as blending[646] within themselves and therefore subject to quantitative variation. For Eriugena once more, these pairs are independent because both hotness and coldness can join with both wetness and dryness (see figure 10).

Eriugena's doctrine of the two elemental states gives rise to additional complications in metaphysics. For example, one passage[647] states that the different qualities are both single and self-identical[648] in all the elements and also pure and distinct from one another.[649] Such a contradiction is typical of the transcendent state according to Eriugenian thought and signifies that the isotopy of internal relation is operative in the discussion. Elsewhere,[650] it is argued that the different qualities are both single and self-identical[651] in all bodies and also more in some than in others.[652] This contradiction accompanies Eriugena's normal depiction of the transcendent as shifting to the immanent state and again indicates the presence of the isotopy of internal relation. Yet the doctrine of the two elemental states has also clarified several ambiguities left by his philosophical forebears. In particular, there had been a question whether elemental qualities are logical contradictories or admit of degrees. Eriugena's response[653] was that coldness contradicts[654] hotness when these are viewed in the transcendent state, but involves a blending[655] with its opposite when the transcendent shifts to the immanent state.[656] Furthermore, there had been a problem whether proportionality connects elements through their qualities or those qualities themselves. The Eriugenian teaching here[657] emphasized the proportional joining of qualities to one another[658] according to degrees of those qualities in the immanent state alone.

Although Eriugena's doctrine of the four elements evolved in response to certain problems of biblical exegesis, it could not have taken its partic-

148 *Components of concord — Ternary relations (ontological)*

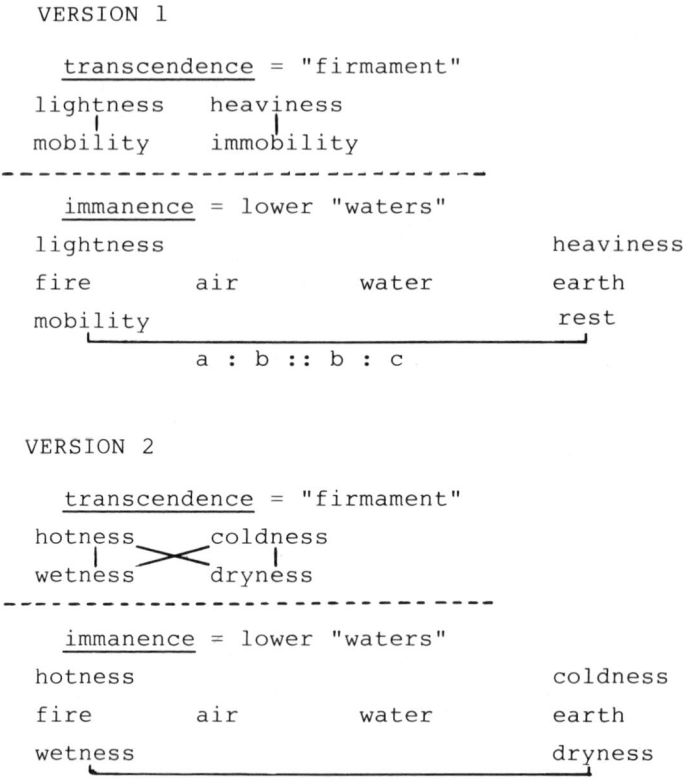

Figure 10. Proportional joining of qualities

ular form without the influence of earlier philosophical sources both pagan and Christian. The notion of a transcendent state of the elements and their qualities is actually paralleled in Calcidius' presentation of the Neopythagorean doctrine of first principles.[659] Of the two versions of the elemental theory, that based on the qualities lightness-heaviness and mobility-immobility goes back to Plato[660] although Eriugena prefers to cite an intermediate patristic source in Gregory of Nyssa. The version of the elemental theory based on the qualities hotness-coldness and dryness-wetness is of Peripatetic provenance[661] although again he ostensibly derives it from the Christian writers Ambrose, Augustine and Basil. Finally, the employment of the term *proportionalitas* to signify the Greek mathematical concept of *analogia* follows Boethius' translation of the Nicomachean arithmetic.[662]

As stated earlier in this section, there is another philosophical question with which Eriugena primarily associates the notion of dialectical mediation:[663] namely, that of generic life. Although the most interesting development of this occurs in the angelology of his ps.-Dionysian commentary, its beginnings among glosses dealing with the world's soul in the commentary on Martianus Capella deserve comment.

In certain passages of the *Annotationes in Martianum*, Eriugena mentions this soul which he has discovered in Calcidius' exposition of the *Timaeus* with reference to its mode of division. As the generic soul of the world,[664] it can be divided[665] into specific souls which are either rational or irrational,[666] and this division is according to multiple and superparticular ratios.[667] Further, the relation between the generic and specific souls constitutes a production under control of the sun.[668] Clearly Eriugena continued to be fascinated by this doctrine since in later years he identified the most universal soul[669] of Plato and the philosophers of this world with the living soul which arose on the fifth day of Biblical creation.[670] In several passages of the *Periphyseon*, he describes the living soul of the Genesis account likewise with reference to its manner of division. Corresponding to the most generic life,[671] it is divisible[672] into specific lives which are either rational or irrational,[673] the rational being further divided into specific lives which are either angelic or human.[674] Here, the relation between generic and specific constitutes a providential distribution analogous to the sun's illumination.[675]

It is obvious that Eriugena is dealing with the same doctrine of generic life throughout these passages. There is the discrepancy that the earlier texts mention a division according to ratios and the later one into angels and men. Yet this is overcome by the *Expositiones in Ierarchiam caelestem* which combine the themes of proportionality and angelic division.

Such developments are best illustrated by the passages where ps.-Dionysian technical terms like "mediation", "analogy", and "harmony"[676] are expanded in commentary. Although this material is widely scattered throughout the *Expositiones*, a selection of three short extracts and one continuous text can represent the entire range of arguments without too much distortion. In some cases, we must quote the ps.-Dionysian lemmata; in others, the Eriugenian commentary; and in others both the ps.-Dionysian lemmata and the Eriugenian commentary.

The first passage comes from Eriugena's comment on a listing of the nine angelic orders:[677]

1. Nec transitorie praeterendum quod perfectissimus cubus et primus imparis numeri, qui ex ternario nascitur ter ducto ter conficitur, in his tribus caelestibus hierarchiis pulcherrime consideratur. Singularum siquidem hierarchiarum tres ordines simul connumerati novem faciunt, in quibus longitudo ternaria et latitudo cubica novena efficitur. Si vero singulas tres hierarchias novennalis latitudinis ter quis multiplicaverit, propter singularum primam et mediam et ultimam virtutem, ut in superioribus summatim est dictum, cubus profecto integer consurget, qui viginti septem numero conficitur... Et cetera quae de cubicis proportionibus et proportionalitatibus disseruntur, non aliunde nisi ex caelestium essentiarum adunationibus, in quibus primo condita sunt, in notitiam humanorum intellectuum provenire crediderim vere.

    [And we should not omit to mention that the most perfect cube and the first of an odd number generated from 3 when that is multiplied by 3 and 3 again, is most beautifully contemplated in these three celestial hierarchies. For the three orders of each hierarchy added together make 9, and in this is comprised the 3 corresponding to the length and the 9 to the breadth of a cube. If one then multiplies each of the three hierarchies within the nine-fold breadth by 3, on account of the first, middle, and last of its individual powers — in the manner summarized earlier — the whole cube corresponding to the number 27 will certainly arise... And all the other things said about the proportions and proportionalities of the cube, I truly believe, come into the knowledge of human intellects from no other source than the unifications of celestial essences in which they were first created].

In the second extract, Eriugena comments on the mediate position of archangels within the last celestial hierarchy. This is followed by a comment on their reception and transmission of illuminations according to "analogy".[678]

2. Archangelorum siquidem ordo medietatis proportionem inter duos extremos, hoc est inter ordinem Principatuum et ordinem angelicum obtinet, quoniam nulla hierarchia est, sive humana sive angelica, quae non habeat et primas et medias et ultimas virtutes. Ordo itaque Archangelorum medius est inter Principatuum quasi superiorem et Angelorum veluti inferiorem. Et nihil aliud est ipsa medietatis proportio, nisi hierarchica, id est pontificalis communicatio... Archangeli... divinas illuminationes hierarchice, id est pontificali ordine, per primas virtutes, Principatus videlicet, qui se praecedunt, suscipit, et eas illuminationes Angelis divinitus annuntiat... Unusquisque enim caelestium animorum ordo iuxta suam analogiam divinarum illuminationum capax est.

Mediation in the cosmology and angelology of Eriugena 151

[Indeed, the order of archangels has the proportion of mediation between two extremes: that is, between the order of principalities and the angelic order, since there is no hierarchy whether human or angelic which does not have first, middle, and last powers. So the order of archangels is in the middle between that of principalities which is as though superior to it and that of angels which is as though inferior, while that proportion of mediation itself is none other than hierarchical or priestly communication... The archangels... receive divine illuminations hierarchically: that is, in priestly ordering through the first powers which precede them — namely, the principalities — and they proclaim these illuminations divinely to the angels... For each order of celestial souls is receptive of divine illuminations according to its analogy].

The third passage comes from Eriugena's comment on the levels of reception characterizing angelic orders:[679]

3. ... superordinati divini animi abundanter sanctas proprietates minorum animorum habent, ultimi vero maiorum universas superpositas proprietates non habent, dum apparentes illuminationes primis primo universaliter in eos, ultimos videlicet, particulariter per primos, et proportionaliter eis, ultimis, distribuuntur. Quod breviter colligendum: copiose habent primi ordines et suas et minorum se divinas primo in se apparentes illuminationes; non autem copiose, id est universaliter, sicut ipsis primis, sed particulariter per primos ultimis, prout analogia eorum exigit, eaedem illuminationes distribuuntur.

[The divine souls of higher rank possess in abundance the holy properties of lesser souls, while those of lowest rank do not possess the transcending universal properties of the higher. For the illuminations which at first appear universally to the first ranks are then distributed through those first ranks to the last in a manner particular and proportionate to the latter. In brief, one should understand: The first orders have plentifully both their own divine illuminations and those of the lower which first appear in them. But those same illuminations are distributed through the first orders to the last not plentifully or universally — as they are to the first orders themselves — but particularly and as their analogy demands].

To these short extracts is added a longer passage which begins with the ps.-Dionysian text itself in Latin translation, continues with a lemma and commentary, and ends with another section of Eriugena's commentary. The context is the tenth chapter of *De caelesti hierarchia* where the characteristics of the three angelic orders are summarized.[680]

4. Ab ipsa autem iterum proportionaliter secunda, et a secunda tertia, et ex tertia secundum nos hierarchia, secundum ipsam bene ornantis taxiarchiae legem, in harmonia divina et analogia, ad simul omnis boni ornatus superprincipale principium et consummationem hierarchice reducitur... superessentialis harmonia... ipsam, per singulas dicendum, dispositionem ipsis divinis harmoniis discrevit.

Ac si diceret: non solum singulas hierarchias videmus in primas et medias et ultimas virtutes divisas, sed etiam dicendum quod superessentialis harmonia ipsam generalem dispositionem omnium caelestium hierarchiarum in ipsis divinis harmoniis, adunationibus videlicet, per singulas hierarchias specialiter discrevit in primas et medias et ultimas virtutes. Hierarchia siquidem Virtutum, Potestatum, et Dominationum proportionalis medietatis inter tres ordines primae et tres tertiae hierarchiae harmoniam possidet. Ut enim a prima praeceditur media, ita media praecedit tertiam; et conversim, quemadmodum praeceditur tertia a media, ita media praeceditur a prima. Et haec praecessio et successio in divinarum illuminationum participationis differentiis intelligitur... non solum generalis omnium hierarchia, et specialium hierarchiarum ordines, ipsique singuli ordines, verum etiam unusquisque caelestis et humanus animus in se ipso speciales habet primas et medias et ultimas virtutes, secundum dictas per unumquodque, hoc est per unumquemque ordinem proprias anagogas, reductiones plane, hierarchicarum illuminationum proportionaliter manifestas, id est illuminatas, per quas proprias anagogas unumquodque eorum quae praedicta sunt in participatione fit... divinitatis...

[(A) "Then to the supercausal beginning and likewise end of all good ordering is elevated hierarchically the second disposition proportionally by the first, the third by the second, and the hierarchy among us by the third. This is according to the very law of that Orderer who arranges well through divine harmony and analogy... (B) The superessential harmony... has divided that disposition — speaking of things separately — according to the divine harmonies themselves." As though he were saying: not only do we see the individual hierarchies divided into first, middle, and last powers, but it should also be stated that the superessential harmony has — in those same divine harmonies: that is, unifications — divided the general disposition of all the celestial hierarchies itself, through individual hierarchies specifically, into first, middle, and last powers. Indeed, the hierarchy of virtues, powers, and dominions possesses the harmony of proportional mediation between the three orders of the first and the three of the third hierarchy. For just as the middle is preceded by the first, so does the middle precede the third; and conversely just as the third is preceded by the middle, so is the middle preceded by the first — this preceding and following being understood in differences of participation in the divine illuminations... (C)

Not only the general hierarchy of all, the orders of the specific hierarchies, and the individual orders themselves, but even every celestial or human soul has in itself specifically first, middle, and last powers. These are according to the stated particular "anagogae" — namely, the elevations of the hierarchical illuminations proportionately manifested or illuminated — through each thing: that is, through each order. Through these particular "anagogae" each of the aforesaid things becomes a participant in the... divinity].

Underlying all these passages is the most highly structured conception of the angelic world in Christian thought. According to Eriugena's commentary in *4C* — which systematizes the sketchier presentation of ps.-Dionysius himself — there is divided into first, middle, and last powers:[681] i. the general angelic hierarchy (producing 3 terms); ii. the specific hierarchies (producing 3×3 terms); iii. the individual angelic orders (making $3 \times 3 \times 3$ terms); and iv. the individual angelic intellects (making $3 \times 3 \times 3 \times 3$ terms), the nine traditional angelic names being assigned at division ii. This massive structuring derives from God himself defined as superessential harmony[682] in *4B*.

The passages are further linked by assumptions that each angelic group or intellect is defined in relation to the entire structure by a proportionality[683] equivalent to an analogy,[684] that angelic groups or intellects which are first or last in a triadic configuration correspond to extremes[685] while an angelic group or intellect which is second in a triple configuration represents a mediator,[686] and that the latter is defined in relation to an individual structure by proportionality of mediation.[687] The proportionalities or analogies defining each group or intellect signify not a spatio-temporal position but a metaphysical determination. This determination represents in the first instance a participation[688] where principles superior in the hierarchy possess their own universal properties together with the particular properties of inferior terms in a universalized manner, while principles lower in the hierarchy possess their own particular properties together with the universal properties of higher terms in a particularized mode (texts *3, 4C*). The determination is also conceived as an illumination[689] in which the epistemological, reciprocal — since mediate groups or angels receive from the higher and transmit to the lower —, and dynamic aspects become apparent (texts *2, 3, 4B, 4C*). Finally, this determination resides especially in the elevation[690] where principles lowest in the hierarchy have their unfolded multiplicity unified through the agency of mediate terms, principles mediate in the hierarchy have their unfolded multiplicity unified through the agency of highest terms, and so forth (texts *1, 4A, 4B, 4C*).

The structured conception of the angelic world in all these passages well illustrates the application of mathematical terms to another sphere. According to Eriugena's commentary in 1 — where he especially departs from the original ps.-Dionysian treatment — the relations in which the one general hierarchy stands to the three specific hierarchies, the three specific hierarchies to the nine orders, and the nine orders to the twenty-seven powers correspond to generations of a length from the point, a breadth from the length, and a cube from the breadth[691] respectively in Neopythagorean geometrical arithmetic. Moreover the principles of constructing a three-dimensional solid were first created[692] in the angelic world and thereupon copied into that of the visible.

Eriugena's intricate reading of *De caelesti hierarchia* exploits the connection between ps.-Dionysian metaphysical *analogia* — the determination of something's nature according to its position within an ontological hierarchy — and mathematical proportionality described by writers like Calcidius.[693] It is well-established that ps.-Dionysius' doctrines reflect those of Greek Neoplatonic schools during the fifth and sixth centuries A. D., and we should not be surprised to find developments surrounding the metaphysical *analogia* also paralleled in such sources. The ps.-Dionysian concept of participation reflects the Neoplatonists' tenet that reality is a graded sequence between the most universal and the most particular in which the former contain properties of the latter more universally and the latter properties of the former more particularly. The notion that principles mediate in the hierarchy receive emanations from the higher and transmit them to the lower, and that reception corresponds to the mediates' passive potency and transmission to their active potency is a Procline teaching underpinning the account of angelic illumination. Ps.-Dionysius' concept of elevation parallels the Neoplatonic theory that in the gradation of reality the more universal cause the return of the more particular to themselves and the reunification of their multiplied potencies. In fact, all the ideas associated with metaphysical *analogia* by the Greek theologian are similarly presented in that treatise which served as his primary inspiration: the *Elementatio theologica* of the Neoplatonist Proclus.[694] Since this work is notable for its application of mathematical method to metaphysics — being constructed in a form deliberately recalling Euclid — the later use of Calcidius' mathematics to explain the ps.-Dionysian derivative is quite appropriate.

But the precise connection between *analogia* and participation in ps.-Dionysius or Eriugena remains obscure. Although participation is said to involve principles superior in the hierarchy possessing their own universal properties together with the particular properties of inferior terms in a universalized manner, and principles lower in the hierarchy possessing their own particular properties together with the universal properties of higher terms in a particularized mode, we need answers to the following questions: How many properties are involved?; What are the properties?; How are the properties distributed?

A response to the first and third questions is that at least two properties are required each of which can appear in either universal or particular form. Given that the principles are configured triadically in descending order of universality, the only viable distribution of properties would be of universal first property and universalized particular second property to the highest term; of particularized universal first property and universalized particular second property to the middle term; and of particularized universal first property and particular second property to the lowest term.

In order to identify these properties, one must recall the only attributes which ps.-Dionysius believes to be characteristic of all spiritual principles — the functions of perfecting, illuminating, and purifying[695] — although these present the obvious difficulty of appearing as a triad rather than a pair.[696]

The response to the first and third questions should therefore be reformulated by changing the two properties which could both occur in either universal or particular form somehow into three. Again assuming that principles are structured triadically in descending order of universality, a possible distribution of properties is of first property, universalized particular second property, and universalized particular third property to the highest term; of particularized universal first property, second property, and universalized particular third property to the middle term; and of particularized universal first property, particularized universal second property, and third property to the lowest term.

Using the identification of properties above, one obtains the final scheme:

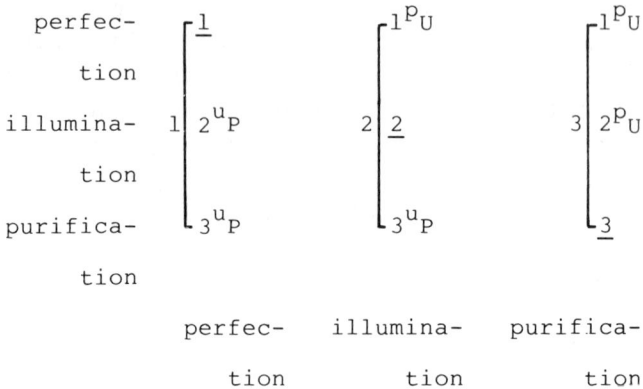

Figure 11. Structure of the angelic world

3.6 The Eriugenian transcendent harmony

In studying the question of ternary or concordant relations, we began with Augustine's explanations of the presence of evil in the world. It will now be useful to return to that discussion from the topic of mathematical mediation applied to physics and psychology and examine further refinements of the Augustinian theory by Eriugena. In some respects the earlier ideas are repeated, in others dramatically transformed by encountering the conclusions of different lines of thought.[697]

Eriugena also presents an analysis of the created world in which assimilation of the concept of relation to those of contrariety and inclusion is a significant factor. Its consequences are a. that discussion of contraries can be fused with that of parts and whole through the shared implication of relationality, and b. that the blending of these discussions yields the concept of a whole containing not simply parts but contrary parts.[698] In addition, Eriugenian texts repeat the three leading ideas that: i. a contrary relates to its contrary ($s_1 \rightarrow s_2$), ii. a part relates to a whole ($s_1 \rightarrow S$), and iii. a contrary together with its contrary relates to a whole (($s_1 + s_2) \rightarrow S$).[699] These ideas are exploited in a variety of situations where they appear either separately or in different combinations with one another.

Eriugena's departures from the Augustinian viewpoint include his understanding of the relation between God and created things. According to this, the creator is simultaneously transcendent of and immanent in what he creates in a basically twofold perspective.[700] Secondly, for Eriugena the relations between parts and whole become in a more strictly logical sense those between particulars and universal. Another deviation from Augustine's standpoint involves perceiving such relations as primarily cognitive in nature — determined through the interaction of divine and human minds — rather than primarily non-cognitive.[701] Fourthly, with Eriugena the relations between contraries are replaced more frequently by those between similars, dissimilars, and contraries. A final departure from the Augustinian viewpoint resides in his account of the relation between God and created things. According to this, the creator is not only simultaneously transcendent of and immanent in what he creates but also transcendentally immanent in an ultimately threefold perspective.[702]

The creator who is simultaneously transcendent of and immanent in the created represents one of Eriugena's most striking conceptions. As developed especially in *Periphyseon* III, the two aspects of divinity are signified by statements that God is *super* [above] created things and therefore the subject of negative predicates, or that he is *in* [in] the created world and thereby the subject of affirmative ones.[703] That these are two simultaneous aspects of a single divine principle is underlined by describing how God transcends created things *dum* [while] immanent in them, or from a status characterized by the negative predication *descendit* [descends] into that characterized by the affirmative.[704]

This discussion should be read in conjunction with another in book I. Here, Eriugena argues that affirmative terms acquire meaning †*opposita...respiciunt* [in relation to opposites],[705] that there exists no thing in opposition to God which could be signified by such an opposite,[706] and therefore that affirmative terms cannot really apply to the creator.[707] However, he continues by suggesting that an affirmative term or its opposite may be predicated of God indirectly by transference from the creature[708] and also that an affirmative term prefixed by *super (hyper)* can be predicated of the creator in direct application to his essence.[709] Finally, he explains that such a super-affirmative term although overtly lacking negation *intellectu negatione pollet* [is strongly negative in meaning][710] and also that it comprehends two branches of theology by being *affirmatio simul et abdicatio* [affirmation simultaneously with negation].[711]

The creator who is simultaneously transcendent of and immanent in the created now presents certain problems of nomenclature. First, his transcendent status seems to be signified not only by negative terms but also by super-affirmative terms and secondly, the super-affirmative terms seem to signify not only his transcendent status but also his simultaneously transcendent and immanent status.[712] The solution to both problems lies in distinguishing the super-affirmative term as something which actually signifies transcendence predominating within a simultaneous transcendence and immanence.

But the precise ontological referent of the super-affirmative terms can be left unspecified while we concentrate on the interpretation of the affirmative terms and their opposites.[713] These divine names are presented throughout the *Periphyseon* in three basic forms: as parts within a whole, as contraries or opposites, and as contraries within a whole. That Eriugena discusses the relations between the affirmative divine names and their opposites in combination with these other relations follows from his attempt to synthesize ps.-Dionysian and Augustinian ideas.[714]

In an important group of passages, attention is focussed on the relation between a part and the whole.[715] Eriugena explains why the punishment of evil angelic and human wills is included in the final resolution[716] of creation into unity by arguing that the blessedness of the righteous is heightened *ex collatione/comparatione* [by comparison with] the torments of the damned.[717] Furthermore, this punishment contributes to the ultimate beauty of creation since what †*in parte...existimari/in partibus...iudicari/in parte...putari* [appears in the part] as evil and deformed †*in toto.../in contemplatione universitatis/in toto...* [is understood in the whole] to be good and beautiful.[718] Although this passage explicitly claims to follow Augustine's authority,[719] there are elsewhere greater deviations from the model. For example, Eriugena replaces the notion that what is evil in the part is not really evil in relation to the whole with the more paradoxical thesis that what is not evil in the whole is not really evil in relation to the part either.[720]

During the introductory section of *Periphyseon* II,[721] a similar argument is applied to the present state of the created world.[722] However, this reveals a further dimension: that the relation between part and whole is viewed in conjunction with that between God and the created.

> ... in superiore libro de universalis naturae universali divisione non quasi generis in formas seu totius in partes — Non enim deus genus est creaturae et creatura species dei sicut creatura non est genus dei neque deus species creaturae. Eadem ratio est in toto et partibus: deus siquidem non est totum creaturae neque creatura pars dei quomodo nec creatura est totum

dei neque deus pars creaturae, quamvis altiori theoria iuxta Gregorium theologum pars dei simus qui humanam participamus naturam, quoniam in ipso vivimus et movemur et sumus metaphoriceque deus dicatur et genus et totum et species et pars. Omne enim quod in ipso et ex ipso est pie ac rationabiliter de eo praedicari potest — sed intelligibili quadam universitatis contemplatione (universitatem dico deum et creaturam) breviter diximus...

[In the earlier book we spoke briefly of the universal division of universal nature not as though it were of genus into species or of whole into parts — For God is not the genus of the creature nor the creature a species of God just as the creature is not the genus of God nor God a species of the creature. The same argument applies to whole and parts, for God is not the whole of the creature nor the creature a part of God just as the creature is not the whole of God nor God a part of the creature. However, from a loftier viewpoint we who participate in human nature are part of God according to Gregory the theologian since "we live and move and exist in him" and in a metaphorical sense God is said to be both genus and whole and both species and part, because everything which is in him and from him can piously and rationally be predicated of him — but by a certain intelligible contemplation of the universe, the universe being God and the creature].

Examination of the principal statements here regarding parts and whole — that 1. God is not the whole of which the creature is a part, 2. The creature is not the whole of which God is a part, 3. God is the whole of which the creature is a part since created attributes can be predicated of him a. in a metaphorical sense or b. by an intelligible contemplation, and 4. Nature consists of God and the creature — reveals a fusion of two conceptual schemes. These are the superficial contrast of *pars...totum* [part/whole] itself in points 1, 2, and 3,[723] and the underlying dialectic of God's transcendence where he *non est...* [is not x] and immanence where he †*et...* [is x] in points 1 and 3 respectively.[724] For Eriugena, the parts correspond primarily to the four species into which God or Nature is divided at the beginning of the treatise although, since the second and third species are further subdivided, they ultimately represent the multitude of primordial causes and effects making up the created world.[725] The *intelligibilis...contemplatio* [intelligible contemplation] linking these parts with the whole corresponds to an explicitly cognitive relation in which the divine or human mind refers the one to the other.

160   *Components of concord — Ternary relations (ontological)*

Other passages shift the focus from the relation between a part and the whole to that between a contrary and its contrary,[726] although at this point the argument becomes embedded in a context of expanded terminology. For Eriugena, the question of the relation between contraries within the created world is not in practice separable from that of the relations among certain other logical categories. These include the *oppositum* [opposite] — treated sometimes as a synonym for contrary but sometimes as a wider category embracing contrary[727] — and the *dissimile* [dissimilar]. In fact, these terms are usually applied in various groupings to characterize that variegation and multiplicity of the created world proceeding from its origins in the divine Word which underlies the ps.-Dionysian system of divine names.[728] Speaking of the original fourfold division of God or Nature, Eriugena explains how the first species is similar to the second as creating to creating, how the first species is dissimilar to the second as not created to created, and how the first species is opposite to the third as creating and not created to created and not creating.[729] Speaking of the subdivisions of the second and third species — the primordial causes and their spatio-temporal effects — he argues that the creator's omnipotence requires the production of things similar, dissimilar, and opposite to him.[730] As examples of the first are mentioned primary being and the genera and species within it which are simple and immutable, and of the second unformed matter which is composite and mutable.[731] It is through this *compaginatio similium et dissimilium, contrariorum et oppositorum* [joining of similar, dissimilar, contrary, and opposite] that all beauty in the created world is fulfilled.[732]

In a final set of passages, attention is focussed on the relation between a contrary together with its contrary and the whole.[733] Eriugena cites the proximity of Hell and the blessed state to arise within the final resolution[734] of all things as instance of a principle that what *contrarium esse putatur* [is considered as contrary] in the part *non contrarium...pulchritudinis augmentum reperitur* [is discovered to be not contrary but an increase of beauty] in the whole.[735] In addition, the nature of the blessedness to be enjoyed by the saints will become more apparent *ex collatione/comparatione* [in comparison with] the torments held in reserve for the reprobate.[736] This argument is elaborated in close dependence on Augustine,[737] and contrasts with others where new tendencies emerge. In one example, Eriugena shifts from the position that understanding of a contrary results from understanding of its contrary with

The Eriugenian transcendent harmony 161

which comparison is made to the stronger view that existence of a contrary is dependent on the existence of its contrary to which it is related.[738]

In the concluding section of *Periphyseon* I,[739] there is a parallel discussion concerning the present state of created things.[740] Again, this reveals a further dimension: that the relation between contraries and whole is viewed in connection with that between God and the created.

> ... omnia quae a summo usque deorsum sunt de eo dici possunt quadam similitudine aut dissimilitudine aut contrarietate aut oppositione quoniam ab ipso omnia sunt quae de eo praedicari possunt. Non enim similia sibi solummodo condidit sed etiam dissimilia quoniam ipse similis est et dissimilis, contrariorum quoque causa est... Est enim ipse similium similitudo et dissimilitudo dissimilium, oppositorum oppositio, contrariorum contrarietas. Haec enim omnia pulchra ineffabilique harmonia in unam concordiam colligit atque componit. Nam quae in partibus universitatis opposita sibimet videntur atque contraria et a se invicem dissona, dum in generalissima ipsius universitatis harmonia considerantur convenientia consonaque sunt.

> [All things which are, from the highest to the lowest, can be said of God by a certain similarity or dissimilarity or contrariety or opposition, since all things derive from him which can be predicated of him. He creates things not only similar but even dissimilar to himself, since he himself is similar and dissimilar and also the cause of contraries.... Indeed, he is the similarity of similar things and the dissimilarity of the dissimilar, the opposition of opposite things and the contrariety of the contrary. For he collects and combines all these things by a beautiful and ineffable harmony into a single concord. Things which in parts of the universe seem opposed to one another, as contrary, and as dissonant among themselves are, when considered in the most general harmony of the universe itself, agreeing and consonant].

On analysis of the main statements here regarding contraries and combination — that 1. Things created by God exhibit various relations to one another, 2. Things created by God exhibit these same relations to him, 3. These same relations can be understood of God himself, and 4. God combines created things a. by a harmony and b. by changing perspectives — another blending of conceptual schemes is disclosed. These are the superficial contrast of †*contrarium...colligere* [contrary, etc./collection] itself in point 4,[741] and the underlying dialectic of God's transcendence where he †*condere* [creates] things similar, dissimilar, and contrary, and his immanence where he becomes *similium similitudo* [the similarity of the similar] etc. in points 1–2 and 3 respectively.[742] For Eriugena, the similar and dissimilar/contrary primarily correspond to virtues and vices and, since the latter are causally dependent on the former, God represents the cause of such dissimilars/contraries in a limited sense.[743] The phrase *dum...considerantur* [when considered] reveals the connection of similar and dissimilar/contrary things with the whole as an explicitly cognitive relation in which the divine or human mind refers the one to the other.

Before studying the affirmative divine names and their opposites in the three basic forms of parts within a whole, of contraries or opposites, and of contraries within a whole, we had left one thing unspecified.[744] This was the precise ontological referent of the super-affirmative terms. As indicated earlier, the divine names prefixed by *super (hyper)* would have to signify a transcendence predominating within a simultaneous transcendence and immanence. But only God as final harmony of creation has this particular status.

The connection between the super-affirmative terms and harmony is made in a passage where Eriugena explains that these terms are uttered *sub...una compositionis harmonia* [in a single harmony of composition].[745] Of course, he is referring to the grammatical structure whereby a preposition is joined with an adjective or substantive to form a compound. However, that the issue is more than purely grammatical seems to follow from several considerations. First, Eriugena normally treats grammatical structure as reflecting ontological relations[746] and secondly, *harmonia* [harmony] is not the usual term for grammatical composition.[747] Even more important is the fact that harmony seems to possess the special properties needed by the ontological referent of the super-affirmative terms.

That harmony represents a simultaneous transcendence and immanence emerges from Eriugena's theory that the entire created world is constituted through a dynamic cycle of procession and return.[748] Within this cycle, the primordial causes unfold into a multiplicity of spaces and times and of genera and species and then return that unfolding to a unified state in a process corresponding to harmony.[749] Each individual stage can similarly be characterized as harmonic. The originating causes initially possess *harmonia universaliter differentium seu similium partium copulationem supergrediens* [a harmony universally surpassing the joining of either different or similar parts],[750] and from this transcendence proceed to the visible world — constituted from different genera, species, substances, and accidents reduced to ineffable unity — in a harmony of similar and dissimilar.[751] The visible effects themselves form *extremitates...medietates...concors harmonia* [a concordant harmony of extremes and mediators],[752] and from their immanence return — together with substances and accidents which are and transcendences and privations which are not — to their causes and creator.[753] Nevertheless, it is the final stage which is understood as harmonic in the fullest sense. Here, there is a harmony *supra rerum naturam...inter ea quae non sunt* [above the nature of things and among those things that are not] which produces its counterpart in the sensory realm.[754]

Consequently, that harmony represents the transcendence predominating within a simultaneous transcendence and immanence also emerges from this theory of the procession and return of created things. For Eriugena, the final resolution of parts into the whole and of contraries into the whole constitutes a state where simultaneous transcendence and immanence is recalled to transcendence through the sublimation rather than the annulment of that immanence.[755] For Eriugena also, final resolution of parts into the whole and of contraries into the whole corresponds to that state where the fundamental elements of harmony achieve their consummation. In fact, Eriugena clearly conceives the ultimate mystery of creation more readily in harmonic than in any other terms.[756]

In discussing this last group of texts, we have encountered lavish use of three ideas drawn from Augustine: i. a contrary relates to its contrary ($s_1 \rightarrow s_2$), ii. a part relates to a whole ($s_1 \rightarrow S$), and iii. a contrary together with its contrary relates to a whole (($s_1 + s_2$) $\rightarrow$ S).[757] Although some of the deviations from Augustine's standpoint have already been mentioned, one should emphasize the most important conceptual transformation of all. This involves the underpinning of the above with three ideas from ps.-Dionysius — a. the transcendent God relates to his creature (s_1),[758] b. the immanent God relates to his creature (s_2),[759] and c. the transcendentally immanent God relates to his creature (S).[760]

To comprehend how these two sets of ideas interconnect requires us merely to reflect that relation of the transcendent God to his creature does not coincide with any relations in the latter; b. the relation of the immanent God to his creature coincides with i. the relation of a contrary to its contrary, ii. the relation of a part to a whole, and iii. the relation of a contrary together with its contrary to a whole; and c. the relation of the transcendentally immanent God coincides with ii. the relation of a part to a whole, and iii. the relation of a contrary together with its contrary to a whole, most of these coincidences being explicitly documented in Eriugena's text.

In comparing this last group of texts with the previous group,[761] we can begin to appreciate the complexity of Eriugena's doctrine of harmony. As argued earlier, the theories concerning the presence of evil in the world and the ordering of the physical and psychological spheres are both harmonic in character, revealing conceptual structures based on inclusion of contraries and mediation of extremes respectively. When these theories which were separate in Augustine and Calcidius come together in Eriugena's thought, the result is a philosophical vision of truly compelling power and originality.

Note

There are striking parallels between the medieval philosophical theories of cosmic order and modern structuralist accounts of myth and society. One area of agreement is the notion of mediation which both interpret as capable of further subdivision, as the dialectical counterpart of mathematical proportionality, and as uniting the contrary and the contradictory.

Further subdivision of the mediator is illustrated by Lévi-Strauss' analysis of the Zuni emergence narrative where the central problem is interpreted as one of overcoming the conflict between life and death. Among elements in this myth, agriculture corresponds to life and its contrary warfare corresponds to death. Hunting represents a mediator by furnishing life (as does agriculture) through the causing of death (as with hunting) but, since it remains to some degree in conflict with agriculture, necessitates the interpolation of additional terms. Hence arise as elements in the myth herbivorous animals corresponding to agriculture and their contraries beasts of prey corresponding to death. Carrion-eating animals now represent the mediator by not killing their food (as do herbivorous animals) which is animal in origin (as with beasts of prey) (Lévi-Strauss 1958: 248–249). This type of analysis, through which mythical elements can be explained as a dialectical process of successive mediations within human consciousness, is similar to that described in 1958: 256 ff.

Expression of mediation as mathematical proportionality is also a common feature of structuralist texts. Such thinking is implicit in Lévi-Strauss' discussion of the avunculate, since the kinship-system which contains it is founded on a law that the relation between maternal uncle and nephew "is to" that between brother and sister "as" the relation between brother and sister "is to" that between husband and wife (Lévi-Strauss 1958: 51–52. Cf. 1958: 54–55). The thinking becomes explicit in the same writer's *Le cru et le cuit* where myths dealing with the punishment of noisy behaviour are associated with others concerned with the punishment of scornful attitudes to food through further connections between noise and the sky and between food and the earth, all of which is encapsulated in the formula

[noise (= violation of x) : sky] :: [violation of food : earth]

(Lévi-Strauss 1964: 317–318). As we have seen, Calcidius' and Eriugena's accounts of divisions within the psychic and angelic worlds are developed along similar lines.

Uniting the contradictory with the contrary through the mediator is also illustrated in Lévi-Strauss' analysis of the Zuni emergence narrative whose central problem was viewed as that of resolving the conflict between life and death. Here, the correlation of agriculture and warfare with life and death reveals an important characteristic of the dialectical process which establishes elements within such myths: namely, that contrary terms with no mediator are usually replaced by terms equivalent to them which admit a third term as a mediator (Lévi-Strauss 1958: 248–249). This process taking place within the myth-making consciousness of tribal societies, technically speaking that of transforming contradictory pairs (s_1, $\bar{s}_1$) into contrary ones (s_1, s_2) is similar to that described in 1958: 242 ff.

An even more striking parallel between the medieval philosophical theories of cosmic order and modern structuralism lies in the deliberate recourse to harmonic language. In his discussion of Amerindian mythological systems, Lévi-Strauss describes how the child born to a married couple emerges as a mediator between two extremes which are discordant in respect of the social group's equilibrium (Lévi-Strauss 1964: 334–335). The child performs a structural role similar to that played elsewhere by cooking fire, since the latter appears as a mediator between the two extremes of sun and earth which become disjunct at the time of an eclipse (Lévi-Strauss 1964: 300–301). Both situations are understood as involving the resolution of disharmony: hence the traditional association of noise-making rituals with wedding nights and obscuring of the sun.

Excursus to Chapter 3

Excursus 1 to section 3.4

Texts:

A. Apuleius: *Peri hermeneias* 5, pp. 86–88.
B. Alan of Lille: *De planctu naturae*, pr. 1, 1–9 + 40–56 + 67 + 68 + 77–78 + 85–86 + 95 – 96.

In passages *A* and *B*, a square of opposition is applied to the classification of categorical propositions — in accordance with Aristotle: *dIn* 7. 17b ff. — rather than to the classification of substances and accidents as in the passages discussed earlier. This square is based on four semes: universal (a_1), not affirmative i.e. negative ($\bar{a}_2$), affirmative (a_2), and not universal i.e. particular ($\bar{a}_1$) which combine to form four sememes: universal and not affirmative ($b_1 = a_1 + \bar{a}_2$), both affirmative and universal ($b_2 = a_2 + a_1$), affirmative and not universal ($\bar{b}_1 = a_2 + \bar{a}_1$), and neither universal nor affirmative ($\bar{b}_2 = \bar{a}_1 + \bar{a}_2$).

Passage *A* contains the earliest known depiction of any square of opposition explicitly by means of a diagram. At some point its diagram of the various categorical propositions and their interrelations was also inserted into manuscripts of Boethius' commentary on *De interpretatione*. This led to a relabelling of the diagram with the Boethian terminology nowadays standard in textbooks of logic and also to incorporation of this relabelled diagram into the modern edition of Apuleius. My translation of passage *A* employs the standard terminology in line with this evolution.

Passage *B* comes from Alan of Lille's description of the personified Natura, and presents a striking fusion of two groups of ideas through the single image of an *X*. The first group is marked by the *X* of the square of opposition linking four types of categorical proposition (cf. Apuleius in passage *A*) and is suggested by the phrases "sophistic dazzle," "petitio principii", "contradictory position", and "contradictory side". The second group is marked by the *X* of the psychic substance curved to form astronomical circles (cf. Calcidius: *iTi* 92, 145. 4 ff.) and is indicated by the phrases "starry body", "lily-white path" — i.e. the Milky Way —, "eternal revolution", etc. The image of an *X* occurs twice in passage *B*: in connection with Natura's headband (second group) and Natura's diadem (first and second groups) respectively. In all, the passage dramatically illustrates the generation of complicated poetical imagery by intertextual means.

A

Now we should say how these four propositions are related to one another, it being quite useful to consider them in a square diagram. As depicted below, let there be universal affirmative and negative propositions on the top line: for example, "Every pleasure is a good" and "Every pleasure is not a good." Let these be called contraries to one another. Similarly, let the particular propositions be inscribed under each of these on the bottom line: "Some pleasure is a good," "Some pleasure is not a good." Let these be called subcontraries to one another. Then let diagonal lines from the angles be drawn, one extending from universal affirmative to particular negative, and the other from particular affirmative to universal negative. Let these which are opposite to one another in both quantity and quality be called contradictories, since it is now necessary that one or the other be true. This is called perfect or complete conflict. But between the subcontraries and the contraries there is divided conflict, since the contraries can never be simultaneously true yet sometimes simultaneously false; on the other hand, the subcontraries can never be simultaneously false yet sometimes simultaneously true. So the refutation of either subcontrary confirms the other, although the confirmation of either does not refute the other. If one posits either of the contraries, one certainly cancels the other. On the other hand, if one cancels either of them, one certainly does not posit the other. But if one establishes either of the contradictories, one certainly refutes the other, and if one cancels either of them, one certainly establishes the other. Moreover, either universal proposition, when established, certainly confirms its particular although, when refuted, it does not invalidate that particular. On the other hand, the particular proposition, when refuted, certainly invalidates its universal although, when established, it does not confirm that universal. That all things are as we have stated is easily shown by the propositions themselves as written below (see figure 12).

It is clear that someone who has proposed something assents to it. But either universal is destroyed in three ways: when its particular is shown to be false or when either of the two others — its contrary or contradictory — is shown to be true. However, it is established in one way: if its

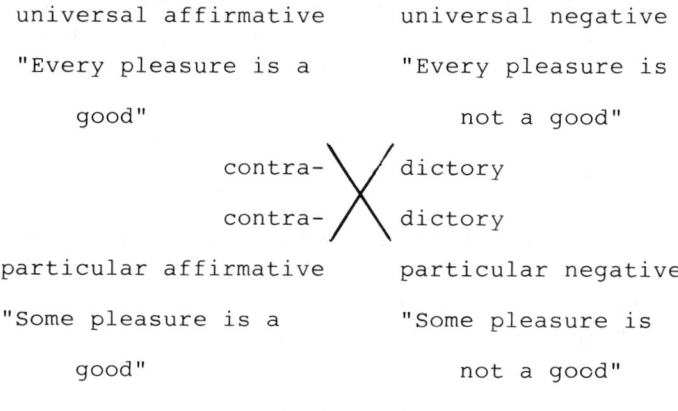

Figure 12. The propositional square of opposition

contradictory is shown to be false. On the other hand, a particular proposition is destroyed in one way: if its contradictory is shown to be true. However, it is established in three ways: if its universal is true or if either of the two others — its subcontrary or contradictory — is false.

B

... a woman glided down from the inner palace of the impassible world and seemed to approach me in haste. Her hair, sparkling with a light not borrowed but its own, not fictively simulating the appearance of light-rays but surpassing their nature with an innate luminosity, formed the maiden's head into a starry body. A double headband parted the hair, not relinquishing the higher realms nor disdaining to favour the earth with a kiss. A sort of extended lily-white path, crossing this headband slantwise in the form of an *X*, divided the factions of her hair — a slant which, in my view, imparted less a detriment than an embellishment to her face... The glowing crown of a regal diadem, sparkling with dancing gems, flashed on the brow of her head. Its golden material was not counterfeit, falling beneath the dignity of gold, and deceiving the eyes with sophistic dazzle: in fact, its very nobility guaranteed authenticity. With a miraculous circling and eternal revolution, that diadem wandered from east to west, being repeatedly brought back to the east. And by retracing the same course endlessly, its motion seemed like the too trifling sameness of a "petitio principii". Some of the aforementioned gems at times offered to our eyes the miracle of a fresh dawn with the new sun of their light, but at times seemed in exile from the palace of the diadem itself through the eclipsing of their glimmer. Other gems, sitting firmly on their thrones, maintained an endless vigil in their sparkling and eternal watch. Among these a circle, shining in the likeness of the zodiac's brightness, and glittering with necklaces of precious stones, interrupted the kisses of stellar conjunction. In this circle, a company of twelve gems — because of their immense magnitude and outstanding brightness — seemed to demand privilege over the others. And in the front part of the diadem itself three precious stones antonomastically outshone the other nine in the audacious confidence of their nature... In this manner, three stones enjoying the status of a secondary rank, placed their thrones in the contradictory position... A benevolent serenity of three gems — revelling in a light which charmed the opposite side — delighted the eyes... On the contradictory side, the starry beauty of three stones sparkled in joyful approbation... Underneath these houses of the twelve stones, a set of seven gems maintained an endless circular motion...

Excursus 2 to section 3.4

Text: A. Abbo of Fleury: *Quaestiones grammaticales* 48–50.

This passage from Abbo of Fleury, which contains an elaborate application of arithmology to the doctrines of Trinity and Incarnation, can be analyzed as follows:

First, the writer appropriates the square of opposition traditionally applied to numbers. This square is based on four semes: generating (a_1), not generated ($\bar{a}_2$), generated (a_2), and not generating ($\bar{a}_1$) which combine to form four sememes: generating but not generated ($b_1 = a_1 + \bar{a}_2$), both generated and generating ($b_2 = a_2 + a_1$), generated but not generating ($\bar{b}_1 = a_2 + \bar{a}_1$), and neither generating nor generated ($\bar{b}_2 = \bar{a}_1 + \bar{a}_2$). These are applied to the numbers 5, 3, 2, 1 (b_1), 4 (b_2), 9, 8, 6 ($\bar{b}_1$), and 7 ($\bar{b}_2$). Given that generation is equivalent to begetting and the latter mentioned in Trinitarian theory, a square of opposition is next applied to the divine Persons. This square is based on four semes: begetting (a_1), not begotten ($\bar{a}_2$), begotten (a_2), and not begetting ($\bar{a}_1$) which combine to form four sememes: begetting but not begotten ($b_1 = a_1 + \bar{a}_2$), both begotten and begetting ($b_2 = a_2 + a_1$), begotten but not begetting ($\bar{b}_1 = a_2 + \bar{a}_1$), and neither begetting nor begotten ($\bar{b}_2 = \bar{a}_1 + \bar{a}_2$). These are applied to the Father (b_1), the Son ($\bar{b}_1$), and the spirit ($\bar{b}_2$) — with ellipse of the second sememe (b_2).

Secondly, two symbolic applications of number to the Incarnation are proposed. 6 is said to symbolize Christ's divinity since this number and Christ's divinity are both perfect; while 8 is said to symbolize Christ's humanity since 8 is less than 9, 9 symbolizes the angels, and humanity is less than the angels.

Thirdly, a series of symbolic equivalents for the numbers 5 to 9 is derived from the foregoing arguments:

Table 4. Symbolic equivalents for numbers

5 →	the Father
6 →	Christ's divinity
7 →	the Spirit
8 →	Christ's humanity
9 →	the Son

His reference to Minerva suggests that Abbo has derived the first stage of his argument from Martianus Capella: *dNPM* VII. 738 — possibly through the mediation of Eriugena.

A

Finally, although many such examples are available, may it suffice to have furnished a proof from numbers whose theoretical science subjoins physical arguments in many ways. It is clearly established that that God "rejoices in the odd number" who appeared as revealer of his own triunity when he disposed all things in number, measure, and weight. For this reason, I believe that the difference within the Trinity can be explained to some extent through the nature of the three odd numbers which follow one another when the even numbers have been skipped. The first odd number is 5, the second 7, and the third 9. The two skipped numbers between these signify the double nature of the single Jesus Christ, since the 6 arises as a perfect number by doubling the first odd number while the 8, arising by quadrupling the first even number, is subject to reduction below the manifestation of a cubic quantity — in order to hint that the perfect God, in the guise of a servant, has a somewhat less pronounced diminution below the angels. Therefore since below the number 10, all numbers — with the exception of 7 — either beget or are begotten, the first of the aforementioned odd numbers begets but is not begotten, the second neither begets nor is begotten, while the third is begotten but does not beget. No religious believer doubts which of these numbers match with which Persons of the godhead, especially since the pagan philosophers attributed the number 7 to Minerva for the reasons stated above and we to that Wisdom which is established by numbering never to have been other than simple. Yet because, in my opinion, I have discussed these matters sufficiently in the small book entitled "On Number, Measure, and Weight" which I once wrote at the urging of my confrères in response to Victorius' "Calculus", I have refrained from saying more at this point.

Excursus 3 to section 3.4

Texts:

A. Gerbert: *De rationali et ratione uti* 8–9, pp. 303–304.
B. Thierry of Chartres: *Commentum in De Trinitate* 2. 28, 77. 70–2. 29, 77. 90.
C. Thierry of Chartres: *Lectiones in De Trinitate* 2. 9, 157. 85–2. 11, 158. 22.
D. Thierry of Chartres: *Lectiones in De Trinitate* 2. 31, 165. 63–2. 32, 165. 88.
E. Thierry of Chartres: *Lectiones in De Trinitate* 2 40, 167. 46–58.

All these texts apply a square of opposition derived from Aristotle: *dIn* 13, 23^a 20ff. (= *Transl. Boeth.* p. 33, 16–21). This square is based on four semes: actual (a_1), not potential ($\bar{a}_2$), potential (a_2), and not actual ($\bar{a}_1$) which combine to form four sememes: actual and not potential ($b_1 = a_1 + \bar{a}_2$), both potential and actual ($b_2 = a_2 + a_1$), potential and not actual ($\bar{b}_1 = a_2 + \bar{a}_1$), and neither actual nor potential ($\bar{b}_2 = \bar{a}_1 + \bar{a}_2$).

In passage *A*, three of these sememes are correlated with types of existent as follows:

Excursus 3 to section 3.4 173

Table 5. Gerbert's ontological scheme

b_1 —	astronomical bodies e.g. the celestial sphere, the sun; physical elements e.g. fire, water; and moral qualities e.g. goodness, equality.
b_2 —	human actions e.g. sitting.
$\overline{b}_1$ —	number and time in the abstract.

In passages *B–E*, these three sememes are correlated with types of existent described in numerous literary sources. This complicated intertextual operation requires the sememe b_2 to be correlated with two levels of being, thereby producing a fourfold scheme not directly identifiable with a square of opposition. The passages, correlations with types of existent, and sources are summarized in the following table:

Table 6. Thierry of Chartres' fourfold scheme

	$\overline{b}_1$	b_2		b_1	
General + Augustine: *dGaL* VI. 17	matter	actual things	forms	God	*B*
Thierry	absolute possibility	determinate possibility	necessity of combination	absolute necessity	*C, D, E*
Aristotle: *dIn.* 13. 23ᵃ	possibility			necessity	*B*
Calcidius: *iPTi.* 27	divided substance			undivided substance	*D*
Boethius: *dTr.* 2. 5–21		object of physics	object of mathematics	object of theology	*C*
Boethius: *dCP* IV. pr. 6			fate	providence	*C, D*

Table 6 (continued)

	$\bar{b}_2$	
$\bar{b}_1$		b_1
Boethius: *iIsPep.* 1. 3. 8, 3–9		object of D soul's intellectibility

A

Aristotle again, wishing actuality to consist of the nature of things subordinate to it as a sort of genus, makes a division and determines its differentiae and species thus: "And some things have actuality without potency — namely, the primary substances. Others have actuality together with potency — these being prior in nature but posterior in time." Some things, he says, have actuality without potency, and others actuality together with potency. Moreover, as things having actuality without potency there are the primary substances. These are called primary because they are principles of things without potency — that is, potency which is capable of producing alternative effects. For the heaven and the sun cannot not move, fire cannot not heat, water cannot not be wet. But things having actuality together with potency descend from the motion of the soul: for example, when I sit, I have come through the motion of the soul to this actuality as one which a potency of sitting has preceded. I would not have sat, if I had not previously had a potency of sitting. And since this potency precedes the actuality in time, this actuality together with potency is said by Aristotle to be prior to potency alone. He speaks of things which "have actuality together with potency — these being prior in nature but posterior in time". This happens because potency, being the beginning of an actuality, is something imperfect. Perfect things are prior to imperfect things both because they excel in the goodness of their nature and because — as goodness or virtue — they exhibit equality. Indeed the equal is prior to the unequal, since every inequality descends from equality. Therefore an actuality in which potency is completed and perfected is prior to a potency which is defective and imperfect before its actuality. Although that potency preceded in time, it flowed down — having a sort of lesser position in respect of its nature — from the perfect.

Excursus 3 to section 3.4   175

"But other things", he says, "never have actuality but potency alone." For number is infinite in potency although it is finite in actuality when you mention any specific number. And the same argument applies to time. For time is infinite in potency yet finite in actuality when you refer to a day, a month, a year, or anything else you choose.

B

So there are, according to Plato, two principles of things: actuality without possibility i.e. God or necessity and — as though placed opposite — matter i.e. possibility. Between these extremes, so to speak, there are the forms of things and actual things. For the forms of things descend from God as though from a first principle, actual things lie underneath the forms, and possibility i.e. matter lies underneath actual things... Aristotle most subtly examined this subtle doctrine regarding actuality and possibility in his treatise "Perihermeneias", and declared that there are some things in actuality without possibility, other things in actuality together with possibility, and other things never in actuality but only in possibility. Actuality without possibility is necessity and therefore eternity as stated above...

C

Since the universe of things, as we have said, is the subject-matter of theology, mathematics, and physics from different viewpoints, this universe of things exists in four ways: one and the same universe exists in absolute necessity, in necessity of combination, in absolute possibility, and in determinate possibility. And these are the four modes of existence of the universe of all things... And this universe is in absolute necessity in that simplicity and quasi-unity of all things which is God; it is in necessity of combination in a certain order and progression — albeit immutably so; it is in absolute possibility — a possibility which is however without any actuality; and it is in determinate possibility — possibly and actually. Absolute necessity is the enfolding of all things in simplicity. Necessity of combination is the unfolding of those things in a certain order, this order being called "Fate" by the physicists. Absolute possibility is the enfolding of that same universe of things in the possibility alone from which they come into actuality, this being called "Primordial Matter" or "Chaos" by the physicists. Determinate possibility is the unfolding of absolute possibility in actuality with possibility. Thus, the same universe of things exists in four ways, and in these ways it is the subject-matter of theology, mathematics, and physics. Theology considers the necessity which is unity and simplicity. Mathematics considers the necessity of combination which is the unfolding of simplicity, since mathematics considers the forms of things in their truth. Physics considers determinate and absolute possibility. Absolute necessity and absolute possibility are the extremes among these things while the other modes are like mediators...

D

For the soul comprehends with its intelligence or intellectibility the undivided substance: the divinity i.e. the universe in simplicity. It has another power by which it comprehends the divided substance: absolute possibility i.e. the universe as it is in that possibility. And the soul has another power by which it comprehends the undivided nature i.e. the universe in necessity of combination which is undivided i.e. immutable. It has a fourth power by which it comprehends the universe in determinate possibility. Thus, the soul conforms itself to four modes of the universe according to different powers and comprehensions because the soul is composed of the four modes of the universe: that is, of powers of comprehending those four modes — as one learns from Plato... Note: if the universe of things were not in the divine providence in absolute necessity and likewise in possibility determined by actuality, what Boethius says in his "Book of Consolation" would not apply. Here, he states that all things are immutable in so far as they exist in providence, but that all these same things are in themselves mutable in so far as they exist in actuality. So it is obvious that Boethius was there maintaining that the universe of things is immutable in divine providence, and that the same universe is mutable in actuality together with possibility. For things are said to be in themselves inasmuch as they are in actuality.

E

There are two things: actuality and possibility which are like extremes and elements of some kind, the one descending from the other i.e. possibility from actuality. Possibility is the mutability which philosophers call "Primordial Matter". Actuality is the immutability and perfection of being which is called absolute necessity by philosophers. But mutability descends from immutability, and therefore possibility descends from

actuality, since actuality is immutability and possibility is mutability —
namely, that aptitude and power of passing from one state to another or
even from non-being to being. Since there are these two things: actuality
and possibility, we should realize that there are two principles of things —
although one of these is the cause of the other and can exist without it:
that is, actuality i.e. immutability can exist without possibility i.e.
mutability. These are principles of things because nothing can exist
without them...

Part IV: The semiotic

Chapter 4

Components of concord — Ternary relations (semantic)

4.1 Eriugena and the triad of signifier, signified, and signification

Of the three unfolded lexemes originally selected for analysis — a. Relation (L) + binary (s), b. Harmony (L) + relative (s) + ternary (s), and c. Signification (L) + relative (s) + ternary (s) — attention should now be focussed on the third. This will complete our undertaking to study the occurrence of the lexeme "harmony" and the actualization of certain of its semes in combination with the lexeme "signification" and the actualization of some of its semes in medieval philosophical texts, as outlined in chapter one. During the interpretative process, it will again be necessary to activate various further semes which are correlated according to principles formulated in the texts although discovered by a method not officially proposed there. This correlation should be based on the squares of opposition involving two generations of terms — each seme taken in sequence is superimposed on the previous seme in the sequence (a_1 on $\bar{a}_2$, a_2 on a_1, $\bar{a}_1$ on a_2, and $\bar{a}_2$ on $\bar{a}_1$) in order to produce four sememes (b_1, b_2, $\bar{b}_1$, and b_2) — which have already been used to analyze the lexeme "relation" into its components.[762]

It will be noted that these operations yield not only three separate schemata[763] applied to semes in the original sememes[764] — that of equivalence where b_2 and $\bar{b}_2$ are present but b_1 and $\bar{b}_1$ absent in the case of existent and cognitive, that of pseudo-hierarchy where b_2, $\bar{b}_1$, and $\bar{b}_2$ are present but b_1 absent in that of dialectical and mathematical, and that of continuity where b_1, b_2, $\bar{b}_1$, and $\bar{b}_2$ are present in that of complex and simple;[765] but also three connected schemata[766] applied to the original sememes as semes[767] — that of pseudo-hierarchy where b_2, $\bar{b}_1$, and $\bar{b}_2$ are present but b_1 absent in the case of relative and harmonic, that of pseudo-hierarchy where b_2, $\bar{b}_1$, and $\bar{b}_2$ are present but b_1 absent in that of relative and significant, and that of equivalence where b_2 and $\bar{b}_2$ are present but b_1 and $\bar{b}_1$ absent in that of harmonic and significant.[768]

182   *Components of concord — Ternary relations (semantic)*

In studying Eriugena's doctrine of signification, we shall come across many indications that a square of opposition can be used for analyzing the lexeme "signification" itself.[769] This study will also suggest that squares of opposition can be used to analyze components of signification in the lexemes "signifier", "signified", and "signification", components of signifier in the lexemes "word", "affirmative predicate", "substantive", and so forth.[770] Now the best approach to Eriugena's theory of signification will be to paraphrase an important section of *Periphyseon* I and then extract its teaching in synoptic form.

In a passage dealing with the problem of divine naming, Eriugena indicates that several types of signification are possible. To Alumnus' question whether the ten Aristotelian categories can be properly predicated of God,[771] Nutritor responds by noting the distinction between apophatic and kataphatic theology — between denying that God is everything that is and affirming that he is everything that is — and by citing the authority of ps.-Dionysius the Areopagite.[772] When Alumnus recalls that those divine names comprising the kataphatic theology are predicated by metaphor or transference from creature to creator,[773] Nutritor elaborates by linking the apophatic and kataphatic theologies with the notion of opposites. Since there is nothing opposed to God, and since both the divine names themselves and those things which they properly signify have opposites, the divine names cannot be properly predicated of God. Alumnus is therefore correct in stating that it is by transference from creature to creator that such names are employed. Illustrations of the divine names are now provided in "Being", "Goodness", "God", "Truth", "Eternity", "Wisdom", "Life", and "Light".[774]

At this point the relevance of the distinction between apophatic and kataphatic theologies to the question of applying Aristotle's categories to God begins to emerge. According to the kataphatic method the divinity is not signified properly by any verb, noun, audible sound, or signified thing. However, it may be signified metaphorically by "Being" or "Truth" or properly — using a specially adapted form of language — by "More-than-Being" or "More-than-Truth".[775]

Alumnus perceives a difficulty in these last remarks, since the admission that God can properly be called "x...y..." in an affirmative predication, albeit of a special variety, seems to conflict with the earlier statement that in an affirmative predication God is only metaphorically "x...y...".[776] Nutritor counters by rephrasing the earlier distinction between the two theologies — the apophatic denies that God can be called "x" properly while the kataphatic affirms that he can be called "x" by transference from creature to creator — and by adding a further argument. Given that significations of the special form "more-than-x" constitute a harmony of the apophatic and kataphatic methods in which the inner meaning is negative although the outer expression is affirmative, the application of such significations properly to God does not contravene the rule that affirmative predications are strictly metaphorical in respect of the divinity.[777]

The relevance of the distinction between apophatic and kataphatic theologies to the question of applying the ten categories to God is finally made explicit after citation of the parallel Augustinian testimony. The kataphatic method states that whatever is properly predicated of created things may be metaphorically predicated of their creator. Therefore, everything properly signified by the categories can be applied to God as signifying not properly what he is but by transference what we should think about him.[778]

Eriugena again discusses types of signification in a passage where the applicability to God of those Aristotelian categories expressed by verbs is under scrutiny. Faced with Alumnus' puzzlement that according to rational argument neither action nor passion can be attributed to God, whereas according to Scriptural teaching he loves and is loved or moves and is moved,[779] Nutritor attempts to reconcile the two by calling upon certain doctrines of his favourite source ps.-Dionysius.[780]

According to the Greek Father, one must combine the reason which demonstrates that no affirmative term applies properly to God with that revelation from which all terminology applicable to the divine nature is derived. Reason consists on the one hand of the apophatic method. Using this, since it holds the creator to be nothing that can be spoken or understood, true conclusions are always achieved. Reason also comprises the complementary kataphatic method. From this, when God is declared to be something definite in the sense of being identical with the latter, false conclusions result, but when he is stated to be a definite thing in the sense of being the latter's cause, the conclusions are true. Revelation supplies us with the terms which may be applied to the divine nature. They include certain highest names — according to nature — like "Life" and "Virtue"; intermediate names taken from the superior portion of the visible world such as "Sun", "Light", "Star" or from the inferior part of visible creation like "Water", "Earth", "Lion"; and various lowest names — contrary to nature — such as "Frenzy" or "Intoxication".[781] Ps.-Dionysius' conclusion is that reason must apply metaphorically to the creator those affirmative terms which Scripture applies properly to created nature or the contrary of created nature.

After these remarks, the question regarding the applicability to God of the Aristotelian categories expressed by verbs is formally resumed. Given that action and passion generically embrace many of the ps.-Dionysian divine names mentioned above, it follows that such categories apply to God in an affirmative and metaphorical sense. In other words, not only nouns signifying the substances but also verbs signifying the actions of created things are applied to God in a transferred manner.[782]

Apart from rendering explicit certain suppressed premises, the foregoing analysis has closely followed the wording of the two passages in *Periphyseon* dealing with divine naming. It only remains now to summarize the essentials of Eriugena's doctrine of signification. Perhaps the most effective way of doing this is against a background of the abstract schema of signifier, signified, and signification described in the introduction.[783] However, some features of Eriugena's doctrine are better expressed in comparison with two more concrete models.

Since the processes of natural language are the most obvious examples of the signifying process, the replacement of the three components in the abstract schema by sign-vehicle, meaning, and sign-function (= "Model 1") has been proposed.[784] This triad can be further analyzed into a plurality of syntactic markers — singular, masculine, verb, etc. — within the sign-vehicle; a plurality of semantic markers — the various sememes and their constituent semes — comprising the meaning; and the association of these pluralities — arbitrary rather than motivated — through the sign-function.[785] The replacement of the three components in the abstract schema by sign-vehicle, meaning, and sign-function is generally useful, although various problems remain concerning the plurality of semantic markers.[786]

And special difficulties are associated with the component of meaning. According to another formulation, a meaning is constituted by an interpretant which enters into relation with an object and a sign (= "Model 2").[787] From a certain viewpoint, there are two parallel dyadic relations — between sign and object and between interpretant and object —; but given that the interpretant is explicitly derived from the sign,[788] selects from among the object's properties,[789] and is the primary communicator of the sign,[790] it is easier to conceive this as one integrated triadic formation — the interpretant determining the relation between sign and object itself.[791] According to the same formulation, the meaning constituted by the interpretant can take a variety of forms. It can be the connotation of an underlying denotation or the further connotation of that connotation;[792] or else the basis of similarity between two semantic units[793] — the sememe and seme whose relation produces metonymy[794] or the seme and seme whose relation produces metaphor[795] —; or indeed any property or properties between an individual seme and the entire semantic spectrum of a lexeme.[796]

Eriugena himself operates with a signifier, signified, and signification which, although having a simple correspondence with the terms of the abstract schema, have a more complicated relation with those of the two more concrete models as follows:[797] His signifier normally subsumes the sign-vehicle and sign-function of model 1 while his signifier, signified, and signification are variously subsumed in the meaning of that model. His signifier normally corresponds with the sign and his signified with the object of model 2 while his signifier, signified, and signification are variously subsumed in the interpretant of that model.[798]

All this can be corroborated by detailed analysis of the Eriugenian signified, signifier, and signification, this order of discussion reflecting his ontological priorities among the terms.[799]

i. The Signified

Of the three components in Eriugena's account of signification the signified — treated as ontological, conceptual, and linguistic — occurred in the two forms of divine nature and of created things. Considered in our purely semantic terms, "God" is a sememe containing negative semes like "non-being", "non-living", "non-knowing", etc. and "the creature" a sememe containing positive semes like "being", "living", "knowing", etc.[800]

ii. The Signifier

The presentation of the signifier was far more complicated. Eriugena's argument posited the following in different contexts — we list these ontological, conceptual, and linguistic items in ascending order of semantic complexity —: (Group a1) 1. Vocal utterances. These correspond to phonemes; 2. Linguistic meaning — corresponding to syntactic markers and semantic markers;[801] 3. Extra-linguistic objects. These correspond to semantic markers. In other contexts he posited combinations of the above: (Group A2) 4. Things — corresponding to types 1, 2, and 3 in the classification above; 5. Words. These correspond to types 1 and 2 in that classification; 6. Designated things — corresponding to types 2 and 3 in the above classification.

Eriugena's discussion also mentioned the following as signifiers: (Group B1) 7. Substantives. These are equivalent to type 5 above with substantival syntactic markers and sememe or sememes;[802] 8. Verbs — equivalent to type 5 with verbal syntactic markers and sememe or sememes;[803] (Group B2) 9. Affirmative predicates. These are equivalent to type 5 above with adjectival syntactic markers and positive seme;[804] 10. Negative predicates — equivalent to type 5 with adjectival syntactic markers and negative seme.[805]

Finally, Eriugena's argument posited the following signifiers in various contexts: (Group C1) 11. Super-affirmative predicates. These correspond to type 5 above with adjectival syntactic markers and positive seme on axis^1 combined with negative counterpart on axis^2 to form sememe on axis^3; (Group C2) 12. Aristotelian categories — corresponding to type 5 with sememe^1 connected to sememe^2 through a common seme, this sememe^2 being connected to sememe^3 through a common seme, etc.[806]

iii. The Signification

Of the three components in Eriugena's account of signification the signification — treated as linguistic only — occurred explicitly in the one form of transference. Considered in our purely semantic terms, a positive seme like "living" contained in signifier type 9 is shifted from the sememe^1 of "the creature" to the sememe^2 of "God". However, signification — again treated as linguistic only — occurred implicitly in the two further forms of combination and transference-combination.[807] Considered likewise in purely semantic terms, semes contained in signifieds and signifiers types 2–8 and 11–12 are associated with one another or else semes contained in signifiers types 7, 8, and 12 are associated with one another and also shifted from sememe^1 to sememe^2.

Having now paraphrased an important section of *Periphyseon* I and also extracted its teaching in synoptic form, we have made a reasonable approach to Eriugena's doctrine of signification.[808] In particular, the analysis has already suggested that squares of opposition can be used to analyze components of signification in the lexeme "combination", components of signifier in the lexeme "super-affirmative predicate", and so

Eriugena and the triad of signifier, signified, and signification 187

forth. Before analyzing the lexeme "signification" itself any further, it may therefore be useful to construct formally a square of opposition for the aforesaid components.

The square of opposition involving two generations of terms provides an easy means of distinguishing between a primary set of "denotative" and a secondary set of "connotative" semantic properties.[809] Assuming that each seme taken in sequence is superimposed on the previous seme in the sequence (A_1 on B_0, B_1 on A_1, A_0 on B_1, and B_0 on A_0), the denotative semes will be A_1 and A_0 and the connotative semes B_1 and B_0 or alternatively the connotative semes will be A_1 and A_0 and the denotative semes B_1 and B_0.[810] Using the example provided by Eriugena where A_1, B_1, A_0, and B_0 correspond to "good", "being", "not good", and "not being" respectively, a sememe b_2 might have goodness as its denotation (A_1) and being as a connotation (B_1), and another sememe ($\overline{b}_1$) non-goodness as its denotation (A_0) and being as a connotation (B_1).[811] Of course, with each seme taken in sequence superimposed on the previous seme in the sequence (A_1 on B_0, B_1 on A_1, A_0 on B_1, and B_0 on A_0), the primary connotative semes could be A_1 and A_0 and the secondary connotative semes B_1 and B_0 or vice versa.[812]

Another type of semantic property which can be analyzed with a square of opposition involving two generations of terms is the super-affirmative predicate. The example of the sememe "living" may be drawn from Eriugena's text.[813] Here, the semes A_1, B_1, A_0, and B_0 correspond to "present", "transcendent", "not present", and "not transcendent" respectively.[814] The sememe b_1 corresponding to "living" is formed first from the superimposition of A_1 on B_0 and secondly from the suppression of B_0, while the sememe $\overline{b}_1$ corresponding to "not living" is formed first from the superimposition of A_0 on B_1 and secondly from the suppression of A_0. Finally, the lexeme "more-than-living" corresponds to the superimposition of b_1 on $\overline{b}_1$.[815] The super-affirmative predicate is unusual in that its denial of the law of contradiction ($b_1 = \overline{b}_1$) necessitates a. a shift between connotative levels ($A_1/A_0 \rightarrow B_1/B_0$), and b. the deactivation of semes ($-B_0$, $-A_0$) within the semantic spectrum itself. As such, it possesses a peculiarly dynamic character much exploited in Eriugena's metaphysics.

4.2 Signification in Martianus Capella: *De nuptiis Philologiae et Mercurii*

The beginnings of creative philosophical activity during the eighth and ninth centuries of the Middle Ages have already been noted. In this so-called "Carolingian" period, various treatises dealing with signification and derived ultimately from the Stoic grammatical tradition became fashionable: especially Augustine's *De magistro*, the *De nuptiis Philologiae et Mercurii* of Martianus Capella, and Isidore of Seville's *Etymologiae*.[816] Although perhaps less familiar to modern writers on the history of semantics, it was the treatise of Martianus which most impressed the Carolingians, since it was treated as a fundamental textbook of the *trivium* and glossed extensively. From this text it was possible to derive the Stoic division of the signifying process into three components — signifier, signified, and referent — but also elements of non-Stoic provenance. In fact, the latter predominate over the former in terms of influence.

Martianus Capella's *De nuptiis* is a work written in that style of Menippean satire latinized by Varro and therefore exploits the blending of playful literary diversion and serious philosophical discourse typical of the genre. Its books I–II comprise an allegorical narrative intended to reveal something about the general status of the seven liberal arts, and its books III–IX an encyclopaedic presentation designed to convey technical information regarding each art in sequence. The fabulous material is obviously more provocative of philosophical reflection but requires us — as it did the medievals — to disengage its meaning through an interpretative process. From the viewpoint of Martianus' theory of signification, it is the figurative meaning of the narrative's protagonists Mercury and Philology which primarily needs to be determined.[817] This meaning is suggested by the following types of narrative association: 1. Mercury → education; 2. Mercury → "verbal" arts; 3. Mercury → oral discourse; 4. Philology → education; 5. Philology → "real" arts; and 6. Philology → written discourse.

In the opening section of book I, various female divinities approached by Mercury in his quest for a bride are listed.[818] Among these the importance of Psyche — to whom Mercury has given *vehiculum...ac volatiles rotas, quis mira posset celeritate discurrere...licet eam auri compedibus illigatam Memoria praegravarit* [a vehicle with swift wheels on which she could travel with amazing speed although Memory bound it with the weight of golden chains] — is particularly stressed.[819] References in the text to swiftness and to Memory's stability seemingly associate Mercury with oral discourse. Mercury addresses himself to Apollo for further recommendations,[820] and the latter proposes a mortal woman called Philology who has refined Psyche's formerly uncultivated state.[821] This passage implies that Philology is a figure of education in general. Mercury and Apollo now ascend heavenwards to seek approval for such a marriage from the council of Olympians.[822] Here, Juno praises the couple's dedication to learning. She describes how Mercury has invited certain women called "Disciplines" into his house and practised rhetoric and music, and how Philology has become pallid through her unremitting studies of astronomy and geometry.[823] References in the text to Disciplines and to various intellectual activities seemingly associate Mercury and Philology with education in general. Jupiter also praises the couple's intellectual attainments. He describes Mercury as *sermo...fida recursio interpresque meae mentis* [my speech, the faithful reflection and interpreter of my mind], and Philology as having intellectual motions whose rapidity surpasses that of the celestial spheres.[824] This passage implies that Mercury and Philology are figures of the verbal and real arts respectively.

In the early pages of book II, Philology is depicted meditating upon the advisability of marriage with an Olympian. She recalls the onset of her passion for Mercury whom she saw running from the gymnasium while she was gathering pre-selected small flowers.[825] The text's references to departure from the gymnasium and to pre-selection of flowers seemingly associate Mercury with the verbal arts. Having satisfied herself that she is compatible with a deity by calculating the numerical values of their two names,[826] she is visited by various divinities. Some of these sing hymns in praise of the couple.[827] The Muse Thalia extols their academic accomplishments by saying that *per vos...nus mentis ima complet; per vos probata lingua fert glorias...* [through you the intellect of the mind fills the depths, and through you the trained tongue brings glory].[828] This passage suggests that Mercury and Philology are figures of the verbal and real arts respectively. A ritual now follows in which Philology brings up certain substances clogging her breast and drinks from a spherical vessel provided by Athanasia.[829] Particularly important are the contents of her vomit — books inscribed with musical notations, *circuli lineaeque hemisphaeriaque cum trigonis et quadratis* [circles, lines, and hemispheres together with triangles and squares], and zoological diagrams — and the collecting of this substance by the Disciplines and Muses.[830] The text's references to books and to preservation of learning seemingly associate

Philology with written discourse. Philology next mounts a palanquin. On this she rises through the celestial spheres under the guidance of Juno, seeing numerous visions of the gods and spirits who inhabit the cosmos.[831] At her arrival in the Milky Way Mercury prepares to hand over as bridal gift the Disciplines invited into his household.[832] This passage suggests that Mercury and Philology are figures of education in general.

It is apparent from even this brief paraphrase that Mercury functions as a fluid symbol[833] of education, the verbal arts, or oral discourse and Philology as an equally flexible symbol of education, the real arts, or written discourse. But in order to understand Martianus' theory of signification as treated by medieval exegetes, we must examine his comments not only on the two protagonists but on the marriage itself. These occur mainly in that continuous passage near the beginning of *De nuptiis* II where Philology examines her compatibility with Mercury through calculation of their respective names' numerical values.[834]

The primary question is: will Mercury *apto sibi foedere copuletur ex nuptiali congruentia* [be joined to her in a fitting bond of nuptial accord]?[835] In determining this she adds the numerical values of the letters in Mercury's and her names (producing 1218 and 724 respectively), reduces each of the numbers so derived by the ninefold rule, and arrives at final numerical values for the two names (3 and 4 respectively).[836] Clearly these two numbers are marked by a *congruens ambobus ratio* [ratio congruent with both][837] for the following reasons. First, the number 3 — which is odd and therefore male — is perfect in itself as consisting of beginning, middle, and end, and as being the foundation of various physical phenomena.[838] There are also three consonances in music.[839] Moreover, the number 4 — which is even and therefore female — is perfect by computation since together with its factors it makes up the perfect decad, and since it is the basis of other physical phenomena.[840] Its factors also form the ratios on which the three musical consonances are based.[841] This *numeri congruentia* [congruence of number] in 3 and 4 separately is further revealed in their sum of 7, as this number is perfect in itself and the foundation of numerous physical phenomena.[842] The congruence inherent in 3 and 4 is finally indicated in the numbers 9 and 8 derived from them by multiplication, since these together make the ratio on which the indivisible and therefore consonant interval of a tone is based.[843] For all these reasons, then *praedictorum nominum numerus concinebat* [the number of the aforesaid names was concordant].[844]

That the marriage between Mercury and Philology has a pronounced harmonic component is also suggested by the symbolism of two further characters appearing in the narrative: Hymen and Harmonia. Because Hymen is the presiding deity of marriage, the placing of a hymn in his honour at the beginning of *De nuptiis* is hardly surprising.[845] However, a quite unexpected feature is the frequent reference to his harmonic functions: he controls the harmony of elements by sustaining †*complexuque sacro dissona nexa* [dissonant bonds in a sacred embrace][846] and that of soul and body by officiating at the instantiation of mind.[847] A converse argument can be applied to the other character. Because Harmonia is the divine personification of harmonies, her association with cosmological and psychological functions of the type described is perfectly reasonable.[848] However, the more surprising feature is the occasional allusion to her nuptial functions — her reappearance on earth is promised at the completion of Mercury's and Philology's marriage[849] and the discourse on her art is placed at the conclusion of *De nuptiis* itself.[850]

If the figurative senses of the narrative's protagonists and the essential nature of their marriage have been interpreted correctly, then these interpretations together probably constitute a fundamental meaning of Martianus' text.[851] This could be summarized as follows: it is harmonic ideas which underlie the educational process, the relation between verbal and real arts, and the relation between oral and written discourse. Since the relation between verbal and real arts is held to reflect that between signifiers and signifieds in general,[852] a further meaning would be that harmony underlies the process of signification itself.

4.3 Eriugena's theory of signification

The further development of this theory of signification can be traced in Iohannes Scottus Eriugena. In his writing, it appears as an element unusually difficult to interpret owing to the adaptation of the signifying relation to a pre-established metaphysical framework, to the combination of frequently divergent textual influences — where Martianus Capella is supplemented by Augustine, ps.-Dionysius, and others,[853] and to the inherent complexity of the signifying relation itself. So a detailed textual analysis should be prefaced by some methodological remarks.

The signifying relation may be compared with the non-signifying relation in its status. A non-signifying relation consists of two terms and, although one can distinguish a referent, a relatum, and a relation,[854] the last possesses no independent existence. A signifying relation basically comprises three terms: a referent or signifier, a relatum or signified, and a relation or signification.[855] The last possesses a quasi-independent existence[856] because of its internality,[857] is determined as both sameness and difference[858] — hence the association with harmony —, and exhibits semantic complexity[859] because of its self-contradiction.[860] Therefore this relation additionally requires a fourth term: the interpreter of the relation or signification.[861] The signifying relation may also be compared with the non-signifying relation for our analysis. A non-signifying relation may be analyzed semantically by articulating the three axes between semes indifferently for referent and relatum, and with no specific attention to the relation.[862] A signifying relation must be analyzed semantically by articulating the axis of existent and cognitive which is equivalent, that of dialectical and mathematical which is pseudo-hierarchical, and that of complex and simple which is continuous separately for signifier and signified, and with special attention to the signification.

That binary and ternary are properties of non-signifying and signifying relations respectively does not prevent them from both being properties of the signifying relation itself. But in the latter case, the binary and ternary must constitute local rather than global actualizations of semes — binarity being suggested in texts referring to a signified and a signifier and ternarity in those speaking of a mediated signified, an unmediated signified, and a signifier[863] — which interact with various Latin lexemes. It is the binary properties of the signifying relation which will form the predominant if not the exclusive topic of this section. Here, the three axes and the four signifying categories must be applied simultaneously: beginning with the existential, simple, and dialectical properties of the signified, shifting from existential to cognitive properties of the signifier while the other axes are unchanged, shifting from simple to complex properties of the interpreter while the other axes are unchanged, and ending with the cognitive, complex, and mathematical properties of the signification.[864]

A binary signification combining the axial position of existent + simple[865] + dialectical and the semantic category of signified is frequently brought into play by Eriugena. Apart from a passage already studied where divine names and their opposites are associated with created things as their proper objects,[866] there are numerous arguments suggesting that sensory signifiers of various types correlate with signifieds which actually exist. For example, there is a passage revealing the fondness for etymology characteristic of medieval writers which argues that the Greek technical term *metochē* exercises more revelatory power than the equivalent Latin *participatio* by having two components *meta* and *echein* signifying the causal dependence and separate existence respectively of each created thing.[867] Elsewhere this realist theory of language is further pursued by explaining how nouns signify the substances or accidents and verbs the motions of created nature.[868] There is also a passage indicating a willingness to make far-reaching deductions from inflexional forms which argues that the verb *sum* can signify either the atemporal existence or the temporal motion of a principle, and that the imperfect tense in the opening sentence of St. John's Gospel: *In principio erat verbum* signifies an object of the former type.[869]

A shift along the axis from existent to cognitive and between the categories of signified and signifier yields a further combination of semantic properties: cognitive + simple + dialectical with signifier. This is especially illustrated by Eriugena's analogy between the transcendence and immanence of the highest principles — the divine nature or primordial causes — and the interiority and exteriority of the human mind.

In one passage occurs the following description of intellect:[870]

> ... dum vero in cogitationes venerit et ex quibusdam phantasiis formam accipit non immerito dicitur fieri. Fit enim in memoria, formas quasdam accipiens rerum seu vocum seu colorum ceterorumque sensibilium... deinde veluti secundam formationem recipit dum quibusdam formarum sive vocum signis (litteras dico quae sunt signa vocum et figuras quae sunt signa formarum matheseos) seu aliis sensibilibus indiciis formatur... dum in cogitationem, ut diximus, venerit quasdamque phantasiarum formas acceperit deindeque in signa vocum seu sensibilium motuum indicia processerit non incongrue dicitur fieri...

> [But when it has entered into thoughts and acquires form in certain phantasies, it is not unreasonably said to come into being. For it comes to be in the memory when it acquires certain forms of things, sounds, colours, and other sensibles... then it receives a kind of second formation when it is formed in certain signs of forms or sounds — I mean letters which are signs of sounds and figures which are signs of mathematical forms — or in other sensible indicators... When it has entered into thought, as I have said, and acquires certain forms of phantasies, and has afterwards proceeded into signs of sounds or indicators of sensible motions, it is not inappropriately said to come into being].

194 *Components of concord — Ternary relations (semantic)*

Here, two quasi-temporal[871] phases in the procession of intellect from its transcendence and interiority to its immanence and exteriority are indicated. The first is that of thinking where intellect appears in non-sensible forms or phantasies, and the second that of signification where it reappears in sensible forms or signs. Of course, the non-sensible forms are forms *of* sensibles in the sense of causing them.

The argument continues in a later passage of *Periphyseon*:[872]

> Et exemplo nostrae naturae illud possumus coniicere. Nam quod intellectus noster in se ipso primum rationabiliter concipit et ad habitum purae perfectaeque intelligentiae perducit semper et in se obtinet et quibusdam signis extrinsecus profert. Verbi gratia si veram cognitionem de aliquo sensibili vel intelligibili sapiens animus perceperit ipsa cognitio et in eo fixa perseverat et <per> phantasias primo in cogitationem, deinde in sensus, deinde in vocum signa aliosque nutus quibus animus secreta sua molimina gradatim descendentia solet aperire... proferre non retardat.

> [And we can infer this from the case of our nature. For that which our intellect first conceives rationally in itself and leads to the condition of pure and perfect intelligence, it always both preserves within itself and expresses outwardly in certain signs. For example, if a wise mind has conceived a true thought of some sensible or intelligible object, that thought remains fixed in it. Yet it also does not delay in putting forth phantasies first into thinking, then into the senses, then into signs of sounds or other gestures by which the mind is wont to reveal its undertakings gradually descending from secrecy...]

The quasi-temporal phases in the procession of intellect from its transcendence and interiority to its immanence and exteriority are now multiplied. In this passage the phases are those of thinking, sensing, and signifying in each of which the intellectual object is expressed in phantasies of the appropriate type.

The same combination of semantic properties is illustrated somewhat differently in a passage where some material from Maximus the Confessor is being summarized. This concerns three universal motions of soul — the first according to mind, having the unknown God as object, and simple; the second according to reason, having the transcendent reasons as object, and simple; and the third according to sense, having the immanent reasons as object, and composite — each motion being analogous to a person of the Trinity.

Eriugena's interpretation of the third motion runs as follows: [873]

> Tertius motus est *compositus, per quem quae extra sunt* anima *tangens veluti ex quibusdam signis apud se ipsam visibilium rationes reformat.* Qui compositus dicitur non quod in se ipso simplex non sit quemadmodum primus et secundus simplices sunt sed quod non per se ipsas sensibilium rerum rationes incipit cognoscere. Primo siquidem phantasias ipsarum rerum per exteriorem sensum quinquepertitum secundum numerum instrumentorum corporalium in quibus et per quae operatur accipiens easque secum colligens dividens ordinans disponit, deinde per ipsas ad rationes earum quarum phantasiae sunt perveniens intra se ipsam eas (rationes dico) tractat atque conformat.

> [The third motion is "composite. It is that through which the soul comes into contact with external things and re-forms the reasons of the visible in itself as if through certain signs." It is called composite not because it is not simple in itself — as the first and second motions are simple — but because it begins to know the reasons of sensible things not through themselves. Indeed, it first receives the phantasies of those things themselves through the exterior sense — which is fivefold according to the number of corporeal instruments in which and through which it operates — and it arranges them within itself by collecting, dividing, and ordering. Next, coming through them to the reasons of those things of which they are phantasies, it handles and shapes them — that is, the reasons, within itself].

Here, another quasi-temporal phase in the procession of intellect from its transcendence and interiority to its immanence and exteriority is indicated: the interior sense. It is important that this phase is associated with signification — which follows from a perceived analogy between the mediating functions of interior sense between reason and exterior sense and of a sign between object and interpreter — since signification was earlier connected with the lowest phase. Clearly signs occur on more than one level of intellect's procession.

At this point, certain general conclusions regarding the theory of the signifier may be drawn from the texts. By combining the first and third passages, we may conclude that thoughts and signs interrelate on the assumption of their commensurability. In other words, a. It is possible for certain things to be understood simultaneously as thoughts and signs, and b. There is no suggestion that the content of thought might exceed the content of the sign or vice versa. According to a. it could perhaps be maintained that every sign is cognitive and every thought semiotic.[874] From the third passage, we may infer that there is a hierarchy within the human soul conceived as a procession of intellect. This consists of i. thoughts: intellect and reason; ii. thoughts as signs: interior sense; and iii. signs: exterior sense, and seems to imply that different levels in soul communicate with one another through the circulation of signs. Finally, a combination of the first and third passages yields various examples of signs: geometrical figures and gestures which are static and mobile signs of thoughts respectively, and written letters which are signs of phonetic sounds.

A shift along the axis from simple to complex and between the categories of signifier and interpreter yields a further combination of semantic properties: cognitive + complex + dialectical with interpreter. This is particularly illustrated by Eriugena's development of the analogy between the transcendence and immanence of the highest principles and the interiority and exteriority of the human mind along different lines.

In one passage occurs the following description of intellect:[875]

> Nam et noster intellectus cum per se sit invisibilis et incomprehensibilis signis tamen quibusdam et manifestatur et comprehenditur dum vocibus vel litteris vel aliis nutibus veluti quibusdam corporibus incrassatur et dum sic extrinsecus apparet semper intrinsecus invisibilis permanet dumque in varias figuras sensibus comprehensibiles prosilit semper statum suae naturae incomprehensibilem non deserit et priusquam exterius patefactus fiat intra se ipsum se ipsum movet, ac per hoc et silet et clamat et dum silet clamat et dum clamat silet...

> [For our intellect too, although it is invisible and incomprehensible in itself, is nevertheless both manifested and comprehended in certain signs when it becomes corporeal in sounds, letters, and other gestures as though in certain bodies. And while it appears thus externally, it always remains invisible internally. While it bursts forth into various shapes comprehensible to the senses, it never abandons the incomprehensible status of its nature. And before it becomes outwardly manifest, it moves itself within itself. So it is both silent and exclaims. And while it is silent it exclaims, and while it exclaims it is silent].

Here, two simultaneous[876] phases in the procession of intellect from its transcendence and interiority to its immanance and exteriority are indicated. The first is that of "thinking" where intellect eludes both non-sensible and sensible forms, and the second that of thinking where it is vested in non-sensible and sensible forms. Apparently, thoughts occur on more than one level of intellect's procession.

The argument continues in the next paragraphs of *Periphyseon*:[877]

> ... et dum sibi veluti quaedam vehicula quibus ad aliorum sensus possit provehi de aeris materia vel sensibilibus figuris efficit mox ut ad sensus exteriores eorum pervenerit ipsa vehicula deserens solus per se ipsum absolutus intima corda penetrat aliisque intellectibus se miscet et fit unum cum his quibus copulatur, et cum peragat semper in se ipso manet et dum movetur stat et dum stat movetur — est enim status mobilis et motus stabilis — et dum aliis adiungitur suam simplicitatem non relinquit.

> [And while the intellect makes for itself from the matter of air or from sensible shapes certain vehicles, so to speak, on which it may travel to the senses of others, it abandons the said vehicles immediately on reaching their external senses and penetrates their innermost hearts as something absolutely in itself alone, and it mingles itself with other intellects and becomes one with those to which it is joined. And when it goes forth, it always remains in itself. While moving it is at rest and while resting it is in motion, since it is moving rest and resting motion. And while it is joined to other things, it does not relinquish its own simplicity...]

The two simultaneous phases in the procession of intellect from its transcendence and interiority to its immanence and exteriority now become three. In this passage, there is no longer a phase of thinking in a sign-emitter contrasted with a phase of signification but a phase of thinking in a sign-emitter contrasted with a phase of signification and a phase of thinking in a sign-receiver.

The same combination of semantic properties is illustrated somewhat differently in a passage where some material from Martianus Capella is undergoing exegesis. This deals with the personal relationship between Mercury and Sophia — one of the female divinities courted by Mercury before he settled on the mortal Philology — which obviously bears an allegorical meaning.

Eriugena's interpretation of the two figures runs as follows:[878]

> In hoc loco si quis leges allegoriae intentus perspexerit, inveniet Mercurium facundi sermonis, hoc est copiosae eloquentiae formam gestare... Mercurius enim dicitur quasi medius currens, quia sermo inter homines currit, non solum infructuosus et inutilis, verum etiam nocivus esse perhibetur, nisi sapientiae pulchra atque modesta virtute... moderetur... Non fabulose igitur sed pulchre et verisimilitudine Cyllenius formatur intemeratam sapientiae pulchritudinem ardere... Quoniam vero sapientiae castitas moderata supervacui sermonis immoderataeque eloquentiae effugit contagium, non immerito ad aeternas virgines describitur migrasse...

[In this place, someone who has carefully observed the laws of allegory will find Mercury serving as a figure of eloquent speech: that is, abundant eloquence... And speech is called Mercury as though "running in the middle", because speech runs between men. It is said to be not only unproductive and useless but even harmful, if not moderated by the beautiful and modest virtue of Wisdom... So the Cyllenian is depicted as longing for the unsullied beauty of Wisdom not fictively but with beauty and probability... But since the moderated chastity of Wisdom flees the taint of superfluous speech and immoderate eloquence, she is described not unfittingly as having migrated to the eternal virgins...]

Here, the two simultaneous phases in the procession of intellect from its transcendence and interiority to its immanence and exteriority again become three: the thinking of the sign-emitter and the thinking of the sign-receiver symbolized by Sophia, and the signification symbolized by Mercury. The reference to Sophia's flight from the embraces of Mercury to the company of virgins is an important detail. It shows that a disparity exists between thought and signification which requires the sign-emitter and sign-receiver to be encoder and decoder respectively of the information passing between them.

At this point, further general conclusions regarding the doctrine of the signifier may be extracted from the texts. By combining the first and third passages, we may conclude that thoughts and signs interrelate on the assumption of their incommensurability. In other words, a. It is possible for certain things to be understood simultaneously as thoughts and signs, and b. There is a suggestion that the content of thought might exceed the content of the sign. According to b. it could perhaps be surmised that every sign requires an interpretation.[879] From the third passage, we may infer that there is a connection between human souls conceived as processions of intellect. This consists of i. the thought of one individual; ii. the sign interpreting that thought; and iii. the thought of another individual interpreting that sign, and complements the view that different levels in soul communicate with one another through the circulation of signs. Finally, the first passage yields a further example of sign: phonetic sounds which are signs of thoughts.

A binary signification combining the axial position of cognitive + complex[880] + mathematical and the semantic category of signification is occasionally brought into play by Eriugena. Apart from a passage already studied where the procession of intellect is identified with the descent of numbers through the proportions and proportionalities forming consonance,[881] there is one argument suggesting that a certain proportional element in human perception is what governs the correlation of signifiers and various types of signified.[882] More specifically, it describes a signifying process in which man can approach such transcendent objects as would otherwise elude his grasp through a *proportio/analogia*, this signifying process allowing him to assert that transcendent objects are at the same time similar to and dissimilar to sensory things: that is, to conjoin and disjoin the semantic properties involved in the two cases. The association here of proportion, similarity-dissimilarity, and signification is a compelling instance of Eriugena's willingness to apply harmonic terms to the cognitive and semantic spheres, and we shall consider some of its further ramifications when we turn from binary to ternary signification in section 4.5.[883]

4.4 Symbolism in ps.-Dionysius' *De caelesti hierarchia*

The Carolingian period is remarkable for its assimilation not only of ancient semantics but also of ancient symbolic theory. At this time, the possibility of two varieties of mediated signification was assumed:[884] Biblical texts signifying natural objects or imaginary objects which themselves signify spiritual truths, and pagan texts signifying natural objects or imaginary objects which themselves signify spiritual truths, although partial and hybrid versions of the above were also conceivable.[885] Works like Origen's *De principiis*, Augustine's *De doctrina christiana*, and ps.-Dionysius' *De caelesti hierarchia* discussed the handling of the first variety, and those like Macrobius' *Commentarius in Somnium Scipionis* the handling of the second. Thanks to the identity assumed between three historically distinct Dionysii, the *De caelesti hierarchia* and other writings of ps.-Dionysius had acquired canonical authority by the mid-ninth century.[886] They were translated from Greek and formally commented upon by Eriugena who paid special attention to their doctrine of Biblical symbolism. According to ps.-Dionysius and Eriugena, the Bible signified natural objects or imaginary objects which themselves signify spiritual truths of two kinds: concerning the divinity itself and the angelic orders.

Ps.-Dionysius' *De caelesti hierarchia* is a systematic treatise on the Biblical depiction of angels divided into fifteen chapters. Chapter 1 discusses the nature of illumination, chapter 2 the importance of dissimilar "symbols", and chapter 3 the nature of hierarchy. After this, the theory of signification by angelic names is explained beginning with the name "angel" in chapters 4–5; and continuing with an account of triadic structure in chapter 6, with the names of the nine orders in chapters 7–9, and with a summary of triadic structure in chapter 10. Next comes a discussion of certain problems in angelic nomenclature: collective application of the name "virtue" to spiritual beings in chapter 11, similar application of the name "angel" in chapter 12, and the purification of Isaiah by the Seraph in chapter 13. Lastly, there are analyses of signification by angelic numbers in chapter 14, and of signification by angelic visual shape in chapter 15. The ps.-Dionysian treatise is a combination of Neoplatonic ontology — based on the providential procession of God and the contemplative conversion of man which together form "illumination"[887] — and a theory of signification — where the encoding activity of a sign-emitter and the decoding activity of a sign-receiver together comprise "interpretation".[888] This theory is perhaps analyzable into the following components: 1. Scripture illuminates man, 2. Angels illuminate man, 3. God relates immediately to man, 4. God relates mediately to man, 5. Scripture mediates, 6. Angels mediate, 7. Mediation is figurative, and 8. Mediation is proportional. Ps.-Dionysius' fusion of ontology and semantics allows these components to be present implicitly as a simultaneous whole in which internal relation (3 = 4), the equation of functional similarity with ontological identity (1 = 2, 5 = 6), and linguistic ambiguity (7 = 8) are unifying factors although as components they sometimes appear explicitly in different contexts.

The first chapter of ps.-Dionysius' treatise *De caelesti hierarchia* begins by describing the spiritual illumination of the world by God as a twofold process: that is, a descent and multiplication of power from the Father and a conversion and unification of that power in the human intellect.[889] It continues by exploring the nature of the second phase in this process in greater detail.

The convertive process itself involves two actions whereby the human mind turns to the illuminations of Scripture and contemplates the hierarchies of angels at the same time.[890] In other words, both Scripture and angels illuminate man. However, the conversion also implies two quasi-temporal phases where the human mind receives divine light first through the angelic minds — God relates mediately to man — and secondly from the divinity itself — God relates immediately to man.[891] During this account, ps.-Dionysius repeatedly stresses that the angelic hierarchies are revealed by Scripture *symbolice...anagogice...in figuratis symbolis* =

symbolikōs...anagōgikōs...en typōtikois symbolois [symbolically and anagogically... in figurative symbols]. In other words, Scripture mediates figuratively. This is because the minds of angels transmit a divine light — they are mediators — which is accessible only *proportionaliter = analogōs* [in proportion] to the human minds which receive it — the mediation is proportional.[892]

The convertive process also implies imitation of the angelic hierarchies by human institutions according to its providential design: that is, God relates through the mediation of angels to man. Since man is elevated from the material to immaterial and formless simplicity so far as he is related *proportionaliter = analogōs* [proportionately] to the latter — the mediation is proportional —, God has revealed the immaterial hierarchies in materiate and composite forms — the mediation is figurative.[893] For example, odours, lights, discursive reasoning, ordering among men, and receiving the Eucharist are material images of the immaterial truths of emanation, illumination, non-discursive thought, harmony with God, and participation in Christ.[894] Moreover, ps.-Dionysius argues that the imitation of the angelic hierarchies by human institutions which the convertive process implies is the primary purpose of Scripture's revelation of those hierarchies: that is, God relates through the mediation of both Scripture and angels to man. This imitation is an elevation simultaneously from the sensible to the intelligible realm and from *sacre figurata symbola = hieroplasta symbola* [symbols sacredly figurative] to a higher simplicity — the mediation is figurative.[895]

The second chapter of *De caelesti hierarchia* turns to consideration of the material or sensory images employed by Scripture in describing the angelic hierarchies. Since unsophisticated people are often misled into believing that higher beings are really endowed with anthropomorphic and bizarre properties, it is essential to grasp why Scripture should resort to images of material or sensible things in such a context. However, ps.-Dionysius' response to this question is best studied together with the lengthy commentary written in Latin by his greatest medieval admirer.

4.5 Eriugena's theory of symbolism

The further elaboration of this theory of symbolism can be traced in Iohannes Scottus Eriugena. In his writing, it appears as an element particularly difficult to interpret owing to the adaptation of the signifying relation to a pre-established metaphysical structure and to the essential complexity of the signifying relation itself. It is set out primarily in the *Expositiones* on ps.-Dionysius' *De caelesti hierarchia*. Since Eriugena's doctrine of symbols is presented not in any independent treatise but in a translation-commentary on earlier material, it is methodologically sound to examine first the part coinciding with the Greek original and secondly the part consisting of paraphrase and exegesis. We shall therefore begin by summarizing the Latin version of ps.-Dionysius' chapter 2 according to the commentator's textual lemmata.[896]

Table 7. Summary of *Expositiones* 2

1–2	*Transition from chapter 1:* nature and purpose of hierarchy
3–8	*Preliminary statement concerning theory of images*
3–4	Sensory images applied to angelic hierarchies by Scripture
5	Mind's ascent to simplicity by contemplating multiplicity in such images
6–7	Sensory images applied to angelic hierarchies by Scripture only indirectly
8	Scripture employs sensory images in manner similar to that of poetry
	Scripture's concession to human weakness
	Scripture's purpose to elevate us from sensory to intelligible
9–17	*Possible objections to this theory*
9–10	Despite acceptance of principle of ascent from lower to higher, Inappropriateness of using sensory images
11–13	Mind's ascent to simplicity better assured by contemplating non-sensory images
14–15	Sensory images degrade higher beings
16–17	Sensory images mislead human minds
18–23	*Preliminary replies to objections*
18	Sensory images do not degrade higher beings
19	Purpose of using sensory images (1): Human mind requires mediator to elevate it,
	A mediator is something lower reflecting the higher,
	These images are mediators
20–21	Purpose of using sensory images (2):
	Concealment of highest truths from unworthy
22–23	Fuller reply to objections:
	Scripture's twofold revelation
24–37	*Theory of similar and dissimilar images*
24	Scripture's application of affirmative terms to God

Table 7 (continued)

25–26	God's transcendence of these terms
27	Scripture's application of negative terms to God
28–29	Superiority of these terms
30	If negative are superior to affirmative terms applied to God, Then dissimilar are superior to similar images applied to spiritual beings
31–32	Superiority of dissimilar images
33	Deceptiveness of similar images
34	Scripture avoids deception by using dissimilar images
35–36	Justification of dissimilar images (1): They do not confine human mind to lower but elevate it to higher, Because they obviously apply indirectly
37	Justification of dissimilar images (2): Even lowest images participate in God
38–50	*Application of dissimilar similarities*
38	Such images apply to a. sensible and b. intelligible in different senses
39–43	Examples of transformation in sense: Application of "anger", "concupiscence", "intemperance", and "irrationality" to higher
44	Such images elevate to higher They are adapted to human level They harmonize with higher as echoes
45	Such images also apply to God
46–48	Examples of a. highest, b. intermediate, and c. lowest images applied to God
49–50	Dissimilar similarities as lowest echoes Purpose of using such images (1): Concealment of highest truths from unworthy Purpose of using such images (2): Avoidance of attachment to lower
51–52	*Personal experiences of the author*
51	His motivations described
52	His perception of dissimilarity forced him to ascend beyond it
53–55	*Transition to chapter 3:* proposal to define hierarchy

This summary has been constructed to display the basic ps.-Dionysian theory of sensory images which Eriugena expands. One immediately discerns from the list of topics that there is a threefold structure in the original argument — of expounding a thesis, of mentioning possible objections to the thesis, and of countering those objections — this emerging despite the treatment of subsidiary questions. Eriugena elaborates this structure at considerable length in his own account of sensory images or symbols.

The relevant parts of *Expositiones in Ierarchiam caelestem* chapter 2 can now be quoted in full:[897]

> Haec enim sunt dissimilia symbola in propheticis visionibus, in eorum prophetarum spiritu administratione angelica plasmata, ad nostram eruditionem et introductionem ad purissimas caelestium essentiarum in semetipsis, remota omni phantastica plasmatione, cognitiones. Quae prophetica figmenta si quis incaute cogitaverit, ita ut in eis finem cogitationis suae constituat, et non ultra ea ascendat in contemplationem rerum intelligibilium quarum illa imagines sunt, non solum ipsius animus non purgatur et exercitatur, verum etiam turpissime polluitur et stultissime opprimitur... reprehendit eos qui divina symbola divinasque imaginationes, quibus sancta scriptura propter nos confecta est, carnaliter ac turpiter accipiunt, arbitrantes ipsa symbola ipsasque imaginationes nec imaginationes esse nec symbola, sed ipsas supercaelestes virtutes per se ipsas, in suis propriis naturalibusque formis quae a conditore omnium factae sunt, in spiritibus apparuisse propheticis, ita ut nullum in ipsis apparitionibus mysticum et allegoricum inquiratur... Siquidem in quantum viles ex vilibus, humiles ex humilibus terrenisque animalibus imagines divinarum virtutum mystice finguntur, in tantum ipsae virtutes et laudantur et exaltantur. Nulla enim maior laus est ea quae ex contrariorum comparatione assumitur... Saepe enim videmus in vilioribus animalium, fructuum, herbarum, speciebus, quam in pulchrioribus maiorem virtutem sapientes laudare... nemo recte intelligentium dixerit, unam singularemque procuratarum formarum et figurarum informium intellectuum carentiumque figuris causam esse, nostram videlicet proportionem adhuc infirmam et mortalem, ac per hoc non valentem absque aliqua medietate interposita ad invisibiles divinorum animorum ascendere contemplationes. Semperque desiderat proprias et connaturales sibi sensibilium imaginum manuductiones quae, cum sint possibiles nobis ad cognitionem, praetendunt, hoc est prius nobis ostendunt, formationes, imagines profecto, informium, carentium videlicet forma... Est, inquit, altera causa sanctarum in scripturis divinis descriptionum decentissima convenientissimaque divinorum eloquiorum mysteriis. Et ea est sacram secretamque veritatem

supermundanorum spirituum occultare, inviamque multis ponere per incomprehensibilia et divina aenigmata, hoc est per difficillimas et inaccessibiles divinas obscuritates, his qui indigni sunt pura caelestium virtutum cognitione... Duo, inquit, modi sunt quibus sanctae manifestationes sanctorum angelorum in divina scriptura per imagines fiunt, quorum unus est qui spiritualium substantiarum intelligibiliumque virtutum, quibus rationalis anima decoratur, absolutis quibusdam convenientibusque imaginationibus formatur... Alter vero, qui bestiarum ferocium superbarumque ut leonis et equi, seu turpium ut ursi et vermis, seu, quod longissime putatur distare, insanientium hominum... configurationibus fingitur. Huc etiam accedit formarum confusio, dum in una eademque imagine species humana, vitulina, leonina, aquilina monstruose miscetur, quod omnino absolutis naturalibusque formis contrarium perspicitur... Si, inquit, depulsiones, hoc est negationes, quas Greci *apophaseis* vocant, in divinis significationibus vere fiunt, non autem intentiones, affirmationes videlicet, quas *kataphaseis* dicunt, eisdem divinis significationibus compactae et convenientes sunt... Profecto obscuritati arcanorum, hoc est ineffabilium, multo aptior est per dissimiles formationes, quam per similes manifestatio. Ac si diceret: si vera est negatio in divinis rebus, non autem vera sed metaphorica affirmatio... quid mirum, si naturalibus simplicibusque formis longe dissimiles, mixtae, confusae, deformesque plus ad divina et ineffabilia valeant significanda, quam absolutae, ac simplices, omnique confusione carentes naturalium formarum imaginationes... Eadem ratione, dum in sanctis visionibus sanctorum prophetarum lego humanam effigiem pulchram, absolutam, omnimodisque naturalem in significatione ipsius, qui super omnem formam et figuram in se ipso absque forma subsistit et figura, plus possem decipi, ut existimem ipsum Deum incircumscriptum humana effigie circumscribi posse, et invisibilem et ineffabilem, visibilem, ac de eo aliquid fari. Dum vero in eisdem visionibus pennati hominis ac volitantis imaginem invenio in significatione caelestium virtutum seu ipsius divinitatis, veluti celeri volatu omnia penetrantis, non facile fallor, quoniam in natura rerum visibilium pennatum hominem et volitantem nec vidi, nec legi, nec audivi. Est enim monstruosum et omnino humana natura alienum... Ac per hoc citius adducor ad negandum tali imagine omnino divinas virtutes ipsumque Deum circumscribi et deformiter formari, — omne siquidem quod contra naturam est turpe atque deforme est, — quam ad consentiendum tales figuras naturaliter in caelestibus esse... Sicut itaque negatio affirmationi praeponitur in significationibus, ita inconvenientes atque deformes species formosis convenientibusque proponuntur in imaginationibus manifestationibusque divinarum rerum... In pretiosis, inquit, hoc est pulchris naturaeque similibus sanctis imaginationibus, facillime possunt seduci qui existimant caelestes substantias aureas habere formas... Non concedens, inquit, theologia, materiale nostrum, hoc est nostrum animum rebus materialibus promptissimum se inserere, in turpibus imaginibus manendo requiescere, inque eis finem cognitionis ponere, ad obscuras indecorasque similitudines pervenit... Oportet nos, inquit, intelligere quod nulla creatura est quae omnino iuxta suam analogiam participatione summi boni privetur. Ait enim scriptura: *Et vidit Deus, et ecce omnia bona valde*. Et si ita est, quid mirum si ex rebus materialibus speculationis intelligibilium occasio sumatur, ut, quoniam omnia summum bonum participant, ex similitudine inferiorum bonorum ad cognitionem sublimium humanus animus possit ascendere?... Si, inquit, omnia summi boni participantia sunt, oportet profecto ex omnibus intelligere, hoc est in omnibus materialibus conspicari bonas immaterialium contemplationes, et ex materiis sensibilibus formare praedictas dissimiles similitudines, ut per eas invisibiles et intellectuales intelligantur virtutes, dum non eodem sed altero modo intelligibilium virtus et sensibilium natura perspicitur... de similitudinibus longe dissimilibus, quae ex naturalibus motibus irrationabilium bestiarum ad rationabiles intelligibilium animorum virtutes significandas sancta introducit theologia, tractatum est... Est itaque, inquit, hoc est oportet formare formas non dissonas, sed convenientes caelestibus significandis essentiis, etiam ex vilibus partibus terrenae mortalisque materiae; nec sine ratione, quoniam et ipsa materia ex summo bono, quod solum vere est, substantiam possidet in omnibus suis materialibus ordinibus, et habet resonantias quasdam, hoc est resultationes intellectualis pulchritudinis. Resonantias autem dico vel resultationes, quas Graeci *apēchēmata* vocant, rerum intelligibilium imaginationes. Sicut enim imago vocis ex rupe quadam seu aliqua concavitate, vel sicut imago corporis ex specilla resultat, ita intellectualis pulchritudinis caelestium virtutum imaginationes ex omni terrena vilissimaque materia respondent. Ideoque possibile est nostrum animum reduci per eas resonantias ad immateriales primas formas, quas Graeci *archetypias* appellant, quarum resultantes imagines sunt, ita tamen ut dissimiliter ipsae similitudines accipiantur in materialibus unde resultant et in immaterialibus quibus resultant. Aliter enim furor in leone diffinitur, aliter in angelo. Et eisdem similitudinibus non eodem modo consideratis, sed iuxta differentias materialium rerum et altitudines immaterialium, compacte autem et pulchre proprietas diffinitur uniuscuiusque in intellectualibus virtutibus et sensibilibus materiis. Verbi gratia, irrationabilitas defectus rationis est in animalibus ratione carentibus, in caelestibus vero essentiis supereminentia rationis et superrationabilitas, qua superant omnem rationem nostram et sensum... Divina itaque symbola sancta sunt, res vero quarum symbola sunt sancta sanctorum, hoc est sancti intellectus sanctorum symbolorum, et dissimilem sanctam figurationem honorant; hoc est: sancta illa divinarum rerum figuratio, quamvis longe dissimilis sit ipsis intellectibus per eam significatis, honoratur a sanctis theosophis atque prophetis. Dum enim eas res quae significantur pure intelligunt, ipsas prius honorant, quoniam divinae et supermundanae sunt. Consequenter etiam earum figurationes, sive ex superioribus materialis creaturae partibus, sive mediis, sive novissimis translatas, non immerito venerantur, intellectualique distinctione et discretione res ipsas suis figurationibus segregant, nec figuras pro veris intellectibus, nec veros intellectus pro figuris approbant, sed omnibus, remota omni confusione, suas diffinitiones et cognitiones distribuunt... redditur causa dissimilium significationum... repertum est, ut neque divina tractabilia sint, hoc est ut neque divini intellectus pervii et patefacti fierent immundis, pollutis videlicet hominibus, delictorum impietatisque vel certe superbiae sordibus contaminatis... neque mirabilium agalmatum studiosi contemplatores tamquam veris remaneant figuris. Ac si diceret: ad hoc etiam obscurae et dissimiles imaginationes factae sunt ut neque remaneant, hoc est neque finem speculationis suae ponant qui studiose mirabilia agalmata, divinas scilicet imagines, contemplantur in ipsis figuris, putantes eas veras esse et non figurativas... Et divina itaque honorificant mysteria sancti theologi veris negationibus, hoc est per negationes quae vere de divinis praedicantur. Ut enim praedictum est, in divinis significationibus verae sunt negationes, affirmationes vero metaphoricae, ac veluti extrinsecus acquisitae, ut omnino incompactae, hoc est non propriae. Et non solum per negationes veras divina honorificant, verum etiam per diversas similitudines vel, ut expressius transfertur, per alienas similitudines compactarum resonantium, hoc est consonantium imaginationum ad novissima, ad materialium videlicet et corporalium rerum formas et species. Ut enim superius confectum est, sicut plus divina honorificari, hoc est expressius significari per veras negationes quam per translatas affirmationes, possunt, ita plus et significantius eadem divina per alienas similitudines novissimarumque materialium rerum imagines quam per pulchras caelestium rationabiliumque rerum formas mentibus humanis insinuatur... Ac per hoc, sicut ipsum magis honorat qui negat eum esse quid, quam qui eum affirmat quid esse, ita plus eum significat atque honorat qui figuram bestialem ipsi circumdat, quam qui in humana effigie auro gemmisque decora, preciosaque induta vestimenta, caelestibusve splendidissimis corporibus circumscripta ipsum imaginat. Fallitur namque animus insipiens dum pulchra de Deo cogitat. Putat enim eum sic subsistere; non autem decipitur, cum de ipso turpesve confusasve formas tractat; naturali enim ingenio veraque ratione ductus omnino eum sic esse fiducialiter negat... in huius quaestionis quae de divinis symbolis est, diligentem investigationem non descenderemus, si non deformitas ac veluti turpido formationum, quae angelicas virtutes in divinis scripturis manifestant, veluti invitos cogeret et extorqueret. Quae deformitas non sinit nostrum animum remanere in dissimilibus divinorum intellectuum formationibus... sed sinit nostrum animum luctari adversus falsas phantasias vana cogitantium, et negare materiales passibilesque spiritualibus carnaliter inesse substantiis...

[(6) For these are dissimilar symbols in prophetic visions, fashioned in those prophets' spirit under angelic control, and designed for our education and our introduction to the purest thoughts of the celestial essences in themselves and remote from all imaginative fashioning. If anyone should conceive these prophetic figments so incautiously as to establish a limit of his thought in them, and not ascend beyond them to contemplation of the intelligible things whose images they are, his mind is not only unpurified and unexercised but even most grievously tainted and most stupidly oppressed... (9) He reproves those who accept in a carnal and base manner the divine symbols and divine imaginings in which holy Scripture has been realized for our benefit, and who believe that the symbols and imaginings themselves are neither imaginings nor symbols but that the supercelestial powers themselves have appeared in the prophetic spirits through themselves and in their own proper and natural forms made by the creator of all things — so that nothing mystical or allegorical is sought after in those same apparitions... (18) As much as base images of the divine powers are mystically derived from base animals and humble images from humble and terrestrial animals, so much are the powers themselves both praised and exalted. For there is no greater praise than that obtained from the comparison of contraries... We often observe the wise praising virtue more highly through baser forms of animals, fruits, and plants than through more beautiful ones... (19) No person understanding rightly would say that there is as the one single cause of the forms and shapes provided to us of the unformed and shapeless intellects our proportionality. This is as yet weak and mortal, and therefore unable to ascend to the invisible contemplations of divine minds without some mediator being interposed. It always needs the guidance of sensory images proper and connatural to itself which, as possible sources of knowledge for us, pre-extend — that is, show to us in advance — the formations or images of the unformed or formless... (20) There is, he declares, another cause of the holy descriptions in divine Scripture which is most fitting and appropriate to the mysteries of the divine utterances. This is the concealment of the holy and secret truth of the supermundane spirits, and its rendering inaccessible through incomprehensible and divine enigmas — that is, through the most difficult and inaccessible divine obscurities — to the multitude unworthy of pure knowledge of the celestial powers... (23) There are, he says, two ways in which the holy manifestations of holy angels are accomplished through images in divine Scripture. One is formed by certain unconfused and fitting imaginations of the spiritual substances and of the intelligible virtues by which a rational soul is adorned... The other is contrived in the shapes of ferocious and aggressive animals like the lion and the horse or of ugly ones like the bear and worm or — at what seems to be the greatest distance — of insane men. To these is also added the confusion of forms when human, bovine, leonine, and aquiline forms are monstrously blended in one and the same image — something perceived as wholly contrary to the unconfused and natural forms... (30) He says that if the denials or negations which the Greeks call *apophaseis* are true when signifying divine things, whereas the positings or affirmations which they call *kataphaseis* are not suitable or appropriate for signifying those same divine things... then indeed manifestation through dissimilar forms is much more fitting to the obscurity of the arcane — that is, the ineffable — than that through similar forms. In other words, if negation is true regarding divine things, while affirmation is not true but metaphorical... it is not surprising that imaginings greatly dissimilar to natural and simple forms in being blended, confused, and deformed are more powerfully significative regarding divine and ineffable things than are those of natural forms which are separate, simple, and lacking all confusion... By the same token, when I read in the holy visions of the holy prophets of a beautiful human shape which is unconfused and totally natural as signifying him who exists above all form and shape in himself without any form or shape, I am more liable to be deceived. I might therefore believe that God himself who is uncircumscribed could be circumscribed by a human shape, and that as invisible and ineffable he is visible and describable in some manner. But when I find in the same visions the image of a winged and flying man as signifying the celestial powers or the divinity itself as though penetrating all things with swift flight, I am not easily deceived. This is because I have neither seen nor read nor heard of a winged and flying man in the nature of visible things, for this is monstrous and utterly foreign to human nature... And through this I am more quickly led to deny that the divine powers and God himself can in any way be circumscribed by such an image and formed in a deformed manner — indeed, everything contrary to nature is ugly and deformed — than to agree that such shapes could exist naturally among the celestial... Therefore just as negation is preferred to affirmation in signifying, so are unfitting and deformed forms placed before beautiful and fitting ones in the imaginings and manifestations of divine things... (33) He says that in holy imaginings of the precious — that is, of things beautiful and similar to nature — they can easily be deceived who believe the celestial substances to have golden forms... (35) He declares that theology, not permitting our materiate aspect — that is, our soul — to place itself most readily within material things, to remain idly among ugly images, and to set the limit of its thinking in them, has recourse to obscure and indecorous similarities... (37) We must understand, he says, that there is no creature which is according to its own proportionality totally deprived of participation in the supreme Good.

For Scripture states: "And God saw it, and behold, everything was very good." Such being the case, how is it surprising that a starting-point for contemplating the intelligibles is taken from material things so that — given that everything participates in the supreme Good — the human mind can ascend to knowledge of the highest from the similarity of lower goods?... (38) He says that if all things participate in the supreme Good, we must understand from all things — that is, we must perceive in all material things — good contemplations of the immaterial. We must form the aforesaid dissimilar similarities from sensible substrates, so that the invisible and intellectual powers may be understood through them, given that intelligible power and sensible nature are perceived not in the same but in different manners... (42) He has discussed the greatly dissimilar similarities which holy theology has introduced from the natural motions of irrational beasts in order to signify the rational powers of intelligible minds... (44) He asserts that one is to form — that is, one must form — forms that are not dissonant but harmonious with the celestial essences to be signified, and take these even from the base parts of earthy and mortal matter. This is not unreasonable since even matter itself has its subsistence from the supreme Good — which alone truly exists — in all the gradations of its materiality, and possesses certain resonances or reverberations of intellectual beauty. I call "resonances" or "reverberations" — what the Greeks call *apēchēmata* — the imaginings of intelligible things. For just as the image of a voice rebounds from some rock or other concavity, or the image of a body from a mirror, so do imaginings of the intellectual beauty among celestial powers answer back from all earthy or base matter. It is therefore possible for our mind to return through these resonances to the immaterial primary forms — termed *archetypiai* by the Greeks — of which they are the reverberating images, with the consequence that the similarities themselves are received in dissimilar ways among the material from which they reverberate and among the immaterial in which they reverberate. Thus, anger is defined in one way in a lion and in another way in an angel. With those very similarities considered not in the same manner but according to differences of material things and levels of immaterial things, the property of each object among intellectual powers and among sensible substrata is defined fittingly and beautifully. For example, irrationality is a defect of reason in animals lacking reason but in celestial essences a pre-eminence of reason and a "more-than-rationality" by which they transcend all our reason and sense... (49) So the divine symbols are holies whereas the things of which they are symbols are holies of holies: that is, holy understandings of holy symbols. The theologians honour the holy figuring which is dissimilar: that is to say, this holy figuring of divine things is honoured by holy theologians and prophets although it is greatly dissimilar to those understandings signified by it. But when they understand the things signified in their purity, the theologians honour them more as being divine and supermundane. So they not unreasonably venerate the figurings of those things — whether transferred from the higher or median or lowest parts of the material creature — and they separate the things themselves from their figurings by an intellectual distinction or discrimination. They do not approve figures in place of true understandings, nor true understandings in place of figures, but assign the appropriate definitions and concepts to all things with every confusion removed... The cause of dissimilar significations is explained... its purpose is that divine things should not be liable to handling: that is, that divine understandings should not be accessible or exposed to the impure — men who are polluted and contaminated by the stain of sins, impiety, and especially pride... nor should those desirous of contemplating wonderful icons remain within figures as though they are truths. In other words, the obscure and dissimilar imaginings have been made to this end: that those who zealously contemplate the wonderful icons — the divine images — should not remain or set a limit to their speculation in the figures themselves by believing them to be true and not figurative... And so the holy theologians honour the divine mysteries with true negations: that is, through negations which are truly predicated of the divine. As stated earlier, in signifying divine things the negations are true but the affirmations metaphorical and — being taken as though from the exterior — like the wholly unfitting and improper. And theologians honour divine things not only through true negations but through differing similarities or — to rephrase in more vivid language — through the divergent similarities of fitting resonances: that is, of imaginations consonant down to the lowest levels, or down to the forms and species of material and corporeal things. As demonstrated above, just as the divine can be more honoured — that is, more precisely signified — through true negations than through transferred affirmations, so are the same divine things introduced into human minds more meaningfully through divergent similarities and images of the lowest levels among material things than through the beautiful forms of celestial and rational things... In this way, just as one honours God more by denying that he is something than by affirming that he is something, so one signifies and honours him more by investing him with an animal shape than by imagining him in a human shape decked with jewels, wearing precious garments, and surrounded by the most splendid celestial bodies. Our unwise mind is deceived when it conceives beautiful attributes of God, for it believes that he exists in this manner. But it is not deceived when it applies ugly and confused forms to him, for it is led by natural intelligence and true reason into confidently denying that he is anything of this kind... (52) We would not penetrate into the careful investigation of this question about divine symbols, if the deformity and ugliness so to speak of the formations manifesting the angelic powers in holy

Scripture did not compel us and tear us away as though against our will. This deformity does not allow our mind to remain in dissimilar formations of the divine intellects... but permits our mind to strive against the false phantasies of those thinking vain thoughts and to deny that material and passible phantasies are present carnally in spiritual substances...]

Having performed a sort of textual distillation with Eriugena's discussion of sensory images, we are left with an informative account of ternary signification. As argued before, that binary and ternary are properties of non-signifying and signifying relations respectively does not prevent them from both being properties of the signifying relation itself, although in the latter case the binary and ternary must constitute local rather than global actualizations of the semes interacting with various Latin lexemes. However, if binarity is suggested in texts referring to a signified and a signifier and ternarity in those speaking of a mediated signified, an unmediated signified, and a signifier,[898] then it is indeed the ternary properties of the signifying relation which will form the predominant if not the exclusive topic of this section.[899] The three axes and the four signifying categories must be applied simultaneously producing a sequence of interactions similar to that described in section 4.3. Thus, discussion begins with the existential, simple, and dialectical properties of the signified, shifts from existential to cognitive properties of the signifier while the other axes are unchanged, shifts from simple to complex properties of the interpreter while the other axes are unchanged, and ends with the cognitive, complex, and mathematical properties of the signification.[900] However, the ternarity implied in the positing of a mediated signified, an unmediated signified, and a signifier naturally adds a further complication to the sequence.

A ternary signification combining the axial position of existent + simple[901] + dialectical and the semantic category of signified[902] is brought into play in several glosses. Thus, among transcendent signifieds God is described as the only true existent[903] although the terminology applied to the angels — nouns like things, essence, substance, and intellect[904] and adjectives like immaterial, intelligible, intellectual, and rational[905] which are associated with higher being by classical Platonism — indicates their existence also. Among immanent signifieds Matter is said to derive subsistence from the supreme Good[906] while further terminology applied to the sensibles — nouns like creature, nature, and substrate[907] and adjectives like natural, material, and corporeal[908] which traditional Platonism has associated with lower being — likewise implies their existence. Eriugena himself shows that the transcendent and immanent realities of the ontological realm correspond to mediated and unmediated signifieds in the semantic sphere by his ambivalent usage of *intellectus*.[909] In gloss 49, this term indicates an "understanding" separated from a "figure" by an intellective process: i.e. a set of semantic properties isolated within and therefore mediated by a further set in a signifying process. But elsewhere in the glosses, the same term indicates an angelic "intellect" which ontologically transcends a sensible object.[910]

A shift along the axis from existent to cognitive and between the categories of signified and signifier yields a further combination of semantic properties: cognitive + simple + dialectical with signifier.[911] This axial position is implied frequently when the glosses describe those sensory images which human beings make for themselves in endeavouring to comprehend the supra-sensible realities and which are contrasted with forms immanent in the external world. The fact that these images are fashioned is one reason for distinguishing them from their non-cognitive counterparts, this fact being indicated by references to them as imaginings, formations, and figurings[912] where psychological activity is implicit in the terminology, or else as images, symbols, forms, and figures[913] where that activity is suggested by the context. The place where these images are fashioned is another reason for distinguishing them from their non-cognitive counterparts, this place being identified in some glosses as the prophetic spirit[914] and in others as the Scriptural text.[915] What Eriugena says here about the location of such images is of some importance. First, it shows that the signifier is either i. a concept, or ii. a graphic substance, or iii. a combination of a concept and a graphic substance and not iv. a phonic substance, or v. a combination of a concept and a phonic substance.[916] Secondly, it shows that the signifier, if understood as iii. a combination of a concept and a graphic substance which are themselves a signified and signifier respectively, is already a complex entity.[917]

A ternary signification combining the axial position of cognitive + complex[918] + dialectical and the semantic category of interpreter[919] is brought into play in several glosses. Thus, the users of sensory images are divided into three groups: angels who transmit them to the prophets,[920] prophets or theologians who receive them in their spirits and transmit them through Scripture,[921] and we ourselves who receive them from Scripture.[922] Eriugena concentrates his attention on the last group, subdividing it according to the manner in which the images are interpreted. According to glosses 6, 9, 20, and 52 we can either remain in the sensory images as though they truly represent the intelligible things of which they are images — this attitude being characterized as thinking or believing[923] — or else ascend above the sensory images as things not truly representing the intelligibles — an attitude described as contemplation or knowledge.[924] According to glosses 30, 33, 35, and 49 the latter approach is facilitated where the images are of a "dissimilar" variety.[925]

A shift along the axis from dialectical to mathematical and between the categories of interpreter and signification yields a further combination of semantic properties: cognitive + complex + mathematical with signification.[926] This axial position is revealed more clearly in these glosses than anywhere else, although it is less easy to separate the category from those invoked earlier. The problem might be stated as follows. Eriugena attributes what is in our terms semantic content on the one hand to the signifier/cognitive image — this is especially apparent in passages discussing the meaning of confused images which cannot correspond to extramental realities[927] — and on the other hand to the mediated signified/transcendent existent or to the unmediated signified/immanent existent or to both. So the normal difficulty of isolating signification is compounded by the presence of an existent-cognitive axis.[928]

The semantic processes themselves are described in considerable detail:

1. Eriugena assigns certain properties to images in general. Translated into modern terminology, he views these as signifiers which contain at least two sememes: A. a sememe^1 corresponding to a sememe^2 in the mediated signified = the transcendent ontological principle, B. a sememe^3 corresponding to a sememe^4 in the unmediated signified = the immanent ontological principle.[929] Now the relation between semes$^{1/2}$ and sememes$^{3/4}$ is one of difference or dissimilarity while that between sememe^1 and sememe^2 and between sememe^3 and sememe^4 is one of sameness or similarity. Two conclusions are therefore drawn immediately. First, the dissimilar and similar elements in the images somehow correlate with the negative and affirmative aspects of the divine names;[930] and secondly, the combination of dissimilar and similar like the combination of negative and affirmative is an instance of harmony.[931]

2. Much is said regarding the "form" of signification implied in the fashioning of images.[932] Eriugena describes operations corresponding to activation of semes — the derivation of images from sensible objects in general[933] — ; combination of semes — the blending in an image of properties both found and not found together in sensible objects[934] —; transference of semes — the application in an image of a property found

in sensible objects to intelligible objects [935] —; and transference-combination of semes — the application of images to intelligible objects in general. [936]

3. Much is also said regarding the "form" and "content" of signification implied in the fashioning of images. [937] Eriugena classifies images into 1a uncombined or 1b combined — where it is a question of form —; and into 2a of the human or 2b of the animal, and into 3a of the psychic or 3b of the physical — where it is a question of content. [938] From these classes the following types can be derived: A. uncombined + human + psychic, B. uncombined + human + physical, C. uncombined + animal + psychic, D. uncombined + animal + physical, E. combined + human-animal + psychic, F. combined + human-animal + physical, G. combined + human + psychic-physical, and H. combined + animal + psychic-physical.

4. Various instances of images fashioned along these lines are given. A combination of semes is clearly implied in all cases, [939] although sometimes several semes in the collection are expressed — e.g. "ugly animal" [940] and sometimes only one — e.g. "anger". [941] The transference of this combination can be treated equally as where a seme is shifted from one sememe to another sememe opposed to it — e.g. "animal" from not transcendent + not beautiful to transcendent + beautiful [942] — or where that seme itself contains the one sememe and the other sememe opposed to it. [943]

5. Eriugena assigns a special property to those images called "dissimilar", [944] reasoning perhaps along the following lines. Since images are signifiers which imply a relation of difference or dissimilarity between sememes $^{1/2}$ and sememes $^{3/4}$, and relations of sameness or similarity not only between sememe ^{1} and sememe ^{2} and between sememe ^{3} and sememe ^{4} but also through the single lexeme corresponding to the image as such, [945] the relation of difference or dissimilarity between sememes $^{1/2}$ and sememes $^{3/4}$ must be increased in order to restore balance to the image. [946] It is this last property which is absolutely central to its harmonic conception. [947]

6. Finally, much is said regarding the enigmatic, obscure, and arcane aspects of dissimilar images: in modern terms the impossibility of definitive closure in their interpretation. [948] Two observations should be made here. First, one should not conclude that the semantic analysis proposed above compromises this aspect. Given that identification of the semic combination implied by a given image is often a matter of personal

judgement,[949] the openness of its signification is hardly diminished. Secondly, one cannot hold that the harmonic component of the theory is a countervailing tendency. Since any harmonic relation underlying the said image is ultimately ternary, semantically complex, and self-contradictory,[950] the openness of its signification is if anything increased.[951]

4.6. Extensions of the Eriugenian theory of symbolism

To pursue the ternary aspect further would require consideration of more elaborate signifying relations: for example, where the signifiers are composed of smaller elements, or where the mediated signifieds have become 2 x....n x mediated signifieds, or the significations connect with larger units.[952] In Eriugena's writing, such signifying relations are best illustrated by the rhetorical devices of *transitus* and *recapitulatio*,[953] and by the exegetical distinction of literal and spiritual[954] all of which appear in non-traditional forms. His usage of the rhetorical devices reveals a prominent duality: they are syntagmatic — i.e. with syntactic-semantic elements distributed through a horizontal segment of text — and also paradigmatic — i.e. with semantic elements distributed through a vertical segment of text.[955]

The syntagmatic notion of transition is employed quite frequently by Eriugena. In *Periphyseon,* when Nutritor interrupts his discussion of the Aristotelian category of place to explain the nature of the visible world, Alumnus characterizes this move as a transition *a principali quaestione in incidentem* [from the principal question to a subordinate one].[956] Likewise, when Nutritor interrupts his exegesis of the *Genesis* cosmogony according to synecdoche to digress on the use of this rhetorical device, he comments on the value of a *transitus...a proposito* [transition from the subject].[957] The paradigmatic notion of transition is also fairly common. For example, in interpreting the stories of the prodigal son and of the ten virgins Eriugena notes a *transitus parabolarum/parabolicae figurae* [transition in the parables/the parabolic figure] from what is signified at the beginning to what is signified at the end of the narratives:[958] that is, from the general return of mankind to God to the special return of the elect.[959] This semantic usage may be compared with a cognitive one. For example, in introducing his account of the special return Eriugena notes the complexity of Scripture which in the course of paragraphs, sentences, and phrases makes *transitus ex diversis sensibus in diversos* [transitions from various senses to various other senses][960] — this movement being equivalent to a progressive ascent in contemplation to the divinity itself.[961] Finally, this cognitive usage can be contrasted with an existential one. In *Periphyseon,* Scripture's teaching that *caelum et terra transibunt* [heaven and earth will pass away][962] is explained by distinguishing two transitions: between things on the same level of being[963] and between things on a lower and a higher level of being.[964] Similarly, the opinion of theologians like Ambrose and Gregory of Nyssa that lower things can be transformed into higher is endorsed by distinguishing three transitions: between bodies and souls, between souls and primordial causes, and between primordial causes and God.[965]

In opposing the syntagmatic sense of *transitus* to its paradigmatic senses, Eriugena raises the possibility that the signified of the syntagmatic chain might itself be that paradigmatic sense.[966] This would extend the theoretical perspectives assumed hitherto, since the signified of the syntagmatic chain would therefore be a signification.[967] Now in opposing the syntagmatic sense of *recapitulatio* to its paradigmatic senses, it is this possibility which is realized.[968]

The syntagmatic notion of recapitulation is employed several times by Eriugena. In *Periphyseon* II there is a recapitulation of the *Genesis* exegesis: the statements "In the beginning God made heaven and earth", "But the earth was invisible and uncomposed", and "And darkness was over the abyss" signify aspects of the primordial causes, while the statement "And the spirit of God was borne above the waters" applies to God as Holy Spirit.[969] Later in the same treatise comes a recapitulation of the fourfold division of nature into creating and not created, both created and creating, created and not creating, and neither creating nor created. The value of recapitulation in discourse is here stated to be that of recalling to memory and *simul* [simultaneously] displaying to the mind what has previously been argued.[970] In *Periphyseon* IV there is another recapitulation of the *Genesis* exegesis: Paradise signifies human nature made in God's image, the fountain Christ, the rivers flowing from the fountain the four cardinal virtues, the all-tree the Word of God immanent in human nature, the tree of mixed knowledge the appetite of carnal senses, the man the human mind, the woman the human sense, and the serpent illicit pleasure.[971] Even later in the same treatise comes a recapitulation of Maximus' fivefold division of nature into not created and created, intelligible and sensible, heaven and earth, paradise and inhabited earth, and male and female. Here, the value of recapitulation in discourse is again said to be that of *in memoriam revocare* [recalling to memory] various arguments set out previously.[972]

The last passage leads to the important conclusion that the syntagmatic chain of recapitulation has as its signified a recapitulation in paradigmatic form. Its signified is a recapitulation because the Maximian fivefold division is inseparable from a fivefold *recapitulatio = anakephalaiōsis* — the latter being both a constituent part of and a principle of unifying the former.[973] Its signified is paradigmatic because the Maximian division and recapitulation are simultaneously existent, cognitive, and semantic in character.

That Maximus' recapitulation is a constituent part of and a principle of unifying the division of existent things emerges from his account of the fivefold division in the *Ambigua* cited at length by Eriugena.[974] According to this description, the *substantia = hypostasis* [substance] of all created things is divisible into not created and created nature, the latter into intelligibles and sensibles, the latter into heaven and earth, and the latter into paradise and inhabited world. In place of the expected division of the inhabited world there is a division of man which takes a more elaborate form. On the one hand, man is divisible into male and female but on the other, he constitutes a recapitulation of all the previous divisions — *medietatem faciens extremitatibus = tois...mesiteuōn akrois* [establishing mediation of the extremes], functioning as an agent of continuity, paralleling the intelligibles and sensibles in his own status, coming between the intelligibles and sensibles in that status, exercising a power of unification, and containing the *harmonia...diversis naturis* [harmony of different natures] — this recapitulation occurring pre-eminently in the humanity of Christ.[975]

To be a principle of unifying the division of cognitive objects is for Eriugena another function of the recapitulation. In commenting upon Maximus' text in *Periphyseon* II, he observes that the unification of inhabited world with paradise perhaps *credatur* [is believed] to take place,[976] and that the unification of sensibles with intelligibles is possibly *in intellectu solummodo* [in intellect only].[977] Given that the recapitulation is a process which the saintly may perform even in the present world, he must understand its phases as possibly cognitive in character. However, Eriugena actually understands them as essentially cognitive in nature, since for him existent things are thoughts primarily of God and secondarily of man.[978] Indeed in his development of Maximus' doctrine in

Periphyseon IV, he argues not only that the human mind contains a *notio* [concept] of all intelligibles and sensibles, but that that concept is the *substantia* [substance] of those intelligibles and sensibles.[979] It is this to which the Bible refers in describing Adam's naming of all the animals.

That Maximus' recapitulation is a constituent part of the division of semantic properties is implied by Eriugena's assimilation of the fivefold division to his own fourfold division.[980] He argues that the two teachings only differ in that the former subdivides those sensibles which correspond to the latter's created and not creating nature ($\overline{b}_1$) into heaven and earth etc., but does not subdivide that not created nature equivalent to the latter's not created nature ($\overline{a}_2$) into creating and not created (b_1) and neither creating nor created ($\overline{b}_2$). The references to mediation and harmony are likewise to ideas elsewhere used in the theory of signification.[981] Finally, that Maximus' recapitulation is a principle of unifying the division of semantic properties emerges from his account of the fivefold division in the *Quaestiones ad Thalassium* quoted on one occasion by Eriugena.[982] According to this argument, the *anguli* = *gōniai* [angles] of the five towers built by Uzziah in Jerusalem represent the five unifications of created things in man — as though the Bible's narrative intimated depiction of created properties as the intersecting points of geometrical axes.

If Eriugena's discussions of *transitus* and *recapitulatio* therefore illustrate the theoretical perspective where what is signified by a syntagmatic chain is itself a signification, his comments on literal and spiritual exegesis reveal a theoretical viewpoint where what is mediately signified by a syntagmatic chain is itself a signification.[983] This material perhaps for the first time suggests an extended if not infinite horizon of semiosis.

One discussion occurs in the *Commentarius in Evangelium Iohannis* where Eriugena understands various details in the Gospel narrative as signifying not the mysteries of the Christian faith but the principles of exegesis themselves: for example, the untying of Jesus' sandal-strap becomes the signifier of interpretative distinction between the literal and spiritual senses of a text.[984] A more extensive development along similar lines occurs in his exegesis of the feeding of the five thousand where the number itself signifies the combination of the literal and spiritual meanings — since 5 is a number associated with sensation and 1,000 a perfect number —;[985] where the distribution of bread signifies the separation of the literal and spiritual meanings — ;[986] where the remnants of the bread gathered up into twelve baskets signify the spiritual meanings collected by holy exegetes — since 12 is a perfect number —;[987] and where the ascending of the mountain signifies the spiritual and the sitting in the grass the literal sense.[988] A comparable discussion occurs in the *Homelia in prologum Iohannis* where Eriugena understands not the literary contents of the Gospel narrative but the physical contents of the created world as signifying the principles of exegesis: so that earth, water, air, and aether become signifiers of the historical, moral, physical, and theological modes of interpretation.[989]

Excursus to Chapter 4

Excursus to section 4.2

Texts: A. Thierry of Chartres: *Heptateuchon,* prol.
 B. Bernard Silvestris: *In Martianum* 2, 1–5 + 22–55.
 C. Bernard Silvestris: *In Martianum* 3, 87–103.

Passages *A*, *B*, and *C* explore the central figurative meanings of Martianus Capella's treatise *De nuptiis Philologiae et Mercurii*, passages *B* and *C* being extracted from a formal commentary on that work written during the early twelfth century.

Al these texts interpret the marriage between Mercury and Philology as a figure of conjunction in its widest cosmological implications. This conjunction takes place in a general sense between the verbal and the rational — interpretation and understanding in *A*, speech and reason in *B* and *C* — and more specifically between the verbal and real arts — trivium and quadrivium in *A*, arts of speech and arts of reason in *B*. Moreover, this conjunction is an instance of concord: a fitting harmony or a massive harmony in *A*, a gift of the goddess Concordia who also confers the celestial harmony in *C*.

Passage *B* goes beyond the explicit pronouncements of Martianus' treatise to the greatest extent. Here, the writer takes pains to justify an interpretation of Philology as reason itself rather than love of reason, and to expand the sexual connotations of Mercury's and Philology's relationship.

A

The prologue of Thierry to the Heptateuchon begins. Marcus Varro was the first among the Romans to compile a volume of the seven liberal arts — something which the Greeks call a "Heptateuchon" —, Pliny following him, and then Martianus. These authors wrote their own material. However, we have joined together in a fitting harmony, as though forming the single body of a book, not our own discoveries but those of the men most learned in these arts; and we have united Trivium to Quadrivium as though in a marital compact for the propagation of a noble race of philosophers. Indeed, both Greek and Roman poets testify that Philology was joined to Mercury in a nuptial rite with an introit of all Hymenaeus' power, with the massive harmony of Apollo and the Muses, and with participation of these seven arts — as though the affair could not be conducted without them. And this is not an unreasonable idea. For since there are as the two primary instruments of philosophy understanding and its interpretation, and understanding illuminates the Quadrivium while the Trivium supplies its elegant, rational, and decorative interpretation; it is clear that a Heptateuchon is the one and only instrument of philosophy as a whole. Philosophy is the love of wisdom, and wisdom the complete comprehension of the truth in existing things which one attains not at all or insufficiently if one has not loved it. Therefore nobody is wise who is not a philosopher.

B

About to discuss the seven liberal arts of which four pertain to reason and three to speech, the philosopher prefaces this with a treatment of the conjunction of reason and speech. For conjunction precedes the teaching of these arts because it is necessary both to comprehend by reason and express what has been comprehended in speech... He calls speech "Mercury" as though "running in between" because speech runs in the middle between speaker and hearer thus: by revealing the thought of the speaker and forming a similar thought in the hearer. Others understand "Mercury" to symbolize "vehicle of merchandise", others "care of minds", and others "lord of merchants" on the grounds that men's minds are drawn to different things by speech and eager salesmen dispose of their wares by the same means. "Philology" is the Greek word for human reason. For just as Pythagoras is read to have employed the name of human wisdom with restraint because most men were abusing it and to have been unwilling to call it "Sophia" but rather "Philo-sophia": that is, "love of wisdom"; likewise, the Aristotelians invoked the name of their discipline with restraint by calling it "Peri-patetic": that is, "around truth" and not "in truth"; and likewise the philosopher Martianus also utters the name of our reason more cautiously by calling it "Philo-logia" rather than "Logos": that is, "love of reason" and not "reason" as such. He described the conjunction of these things as a "marriage". For a marriage is the conjunction of two things of the same nature but of different sexes made with hope, pleasure, and constancy. And these two, being human goods, are of the same nature but of different sexes. We discern such things here because speech is active and reason passive when speech expresses, according to its will, that which reason grasps. And Mercury engenders sons in Philology through the emission of semen when speech forms the sciences in our reason through the transference of teaching. So the one is expressed by a masculine and the other by a feminine name, since "speech" or "Mercury" is named as something male and "reason", "discernment", or "Philology" as a woman. These two are united not without hope: that is, without expectation of future offspring. Moreover, this bond has its own pleasure. For what greater pleasure is there for a man than if he perceives his speech vehemently resisting reason but reason as his lawfully pregnant wife truly filled with the teaching of speech as though with some male semen and producing as offspring the fruits of the sciences? This marriage also has its own constancy. For it is the condition of natural goods that, once they have come together, they can by no means easily be separated. So here we have the subject-matter of this volume: the conjunction of speech and reason.

C

"The commencement of the song". At the beginning of a work one usually takes the auspices, and so it became customary to employ the word "auspice" in place of "beginning" — we shall say what an auspice is in making the division of magic. The starting-point of this volume is the conjunction of speech and reason which is discussed before the liberal arts. The meaning is this: the fact that you, O Concord, bestow celestial harmony indicates that you can also confer the marriage of Mercury and Philology. This union, indeed, is the commencement of my song. Again, the context is: "you assent whom, as sacred bond, they declare" — that is whom, as marriage, they testify — "to be the god who sings at weddings". We say that any conjunction of two things of the same nature but of different sexes is a "bond" yet, because adulterous fornication has all these characteristics, "sacred": that is, legitimate is added. They are "sacred" because it is sacrilege to dissolve them: "For what God has joined, let no man separate." Hence, we also read elsewhere: "Are you bound to your wife? Do not seek dissolution." Moreover, the Lord reveals marriage to be sacred, since he deigned not only to attend a wedding but also to gladden those nuptials with his first miracle.

Excursus to section 4.4.

Texts:

A. Hugh of St. Victor: *In Hierarchiam coelestem* III. 969C–970B.
B. Alan of Lille: *Expositio Prosae de angelis*, pp. 200–201.
C. Alan of Lille: *Hierarchia*, pp. 224–225.

Of these three passages dealing with symbolic theory the first is a commentary on ps.-Dionysius which begins amidst the difficulties of understanding the latinized Greek grammar of Eriugena's translation. It explains that one reason for using symbols i.e. visible, corporeal, and shaped representations of invisible, incorporeal, and shapeless things is our proportionality. Proportionality is then defined on the one hand as the human status of corporeality etc. — in accordance with ps.-Dionysius' explicit statements — and on the other as human beings' similarity, agreement, and equality in that status — a notion derived rather from the grammatical theory concerning proportionality (= analogy). The text will continue by explaining that another reason for using symbols is the need to conceal the highest truths from those unworthy of them.

The second passage is an informal response to ps.-Dionysius who is nevertheless cited by name. Here, its author enumerates various senses of the word "symbol" among which one is isolated as particularly relevant: that of an utterance containing lower and higher levels of meaning. This interpretation is again in agreement with ps.-Dionysius' explicit statements, although the etymology — "syn" + "olon" = "together" + "whole" — is more typical of his non Greek-speaking commentator.

The third passage is another informal response to ps.-Dionysius who is not cited by name. The author here underlines one application of the word "proportionality": namely, to the angelic order. Given that proportionality implies the balance of a middle term between two extremes, while the angelic hierarchy is mediately poised between the divine and human orders, such proportionality may rightly be associated with those spiritual beings.

A

"For anyone would not say our proportionality is the one reason that forms are beautifully supplied of things lacking form and shapes of things lacking shape…" Contrary to the Latin usage but according to the idioms of the Greek language the writer has amassed conjunctions. Or if "that" is read as "why", the resulting meaning here is: For anyone, i.e. someone would not say there is as the one reason that proportionality of ours i.e. would not say there is as the only reason our proportionality why there are beautifully supplied i.e. fittingly from sacred Scripture forms of things lacking form and shapes of things lacking shape i.e. why in sacred Scripture forms and shapes are attributed to those celestial spirits which in their own nature have neither corporeal forms nor shapes. To repeat, for anyone would not say there is as the only reason our proportionality i.e. our status which is otherwise unable to achieve knowledge of invisible things and is unable to achieve it immediately: i.e. does not extend through intellect to invisible contemplations i.e. to contemplations of the invisible without some mediation. Our proportionality, indeed, also demands proper and connatural elevations i.e. to be elevated to knowledge and contemplation of the invisible through those things which are proper and connatural with it i.e. the visible and corporeal which as corporeal bring forward i.e. posit formations of the things lacking form i.e. the spiritual and supernatural speculations i.e. the speculations exceeding our nature and wholly incomprehensible to us except as demonstrated and suggested to us through those passible formations. By proportionality he means the human status, since proportionality is a property according to a rule and the agreement of many similar things in a unity. Thus, grammarians are accustomed to assign proportionality to words in accordance with the similarity of many things falling under a single property. And so the proportionality of human nature i.e. its status or property or agreement is the ability and knowledge which pertains to man and which man has received as his existence and capacity. The ability and knowledge to investigate celestial things also which is above our proportionality i.e. our agreement and equality has been received only where we are instructed through those things which are among us as visible and known to us. Therefore, this proportionality i.e. human status is the reason why sacred Scripture has posited visible signs for the education of human minds regarding the invisible...

B

After enumerating the functions of celestial spirits in general, a certain special function of theirs is next expressed when the words are added: "they categorize theological symbols". A symbol is literally speaking a gathering of some dinner-guests where each one contributes his own portion of the expenses. Hence it is called a symbol from "syn" i.e. together and "bolos" i.e. portion because each one contributes his own portion of the expenses. Metaphorically, an inventory of the articles forming the Christian faith like the "Quicumque vult" and the "Credo in Deum" is called a symbol, because the various portions or articles of the Christian faith are contained in it. So the aforesaid ranks have this special function: that, being themselves "divided by three times three" i.e. into nine orders, they "categorize" i.e. preach to us "through their separate functions" i.e. according to their assignment to individual functions. To categorize is the same thing as to preach — hence a categorical proposition is said to be predicative and the predicative is called a category. The "symbols" i.e. articles of the Christian faith are indeed "theological" symbols i.e. those in which a "logos" i.e. a discourse is made about "theos" i.e. about God, for "theos" in Greek is translated as God in Latin. And it is often through angelic intervention that what they should think about God is imparted to human minds. Alternatively, "symbols" may be understood as enigmatic utterances which display one meaning on the surface of the letter but keep within a loftier meaning for the understanding. For example, when it is read that the angels have fiery chariots or wings or things of this kind, the utterance is symbolic — hence Dionysius in his "Hierarchy" calls such utterances symbolic. Utterances of this kind are called symbols from "syn": that is, together and "olon": that is, a whole because a multiple knowledge is contained in these utterances, and because a literal understanding resounds on the surface of the letter while a tropological and anagogic understanding is enclosed within. Because angels have often spoken to orthodox Fathers like Daniel, John the Evangelist, and others of hidden celestial things by using symbolic utterances, they are said to "categorize theological symbols" for us. And because the writer has said that the celestial spirits are divided into nine orders, he has distinguished those same orders more clearly by assigning individual names to them and by suggesting their functions through the interpretations of those names...

C

A discussion of the celestial hierarchy follows. The celestial hierarchy is the balanced secondary power of the celestial spirits in a relation of similitude to the highest, having gradation, subject to differentiation, and allowing comparison; after the highest Trinity it is distinguished by a threefold division — according to adoption, participation, and ranking — in proceeding from the first but not receding from it, in being obedient to the first, and in turning towards the first. It is rightly called "balanced" because the angels proportionately possess gifts, functions, and powers. It is called "secondary" through its similitude to the highest, since the first similitude is in the Trinity and the second in the angels. It "has gradation" because there are grades and differences among the angels. Hence follow the words "subject to differentiation and allowing comparison" since one angel is greater than another; "after the highest Trinity distinguished by a threefold division" since the nine orders of angels are reducible to three hierarchies; "according to adoption" since the angelic nature is adopted through grace, "according to participation" since it participates in the Lord's goodness, and "according to ranking" since God, through his embellishment and disposition of the angelic nature with so many gifts, has the highest ranking; "proceeding from the first" because it has proceeded from God in creation, restoration, and conservation, "not receding from the first" either in space or dissimilarity because, wherever it is sent, an angel is confined beneath the Lord's immensity, "being obedient to the first" because all angels are administering spirits and serve God in all their functions, and "turning toward the first" because, whatever they do, they do in the sight of God.

Excursus to section 4.6.

Texts: A. Vitruvius: *De architectura* V, pr. 1 + 3–4.
        B. Macrobius: *In Somnium Scipionis* II. 3, 4–6.

Complex signifying relations where a syntagmatic chain has as its signified the paradigmatic sense of the same type of relation occur in two late antique texts. In the first, numbers govern the unfolding of a discourse which itself describes the metaphysical properties of number and in the second, opposition governs the unfolding of a discourse which itself describes the opposition of astronomical motions.

A

Those men, My Emperor, who have set forth the thoughts and precepts of their minds in more ample volumes, have added a considerable and exceptional authority to their writings. Moreover, even in our discipline the subject-matter might permit the authority contained in its precepts to be increased through amplifications. Yet this is not as useful as it is thought to be. For architecture is not written about as history or poetry is written. Histories through themselves engage their readers since they entertain various expectations of new information. And in poetry, the metres and feet of the songs, the elegant disposition of words and of thoughts among different characters, and the sound of the verses enticingly leads on the readers' minds without impediment to the final conclusion of the text. However, this cannot happen when writing about architecture… Furthermore, Pythagoras and those who belonged to his sect were pleased to write the precepts in their volumes according to cubic measures. They established 216 verses as the cube and believed that there should not be more than three of these in one composition. A cube is a body with squares on all sides and surfaces of equal dimension. When a cube is thrown, it maintains an unmoved stability on whatever side it rests, provided it is untouched — just like the dice which players cast onto the gaming-board. The Pythagoreans seem to have drawn this analogy from the fact that this number of verses — like a cube — produces an unmoved stability of memory in whatever sense it falls upon. Moreover, the Greek comic poets divided up the space of their plays through the interpolation of songs performed by the chorus. By making the parts with a cubic measurement, they bring respite with interruptions in the delivery of the authors' texts.

B

The Etruscans also understand the Muses as the song of the universe, and called them "Camenae" as though "Canenae" from "canere". It was therefore in confirmation of the heaven's song that the theologians incorporated musical sound into their rituals, the latter being usually performed on the lyre or cythara in some countries and on pipes or other musical instruments elsewhere. Moreover, in the hymns of the gods metres based on strophe and antistrophe were applied to the sung verses so that the forward motion of the astral sphere might be declared through the strophe, and the various backward motions of the planets through the antistrophe. From these two motions, the first hymn of nature addressed to God took its origin…

Part V: Translations and commentary

Chapter 5

The notion of concord in ancient and medieval philosophy

Chapter Five collects a number of passages explicitly treating the notion of concord. These have been arranged in terms of various isotopies.[990] 5.1 deals with concord among angels and saints, 5.2 with that of the spiritual world, 5.3 with that of the world soul, 5.4 with that of the elements in the world, 5.5 with concord among planets and stars, 5.6 with that of the celestial world, 5.7 with that of the human soul, and 5.8 with that of the elements in man. The passages are selected from authors of later antiquity — Pliny the Elder, Origen, Censorinus, Macrobius, Favonius Eulogius, and Martianus Capella —, from Carolingian writers — Eriugena, Remigius of Auxerre, and an Anonymous —, and from authors of the eleventh to twelfth centuries — Bovo of Corvey, Otloh of St. Emmeram, Adalbold of Utrecht, Honorius Augustodunensis, Hugh of St. Victor, William of Conches, Bernard Silvestris, and ps.-Hermes Trismegistus.

In these passages, a cluster of semantically-related Latin lexemes occur: 1ª *concordia*, 1ᵇ *concors*, 1ᶜ *concordare*, 1ᵈ *concorditer*, 2 *concentus*, 3ª *consonantia*, 3ᵇ *consonans/ consonus*, 3ᶜ *consonare*, 4ª *convenientia*, 4ᵇ *conveniens*, 4ᶜ *convenire*, 4ᵈ *convenienter*, 5 *consensus*, 6 *harmonia*, and 7 *symphonia* which I have translated using the English terms "concord", "consonant", "harmonize" etc. according to syntactic requirements.[991] It should be noted that in the Latin lexemes 1ᵃ⁻ᵈ, 2, 3ᵃ⁻ᶜ, 6, and 7 the semes connected with the encyclopaedia of "music" are normally actualized to the highest degree, whereas in the lexemes 4ᵃ⁻ᵈ and 5 these semes normally have a lesser degree of actualization which can however be converted to a greater degree of actualization by the surrounding context.

Yet the isotopy of concord itself must be understood not only by enumerating the various Latin lexemes but by observing their use. From such observation we discover two facts: A. That the isotopy connects a number of different usages, and B. that one usage parallels the modern semiotic "code".

A. *Concordia* and its cognates can designate:
1. Any logical relation or mathematical ratio i.e. involving 2 terms (5.1).
2. A combination of sameness and difference (5.2, 5.3).
3. Mathematical ratios based on the lowest integers i.e. 2:1, 3:1, 4:1, 3:2, 4:3 (5.1, 5.6).
4. Any logical relation or mathematical proportionality i.e. involving 3 terms (5.4, 5.8).
5. A structure i.e. group of 4 or more terms consisting of ratios (5.3, 5.5, 5.7).
6. A structure i.e. group of 4 or more terms consisting of numbers (5.3, 5.7).

These applications reveal a systematic organization of semantic properties:

a. Mathematical vs. dialectical. Axis of opposition determining 1 and 4 above.[992]
b. Number (1 term) vs. ratio (2 terms). Axis of opposition dividing 5 from 6 above.
c. Ratios based on the lowest integers (2:1, 3:1, 4:1, 3:2, 4:3) vs. ratios based on higher integers (5:4, etc.). Axis of opposition determining 3 above.
d. Structure (group of 4 or more terms) vs. non-structure (group of 3 or less terms). Axis of opposition dividing 1–4 from 5–6 above.
e. Ratio (2 terms) vs. proportionality (3 terms) vs. structure (4+terms). Axis of continuity dividing 1–3 from 4 and from 5–6 above.
f. Sameness vs. difference. Axis of equivalence determining 2 above.

B. Since *concordia* etc. frequently designate a group of ratios — see especially the passages in 5.5 — while the ratios are treated as signifiers — see especially the passages in 5.3 and 5.7 —, this usage parallels the modern semiotic "code". Such a code provides the means for correlating two systems which may be described as those of signifiers and signifieds or of expression and content respectively.[993] Moreover, the signifying or expressive system may comprise distinctive and meaningless units, or distinctive and meaningful units, or both distinctive and meaningless and distinctive and meaningful units. In this manner the *concordia* designating a group of signifying ratios — see also the passages in 5.1 — would parallel the international maritime flag code and the like, being a collection of distinctive but meaningless units.

5.1 Concord among angels and saints

Texts:

A. Otloh of St. Emmeram: *De tribus quaestionibus* 40, 116B–117A.
B. Otloh of St. Emmeram: *De tribus quaestionibus* 41, 118B–117D.
C. Otloh of St. Emmeram: *De tribus quaestionibus* 41, 118D–43, 120A.
D. Otloh of St. Emmeram: *De tribus quaestionibus* 45, 123B–D.

A first group of passages — drawn from Otloh of St. Emmeram — illustrates the application of concord to the angels and saints. The writer starts from a division of numbers into two classes: numbers in themselves (or dissonant numbers) and numbers in relation (or consonant numbers) (passages *B*, *C*). The second class is considered superior because Christ's incarnation involved the relation of divine to human (*C*, *D*). The writer next argues that the numbers in relation apply not only to sounds but to all ordered things (*C*, *D*). So illustrations of their application to spiritual beings are given: the ratio of 9:8 in the "equality" of angels and saints (*A*); the ratios of 9:8, 3:2, and 4:3 in the relative positions according to moral worth of different saints — higher pitch corresponds to greater and lower pitch to lesser merit (*D*) —; and the ratio of 2:1 in the single wisdom or charity of spiritual beings (*D*).

A

The number 8 also signifies perfection, but only that promised after the seven-day cycles of this life. But this is fitting enough. For just as the number 8 follows straight after the number 7 signifying rest, similarly one who rests in freedom from this life's wicked acts will merit the attainment of perfection in eternal blessedness. Hence, our Lord in the Gospel promised eight types of blessedness to his followers and thereby signified the perfection of eternal life... But now reaching the number 9 I shall also — so far as my limited understanding permits — describe its mystery. In that this number, as it seems to me, is surrounded by the greater perfection of the two numbers 8 and 10, so does it reflect the value of a superior mystery. For it signifies the angelic orders given that, as holy Scripture proclaims, there are nine orders of angels. Of these, some are called angels, but others archangels, and others principalities; some are called powers, some virtues, and some dominations; while some are called thrones, but many cherubim, and many seraphim. One should also observe how great a numerical consonance there is with this mystery, since all those who achieve the perfection of the number 8 become equal with the number 9: that is, the angelic order. The Lord witnesses this when he says in the Gospel: "Those who will be considered worthy of the future world and resurrection from the dead will neither be married nor marry. No more liable to death, they are equal to the angels and sons of God, being sons of the resurrection." The 9 is also venerated because, when every number multiplied by itself to produce another is like a parent while the number generated through that multiplication can be called the offspring, the 9 arises as offspring of that 3 fitting with it which signifies the holy Trinity. For if you say 3×3 — thereby forming the multiplication of a number by itself — the 9 is generated: from which one concludes that both the holy angels and those following the angelic life are fittingly called sons of God being sons of the holy Trinity…

B

… I should like to divide all numbers into two classes. One will consist of those so arranged by arithmetic that they are joined by no harmonious proportion but described only in relation to themselves: for example, 2, 5 and 7 or 3, 7 and 10 or any similarly dissonant group. The other will consist of those described according to music as relative to a consonance produced with another number: for example, 3, 4, 6, 8 and 12. In fact, of the numbers so arranged that middle compared to lowest produces the ratio of $4:3$, highest to middle that of $3:2$, and highest to lowest that of $2:1$ — these being specifically associated with harmonic consonance — I as one about to speak here of this consonance's mysteries should provide a graphic illustration (figure 13).

So great a power of mystery seems contained in the aforesaid division into these two classes, that even one most learned among the holy Fathers could scarcely disclose it fully…

C

Any knowledgeable person can appreciate the difficulty of comprehending all these things with mind or reason. But although I can explain none of them in a manner which befits, I may nevertheless present something modest: especially — and as a first task — what the two opposite numbers: namely, that which is described as in itself and that which pertains to consonance with another signify. Next I want to disclose the mystery of

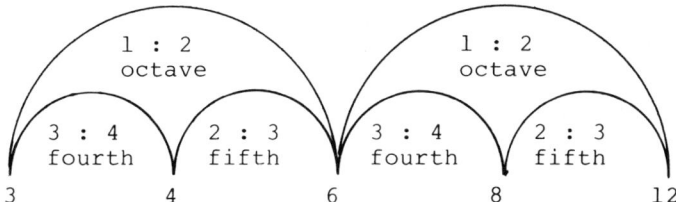

Figure 13. The consonant numbers.

that number subject to consonance alone, striving to demonstrate after a fashion in what great consonance everything both earthly and heavenly has been made by God, although man alone opposes it continually with his vices. (42) So all number which, pertaining only to itself, produces no consonance fittingly signifies the carnal man. For he esteems only what is pleasing to himself — the temporal, visible, and carnal — and nothing delights him except things suggested by his own concupiscence and will. Everything consonant or fitting to others displeases him, and he believes himself born for the sole purpose of serving his own desires to the utmost. He imitates that rich man who, as narrated in the Gospel, lives only for himself so much that he does not bother to give crumbs falling from his table to the other needy man who begs them. But the number which is referred to another signifies the spiritual man, since anyone spiritual counts other men's losses or gains as his own, conforming and adapting himself to the habits of others. He continually reflects on the words: "Bear one another's burdens" and "Let no man seek what is his" alone "but what is another's." Hence the apostle Paul, wishing to benefit not only himself but others also said: "I was made all things to all men, so that I might gain them all." Furthermore, our Lord and Saviour, since he deigned to be incarnated and suffer not for himself but for our salvation, was willing to be relative. (43) Having made these brief opening remarks about the contrast of the two classes mentioned, I now wish — as one who has at times played musical instruments and willingly heard the sweetness of all kinds of melody — to play in spiritual and intellectual harmony as much as the Lord allows. I shall explain what great sweetness of mystical consonance may be understood in all those things described earlier. But before you hear something of this consonance, you must grasp more fully what consonance itself is. Since consonance is produced not only among sounds joined by the relative proportion of numbers but among all sorts of things ordered well, while everything subsisting in an ordered manner is surely produced as agreeing and fitting, one can apparently give as definition of this consonance "the agreement of dissimilar things". Similarly, if there is consonance in any type of agreement, and all creatures however dissimilar among themselves are in agreement through God's ordering, then consonance may be understood in every creature.

D

... and I believe everything I have stated about the consonances of this life and every instrument ever used in the art of music to represent great proofs of the celestial harmony. For just as various differences of pitch on the organ or monochord — these being the primary elements in such an art — irrespective of the manner in which they precede or follow one another are brought to unity in the octave, so I believe it occurs in the celestial kingdom as follows: There, although through differing merits one saint is as if to another in the ratio of $9:8$ or the whole tone, while another is related to another in that of $3:2$ or the fifth, and another to another in that of 4:3 or the fourth; nevertheless all the saints have a single wisdom and sound in unity through charity's concord as if through an octave. There, the saints' praise and action in goodness is both with respect to the consonances of God with man — since God was made man — or of all ages or elements or things, and with regard to their own rewards of happiness, akin to some everlasting harmony. This contains various differences in holiness corresponding to various modes of different voices, and also has all the most saintly assigned to higher pitches and the less saintly to the lower.

5.2 Concord in the spiritual world

Texts: A. Origen: *De principiis* I. 6. 3, 202. 122–131.
B. Origen: *De principiis* II. 1. 1, 236. 22–II. 1. 3, 238. 64.
C. Origen: *De principiis* II. 9. 1, 352. 16–354. 30.
D. Origen: *De principiis* II. 9. 4, 358. 107–360. 116.
E. Origen: *De principiis* II. 9. 6, 364. 183–366. 204.
F. Origen: *De principiis* II. 10. 5, 386. 174–185.

Passages in Origen's *De principiis* explore the concordant character of the spiritual world. Passages *C* and *D* argue that number, measure, and justice pervade all things created by God. Three phases in the cosmic history of rational substances are described in passage *B*: the original concord in which they were created by God, the consonance retained despite the diversification associated with their acts of will, and the final harmony to which they are recalled. Likewise, three phases are mentioned in passage *E*: the initial equality or similarity in which they were fashioned by the creator, the diversity concomitant with their lapses into sin, and the final consonance to which they are recalled. Passages *A* and *F* discuss the nature of the last phase. This is either the unity and harmony of salvation or else the disruption yet consolidation of harmony in punishment through eternal fire.

A

But whether any of those orders acting under the devil's rule and complying with his wickedness could sometime in future ages turn to goodness in accordance with their inherent power of free will; or whether an enduring and hardened wickedness will turn from habit into a kind of nature, you the reader must judge. That is whether, neither in the visible and temporal ages nor in the invisible and eternal ones, this portion of creation will be utterly and totally distinct from that final unity and harmony.

B

If indeed this argument seems cogent, what cause of such great diversity in the world shall we assume other than a diversity and variety in motions and declines among those who lapsed from that original unity and concord in which God first created them? Stirred and distracted from that state of goodness, and then agitated by different motions and desires of their souls, they brought down that single and undivided goodness of their nature into varying intellectual qualities according to their diversity and inclination. Yet God who, through the ineffable art of his wisdom, transforms and restores all things — in whatever form they occur — to a useful purpose and the common advantage of all, recalls these same creatures so different among themselves in variety of soul to a single harmony of activity and endeavour. This in order that they might complete the plenitude and perfection of a single world — albeit with different motions of souls — and that the variety of intellects itself might tend to a single end of perfection. For there is a unitary power which binds and contains the entire diversity of the world, directing various motions to a single task lest such an immense work as the world be dissolved by divisions among souls. And for this reason, we think that God the father of the universe has so arranged everything, for the salvation of all his creatures through the ineffable plan of his Word and wisdom, that each individual spirit or soul — or whatever the rational substance may be called — should not be forcibly compelled against its free will to any object other than that to which its own intellect's motion directs. In this way, the power of free will would appear to be removed from them — thereby producing a change in the very quality of their natures. God has also arranged that the different motions of their intentions should combine suitably and usefully into the consonance of a single world. While some rational substances need assistance, others can give it, while yet others establish contests and struggles for those making progress. The latter's diligence will be considered more proven and their position in a rank recovered after victory will be held more securely having been gained through difficulties and tribulation. So, although it is arranged in different functions, the state of the whole world should not be understood as something dissonant and conflicting with itself. But just as our single body is composed of many members and is held together by a single soul, so — as I believe — should the entire world be thought like some immense and fearsome animal sustained through God's power and reason as if by a single soul...

C

Moreover, as Scripture says that God created all things in number and measure, so will number rightly be applied to rational creatures or intellects since they are as many as can be arranged, ruled, and contained by God's providence. Measure will consequently be linked with corporeal matter which we should believe created by God in a quantity he knew to be sufficient for ordering the world. So these things are what should be considered as created by God in the beginning: that is, before all else. We should also think these facts indicated by the beginning which Moses cryptically introduces when he says: "In the beginning God made heaven and earth." For this is certainly not a reference to the firmament nor the dry land but to that heaven and earth from which the heaven and earth which we see afterwards took their names.

D

So because Christ — as he is Word and wisdom — is also justice, it will undoubtedly follow that those things made in the Word and wisdom should also be described as made in that justice which is Christ. Therefore, we should see that there is nothing unjust or fortuitous among those things which were made, and we should teach that everything is as the principle of equity and justice demands. But how such a great variety and diversity of things may be understood as most just and most equitable cannot, I am certain, be explained by human intelligence and discourse unless...

E

And when "in the beginning" he created those things which he wished to create: that is, the rational natures, he had no other reason for creating them than himself: that is, his goodness. Since he was himself the cause of those things to be created, and in him there was neither any variation nor mutability nor incapacity, he created all his creatures equal and similar. There was indeed no cause of variety or diversity in him but, since the rational creatures themselves — as we have frequently shown and will again in the appropriate place — were endowed with a power of free will, this freedom of will either stimulated each one to progress through imitation of God or allured it towards decline through negligence. And this, as we have already said, was the cause of diversity among rational creatures, a cause taking its origin not from the Creator's will or judgement but from an individual's free choice. Yet God, to whom it now seemed just to arrange his creature according to its merit, gathered the diversities of intellects into the consonance of a single world in order to furnish as it were a single house, in which not only gold and silver but also wooden and earthen vessels had to be present with some for honour and others and dishonour, using these diverse vessels or souls or intellects.

F

But I think that another type of punishment may also be understood here. Just as we feel the body's limbs, when loosened and torn from their interconnections, producing the torment of an immense pain; so must the soul, when found outside order, connection, or that harmony in which God created it for good action and useful thought — being not consonant with itself through its rational motions' interconnections —, be thought to sustain the punishment and torment of its own separation within itself and feel the penalty of its inconstancy and disorder. But when this dissolution and dismemberment of the soul has been tested by means of the fire applied, it will undoubtedly be consolidated into a firmer connection and renewal within itself.

5.3 Concord in the world soul

Texts:

A. William of Conches: *Glosae super Boethium* 2, pp. 75–76.
B. Macrobius: *Commentarius in Somnium Scipionis* I. 6. 2–5 + 45–47.
C. William of Conches: *Glosae super Macrobium* 2A, pp. 144–147.
D. William of Conches: *Glosae super Macrobium* 2B, pp. 149–157.
E. William of Conches: *Glosae super Macrobium* 6B^2, pp. 241–248.
F. Macrobius: *Commentarius in Somnium Scipionis* II. 2. 14–18.
G. William of Conches: *Glosae super Macrobium* 9AB, pp. 256–260.
H. William of Conches: *Glosae super Platonem* 71, pp. 144–146 + 74, pp. 148-149.
I. William of Conches: *Glosae super Platonem* 77, pp. 153–154 + 78, pp. 155-156.
J. William of Conches: *Glosae super Platonem* 80, p. 158 + 82, p. 162.

These passages from Macrobius and William of Conches associate the world soul with concord through its numerical composition. Speaking both metaphorically and literally, the authors outline two basic arguments. First, the world soul which is possibly equivalent to the Holy Spirit corresponds to concord (*A*, *E*, *H*) because it is present to bodies proportionately (*E*, *H*) — a feature associated with its being identical according to its substance but different according to its activities in all physical things —; and because it is present to bodies consonant with one another in their properties (*A*). Secondly, the world soul corresponds to concord because it is described through an "integument" i.e. simile as composed of numbers (*C*, *D*, *F*, *G*, *I*).

According to Macrobius (*B*, *F*), soul is fashioned from a set of numbers — representing quantities of psychic substance — which can be illustrated with the diagram:

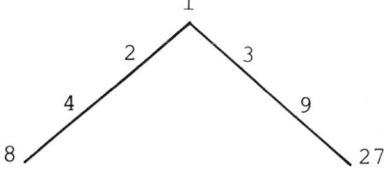

Figure 14. Numbers and psychic substance (first series)

In response to this, William argues that the numerical composition is intended to suggest the perfection of soul since the linear numbers 2 and 3 designate soul's ability to move bodies in length, the plane numbers 4 and 9 its ability to move them in breadth, and the solid numbers 8 and 27 its ability to move them in depth while the odd numbers indicate its ability to move celestial things and the even numbers its ability to move terrestrial things. William also argues that the numerical composition is intended to signify the soul's concordant movement of all things since between 2 and 1 is the ratio producing the octave, between 3 and 1 that producing the octave and a fifth, between 4 and 1 and between 8 and 2 that producing the double octave, between 3 and 2 that producing the fifth, between 4 and 3 that producing the fourth, and between 9 and 8 that producing the tone. Moreover, the ratio of 2:1 contains the ratios of 3:2 and 4:3 and the ratio of 3:1 those of 2:1 and 3:2. Finally, between 1 and 2 when multiplied by 6 to make 6 and 12 the harmonic and arithmetical means of 8 and 9 can be inserted, thereby leading to a series 6, 8, 9, 12 within which all the ratios producing consonances can be found (*J*). This last point implies an expanded diagram.

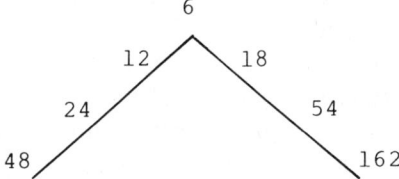

Figure 15. Numbers and psychic substance (second series)

A

The world soul is a natural force through which are enabled some things only to move, some to grow, some to sense, and some to discern. Yet there is a question what this force is. In my opinion, this natural force is the Holy Spirit: namely, the divine and beneficent concord which is that from which all things derive their being, motion, growth, sensation, life, and discernment. It is well described as natural force because all things grow and flourish through divine love. It is well described as the world soul because all things existing in the world live and derive life from the divine love and charity alone. Having seen what the world soul is, we should examine its properties in association with body. These are as follows: sensitivity, vitality, and reasoning. For it renders certain bodies vital and makes them grow — as in the case of plants and trees; it makes certain bodies sense — as with dumb animals; it makes certain bodies discern — as in the case of men. It remains one single soul, but does not exercise the same power in all these cases, since the sluggishness and nature of bodies takes its toll. Hence, Virgil writes: "To the extent that no harmful bodies delay"... We should now comment word by word: "You resolve through consonant members" since you distribute the soul in its power through members and among bodies which are called members — that is, parts — of the world. "Consonant" or fitting in terms of its properties, since the divine love confers on all things what is fitting to them. "Connecting the soul" or joining it to bodies themselves. "Mediate" or communal, since nothing exists or could exist without the divine love and will.

B

This is why Plato's "Timaeus" recalls that the God who fashioned the world soul interwove its parts from even and odd numbers — namely, 2 and 3 — so that from 2 to 8 and from 3 to 27 an alternating derivation might be established. For these are the first cubes arising on either side: among the even numbers 2×2, which are 4, produce a plane; $2 \times 2 \times 2$, which are 8, make a solid body; among odd numbers 3×3, which are 9, produce a plane: $3 \times 3 \times 3$ or 3×9, which are 27, similarly make the first cube on the other side. So we are given to understand that these two numbers — I mean 8 and 7... have alone been judged suitable for producing the world soul, for there can be nothing more perfect than this after the Creator. And something else should be noted. In asserting the general status of all numbers earlier, I showed that they are prior to the plane, its lines, and all bodies. Further, my ensuing discussion concluded that numbers, from which the most lofty account of the "Timaeus" — a witness and confidant of Nature herself — showed the world soul to be woven, were even prior to the latter. This is why learned men have not hesitated to proclaim soul as a number moving itself... The number 7... for the world soul was generated through this number first of all, as Plato's "Timaeus" taught. The number 1 was placed at the apex, and from this sets of three numbers flowed down on both sides: here the even and there the odd. In other words, after 1 came 2, then 4, and then 8 on one side; and 3, then 9, and then 27 on the other, the interweaving of these numbers producing the generation of soul at the Creator's behest. Given that the foundation of the world soul is constituted by seven terms, the not insignificant power of this number is hereby demonstrated.

C

Thus Plato, in his usual manner of speaking about the world soul, shifts to an integument... And so we should consider the truth and essence of this integument. Through the shape pointed at the top, Plato wished to indicate the indivisibility of soul, since soul is indivisible in its essence. Yet it is divisible through its powers, and so the figure is extended sideways to designate soul's divisibility through those powers. Similarly, through the number 1 placed at the top is indicated the soul's undivided essence. But since soul moves body in length, breadth, and depth, he placed even numbers along one side: namely certain linear numbers — for example 2 — to designate soul's motion in length, plane numbers to designate its motion in breadth, and solid numbers to designate its motion in depth... Likewise by placing odd numbers along the other side — some linear, some plane, and some solid — he designated the same motions of soul. If someone asks why he did not employ just even or odd numbers, given that he could have indicated all this with even or odd numbers alone, we reply that his recourse to both types was not without purpose. Through even numbers he indicated that soul moves terrestrial things which are dissoluble, and through odd numbers that it also moves the celestial and indissoluble... "And something else should be noted." Just as the greatest fulness of numbers was shown earlier by saying that numbers are prior to plane and lines, so does Macrobius imply by his statements a great fulness on the part of numbers owing to their priority to the world soul... "This is why" since number is more worthy than soul and soul is composed from it...

D

He says that God created the world soul thus from numbers, because he placed the number 1 first and after that the even numbers along one side and the odd numbers along the other... And since he here makes reference to this composition of soul, we should therefore briefly say something on the topic sufficient for understanding this chapter. Indeed Plato observed that bodies live and move but that, since they are naturally sluggish, they cannot have life or motion through their own nature. He therefore proposed that there exists in them some communal spirit in conjunction with which they acquire vitality and motion. Since this spirit exercises a certain power in different parts of the world, he called it "the world soul". Furthermore, his custom was to express truth in figurative language and so, in order to reveal the world soul's suitability for moving all substances — be they the same or different in nature — with some kind of motion, he said that it consisted of every substance and every nature... And there is another reason why Macrobius said that soul was constituted from these numbers. It was constituted from numbers so that the perfection of soul itself might be designated through such numbers than which nothing more perfect can be found after God; it was constituted from these numbers because among them are found the ratios which can produce concord in things. So he also notes here that soul is concordantly structured and moves all things concordantly... "And something else should be noted." Earlier Macrobius said that number was prior to the boundaries of bodies, but now he shows that the world soul consists of numbers. Anything which constitutes is prior to that which is constituted, and so number is prior to soul itself. So he notes the status of soul. "Prior to soul" not in time but in status...

E

Solve this problem by saying that Plato spoke in an integument when he declared that soul was a creature, understanding by this simply that it penetrated all things made according to number. But if he spoke openly, he was making these remarks about that certain spirit established proportionately in order to vivify bodies more effectively which Augustine mentions in the passage of his commentary on Genesis where he says: "The Spirit of God was borne above the waters." Augustine says that these words could have referred to three kinds of spirit: either that air which is like a breeze or breath borne along the surface of earth or water; or that certain spirit which, although corporeal, is more stable than any aetherial body and by passing through vivifies all the elements in their combination and recombination...; or that spirit which we venerate in the Trinity... "Minds". Macrobius refers to the plural so that, although there is also one reason as there is one world soul, he could demonstrate that every body is not equally suitable to exercise reason. The world soul is present in all things in the same proportion, although in a given body like a stone it is not active... One asks why Plato referred to a world soul and also maintained that human and individual souls were born from its remnants? ...Plato did not give two opinions in his own person but alludes to the fact that some maintained the existence of individual souls but others a single great soul — which penetrated all things — or world soul. By the latter he was referring to none other than the Spirit of God which is as a whole everywhere just as the soul is thus in individual parts; or else to that subtle corporeal spirit...

F

Plato's "Timaeus", expressing the divine plan in the fashioning of the world soul, says that soul was interwoven through those numbers which produce the cube or perfection of solidity as being both even and odd. He did not mean that this soul had some corporeality. Rather, it was constructed from solid numbers so that it might penetrate the universe with animation and fill the world's solid body. Now let us come to Plato's own words... Some have taken these words of Plato to mean... This fabrication of soul proceeded so that it should be born from even and odd or male and female numbers since it was to give birth to all things, and it should proceed up to the solidity of each type of number since it was to penetrate the world as though a solid. And then it had to be composed of those numbers which alone embody joining proportion, since it was itself to provide joining concord to the entire world...

G

"He did not mean that." He shows the reason why Plato viewed soul as interwoven through these numbers. This was not to prove it a solid body but to signify, by the linear, plane, and solid numbers placed there, that the world soul moves in length, depth, and breadth. "The universe": that is, the world. It is called the universe for the same reason that it is called Pan or the all. Hence, it is also imagined in myths that this world has a fawn-skin or multi-colored hide around its neck because of the variegation of different stars in the world's upper part or the firmament, a reddish face because of the fire in the world's face or its superior and higher part, shaggy legs because of the woods, goat-like or horny feet because of the earth's solidity, a pipe fashioned from seven reeds because of the seven planets' harmony, and a sheep-hook or shepherd's crook because of time's circularity. Pan is said to have loved the nymph Syrinx or concord, since as world he was made so concordantly and proportionately... "And then of those numbers". He appends another reason why Plato interwove soul from these numbers: namely, because musical consonance is born from such numbers. So, in order to show that soul moves all things proportionately and concordantly, he said that those numbers which produce musical consonances are in the fabric of soul.

H

The world soul is a certain spirit implanted in things which confers on them motion and life. It is everywhere whole and complete, although it does not operate equally, as indicated by Virgil's words: "to the extent that no harmful bodies delay". Some maintain that this spirit is the Holy Spirit — a notion which I neither deny nor affirm... "In the middle". That is, in the communal, since the middle is often interpreted as the communal. For one and the same world soul is wholly in the planets — where it produces motion —, in plants and trees — producing vitality —, in dumb animals — producing sense —, and in man producing reason. It thus operates in individual things according to the nature of each one, existing in them as a whole but not exercising all its powers... Since God wished the world to be an intelligent animal, and it could not have been intelligent without a soul, he therefore contrived a soul. It was right that he said "contrived" rather than "created" according to the view that this soul is the Holy Spirit, since the Holy Spirit is neither made nor created nor begotten by God but proceeds...

I

After showing from what components the world soul was contrived, he turns to the manner of contrivance while remaining within the integument. The essentials of this theory are... He therefore set down numbers to suggest the perfection of soul, for there is nothing after God — as I have stated at the beginning of this work — so perfect as the perfect number. This type of number he especially set down... So there is in soul's composition the number 1 to signify the indivisibility of psychic essence through its indivisibility, the numbers 2 and 3 which are linear to show soul's power of moving body in length, the numbers 4 and 9 which are plane to show its power of moving in breadth, and the numbers 8 and 27 which are solid because of its power of moving in depth. But someone will say that linear, plane, and solid numbers among either the even or the odd alone would suffice to designate this. To this I reply that some bodies are dissoluble and some indissoluble, and that even numbers — capable of division into two equal parts — correspond to the dissoluble while odd numbers — not capable of division into two equal parts — correspond to the indissoluble. Hence Virgil's statement: "God rejoices in the odd number." So, in order to indicate that one and the same soul could move dissoluble and indissoluble bodies in length, breadth, and depth, he placed linear, plane, and solid numbers among both the even and the odd in its composition. There is another reason why he set down these numbers, for among them are found the ratios which produce every consonance. Along one side, is the double ratio from which the octave comes and along the other the triple from which the octave-and-fifth derives. Between 4 and 1 and between 8 and 2 is the quadruple ratio from which the double octave arises. Between 3 and 2 is the sesquialter ratio from which the fifth comes, and between 4 and 3 the sesquiterce from which the fourth derives. Between 9 and 8 is the sesquioctave ratio from which the tone arises. So, in order to signify that soul moves body concordantly, he placed concordant numbers in its composition...

J

Still holding to his integument, Plato says that because the intervals — after the division of soul's substance into parts double along one side and triple along the other — stood open and wide, God filled out each one with two means. In this integument, Plato designates not a power of soul but the properties of double and triple ratios which he has mentioned, for within the double are always contained the two ratios of sesquialter and sesquiterce and within the triple the two ratios of double and sesquialter. Since we cannot indicate this with the first figure — there being nothing between 2 and 1 — let us change this into a figure with 6 at the top and underneath that three doublings of that number: namely, 12, 24, 48, with three triplings of the same number along the other side: namely 18, 54, 162... And we should note that between 6 and 12 all proportionalities are revealed in the aforesaid manner, and hence the greatest harmony. So the latter is justifiably placed in the composition of a soul which is to provide concord to bodies...

5.4 Concord of the elements in the world

Texts: A. Bovo of Corvey: *In Boethii Consolationem* 8, p. 387–11, p. 389.
B. Bernard Silvestris: *Cosmographia* I. 1. 18–22.
C. Bernard Silvestris: *Cosmographia* I. 2. 7–10.
D. Bernard Silvestris: *Cosmographia* II. 1. 2.
E. Bernard Silvestris: *Cosmographia* II. 2. 7–16.
F. ps.-Hermes Trismegistus: *De sex principiis* 109–112.
G. ps.-Hermes Trismegistus: *De sex principiis* 124–132.
H. ps.-Hermes Trismegistus: *De sex principiis* 180–188.

This section consists of passages dealing with the concord of elements in the world. Here, concord is envisaged either between their physical qualities or between their spatial positions, the latter being determined either concentrically or radially. The reference to concord is usually marked by the occurrence of terms like "mediation", "proportion", and "harmony".

Passage *A* establishes the analogy between mathematical mediation — e.g. of 2 and 3 between 1 and 4 — and physical mediation — of water and air between earth and fire — on which the notion of elemental concord is based. The four elements are presented in terms of their qualities where one is dry and cold, another wet and cold, another wet and hot, and another dry and hot. Water is said to be the mediator between earth and air by sharing cold with the former and wetness with the latter, and air the mediator between water and fire by sharing wetness with the former and hotness with the latter, the interrelation being termed a harmony. The physical elements are also presented in terms of their qualities when arranged in a series between heaviest or densest and lightest or rarest. Here, the difference in heaviness or density between earth and water is said to be proportionate to the difference between water and air, and the difference in heaviness or density between water and air to be proportionate to the difference between air and fire. Finally, the four elements are presented in terms of their concentric positions when arranged in a sequence between lowest i.e. innermost and highest i.e. outermost.

In passages *B*, *C*, *D*, and *E* matter is contrasted with the elements as the discordant with that exhibiting mediation, proportion, and harmony. In passage *C*, the four elements are presented in terms of their qualities and the mediation or proportion between qualities; and in terms of their concentric positions.

In passage *F*, the four elements are presented in terms of their qualities of dry, cold, wet, and hot and the harmony between qualities, being associated with the twelve zodiac signs. Passage *G* further associates them with the seven planets. In passage *H*, the four elements are presented in terms of their qualities and the harmony between qualities; and in terms of their radial positions (see figure 16).

A

"You bind the elements with numbers, so that the cold may agree with the flaming and the dry with the fluid." We frequently discover in Latin authors how much the Greek philosophers and that most excellent of them Plato in his "Timaeus" discoursed upon the power of numbers and that harmony of elements divinely produced through them which is indeed the construction of the entire universe. Such authors reflected on the discourses derived from these sources, thinking that this contributed greatly to the progress of learning. From among them, I have decided to insert here this one passage as sufficient for the present exposition. Ambrosius Macrobius, who outstandingly commented on the dream of Scipio described in two books by Cicero, writes as follows in his first volume: "We know through Plato — that is, through the secret teaching of truth itself — that those things to which an interposed mean provides the firmness of binding are joined among themselves with a strong bond. But when that mean itself is doubled, the things constituting the extremes are bound not only firmly but even indissolubly. So the number 3 is the first to which accrues reception of a mean between two extremes capable of binding it. The number 4 is the first of all the numbers to obtain two means. Deriving the means from this number, the God who is the artificer and creator of the world's substance joined the elements among themselves with an indissoluble bond, as affirmed in Plato's 'Timaeus'. In no other way could things so opposed to one another, conflicting, and rejecting community of nature be blended — I refer to earth and fire — except by being joined through the

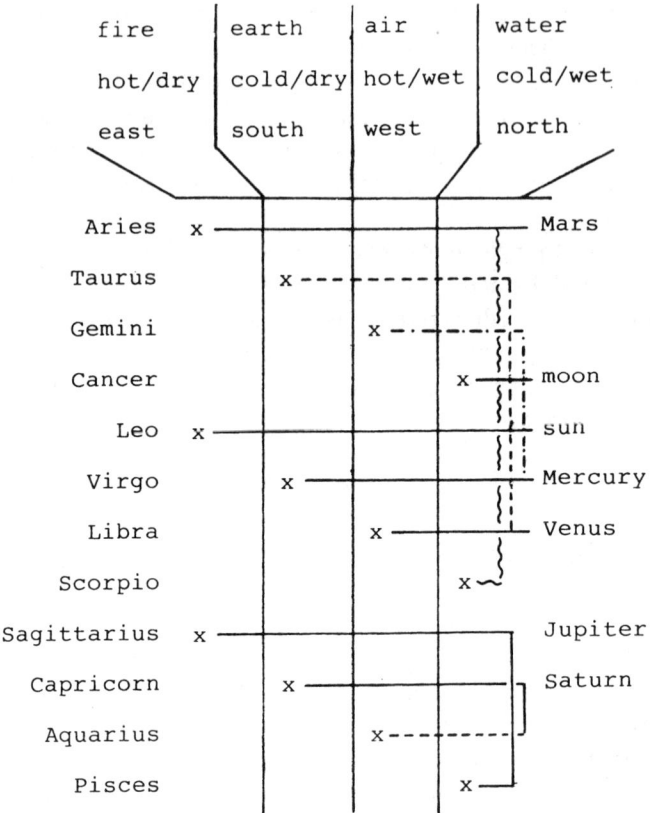

Figure 16. Elemental qualities and zodiac signs

two mediating connections of air and water." It is clear from these words of Macrobius, unless I am mistaken, what "you bind the elements with numbers" means. (9) The subsequent words: "so that the cold may agree with the flaming and the dry with the fluid" can easily be understood, for by that same number through which the elements themselves subsist do the differentiating properties of the selfsame elements. There are four of the latter: the cold, the hot, the dry, and the wet which by coming together in pairs to form individual elements produce a certain fitting connectedness even among things seemingly contrary. To illustrate by beginning with the lowest element: — earth's nature is dry and cold while air by being wet and hot is contrary to it. As mediator between these is placed water which is cold and wet and therefore connected with earth by cold and with air by wetness. Similarly, because the cold and wet nature of water conflicts with fire which is hot and dry, air is interposed between them and joined to water by the wet and to fire by the hot. Moreover, just as fire is demarcated from earth by the hot, so is it concordant with it in the dry. Therefore all the elements together with their differentiating properties are varied and arranged by a definite law of numbers since, through the concordance of the contrary and the alliance of the conflicting, they are joined and connected to one another in an indissoluble bond... (10) And one should carefully note the subsequent words: "lest fire too pure should fly aloft and earth sink down overwhelmed by weight" for, just as earth and fire are the elements most separated from one another in spatial position whereby earth is the lowest and fire the highest — indeed fire's natural place is in the aether which is agreed to be of fiery nature and which every flame rising upwards is also observed to seek — in the same manner are they most separated by certain differentiating properties other than those mentioned above: namely, lightness and heaviness, rarity and density. Of these elements fire is the rarest and lightest, while earth is known to have more density and heaviness than the others. So also, lest such great diversity should totally separate fire and earth in irreconcilable conflict, a double mediation has been supplied which may connect the extremes with an indissoluble bond as shown above. This bond is water and air which, blended through a certain fitting participation in each of these contraries, reconciles the lightness of fire with the heaviness of earth. For each of the mediators shares some lightness with fire and some heaviness with earth, although air is closer to fire in its lightness while water more approaches the earthly heaviness. (11) But as much difference because of density and heaviness as there is between water and air, so much is there between air and fire. Again, as much difference because of rarity and lightness as there is between air and water, so much is there also between earth and water. Likewise, as much difference because of density and heaviness as there is between earth and water, so much is there between water and air. And as much difference as there is between water and air, so much is there between air and fire. Not only are neighbouring and compatible elements similar, but the same equality is preserved in alternate steps since, just as earth is to air, so is water to fire. And wherever you begin the sequence, you will find the same joining proportion through which they are associated among themselves in equality of diversity. And this is why he says: "lest fire too pure..."

B

Inflexible Silva, the formless chaos, the obstinate coalescence, the variegated likeness of substance, the mass dissonant with itself, yearns in her turbulence for tempering, in her crudity for form, in her roughness for refinement. Longing to emerge from her ancient commotion, she demands the creative numbers and musical bonds...

C

So divine Providence, to apply the needed remedy to this situation, looked around herself, compared her sensations with her thought, and called forth her intelligence. Since a discordant union, a dissonant mass, and a yoking of the hostile seemed thus established as foundations, she provided for the mixed with separation, for the confused with order, and for the unformed with refinement. She imposed laws and curbed licence. Despite their crudeness, she produced equilibrium among the undisciplined and recalcitrant materials in their qualities. She connected them through mediators, and bound them with numbers. So after insertion of conciliating amity's bonds — according to the innermost deliberations of Providence — the roughness of Silva changed its hardness to pliability and reduced its inborn conflicts to harmony... When each element had taken up that residence to which it was borne most readily in harmony with its material, earth stood at rest, fire sprang forth, and air and water took the middle position. That tie and mediating connection was interposed by whose peaceful gift the elements bordering one another assumed the proportions of amity and compliance. Fire, the more glowing and lighter body, might perhaps have disrupted the joining of the work undertaken, had not water and air prevented this through their fraternal alliance and pledged cooperation. The dry stood opposed to the wet, and the heavy shackled the light. Earth bursts into flower from its natural aridity through the water nearby, and sustains itself through the breathing of air, lest it should descend below its lawful boundary weighed down by bodily substances. The differences of the various kinds of body were in this way forbidden to introduce difference into that work, in order that the differences might come into agreement. And so the contentious and discordant multitude, as when combatants have laid down their arms, entered into peaceful unity.

D

I shall not mention with what great turmoil Silva's roughness responded to my handling, nor what efforts I exerted against her furious recalcitrance until it grew accustomed to the artificer's hands. I shall not mention with what implement I scraped away the rust from the ancient elements and forged their essences anew with the splendour which befitted them. I shall not mention how a sacred embrace made allies of disparate genera, and how the mediation born there brought unequal powers into balance. I shall not mention how forms supervened on substances and how life arose on the earth, in the ocean, in the air, and in heaven's vault.

E

I count it as my glory and renown, O Nature, that I have refined coarse materials so well. I have introduced forms into things and bound the elements with a number producing harmonious trust. I have given law to the stars and ordered the planets to run a perpetual and invariant course. I have restrained the sea with boundaries. Lest it should fall, the earth sits fixed by its weight in the centre. I have decreed that etherial heat should produce plants, and that moisture should nourish what the etherial heat has brought to birth...

F

Note that Aries, Leo, and Sagittarius are fiery signs; Taurus, Virgo, and Capricorn earthy; Gemini, Libra, and Aquarius airy; and Cancer, Scorpio, and Pisces watery. But the fiery and airy signs are hot, masculine, and diurnal; the earthy and watery cold, feminine, and nocturnal. The earthy and watery, and the airy and fiery groups are discordant among themselves, although the watery harmonizes with the earthy and the airy with the fiery. Moreover, stars of the signs which are airy and fiery are bad, and stars which are earthy and watery good...

G

All the planets are borne through these signs, not that they are in them but that they are borne under them. And in alignment with them, Saturn is higher and slower in his course, being cold and dry in nature, and of an iron colour. This is because his house i.e. Capricorn is shown to be melancholic in nature — It is read that this sign harmonizes with him in nature and that he therefore desires it more. His accidental house is Aquarius, by whose quality the heavy quality of Saturn is sometimes tempered. Jupiter follows, being hot and wet, and of an amber colour. This is established through the natural harmony between his houses: that is Sagittarius a hot sign and Pisces a wet sign. Mars is hot and dry, and of a copper colour. His natural house is Aries, a hot and dry sign, and his accidental sign Scorpio, a cold and wet one. But the sun, following in the fourth position, is of a temperately hot nature, and of a gold colour. This is understood from the hot sign Leo which has affinity with him. Venus is of a cold and temperately wet nature, and of a tin colour. Her natural house is said to be the hot and wet i.e. tepid Libra and her accidental sign Taurus whose coldness together with dryness moderates the tepidity of Venus. Mercury is temperately cold, and of a lead colour. The house naturally proper to him is Virgo, his accidental house being Gemini which is hot and wet in relation to that temperateness. But the moon, placed after all the others, is of a cold and wet nature, and of a silver colour. Her nature is brought into harmony with the cold and wet Cancer as her proper house…

H

The triplicities of the signs, in which the active powers of the planets are shown to subsist, are distinguished as follows: every group of three signs which seem to be concordant in a single nature makes a triplicity. Aries, Leo, and Sagittarius make the first triplicity, since each of these signs is fiery, choleric, masculine, and diurnal. This is the eastern triplicity whose rulers are the sun by day and Jupiter by night, together with their partner Saturn by day and night. Taurus, Virgo, and Capricorn make the second triplicity being of a single nature as earthy, melancholic, feminine, and nocturnal. This is the southern triplicity whose rulers are Venus by day and the moon by night, their partner being Mars by day and night. The third triplicity arises from the signs of the same nature Gemini, Libra, and Aquarius, these being airy, sanguineous, masculine, diurnal, and western. The rulers of this triplicity are Saturn by day and Mercury by night, their partner being Jupiter by day and night. The fourth triplicity arises from Cancer, Scorpio, and Pisces, since these signs are watery, phlegmatic, feminine, nocturnal, and northern. Its rulers are Venus by day and Mars by night, their partner being the moon by day and night…

5.5 Concord among planets and stars

Texts:

A. Pliny: *Naturalis historia* II. 19–20.
B. Censorinus: *De die natali* 13. 1–5.
C. Macrobius: *Commentarius in Somnium Scipionis* II. 3. 12–16.
D. Favonius Eulogius: *Disputatio de Somnio Scipionis* 25. 1–5.
E. Martianus Capella: *De nuptiis Philologiae et Mercurii* II. 169 + 171 + 181 + 182 + 194 + 196 + 197 + 198–199.
F. Anonymous: *Epistula ad B.*, p. 198. 5–39.
G. Eriugena: *Glosae Martiani* p. 118. 25–119. 8, 119. 18–23, 126. 21–127. 17, 128. 24–129. 11.
H. Eriugena: *Periphyseon* III. 715C + 718C–D + 722A–D.
I. Honorius Augustodunensis: *De imagine mundi* 86 + 88.
J. William of Conches: *Glosae super Macrobium* 10AB, pp. 265–267.

A fifth group of passages — drawn from writers active between late antiquity and the twelfth century — illustrates the application of concord to the planets and stars. After equating the distance between the earth and the moon with a tone (passages *A, B, D, E, G, H, I*), the writers establish various types of planetary-distance scale. In one type, the distance between any two successive planets is calculated as some multiple of that between the earth and the moon (*A, B*), producing a scale (see figure 17), this scale being calculated sometimes correctly (*B, D, G*) and sometimes incorrectly (*A, E, I*). Another type of planetary-distance scale is based entirely on octave (2:1) ratios. It postulates either an octave between moon and sun, an octave between sun and Saturn, and therefore two octaves between moon and Saturn (*G*) or alternatively an octave between earth and sun, an octave between sun and stars, and therefore two octaves between earth and stars (*D, H*). In another type, the distance between the earth and any successive planet is calculated as some multiple of that between the earth and the previous planet (*C, F, J*), yielding a scale (see figure 18).

After establishing the various types of planetary-distance scales, the writers also consider ratios between non-successive degrees (*C, D, F*). Finally, the distance corresponding to the tone itself is sometimes declared to be 126,000 stades (*A, B, C, E, G, H*) — i.e. 15,625 miles (*I*) — the distance corresponding to the correct first scale therefore totalling 756,000 stades (*H*) — i.e. 93,750 miles. However, the distance cor-

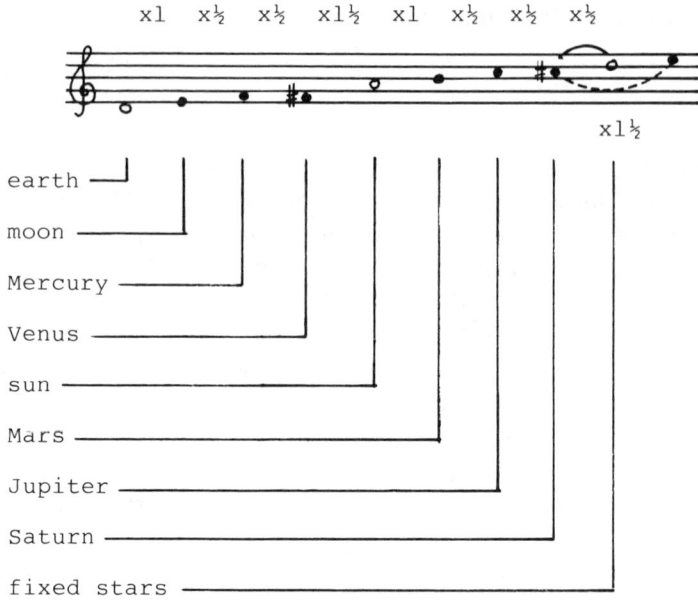

Figure 17. Planetary scale (small-interval)

responding to the incorrect first scale totals 882,000 stades — i.e. 109,375 miles (*I*).

A

Many have also tried to investigate the distances of the planets from the earth, and have reported that the sun is distant from the moon 19 times as much as the moon itself from the earth. But Pythagoras, a man of acute intelligence, concluded that there are 126,000 stades between the earth and the moon, double that amount between the moon and the sun, and three times that amount between the sun and the twelve zodiac signs — a view also held by our compatriot Sulpicius Gallus. Yet Pythagoras sometimes applies a musical argument, calling the distance from the earth to the moon a tone, that from her to Mercury half that distance, that from him to Venus the same, that from her to the sun one and a half times that distance, that from the sun to Mars a tone — i.e. the same distance as from the earth to the moon — that from him to Jupiter half that distance, that from him to Saturn half that distance, and that from here to the zodiac one

```
earth to moon     1 t.
                                    x2
earth to sun      2 t.
                                    x3
earth to Venus    6 t. = 1 oct.
                                    x4
earth to Mercury  4 oct.
                                    x9
earth to Mars     36 oct.
                                    x8
earth to Jupiter  288 oct.
                                    x27
earth to Saturn   7,7776 oct.
```

Figure 18. Planetary scale (large-interval)

and a half times that distance — what they call the "diapason harmonia" i.e. the totality of harmony being thus produced with seven tones. In this harmony, Saturn moves in the Dorian mode, Jupiter in the Phrygian, and so forth with the other planets — the subtlety here being aesthetic rather than logical.

B

In addition, Pythagoras has reported that this whole universe is fashioned according to musical principles, and that the seven planets wandering between heaven and earth and controlling the reproduction of mortal things have a "rhythmical" motion and distances corresponding to musical intervals… For just as Eratosthenes concluded from geometrical reasoning that the greatest circumference of the earth is 252,000 stades, so did Pythagoras indicate what the number of stades was between the earth and each planet… So Pythagoras thought that from the earth to the moon is roughly 126,000 stades corresponding to the interval of a tone; from the moon to Mercury — which is called "Stilbon" — half of that amount as though a semitone; from here to "Phosphorus" which is Venus about the same i.e. another semitone; from here to the sun three times that amount as though one and a half tones. Therefore the sun is three and a half tones distant from the earth — this being called the "diapente" interval — but two and a half tones distant from the moon — this being the "diatessaron". Pythagoras thought that from the sun to Mars — whose name is "Pyrois" — is the same distance as from the earth to the moon, thereby making a tone; from here to Jupiter — which is called "Phaethon" — half of that amount, thereby making a semitone; from Jupiter to Saturn — whose name is "Phaenon" — the same amount i.e. another semitone; and from here to the highest heaven where the zodiac signs are likewise a semitone. So from the highest heaven to the sun is the interval of a "diatessaron" — that is, two and a half tones — and from the same heaven to the highest point of the earth six tones in which occurs the consonance of the "diapason".

C

But one must inquire whether the balanced measurement of the world's body itself has also maintained those intervals which in the incorporeal soul are evaluated by reason alone and not by sense. Indeed, Archimedes believed that he had discovered the number of stades by which the moon was separated from the earth's surface, Mercury from the moon, Venus from Mercury, the sun from Venus, Mars from the sun, Jupiter from Mars, and Saturn from Jupiter. He also thought that he had measured by reason the whole space from Saturn's sphere to the star-bearing heaven itself. Yet Archimedes' measurement was rejected by the Platonists for not being based largely on double and triple intervals. They decided that one should believe: that the distance between the earth and the sun is double that from the earth to the moon, that the distance between the earth and Venus is triple that from the earth to the sun, that the distance between the earth and Mercury's star is four times that from the earth to Venus, that the distance between the earth and Mars is nine times that from the earth to Mercury, that the distance between the earth and Jupiter is eight times that from the earth to Mars, and that the distance between the earth and Saturn's sphere is twenty-seven times that from the earth to Jupiter. Porphyry included this opinion of the Platonists in those books where he cast a little light on the obscurities of the "Timaeus". He also says they believe that the intervals in the world's body which are filled out by the ratios of $4:3$, $3:2$, and $9:8$, by semitones, and by the "leimma" are a reflection of the soul's structure; and that there comes forth in this manner a harmony whose proportions are woven into the substance of the soul and also inserted into that world's body which is moved by the soul.

D

But because the world's harmony is, according to tradition, established not with four circles but with eight, it sounds not with the consonance of the diapason but with that of the double diapason as though through the coming-together of two tetrachords. That most learned man Pythagoras has revealed their intervals, recognizing that from the earth to that highest point which is called "aplanes" there extend twelve semitones — a division which is associated with the duple ratio if one is prepared to relate the eight to a four. For he says that there is a tone from the earth to the moon, a semitone from the moon to Mercury's circle, from there to Venus' circle a semitone, from there to the sun three semitones; and that there is a tone from the sun's sphere to Mars' circle, a semitone from there to Jupiter, from there to Saturn's circle a semitone, and from there to the zodiac circle likewise a semitone. Thus, it transpires that the heaven is separated from the earth by six tones i.e. twelve semitones, and that the traditional consonances arise among these. For the "diatessaron" consonance resounds between the earth and the sun's circle, the "diapente" between the sun's and the zodiac circle, and the "diapason" arising from the first two consonances in the whole. Just as there are two hemispheres: higher and lower, the sound of the entire world echoes also as a double diapason i.e. twenty four semitones. You may also associate this with the duple ratio for, just as eight differs from four, so does twenty-four differ from twelve — the larger numbers contain in themselves those same smaller numbers and others similarly duplicated, this being the nature of a doubled term. And so through these tones which are blended by overlapping and joining in the ratio of nine to eight is produced an uninterrupted modulation of joined consonance.

E

Then the bearers picked up the goddess' palanquin and bore it aloft with great effort. And when they had ascended 126,000 stades supported by the lightness of the air and completed the first tone among the celestial notes, the maiden entered the moon's circle... Next, by half of the interval through which she had ascended to the moon, she came to the Cyllenian's circle... With a rapid ascent from here, the crossing by flight to Venus' circle is completed in a semitone... Soon she was eager for the journey to the sun's circle — a laborious one since that circle, believed to comprise a tone and a semitone, wearied an ascent with its interval of one and a half... But when she has ascended by a semitone, the "Pyrois" circle brings a delay... When this circle had been crossed — for it was no labour to cross the interval of a semitone — they arrived at the brightness of Jupiter's planet. Its circle resonated in the Phrygian mode... And when she had crossed this circle by a similar interval, she spied from on high the creator of the gods stiff with the cold and snowy frosts to which he clings. This god, whom she tried to circle around, tinkled with the Dorian melody of his sphere... From there they rose with the greatest effort by a journey's interval of one and a half. For they arrived through a tone and a semitone at the globe of the celestial sphere itself and the circumference studded with stars. They were exhausted by their ascents through the six tones and by the utter wearisomeness of the stades. But when they realized that the space they had crossed was resonating as an octave consonance in the perfection of absolute modulation, they rested a little refreshed after the greatest exertions.

F

According to the opinion of the Egyptians whom Plato also follows, the circle of the moon is the first after the earth. The sun's circle follows this, Mercury is placed above this, Venus is situated above this, and Mars is located above this. Jupiter and Saturn are elevated above this in the sixth and seventh circles. It is therefore said that the space by which the moon is separated from the earth multiplied by two is the space between the earth and the sun: a ratio which is called the "diapason" consonance. The space by which the sun is separated from the earth multiplied by three is the space between the earth and Venus. If you compare triple and duple: that is, 2 which is 2 times 1 and 3 which is 3 times 1, the ratio of 3:2 — which is called the "diapente" consonance — arises. The space by which Venus is separated from the earth multiplied by four is the space between the earth and the star of Mercury. If you consider the quadruple and the triple, you will see that 4 contains 3 in itself and a third part of the 3: that is, 1 since 3 times 1 makes 3. This ratio of 4:3 is called the "diatessaron" consonance. The space by which Mercury is separated from the earth multiplied by nine is the space between the earth and Mars. If you measure 9 and 4, these are joined in neither the ratio of 2:1 nor that of 3:2 nor that of 4:3, and produce neither the "diapason" nor the "diapente" nor the "diatessaron" consonance. For this reason, Mars is judged to be incompatible with propitious things. I am not unaware that 4 and 9 are the first square numbers, since 4 arises by taking 2 times 2, and 9 by taking 3 times 3. Moreover, the former is a square of the first even number, the latter generated from the first odd number. Nor does it escape my notice that 9 and 6 are joined to one another in a ratio of 3:2, and 12 and 9 in a ratio of 4:3, although 4 and 9 are connected by nothing comparable with this. The space by which Mars is separated from the earth multiplied by eight is the space between the earth and the sphere of Jupiter who comes next. If you are willing to compare 9 and 8, you will find the ratio of a tone. For by the same amount that 9 is separated from 8: namely 1, so is a tone separated from a consonance. Finally, the space by which Jupiter is separated from the earth multiplied by twenty seven is the space between the earth and the sphere of Saturn. If you compare 8 and 27, you will see 8 multiplied by 3 making 24 plus a remainder of 3, but the 8 and 27 joined neither by the ratio of 2:1, nor by that of 3:2 , nor by that of 4:3. And if you apply 7 to the completion of this sum, you will find 7 multiplied by 3 together with a further 6 combining to form the 27. If you apply 5, you will find 5 multiplied by 5 and a remainder of 2. However, between 4 and 8 there is only one relation where the latter is achieved by doubling the former. 27 is measured by 3 multiplied by 9… We can therefore see from these combinations of numbers why this or that planet is held to be the promoter of good or bad fortune. The star of Jupiter which is more conformable with the sun and that of Venus which is joined more to the moon by a certain principle of nature or of number are held to be more conducive to man's well-being…

G

He states this because some say that there are whole tones between the sun and the moon. There are again said to be whole tones between the sun and Saturn. Thus, it is concluded that the sun is the "mese" i.e. holds the middle position, since there is believed to be the same distance between the sun and the moon as there is between the sun and Saturn. Some, however, bring up the "leimmata" i.e. semitones: for example, the semitone between the moon and Mercury, and so forth… Therefore the space between Saturn and the sun represents a duple: that is, "diapason" ratio. Again, that between the sun and the moon represents a diapason, i.e. duple ratio. However, the space between Saturn and the moon is constituted as a double diapason, i.e. twice duple ratio, just as 8 is in duple ratio to 4. Moreover, the 8 of the double diapason represents the fulness of the celestial harmony between the earth and the sun, for there are 8 sounds, 7 spaces, and 6 tones… A "diapason" can therefore be found above the sun in level of pitch and below the sun in spatial position as is apparent to mortal senses. The sun connects with the celestial sphere in a diapason. But it initially has a "diatessaron" ratio to the moon, while Venus is first consonant with it in a tone, Mercury to Venus in another tone, and the moon to Mercury in a semitone. There is also a "diapente" ratio in the same spaces, when Venus responds to the sun in a tone, Mercury to Venus in a tone, the moon to Mercury in a semitone, and this sphere to the moon in a tone. And it should be noted that those tones which are calculated between the earth and a sphere: for example, the tone between the earth and the moon are not in auditory ratios but in spatial distances. For there are many kinds of tone. Indeed, tones are the distances between stars: i.e. the extent to which each one's distance from another is a multiple of the moon's distance from the earth, these tones varying in accordance with the diversity of absides and circles. Martianus defines this kind of tone when he says "a tone is a space of appropriate quantity." This type of tone is called a "diastema" in music... Ignorance about tones becomes a cause of error for many people, since they think that the tone by which the moon is separated from the earth relates to the ratios of the celestial sounds. They do not realize first, that a musical tone can only arise between two sounds and that, since the earth is static and produces no sound, there is consequently no musical tone between the earth and the moon; secondly, that musical intervals are never measured by the number of stadia but only by the increase of tension measured according to numerical rules. For it is one thing to measure 126,000 stades between the earth and the moon, another thing to count 24 units between 192 and 216. In the first case, a tone is 126,000 stades and in the second, a tone as the eighth part of the lesser number is 24...

H

Some of the celestial bodies are established not far from the earth — like the moon which is elevated 126,000 stades above the earth's mass according to Pythagoras and is therefore called the neighbour of the earth... And the philosophers call that distance by which the moon is separated from the earth a "tone": that is, a space of rational quantity. Indeed, those who are expert in the harmony of sounds speak of tones in two ways, since they call tones both the "diastemata" i.e. the intervals of sounds and the "analogiae" i.e. the ratios of sounds... Hence, it is not unreasonably claimed by the philosophers that the distance between the moon and the earth and the circumference of the whole earth are contained in the ratio of a tone.

For 14,000 stades multiplied by 18 makes 252,000 corresponding to the earth's circumference, while 7,000 stades multiplied by 18 completes the earth's diameter and the moon's distance from the earth. But 10 + 8 compared to 10 + 6 — the latter being measured twice by 8 — produces the ratio of a tone, since the larger number contains the whole of the smaller together with the latter's eighth part — which is 2. According to harmonic theories, 10 + 8 is connected to 10 + 6 in the same way as 9 to 8: i.e. through the "epogdoos" ratio. For every greater number which contains a number smaller than itself together with an eighth part of the latter is called "epogdoos" in numbers and "tone" in music... The first of all philosophers, as he is called, Pythagoras declared the distance between the earth and the moon to be 126,000 stades. Later Eratosthenes, as I have stated, decisively proved this fact through the earth's shadow and the lunar eclipse. The same Pythagoras is said to have taught that the sun is elevated above the moon in a duple ratio to this distance, although many people have different views concerning his reasons for holding this belief. But since he tried to prove by cogent arguments that the construction of the entire universe both rotates and is measured according to musical principles — something which divine Scripture also does not deny when it says: "And who will put to sleep the symphony of heaven?" — we may suggest that he said this for no other reason than to reveal the rational ratios of musical intervals in the distances between the stars. Therefore, recognizing that the sun's circle is in the middle of that entire space between the earth and that highest sphere by which all sensible things are encompassed, he not unreasonably believed that there was one "diapason" from the earth to the sun and another from the sun to the extreme circumference of the universe. A diapason is modulated by a duple ratio. As in the diatonic genus, to take one example of the harmony of sounds, the double diapason is adjusted by taking the duple ratio twice, the first diapason extending from the principal of the principals to the "mese" — that is, the middle — but the second diapason from the mese to the "nete hyperbolaion" — that is, the highest of the excellents; so also the entire space between the earth and the sun is adjusted to the ratio of the diapason — since the sun occupies the middle position — , while between the sun and the twelve constellations — that is, the outermost motion of the stars — another diapason is connected. He therefore believed, according to the arguments of what is termed "harmony", that there is a double diapason interval between the earth and the sphere. Through this it is concluded that the diameter of the earth multiplied by three is as equal to the distance between the earth and the sun as it is to the diameter of the lunar circle. Accordingly, the same space will be measured both in the diameter of the lunar circle and in the distance between the earth and the sun. For in both cases 378,000 stades are calculated. Therefore, by doubling this number you will find the distance between the earth and the outermost sphere to be 756,000 stades. You will be amazed at the concord of nature since, as many thousands of stades there are in the length of the moon's orbit, so many are there in the vertical space between the earth and the signs. In both cases, 756,000 stades are computed.

I

Celestial Music. If the gamut is placed in the earth, an A in the moon, a B in Mercury, a C in Venus, a D in the sun, an E in Mars, an F in Jupiter, and a G in Saturn, the measure of music is discovered to perfection. Hence, seven tones are found between the earth and the firmament. For from the earth to the moon is a tone, from the moon to Mercury a semitone, from Mercury to Venus a semitone, and from there to the sun three semitones. From the sun to Mars is a tone, from there to Jupiter a semitone, from there to Saturn a semitone, and from there to the zodiac three semitones. When these are joined together they produce seven tones. The tone contains 15,625 miles, the semitone $7,812\frac{1}{2}$ miles. Hence, the philosophers imagined that there were nine Muses, since they discovered between the earth and the heaven nine consonances which they found naturally inborn in man... From the earth to the moon there are 126,000 stades which make 15,625 miles. From the moon to Mercury are $7,812\frac{1}{2}$ miles, from there to Venus the same, and from there to the sun $23,437\frac{1}{2}$ miles. From the sun to Mars there are 15,625 miles. From there to Jupiter $7,812\frac{1}{2}$ miles, from there to Saturn the same, and from there to the firmament $23,437\frac{1}{2}$ miles. So there are from the earth to the heaven 109,375 miles...

J

"But those intervals". He had said that there are certain intervals in the composition of the soul, and likewise in the sounds which are produced in the spheres of the firmament and planets through the agency of the soul. He therefore inquires whether the measurement of intervals is maintained in the universal body as it is in the composition of the soul. "Yet Archimedes' measurement". Although Archimedes thought that he had measured the spaces which existed between the individual planets, this measurement was useless and futile and was "rejected by the Platonists". "Double and triple". Because he had not maintained double and triple intervals in that measurement as there were in one part of the soul's composition doubles and in another part triples. "That one should believe" not that we should affirm this. He adds what this is. "This opinion of the Platonists". Because the Platonists thought they had thus grasped the measurement of the intervals, he supports this opinion with the authority of Porphyry who expounds Plato's "Timaeus". "He included this...on the obscurities". Because he had cast light on the obscurity of the words with his exposition. "A harmony": that is, the sound of concord. "Whose proportions": that is, of the intervals which are filled out by the ratios of 4:3, 3:2, etc. "Into the substance of the soul": that is, into the composition where all these intervals are. "Inserted into the body". Because as these intervals are in the composition of the soul, so also are they in the universal body...

5.6 Concord in the celestial world

Texts: A. Macrobius: *Commentarius in Somnium Scipionis* I. 19. 20–27.
B. Adalbold of Utrecht: *Musica* 3. 1–12.

Passages in Macrobius' *Commentarius in Somnium Scipionis* and Adalbold of Utrecht's *Musica* explore the concordant character of the celestial world. These argue that, when concordant ratios arise between segments of the 360° circles traced by various heavenly bodies, effects beneficial to man will be produced. According to passage *A*, Venus and Jupiter are aspected to the sun and moon in the concordant ratios of 4:3, 3:2, 9:8, 2:1, 3:1, 4:1 and are therefore considered benevolent, while Saturn and Mars are not aspected to the two luminaries in the same ratios and are therefore thought malevolent. According to passage *B*, the ratio between the trine (120°) and quartile (90°) aspects in general is the concordant 4:3 (making a fourth); that between the quartile (90°) and the sextile (60°) and between opposition (180°) and the trine (120°) the consonant 3:2 (making a fifth); and that between the trine (120°) and the sextile (60°) and between opposition (180°) and the quartile (90°) the consonant 2:1 (making the octave).

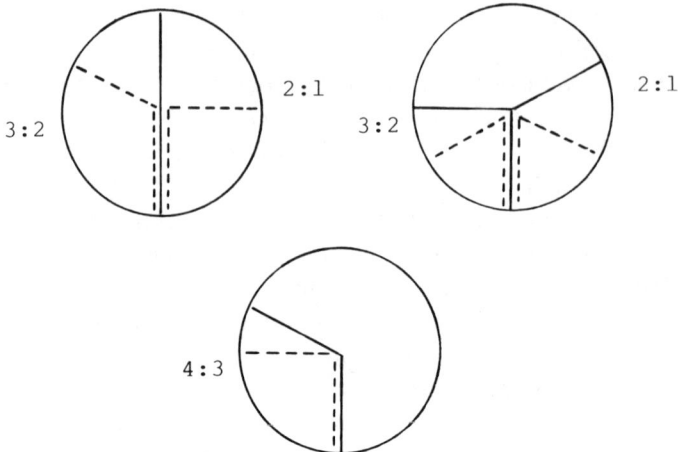

Figure 19. Concordant ratios in the celestial world

A

If perchance someone should seek a deeper reason why malevolence is attributed to the divine so that a planet can be described as harmful — this is believed in the cases of Mars and Saturn — or why Jupiter and Venus are more known for benevolence among astrologers even though there is a single nature among divine things, I shall report an explanation found in only one writer to my knowledge. For Ptolemy revealed the cause in the three books which he wrote "On Harmony" and I shall explain it briefly. There are certain ratios, he says, through which a joining proportion arises among all things which agree, join, or adapt to one another, nor can anything agree with anything else except through these ratios: namely, 4:3, 3:2, 9:8, 2:1, 3:1, and 4:1. At this point, I would have you remember temporarily these mere names of ratios, although later when my discussion turns to the harmony of the heavens I shall more opportunely reveal these ratios' nature and power. Let the fact suffice for now that there can be no conjoining nor concord without these ratios. The sun and moon principally govern our lives, for the two faculties of sensation and growth are peculiar to mortal bodies, while this "aisthetikon" or nature of sensation comes to us from the sun and the "phytikon" or nature of growth from the lunar sphere. So that life which we enjoy is sustained through the two luminaries' beneficence. Our personal dealings and the successes of our endeavours are related as much to these two luminaries as to the five planets. However, the intervention of the ratios mentioned above readily joins and associates some of these planets with the luminaries, whereas no bond of ratio connects others to the luminaries. Thus Venus and Jupiter are associated with both luminaries in these ratios. Yet Jupiter is joined to the sun in all of them but to the moon in many, while Venus is joined to the moon in all of them but to the sun in many. Hence, although both are considered beneficent, Jupiter is more conformable with the sun and Venus more with the moon, these planets being especially favourable to our life as though concordant in numerical ratios with the luminaries which are authors of our life. Conversely, Saturn and Mars have no proportion with the luminaries, although by some remote numerical relation Saturn is aspected to the sun and Mars to the moon. So they are considered less favourable to human life, as though not closely joined by numerical ratios with the authors of life. But how even these are believed sometimes to bring wealth or fame to men should be discussed in another treatise, it being enough here to have revealed why one planet is thought fearful and another beneficial. Indeed, Plotinus declares in his treatise entitled "Are the stars causes?" that nothing accrues to men through the stars' force or power, but that what fatal necessity appoints for individuals is revealed by the progression, station, and retrogradation of these seven — just as birds in flight or at rest unwittingly signify future events with their wings or cries. Similarly, then, one planet will rightly be called beneficial and another fearful since fortunate outcomes are signified by the former and unfortunate by the latter.

B

Let us taste a little of the sweetness in cosmic music… In the heavens are said to be four aspects primarily: sextile, quartile, trine, and opposition. The sextile controls a sixth part of the heaven — namely, 60 degrees — to which the entire circuit is in the ratio 6:1. The weight of the last of the 19 strings is similarly related to that of the first. The quartile aspect controls a fourth part of the heaven — that is, 90 degrees — whose ratio to 60 is that of 3:2 which is called the fifth in music. The trine aspect controls a third part of the heaven — namely 120 degrees — whose ratio to 90 degrees is 4:3 which is called in music the fourth. Therefore, the degrees of the trine aspect produce a fourth in relation to those of the quartile, those of the quartile aspect a fifth in relation to those of the sextile, and those of the trine aspect an octave in relation to those of the sextile. Similarly, opposition produces an octave in relation to the quartile aspect and a fifth in relation to the trine, while the trine to the quartile is said to produce a fourth. Further, there are two kinds of sextile aspect, and likewise two each of quartile and trine. One kind of trine contains a third part of the heaven according to the sequence of signs, the other kind the whole outside that third according to the sequence. The latter comprises 240 degrees whose ratio to the degrees in opposition is 4:3 — that is, the fourth. Similarly, one kind of quartile contains a fourth part of the heaven according to the sequence of signs, and one kind of sextile a sixth part. Indeed, they produce all musical consonances according to the sequence of signs although not all are completely consonant. This is why philosophers maintain that the first sextile aspect is superior to the second in amity and advantage, the second more powerful than the first in all manner of harmfulness, a similar theory being applied to the other aspects. According to such aspects do the rays of the sun, reflected in the moon and striking the lower, produce now one effect and now another. In the brain and bones, these effects are obvious to physicians; in the tides and shellfish as also in climactic conditions, they are clear to fishermen; in plants, trees, illnesses, and many other things, they are obvious even to laymen and the uneducated. But the rays of all the planets, reflected back from one another according to the aspects mentioned above, seem sometimes to modify and sometimes to maintain the conditions of everything below. The Lord thought fit to reveal this not to all men but to philosophers alone.

5.7 Concord in the human soul

Texts: A. Macrobius: *Commentarius in Somnium Scipionis* I. 6. 41–44.
        B. Hugh of St. Victor: *Didascalicon* II. 4, 753D–754D.

These passages from Macrobius and Hugh of St. Victor associate the human soul with concord through its numerical composition. Speaking both metaphorically and literally, Macrobius applies the numbers 4 and 3 to the soul. Thus, 4 is applicable to the soul's perfection and 3 to its division into rational, spirited, and desiring. Moreover, 4 and 3 apply to the soul's consonant structure since soul is composed of an octave, the fourth (4:3) and fifth (3:2) together make an octave (2:1), and 4 is the basis of the fourth and 3 of the fifth. Speaking metaphorically, Hugh of St. Victor applies the number 4 to the soul. Here, 4 is applicable to certain "progressions" or multiplications by 3: a first progression ($1 \times 3 = 3$) which signifies the soul's simplicity by the 1, its indissolubility by the 3, its division into reason, anger, and concupiscence by the 3, and its indivisible presence in each of these by the 1×3; a second progression ($3 \times 3 = 9$) signifying the soul's descent from simplicity; a third progression ($3 \times 9 = 27$) which signifies the soul's exercise of sense-perception; and a fourth progression ($3 \times 27 = 81$) signifying the soul's return to simplicity.

A

And not only do these two numbers display a common disposition towards the formation of bodies. In fact, the Pythagoreans so much venerate the number 4 among their secrets — they call it the "tetractys" — as though applying to the perfection of the soul, that they have also fashioned from it a religious oath for themselves: *ou ma ton hāmeterai psychēi paradonta tetraktyn* — "By the very person who gave the fourfold number to our soul". But the number 3 attributes the soul's completion to its three parts, the first being the rational which they call "logistikon", the second the spirited which they term "thymikon", and the third the desiring which they name "epithymetikon". Similarly, no wise man has doubted that the soul also subsists through musical consonances among which that called "diapason" is of no small power. This consists of two consonances: that is, of the "diatessaron" and the "diapente". The "diapente" arises from the ratio of $3:2$ and the "diatessaron" from that of $4:3$, 3 being the first number to enter into a ratio of $3:2$ and 4 the first to enter into a ratio of $4:3$ — we shall explain why things occur in this way more fully at the appropriate juncture. Therefore, through these two numbers subsist the "diatessaron" and the "diapente" from which the consonance of the "diapason" is produced. And for this reason Virgil, who was deficient in no branch of learning, and who wished to express how men were fully and totally blessed declares: "… O three times and four times blessed".

B

On the number 4 in the soul. And number itself also teaches the manner of this progression and reversion. Say "3×1 makes 3," or "3×3 makes 9," or "3×9 makes 27," or "3×27 makes 81." Behold how the first number 1 occurs in the fourth term. And you will see the same thing happen if you take the multiplication to infinity: namely, that the number 1 is always apparent in the fourth term. Indeed, the simple essence of the soul is most rightly expressed by the monad which is itself also incorporeal. Moreover, the number 3 is fittingly referred to the soul because of the indissoluble bond of its mediating 1 — just as the number 4 which has two mediators and is therefore dissoluble applies properly to the body. So the first progression of the soul is where it unfolds itself from its simple essence which is represented by the monad into a threefold power, here now seeking something through concupiscence, now despising something else through anger, and now distinguishing these two things through reason. And it is rightly said to flow forth from a monad into a triad because every essence is naturally prior to its power. Moreover, that the same number 1 is found three times by multiplication in the number 3 signifies how the soul subsists not in parts but as a whole in each of its powers. For we cannot say that reason alone or anger alone or concupiscence alone is a third part of the soul, since reason is substantially neither other nor less than the soul, anger neither other nor less than the soul, and concupiscence neither other nor less than the soul — rather one and the same substance acquires different names according to its diverse powers. Next, the soul descends from its threefold power by a second progression to the regulation of the human body's music which is composed of the number 9. For there are nine openings in the human body through which everything whereby that same body is animated and controlled flows in or out according to the natural temperament. There is order here also, since the soul has its natural powers prior to its blending with the body. Next, by a third progression the soul, now flowing forth externally through the senses to those visible things whose regulation is represented by the number 27 — a solid number extended in three dimensions after the likeness of body — , is dispersed in the infinity of its actions. But in a fourth progression the soul, liberated from the body, returns to the pure state of its simplicity. Therefore the number 1, in a fourth multiplication where 3×27 produces 81, appears at the extremity. This is to show clearly that the soul after the end of this life — which is designated with the number 80 — returns to the unity of its simplicity from which it had previously departed in descending to the regulation of the human body. Because the boundary of human life stands naturally in the number 80, the prophet declares: "If men have eighty years through strength, even greater is their labour and sorrow." Some think that this fourfold progression is to be understood as the number 4 in the soul of which I spoke above, and that it is called the number 4 in the soul to distinguish it from the number 4 in the body.

5.8 Concord of the elements in man

Texts: A. Remigius of Auxerre: *In Boethii Consolationem*, pp. 32–33.
B. Bernard Silvestris: *Cosmographia* II. 13. 4–9.

This section consists of passages dealing with the concord of elements in man. However, concord is here envisaged not only between their physical qualities in man — where it is technically a question of "humours" — nor only between their physical qualities in the world — where it is simply a matter of "elements" — but also between their physical qualities in man and their physical qualities in the world. Passage *A* speaks explicitly of concord by using the terms "concord", "consonant", and "harmony". This occurs between the cold in black bile and the cold in phlegm, between the cold in earth and the cold in water, between the cold in black bile and the cold in earth, etc. Passage *B* refers implicitly to concord by using the terms "complexion" and "mixture". This arises between the cold in black bile and the cold in phlegm, etc.

A

"Soul in the middle" ... But the more learned interpreters think that the rational soul which has a great concord with the world should rather be understood in this passage. Hence also, man is called "microcosmus" in Greek, i.e. "lesser world". For just as the world consists of four elements and four seasons, so also does man consist of four humours and four ages. Let us therefore examine the concord between the world and man. There are four elements: air, fire, water, and earth. Air is hot and wet, and similarly spring hot and wet. And the blood which occurs in a boy is equally hot and wet, for boyhood is hot and wet. Fire is hot and dry, and summer hot and dry. The red bile which abounds in an adolescent is hot and dry, since adolescence is hot and dry. Earth is cold and dry, and autumn cold and dry. The melancholy i.e. black bile which occurs in young men is cold and dry, since youth is cold and dry. Water is cold and wet, and winter cold and wet. The phlegm which abounds in old men is cold and wet, for old age is cold and wet... "Through consonant members". For the human body is composed according to the science of harmonics. Hence, Sedulius says: "He summons back the life-breath and attunes it to its sinews." When the body is healthy, that harmony is consonant, but as soon as it becomes dissonant, the body grows sick...

B

Physis...decided to return to the matter which underlies her work. In it she observes only the images of the elements and not their truth in the integrity of a purer substance; not the elements which bring to completion but sedimentary essences of elements and cruder remnants of simple things. Taking hold of the fiery, the earthy and the rest with sensation — which is cruder —, she perceives that their powers are full and complete where they themselves are full and complete. And from the materiate substratum which lies before her gaze she elicits the qualities of wet, dry, hot, and cold, either unfolding them individually or blending them through their affinities — for this had been the great plan of the creator. She unfolded individual qualities which had been simple: that is, from their substantial and original state. She blended them through their affinities in order that they might become composites in joining. With fire and water, if the dry and the wet are joined in alliance with the hot of the one and the cold of the other, a certain kinship is found in this adhesion and juxtaposition. With air and earth, if the hot and the cold are joined in alliance with the wet of the one and the dry of the other, this kind of association is called a mixture. Physis pursues this blending of qualities with considerable diligence since this was relevant to the immediate task, and certainly not an idle question. She recalled that in the anatomy of the human body, some parts were formed from simple qualities and others from combinations. So when the elements aligned themselves with one another through contiguity and proximity in this manner, that coherence which is called a "complexion" in an animate thing was effected. She applies elemental complexions to the fabrication of humanity in such a way that they lineally reflect the principles by which they are engendered. Melancholy is a product of earthy weight, and phlegm of watery lightness while choler is raging like fire, and blood mild like air. Moreover, that diligence of Nature in respect of man is not found in relation to other living things. For an unbalanced combination of humours is often wont to corrupt the complexion in beasts, the ass being stupid through phlegm, the lion irascible through choler, and the dog totally infected by the airy sensation of smell.

Alone and unique, the human condition is made from a combination of humours which is moderated in both quality and quantity. Humanity is fashioned with the greatest care, with defect and excess attacking the felicity of the work to a far lesser degree. Indeed, it was not fitting that the future abode of intellect and reason should suffer through inequality or hesitancy disturbing the design. So when the humours had been balanced and their powers equalized, and when the qualities as qualia had completed the essence of substance, that plenitude of parts which forms the body supervened.

Notes

1. For a general perspective on this see de Gandillac — Goldmann — Piaget 1965. Cf. p. 232.
2. The structured terms can also be treated as mental concepts. See pp. 7–8. In practice, this approach frequently turns into a variant of the ontological.
3. See Eco 1968: 63, 361, 395; Greimas 1970: 39; Eco 1976: 83–84; Greimas — Courtés 1979: 311–313.
4. This position is hypothetical since we shall assume that there is no totally non-semiotic state. Cf. pp. 5–6.
5. See Lévi-Strauss 1958: 40; Greimas 1966: 19.
6. According to the normal usage in logic.
7. See Lévi-Strauss 1958: 305–306; Hjelmslev 1971: 100. For the origins of this conception in Saussure — for whom however it is the *valeur* [value] of each linguistic term which is constituted by its relation to all other terms rather than the "structure" — see Saussure 1967–1974: 251 ff.
8. According to a common usage in linguistics.
9. See Lévi-Strauss 1958: 56; Hjelmslev 1971: 32; Greimas — Courtés 1979: 314–315.
10. That Derrida's *différance* is remote from the logical concept of difference is shown by the former's spelling with an *a*; its substitution for gram, trace, spacing; and its alternation of singular and plural, etc.
11. Eco 1984: 169–171, 179. Eco also mediates his dichotomy of structure and code with something called an "s-code". This anticipates our response below yet undermines his own argument against Jakobson.
12. Cf. n. 4.
13. Saussure 1967–1974: 146 ff.
14. *réseau*. See Kristeva 1969: 175, 183–184.
15. Kristeva 1969: 150, 157–158, 183.
16. Kristeva 1969: 8–9, 11–13, 49, 54, 183–185, 279. The regenerate semiotics is to be called *sémanalyse*. See Kristeva 1969: 9, 279–280, etc.
17. Kristeva 1969: 175 ff., 185. Saussure had analyzed certain Latin poems by arguing that key words — for example, the names of gods — were fragmented syllabically and diffused through the texts. See Starobinski 1971; Wunderli 1972 on these *anagrammes* or *paragrammes*. Of the various parallels between this analysis and poetic practice in general detected by Kristeva, that of syllabic dispersal = relational network is the most important here.
18. Kristeva 1969: 28–34, 44, 50–54, 174, 198.
19. Cf. n. 17.
20. Kristeva 1969: 183 *formalisation des relations*. At Kristeva 1969: 29 she defines a model as an interpretative structure isomorphic with an object

structure, and notes the etymological connection with the Latin *modus* (=measure, musical mode, etc.). Cf. Kristeva 1969: 191, 198.
21. Kristeva 1969: 183. Her preliminary classification is actually simpler than the one described below, since she distinguishes only — as partial grams within the grams — writerly and readerly (notated A, B) and — as subgrams within the writerly partial grams — phonetic, semic, and syntagmatic (notated A1, A2, A3). However, the more complex classification is logically required and implicitly used.
22. Kristeva 1969: 184 *grammes...grammes partiels...sous-grammes*. Cf. n. 21.
23. Kristeva 1969: 181–183, 185, 186 ff., 194 ff. *grammes scripturaux...grammes lecturaux*. Cf. Kristeva 1969: 143–145, 181–182. Cf. n. 21.
24. Kristeva 1969: 182, 184–185 *grammes phonétiques...sémiques...syntagmatiques*. Cf. Kristeva 1969: 186–187 (phonetic), 186 (phonetic and non-phonetic), 187–191 (semantic), 187 (semantic and non-semantic), 191–194 (syntactic). Cf. n. 21.
25. The models are frequently expressed in quasi-mathematical language — she speaks of a *numérologie paragrammatique* (Kristeva 1969: 193) which i. employs, ii. subverts, iii. transforms normal mathematics (Kristeva 1969: 32, 174, 201, 206) — this language being either quasi-arithmetical or quasi-geometrical. In the former case, relations may be depicted as binarities of 0/2 (Kristeva 1969: 150 – 153, 183, 185, 193, 197, 202–203) or as equalities which are not equalities (Kristeva 1969: 191); and in the latter, as lines plotted in 3-dimensional space (Kristeva 1969: 182–183, 189, 193, 197–198, 278–279).
26. Kristeva 1969: 11, 143, 174, 280. Cf. Kristeva 1969: 194 (versus form), 280 (versus structure), 187 (versus signifier-signified distinction).
27. Kristeva 1969: 11, 13–15, 22–23, 30–31, 175, 189. Cf. Kristeva 1969: 56 (versus system).
28. These terms are borrowed from the generative grammar theory of S. K. Shaumyan. See Kristeva 1969: 284, n. 8.
29. Kristeva 1969: 280–281, 284–285.
30. Kristeva 1969: 280, 282, 284, 288, 293–294.
31. Kristeva 1969: 280, 284, 293–294.
32. Kristeva 1969: 284 *le dispositif de l'histoire de la langue et des pratiques signifiantes qu'elle est susceptible de connaître*.
33. Kristeva 1969: 283.
34. Kristeva 1969: 281–282, 285. This and the previous feature of the geno-text are the most important from the viewpoint of the history of philosophy. Similarly Derrida 1972[3]: 30–31, 41, 43–44 argues for a signifying difference (linguistic) not preceded by a transcendent signified (conceptual/ontological).
35. Kristeva 1969: 282–284.
36. Kristeva 1969: 282–283.

37. Kristeva 1969: 280 *le texte imprimé*.
38. Kristeva 1969: 284. The reference is to the textual analysis practised by Greimas and his circle.
39. Kristeva 1969: 294. Cf. n. 38.
40. Kristeva 1969: 293–294.
41. Kristeva 1969: 280–281.
42. Kristeva 1969: 298.
43. *la différentielle signifiante*. See Kristeva 1969: 298.
44. Kristeva 1969: 298–299.
45. Kristeva 1969: 298.
46. Kristeva 1969: 298.
47. Kristeva 1969: 301.
48. See n. 16.
49. Kristeva 1969: 291–292.
50. Kristeva 1969: 292–293.
51. Kristeva's networks or paragrams are, of course, structures in a special sense: that is, as dynamic and infinite. In the same spirit, Derrida 1972³: 39 can write: "la différance, n'est pas a-structurale."
52. See n. 13.
53. See p. 5.
54. On relation see further pp. 45–55.
55. This terminology will be employed on p. 181 ff.
56. i.e. as existents, concepts, or words.
57. Peirce 1931–1958, 1: ss. 540–541; 2: s. 274, etc.
58. Hjelmslev 1961: 55–56, etc. For Hjelmslev's discussion of sign-function, substance of expression, form of expression, substance of content, form of content, and purport see Hjelmslev 1961: 47–57. Hjelmslev's ontological views are actually quite ambivalent. The conceptual status of both substance of expression and substance of content is admitted along orthodox Saussurian lines at Hjelmslev 1961: 77–79. Yet a reduction of all the components to a purely linguistic status is indicated as an ideal yet to be realized.
59. Hjelmslev 1961: 55–56, etc.
60. Hjelmslev 1961: 47–48, 54, 57–58, etc.
61. Frege 1892.
62. Hjelmslev 1961: 52, etc.
63. Hjelmslev 1961: 52, etc.
64. To these dyads and triads the interpre*ter* — who relates the signifier to the signified — is always added as a further term.
65. Hjelmslev's system is essentially dyadic and based on the functives expression and content.
66. On Peirce's triadic system see further p. 16.
67. According to these criteria, the main ancient philosophical systems can be understood as follows: Plato → transcendent *ideae* are both ontological and

conceptual realizations of c; Aristotle → words are linguistic realizations of a while c is conceptually realized as thoughts and ontologically realized as things; the Stoics → a and c are both linguistically realized as *sēmainonta* and *sēmainomena* (= *lekta*) respectively.
68. See p. 4.
69. This expansion and contraction using linguistic units was the underlying principle of J. Kristeva's paragrammatical theory summarized above.
70. Eco 1984: 23–26. The critique is explicitly directed against Lacan, Kristeva, and Derrida.
71. One can therefore speak of structures as consisting of signifiers alone in a convenient shorthand.
72. See p. 4.
73. See n. 3.
74. The modern semantic theory of structure will be applied to the ancient ontological theory of structure in chapters two and three; and to the ancient ontological and semantic theories of structure in chapter four.
75. According to L & S, in the classical period *structura* only signified a physical building. When Cicero occasionally applied it to the arrangement of words, he noted that this was a strictly figurative usage (*quasi structura*...) Cf. Lausberg 1960, 2: 818.
76. The meanings of the terms "harmony/harmonic" will not be defined at the outset but will rather emerge in the process of analysis. One clarification should, however, be made immediately: that "equivalence to concord/concordant" and not "opposition to melody/melodic" is the leading idea. Cf. pp. 231–232.
77. Aristotle: *Po.* 22, 1459^a 6–8.
78. See Jakobson 1932, 1980: 17–18 — based on similar remarks in Saussure 1967–1974: 53–54.
79. See Lévi-Strauss 1964: 34–36. There is a critique of this theory in Eco 1968. For another analogy between semiotic and harmonic elements see Barthes 1970: 35–37.
80. Augustine: *dGLI* 5. 25. See pp. 35–38.
81. Since texts are our object of study, the process of analysis into minimal components followed by synthesis of such components will be founded on *textual* units: lexemes, sememes, and semes. Distinction of these three levels — implying that semantic features a. connect not directly to words or morphemes but indirectly through sememes and lexemes, b. are not only collections of terms but also networks of relations — best accords with the postulate of family resemblances. See p. 16. According to Greimas' formulation, semes, sememes, and lexemes can be defined as follows: A. Seme (= semantic feature/property). A semantic unit which is i. minimal, ii. distinctive. iii. combinable (Greimas 1966: 103–104). B. Sememe. A combination of semes producing an "effet de sens" (Greimas 1966: 45).

In a kind of horizontal relation to texts, a sememe can be outside a lexeme: it undergoes expansion or condensation (movement from defined term to definition or vice versa) (Greimas 1966: 36, 39, 72 ff.). In a corresponding vertical relation to texts, a sememe can be inside a lexeme: it is concrete or abstract (containing relatively many or few constituent semes) (Greimas 1966: 110–111). The combination of semes can involve a. nuclear, b. contextual semes — see p. 69f. — a "sememe" containing both a and b, a "metasememe" b only (Greimas 1966: 45–46, 50–51, 79–81, 102–103, 107, 119–120, 126–127). C. Lexeme. A collection of semes which is i. arranged in relation to a centre (Greimas 1966: 34–39, 43–45), ii. prior to phonic or graphic substance (Greimas 1966: 38, 51). We shall generally follow these definitions, although a few precisions should be inserted here. First, the distinction between sememes and lexemes is only implied by Greimas. A sememe is initially described as a grouping of semes in a lexeme corresponding to one of the latter's lexical senses (see Greimas 1966: 44 ff.). However, in practice the distinction between sememe and lexeme is difficult to sustain because seme, sememe, and lexeme are quantitatively — representing increasing degrees of combinatory complexity — rather than qualitatively different. Secondly, the mechanism by which semes interconnect is not explained by Greimas. Semes are once described as connected by their presence in a single lexeme (see Greimas 1966: 38–39). However, this effectively deprives the semes of any relations among themselves — making them approximate a mathematical set — and renders the notion of sememe totally redundant. On lexemes, sememes, and semes see also Greimas — Courtés 1979, 1: 207–208, 332–335.

82. A "universal" would be a collection of semes permanently stable in all linguistic usages. Although it is doubtful that this stability occurs in natural languages — a conclusion indicated by Wittgenstein's later work — discourse and communication require some uniformity in order to function. A "pseudo-universal" would therefore be a collection of semes temporarily stable in certain linguistic contexts. On universals in language see Greenberg 1966; Bach — Harms 1968. On linguistic vagueness see Black 1949; Quine 1951; Lakoff 1973; Putnam 1975.

83. For the use of conventional dictionaries as starting-points see Greimas 1966: 13–14, 72–74, 82 ff. For the modern reform of the dictionary see Eco 1984: 46 ff.

84. The *Merriam-Webster* dictionary gives under "signify" 1. "mean, denote, imply"; 2. "to show especially by a conventional token (as word, signal, or gesture)".

85. See p. 7–8. The issues are also summarized by Barthes 1985[1]: 36–53; Derrida 1972[3]: 27–35.

86. Although discussion of this triad has been more critical than favourable during the last twenty years, few theorists of linguistics and semiotics have

been able to dispense with it entirely. One set of problems surrounds the status of the three terms. In a first sense, the signifier, signified, and signification have been identified with a sign's perceptual aspect, its nonperceptual aspect, and the relation between the two. The status of the signified is controversial since, although its identification with an external object would be universally denied, its identification with a mental concept is advocated by Saussure (see Saussure 1967–1974: 42 ff.) but with a linguistic component by Barthes (see Barthes 1985^1: 36–38, 41–42, 45–48). In a second sense, the signifier, signified, and signification have been equated with a first set of semantic properties, a second set of such properties, and the relation between the two. However, the status of the entire triad is controversial since Hjelmslev (see Hjelmslev 1961: 46) rejects the equation of signif*ieds* and semantic properties, whereas Eco (see Eco 1976: 68–72) accepts that of signif*iers* and semantic properties, and what is true regarding the signified is true regarding the signifier and vice versa. Another set of problems surrounds the relation between the three terms. In particular, Derrida has corrected naive misunderstandings of the theory by showing i. that the relation between signifier and signified is an unresolvable sameness-in-difference — the signified cannot be separated from the signifier because such separation constitutes an unacceptable metaphysical transcendence (see Derrida 1967^1: 23–27). However, the signified must also be separated from the signifier in order to permit discussion of the signifier *qua* signifier (see Derrida 1967^1: 16, 1972^1: 4–5, 1972^2: 187); ii. that the relation between signifier and signified is an infinite chain — the difference grounding the distinction between signifier and signified is itself a signifier requiring a signified, and so forth *ad infinitum* (see Derrida 1967^2: 411, 1972^2: 108, 147). On this question see also Lacan 1966: 501 ff., 557.

87. See n. 83.
88. The *Merriam-Webster* dictionary gives under "harmony" 2. "the combination of simultaneous musical notes in a chord"; 3. "pleasing or congruent arrangement of parts". Cf. n. 76.
89. Such semiotic equivalence corresponds to the phenomenon of "participation" observed by students of primitive mythology and modern linguistics. This phenomenon amounts to a conceptual process whereby the variety of relations constituting the external world is reduced to a single relation: that of identity. In the sphere of mythology, Cassirer has shown how ancient cosmological systems frequently operate with an ambivalent notion of "part" as 1. part (vs. whole) and 2. part (= part + whole). For example, the dimension of space involves a "here" which is 1. here (vs. another place) and 2. here (= here + another place), that of time a "now" which is 1. now (vs. another time) and 2. now (= now + another time) (see Cassirer 1955–1957, 2: 60–82, 83 ff., 104 ff.). Of course, such conceptual processes violate the law

of contradiction. In the sphere of linguistics, various theorists have noted the existence of a kind of sublogic. On the level of a simple relation between two terms, this explains how a word like "man" can ambivalently represent 1. man (vs. woman) and 2. man (= man + woman) — to quote the discussion of Hjelmslev (see Hjelmslev 1935, 1937); on the level of more complex relations between two terms, it explains how linguistic categories like imperative, subjunctive, indicative, and optative can represent stages between 1. x (vs. y) and 2. x ($= x + y$) — to quote that of Brøndal (see Brøndal 1943: chapter 3). On the phenomenon of participation in general see also Lévy-Bruhl 1922: 68ff.; Togeby 1965: 104–105. Cf. Blanché 1966: 21ff.

90. These ideas are summarized in various places. For 1–4 see pp. 120–121, for A p. 118, and for B p. 121 ff. For 5–7 see pp. 191–192, 212, nn. 898–899, for C pp. 162, 187, for D p. 214. See also pp. 198–199, 218–219.

91. To suggest that the identity is merely that between a metaphorizing and a metaphorized term is not really to propound an alternative solution. As conceived by modern theorists like Richards (see Richards 1936: 93) and Greimas (see Greimas 1966: 135–136), metaphor is simply another form of the participation described in n. 89. More importantly, the evidence points to a similar conception in Eriugena and other Neoplatonic writers. See p. 181 ff.

92. On the notion of "seme" see n. 81.

93. Semes are defined in relation to other semes. See n. 517.

94. A "semantic element" is normally either a. a seme or b. a sememe. However, it is sometimes both a. a seme and b. a sememe.

95. In contrasting intensional and extensional semantics, one necessarily takes a position relative to an age-old debate concerning the meanings of words. The medieval terminists had distinguished i. *suppositio* as relation between a word and an external object, and ii. *significatio* as relation between a word and our concept. In the same way Saussure distinguished i. the referent or thing to which a linguistic sign refers, and ii. the signified or concept which the linguistic sign produces (see Saussure 1967–1974: 146ff.) — this distinction being close if not equivalent to Frege's between i. *Bedeutung* or the object which a linguistic expression designates, and ii. *Sinn* or the manner in which the linguistic expression designates (see Frege 1892). Modern theorists once again distinguish i. the reference as relation between a word and an external object, and ii. the signification or relation between a word and our concept. However, they pursue the development further by de-psychologizing the signified. This becomes a unity of linguistic application only and the object of intensional semantics. On reference and signification see Eco — Marmo 1989: 43 ff. for the medieval, Strawson 1950 for the modern period. On intensional semantics see Eco 1976: 58 ff.

96. In the medieval period, conscious semantic analysis which is independent of logic and ontology begins with thirteenth-century modists like Siger of Courtrai and Thomas of Hereford. However, there was an unconscious semantic analysis of this type during the pre-Scholastic period here evoked as the "zero-degree" of ontology.

97. Perhaps the most successful discussion of semantic fields in general occurs in Eco's writings. The initial premiss of his theory is that the semantic expansion constituting interpretation involves the selection and amalgamation of semantic features (Eco 1979: 18–19, 176). According to a traditional model, such features are arranged hierarchically within a system of genera and species. Calling this a "dictionary" (Eco 1984: 47–68, 80), he subjects it to criticism (Eco 1984: 65–68, 84). Eco proposes an alternative model, where semantic features are arranged non-hierarchically within a system of family resemblances. He terms this an "encyclopaedia" (Eco 1984: 67–70, 76, 80–84), according it a pre-eminent status (Eco 1984: 77–78). The final conclusion of his theory is that the semantic expansion constituting interpretation is potentially unlimited (Eco 1979: 24, 39, 176, 1984: 78). However, it is possible to limit it with the cooperation of a reader who employs his own pseudo-dictionary (Eco 1984: 73–74, 84–86).

98. The theory is the most important achievement of the later Wittgenstein. For applications of the term family resemblance see Wittgenstein 1953: ss. 77, 108, 1958: 17, 125, 145. These involve the notions of relation (Wittgenstein 1953: ss. 65–66, 108), similarity (Wittgenstein 1953: s. 130, Wittgenstein 1958: 19), selection of features (Wittgenstein 1953: s. 73, 1958: 125, 145), overlapping of features (Wittgenstein 1953: ss. 66, 76, 1958: 17, 20, 87), connection (Wittgenstein 1953: s. 122), mediation (Wittgenstein 1953: s. 122, 1958: 129), and structure (Wittgenstein 1953: s. 108, 1958: 19). For comparison with threads and nets see Wittgenstein 1953: ss. 66, 67, Wittgenstein 1958: 87. Application of this theory to formal semantics is legitimated by Wittgenstein himself for whom all thinking is the manipulation of signs. See Wittgenstein 1958: 6, etc.

99. The arrangement might be illustrated (see figure N1). Cf. Bambrough 1976.

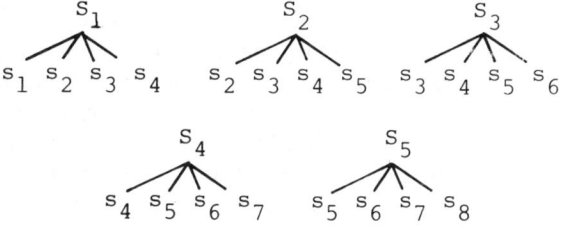

Figure N1. Semes, sememes, and family resemblances

100. Wittgenstein would have suspected this schematization since "sameness", "difference", "mediation", etc. are themselves family resemblances. See Wittgenstein 1958: 86, 133, 150ff., 181.
101. This summary closely paraphrases Peirce 1931–1958, 2: ss. 228, 274. Peirce's theory is refashioned from a less psychologistic standpoint by Eco 1979: 180–183.
102. Peirce sometimes equates a "sign" and a "representamen" and sometimes distinguishes them. In the latter instance, a sign is a representamen with a mental interpretant. See Peirce 1931–1956, 2: s. 274. For Peirce, a sign or representamen exemplifies what he terms "firstness".
103. According to Peirce, an interpretant exemplifies "thirdness".
104. Peirce notes that the sign or representamen may have a plurality of objects. See Peirce 1931–1958, 2: s. 232. For Peirce, an object exemplifies what he terms "secondness".
105. Elsewhere Peirce treats the ground as a selected attribute of the object. See Eco 1979: 181–182.
106. Peirce 1931–1958, 2: s. 274. Cf. Eco. 1984: 68–69, 83–84.
107. Strictly speaking, Peirce's interpretants can be anything from simple properties to complex arguments. See Peirce 1931–1958, 1: s. 615, 2: s. 330; Eco 1979: 187–191, 196–197.
108. See Eco 1984: 44, 113–118, 130.
109. See Eco 1984: 113, 123–124, 127–129. Of course, the important point is that sameness and difference occur in linguistic application rather than in ontological or psychological properties.
110. The doctrine is elaborated by Greimas after suggestions by Brøndal, Jakobson, and Lévi-Strauss. Convenient summaries may be found in Greimas 1970: 135–155, Greimas — Courtés 1979, 1: 29–33. Cf. Greimas 1983: 93–102.
111. On the relational axes see further pp. 20, 139ff.
112. There is some obscurity surrounding presentations of the semiotic square because a. squares may be individual or superimposed, b. their terms may be expressed or unexpressed. Thus, Greimas speaks of a first-generation square (see figure N2). Derived from this is i. a second-generation square which involves superimposition of a second square shifted by one position and expression of all eight of the constituent terms (figure N3). ii. a third-generation square which involves the superimposition of a second square shifted by one position and expression of only six of the constitutent terms (figure N4). In Greimas 1966, the third-generation square is implicitly treated as standard — a_1 ($\bar{a}_2$) is called the positive term, ($\bar{a}_1$) a_2 the negative term, a_2 a_1 the complex term, and $\bar{a}_2$ $\bar{a}_1$ the neutral term — although in Greimas — Courtés 1979, 1: 32, it is declared problematic. In Greimas 1970 and elsewhere, the first and second-generation squares are explicitly treated as basic.

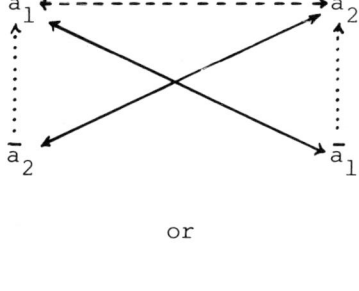

or

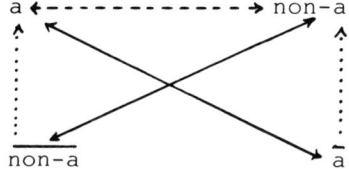

Figure N2. Greimas' first-generation semiotic square

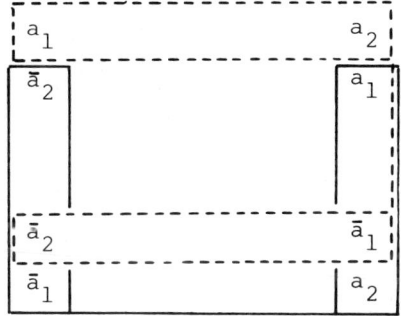

Figure N3. Greimas' second-generation semiotic square

a_1 a_2
$(\bar{a}_2)$ a_1

$\bar{a}_2$ $(\bar{a}_1)$
$\bar{a}_1$ a_2

Figure N4. Greimas' third-generation semiotic square

113. On the relational terms see further pp. 20, 139 ff. Greimas' account presents difficulties because a. the relations differ from those in logical squares of opposition, b. the relations vary in accordance with the generation of the square. However, in the second-generation square contradiction = addition or substraction of two semes, while contrariety and implication = addition or subtraction of one of two semes.
114. The semiotic square will be discussed further on pp. 20, 139 ff.
115. The third term or interpretant would coincide with the axes of the semiotic square.
116. The contrary, contradictory, and implicated in the semiotic square would also coincide with sameness and difference in the family-resemblance structure.
117. In theory, they *should* be simultaneously applicable.
118. See p. 69 ff.
119. See Derrida 1967[1]: 128.
120. Barthes 1970 has shown that a text is not primarily denotative in character (Barthes 1970: 11–12, 14–16, 20–21, 133–134). He distinguishes texts as modern or classic according to the relative liberation or restriction of language's semantic possibilities (Barthes 1970: 11–12, 18–20, 35–37, 125–126, 216–217, 222–223).
121. Barthes 1970 has shown that a text is not simply communicative in nature (Barthes 1970: 150–151, 157–158). He distinguishes text as "scriptible" and "lisible" according to the relative productivity or unproductivity of the reader's role (Barthes 1970: 9–10, 27–28). For a systematic exploration of the reader's contribution see Eco 1979: 3–43.
122. Barthes 1970 argues that the identity of the reader is constituted by his own textuality — the "intertexte" (Barthes 1970: 16–18, 216–217). For Kristeva's theory see pp. 6–7.
123. See Derrida 1967[1]: 15–17, 68–70, 96–98, 1967[2]: 409 ff., 418–421, 423, 1972[1]: xiv ff., xviii–xix.
124. Here, "semiotic" is synonymous with "semantic" or "signifying".
125. By "coordinate" is meant "within the same semantic category". Coordinate with binary and ternary are "quadruple", "n-tuple", and other terms; coordinate with relative is "absolute" only.
126. The semantic structure might be illustrated as follows (figure N5). Diagrams of interrelations among semantic properties are notoriously difficult to construct, since such terms are not the genera and species of a Porphyrian tree but elements within a "family resemblance". Attempts to depict such relations can be found in Greimas 1966: 31–34; Eco 1976: 121–125. In the second reference, the author rejects certain proposals of Katz and Fodor in favour of a model suggested by Quillian (= the "Model Q").
127. The terms "opposition" and "relation" are often treated as equivalents in linguistic and semiotic literature. See Barthes 1985[1]: 65–66.

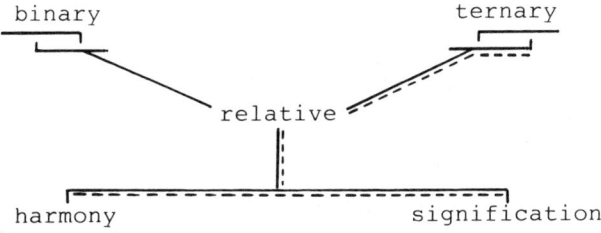

Figure N5. Semantic structure of medieval writing and modern reading

128. Thus, French *mange-mangeons*.
129. Thus, English *foot-feet*.
130. Thus, written characters E–F.
131. Thus, written characters P–R. These four illustrations are given by Barthes 1985¹: 67–69. The privative and equipollent oppositions — together with a third type of graduated opposition (German /u/–/o/) — were postulated by Trubetzkoy, while the bilateral and multilateral oppositions were explored by Cantineau.
132. See p. 69 ff.
133. See Barthes 1985¹: 53–54, 60; Jakobson 1971: 74–75. The image derives from Saussure and is much favoured by Lévi-Strauss.
134. The reciprocity implied by spatial oppositions is discussed by Jakobson 1980: 25.
135. The illustration — but not this application — is supplied by Russell 1956: 225.
136. See pp. 16–17.
137. On this version of the square see Greimas — Courtés 1979, 1:31–32.
138. See p. 139 ff.
139. See Barthes 1970: 20–21, 1985¹: 58–60.
140. Augustine cites the Greek term *harmonia* and translates it as *coaptatio* at *dTr.* IV. 2. 4. On the history of terminology see Meyer 1932; Nebois 1940; Mathiesen 1976.
141. Augustine: *dMECdMM* II. 6. 8. In Plotinus, the creative Logos — closely associated with *pronoia* [providence] — is a similar principle of concord or harmony. See *En.* III. 2. 2, III. 2. 16–17, III. 3. 1, III. 3. 4. Much of the Augustinian theory discussed in this chapter is dependent on Plotinus' analysis at *En.* III. 2–3. Cf. *En.* I. 6. 2–3, IV. 4. 41. The Plotinian teaching is studied by Witt 1938; Schubert 1968; Früchtel 1970; Parma 1971; Turlot 1985.
142. Extensive discussions occur at Augustine: *dOr.* I. 1. 1–I. 11. 33, II. 1. 1–II. 7. 23, *dLA* III. 5. 12–III. 9. 28. Rief 1962 makes a useful collection of passages. Cf. Hübner 1987.

143. Augustine: *dMu.* VI. 17. 56. Plotinus: *En.* III. 2. 12 explains how the creative Logos contains *homoia* [similars] within itself.
144. Augustine: *dCD* XIX. 13. The definition recalls Cicero's of *concentus* at *dRe.* II. 42. 69. Cf. Augustine: *En.* 90. Plotinus: *En.* III. 2. 16–17 speaks of the *diaphora* [difference] within the creative Logos. Cf. En. III. 3. 3.
145. Augustine: *cFM* XXI. 11. Plotinus: *En.* III. 2. 16–17 explains how the creative Logos contains *enantia* [opposites] within itself.
146. It had been employed by Biblical commentators before Augustine. Examples include Philo: *dSo.* II. 193–194; Irenaeus: *aHa.* IV. 4. 2; Clement of Alexandria: *Pr.* 6; Origen: *dPr.* IV. 4. 8; Basil: *iHe.* 3. 5; Ambrose: *iHe.* II. 3. 12. Peri 1983 discusses the early tradition.
147. For this triad in Augustine see *cA* I. 8. 6, *cFM* XX. 7, *dTr.* III. 9. 16–18, XI. 11. 18, *dGaL* IV. 3. 7, *En.* 29. La Bonnardière 1970 provides a list of passages; du Roy 1966 and Beierwaltes 1969 some philosophical commentary.
148. Augustine: *dLA* II. 20. 54, *dGcM* I. 16. 26, I. 20. 32, *cFM* XXI. 6.
149. Augustine: *dNB* 3, 5–6, 8–10, 13, 23. Here, the first member of the triad is *modus* rather than *mensura*.
150. Augustine: *dQA* 36. 81, *dMu.* VI. 17. 56, *dVR* 7. 13, *dTr.* VI. 10. 12.
151. Augustine's interpretation of the triad influenced much medieval speculation. Examples include Claudianus Mamertus: *dSA* 111. 15–113. 21; Cassiodorus: *In.* II, pr. 3; Isidore of Seville: *Et.* III. 4; Bede: *iGe.* 1; Eriugena: *Pe.* V. 1013A; Abbo of Fleury: *QG* 48; Adalbold of Utrecht: *Mu.*, in.; Thierry of Chartres: *dSDO* 35. The twelfth-century material is discussed by Parodi 1984.
152. Augustine: *dMu.* VI. 17. 57–58. Cf. *dDC* I. 5. 5. In Plotinus, the triad of which the creative Logos is the third member is also associated with *harmonia* [harmony]. See *En.* III. 2. 16–17, III. 3. 1–3.
153. For "isotopy" see p. 69 ff.
154. Eriugena: *Pe.* II. 533 A–B. In citing *Periphyseon*, we shall employ the text of Sheldon-Williams for books I–III, and that of Floss for books IV–V. On the former edition see Sheldon-Williams 1961. Unfortunately Sheldon-Williams edited books I–III using many dubious criteria, and so it is sometimes necessary to return to Floss there also. See the review of Lucentini 1976. In studying Eriugena's writing, it will be important to understand his use of earlier materials. This textual dependence is documented by Madec 1986.
155. Eriugena: *Pe.* III. 681A–B. Eriugena's notion of *ordo* is influenced not only by Augustine but by ps.-Dionysius' concept of *taxis*. See Eriugena: *iDdCH* 3. 204 ff.
156. Eriugena: *Pe.* III. 630A–631A.
157. See Boethius: *dIA* II. 40, 137. 1–II. 54, 173. 7.
158. Eriugena: *iDdCH* 9. 159–163.
159. Eriugena: *Pe.* III. 637B–638A. Cf. *Pe.* I. 517B–C.

160. Eriugena: *Pe.* V. 1013A. Cf. *Pe.* III. 652A, III. 656B.
161. Eriugena: *iDdCH* 1. 107–116.
162. See n. 140. For lexical information see Catalogus 1976+.
163. For lexical information see Allard 1983. On Eriugena's knowledge of music in general see Handschin 1927; Hüschen 1954; Wiora 1971; Münxelhaus 1976: 107–109, 199ff., 1977; Waeltner 1977; Viret 1980. Eriugena's activity as glossator of musical materials in Martianus Capella and Boethius is studied by Jones 1957; Leonardi 1977; Duchez 1980. Eriugena's use of musical terms in elaborating philosophical arguments is studied by Coallier 1986. On Eriugena's concept of musical aesthetics see Beierwaltes 1976.
164. See Merguet 1961. For Cicero, *concordia* mostly has a political sense as at *dRe.* I. 32. 49, *dND* III. 24. 61, etc. *dRe.* II. 42. 69 contrasts *concordia* (political) with *harmonia* (scientific). *Harmonia* is generally used in scientific contexts as at *dRe.* II. 42. 69, *TD* I. 18. 41, *dND* III. 11. 27, etc. *Ti.* 5. 15 links the technical sense of *concors* with *amicitia* and *caritas*. Cf. n. 144.
165. For Boethius see Bernhard 1979.
166. Augustine: *dGcM* I. 21. 32.
167. Augustine: *dGLI* 5.
168. Augustine: *cEMF* 41.
169. Augustine: *cSM* 15.
170. Augustine: *dNB* 8.
171. Augustine: *dNB* 16.
172. Augustine: *Ep.* 166. 13.
173. Augustine: *cALP* I. 6. 8.
174. Elsewhere, Augustine emphasizes other features of the song. At *Co.* XII. 29 and *cALP* I. 12. 9 he correlates unformed voice and articulated melody with cosmic matter and form, and at *dOr.* I. 7. 18 and *dCD* XI. 18 the placing of antitheses in discourse with the presence of opposites in the universe.
175. *Gen.* 1. 4 and *Dan.* 3. 72 (Vulg.).
176. See *D, G* above.
177. See *G* above. Human melody relates to divine *ad admonitionem magnae rei*. The isotopy of creation present throughout these passages also contributes to such an interpretation.
178. See *H* above.
179. The philosophical exploration of music by Augustine and Boethius is a typical product of the late antique intellectual milieu. The best general studies of the latter are Gérold 1931 and Wille 1967.
180. Boethius: *dIM* I. 2, 187. 20–189. 9. Chamberlain 1970 has demonstrated Boethius' use of this theory also in his *De consolatione philosophiae*.
181. This conforms to the ancient distinction between *harmonia* [harmonics] and *mousikē*. See Mathiesen 1976.
182. This approach is illustrated by Alan of Lille. See pp. 65–66.

183. This approach is illustrated by Regino of Prüm. At *dHI* 3. 232 ff. he divides music into *naturalis* [natural] and *artificialis* [artificial], the first being subdivided into *caelestis* [celestial], *humana* [human], and *in irrationabili creatura* [in the irrational creature].
184. See Pietzsch 1929: 14, 39 ff.; de Bruyne 1946, 1: 310–318, 2: 112 ff.
185. For the sounding planet theory see Aurelian of Réôme: *MD* 3, Eriugena: *iMCdNPM* (O) 123. 3 ff., Remigius of Auxerre: *iMCdNPM* IX. 476. 15 ff., Bernard Silvestris: *iMCdNPM* 3. 75–85. For the planetary distance interpretation see section 5.5.
186. See pp. 60–63, etc.
187. See Hugh of St. Victor: *Di.* II. 12 discussed on p. 64.
188. See Berno of Reichenau: *PiT* 4. 65–66.
189. For the structural affinity theory see Hugh of St. Victor: *Di.* II. 12, Bernard Silvestris: *iMCdNPM* 3. 38–39, Anonymous: *dPP* 183. 4 ff. For the external expression viewpoint see the glosses on Boethius: *dIM* edited in Pizzani 1980: 334–335.
190. Some sources by identifying human music with vocal performance abandon the metaphysics entirely.
191. See Hugh of St. Victor: *Di.* II. 12 discussed on pp. 114–115.
192. Boethius: *dIM* I. 27, 219. 4–28.
193. See p. 39.
194. See p. 40.
195. Boethius: *dIM* I. 2, 188. 12–26.
196. See p. 14 ff.
197. The following summary is based on the various writings of Russell which remain the best statement of relational theory to date. For more technical discussion of most questions see — in addition to passages cited nn. 198–204 — Russell 1938: index, under "Relation, Relations".
198. See Russell 1919: 48–49.
199. See Russell 1919: 42 ff., 1926: 56–60.
200. See Russell 1919: 15, 45–51.
201. See Russell 1919: 16, 32, 45–51.
202. See Russell 1926: 56–60.
203. See Russell 1919: 31–32.
204. See Russell 1919: 52 ff. In recent times, the various relations occurring in linguistic structures have been extensively discussed by Hjelmslev who however speaks rather of various "dependencies" (Hjelmslev 1961: 22 ff.). For this writer, dependence fulfilling the conditions for an analysis is a "function" (ϕ) (Hjelmslev 1961: 33, 40, n. 9). The terminal of a function is a functive which can be either a "constant" (c) whose presence is a necessary condition for the presence of the functive to which it has function, or a "variable" (v) whose presence is not a necessary condition for the presence of the functive to which it has function (Hjelmslev 1961: 35). On this basis, "inter-

dependence" (c ↔ c) is defined as a function between two constants, "determination" (v ↠ c or c ↞ v) as one between a constant and a variable, and "constellation" (v | v) as one between two variables (Hjelmslev 1961: 24–25, 35). Now the logical distinction between the both-and function and the either-or function — Hjelmslev calls these "relation" (R) and "correlation" (:) respectively — is important for establishing the linguistic difference between process and system (Hjelmslev 1961: 36, 38–39). Interdependence between terms is therefore called in a process "solidarity" (c ~ c) and in a system "complementarity" (c ⊥ c); determination in a process "selection" (v→c or c←v) and in a system "specification" (v⊢c or c⊣v); and constellation in a process "combination" (v–v) and in a system "autonomy" (v†v) (Hjelmslev 1961: 24–25, 36). Various examples of these functions among the elements of language are provided (Hjelmslev 1961: 25ff.).

205. See pp. 71, 75, 88–89, 105.
206. See pp. 75, 81, 84, 88, 105–106.
207. See pp. 80, 82, 85.
208. See pp. 80–81, 82, 93–96.
209. See pp. 88, 105.
210. Cf. Table 1, n. 10.
211. Eco 1984: 23 describes this phase of the interpretative process as the "blowing-up" of semantic properties. The opposite phase is the "narcotizing" of such properties.
212. On relation and propositional functions see Russell 1919: 155ff., 1956: 230, 237–238. Descriptive functions differ from propositional functions but are also relational. See Russell 1919: 46–47, 180.
213. On contextual selection see Greimas 1966: 44–50; Eco 1976: 105ff., 1979: 19, 23ff. On encyclopaedia see n. 261.
214. See n. 211.
215. According to Aristotelian principles, highest genera — like the categories — cannot be genuine unities or objects of definition. This position was, of course, metaphysically unacceptable to Platonists. See n. 217.
216. See Porphyry: *iACa*. 111. 21–29. Cf. Plotinus: *En*. VI. 2. 16, 1–13.
217. See Porphyry: *iACa*. 121. 20–28. Cf. Plotinus: *En*. VI. 1. 6, 1–2, VI. 1. 7, 21–23, VI. 1. 8, 5–8, VI. 1. 9, 25–39 together with Simplicius: *iACa*. 168. 16ff.
218. The Greek commentary-tradition from Porphyry to Simplicius will be our guide here. Although these works were not available in western Europe during the earlier Middle Ages, they influenced or are related to certain Latin treatises which were. So Greek commentators are important indices of the Aristotelianism in Augustine, Eriugena, and the like. On the Neoplatonic treatment of relation see Rutten 1961: 93–103; Conti 1983; Evangeliou 1988: 79–84, 161–162.

219. Plotinus: *En.* VI. 2. 8, 25–43, VI. 2. 16, 1–13.
220. Simplicius: *iACa.* 172. 23–27. Cf. *iACa.* 160. 9–33, 174. 46–49, 202. 21–203. 13, 205. 22–35.
221. See Simplicius: *iACa.* 202. 21–203. 13. See n. 224.
222. Aristotle: *Ca.* 7. 6^a 36–37 *hosa auta haper estin heterōn einai legetai, ē hopōsoun allōs pros heteron.*
223. Aristotle: *Ca.* 7. 8^a 32 *hois to einai tauton esti tōi pros ti pōs echein.*
224. Porphyry: *iACa.* 112. 2–21. There is a tendency among the Neoplatonists to interpret the earlier definition as a linguistic or multiple characterization of relation, and the later as an ontological and unitary characterization. Since the ontological and unitary was understood as the cause of the linguistic and multiple, Aristotle's sequence of writing could be treated as itself reflecting the metaphysical structure of causation. This whole interpretation is post-Porphyrian according to Simplicius: *iACa.* 159. 9–14, 198. 12ff. Cf. Ammonius: *iACa.* 77. 28–78. 16, Boethius: *iACa.* 235B–237A.
225. Simplicius: *iACa.* 162. 12–35.
226. Plotinus: *En.* VI. 1. 6, 13–36, VI. 1. 8, 8–16.
227. Plotinus: *En.* VI. 1. 9, 1–21.
228. Plotinus: *En.* VI. 1. 6, 17–36, VI. 1. 8, 19–21.
229. Simplicius: *iACa.* 174. 30–32, 202. 25–29. Cf. *iACa.* 171. 9–17, 172. 25–27, 205. 22–35.
230. Simplicius: *iACa.* 168. 16–36. Most later Neoplatonists include defences of the reality of relation in their commentaries on the *Categories*: see Ammonius: *iACa.* 66. 21–67. 11 and Simplicius: *iACa.* 169. 1–30. Simplicius argues that since relation is the basis of *koinōnia* [communion] and *harmonia* [harmony], while the latter are the foundations of both dialectic and mathematics, the objectivity of relation is a necessary postulate of scientific research.
231. See n. 222.
232. Porphyry: *iACa.* 125. 16–19. Cf. Plotinus: *En.* VI. 1. 7, 33–38, Simplicius: *iACa.* 190. 12–25.
233. Simplicius: *iACa.* 203. 14–204. 11.
234. See pp. 48–49. On the historical filling and emptying of lexemes see Barthes 1957: 224–245; Greimas 1966: 38.
235. The debate is, however, only indirectly with Hegel. In that Hegel distinguishes internal and external relations and assigns primacy to the former, his philosophical position is close to that of the Neoplatonic Aristotelian commentators. See pp. 53–55.
236. See pp. 45–46.
237. According to Russell 1959: 54 the terminology "internal" and "external" was adopted in response to Bradley.

238. See Russell 1910: 142.
239. See Russell 1959: 54.
240. See Russell 1910: 131, 139–140, 146. Russell 1956: 206 ff. speaks of a reduction of dyadic to monadic relations here.
241. See Russell 1956: 335.
242. See Russell 1910: 140.
243. See Russell 1956: 335.
244. On this theory see Russell 1956: 178–179, etc.
245. See Russell 1919: 44, 1956: 206–207. An illustration from Plato has been substituted for that from Berkeley and Hume given by Russell.
246. See Russell 1919: 44, 1926: 58–59, 1956: 207, 1959: 55.
247. See Russell 1919: 44–45.
248. On this theory see Russell 1956: 332 ff. Russell acknowledged the influence of Wittgenstein here.
249. See Russell 1956: 332–336.
250. See Russell 1956: 337–338.
251. See Russell 1956: 332–333.
252. See Simplicius: *iACa.* 205. 22–35.
253. See Simplicius: *iACa.* 175. 4–11, Boethius: *iACa.* 236A–B.
254. This is Iamblichus' interpretation quoted as Simplicius: *iACa.* 203. 21–25. The same move occurs at Plotinus: *En.* VI. 1. 7, 24–38.
255. See pp. 13–14, 18 ff.
256. This is because semes are often — perhaps usually — contained in but not expressed by their lexemes. Greimas names the process whereby a lexeme is dissolved into semes which are then represented by further lexemes "lexicalisation" (Greimas 1966: 112–113). He advocates a uniform procedure of converting all terms — whether actants or predicates — into substantives with the appropriate suffixes: *-ité, -itude*, etc. (Greimas 1966: 157–158). We shall adopt the standardized method of converting all terms into either a substantival form: *-icity*, etc. or an ambivalently substantival and adjectival form: (*the*) + adjective.
257. Greimas calls the products of this first level of amalgamation "classèmes" (Greimas 1966: 52 ff., Greimas — Courtés 1979, 1: 37). This definition causes certain problems since of the sememes' two components amalgamation is associated with the contextual semes — the classemes — and invariance with the nuclear semes, although amalgamation is really operative in either case. Such difficulties are inevitable in attempting to find a genuine universality within the family-resemblance structure of sememes. Nevertheless, classemes are described i. as *plus large* [wider] than lexemes (Greimas 1966: 53, 78, 113) i.e. attached to several nuclei, ii. as *identique* [identical] (Greimas 1966: 52, 79) i.e. in meaning, iii. as *itératif* [iterative] (Greimas 1966: 53, 78) i.e. in occurrence. Classemes are illustrated by "unitary", "integral", "discrete", "static", "dynamic", "causing",

"caused", "inanimate", "animate", etc. (Greimas 1966: 71–72, 79–82, 121–123).

258. Greimas calls the products of this second level of amalgamation "isotopies" (Greimas 1966: 69 ff., Greimas — Courtés 1979, 1: 197–199). His theory might be summarized as follows. The existence of an isotopy is revealed by the redundant presence of a seme (Greimas 1966: 80), this isotopy being defined as a. a sequence of discourse whose elements have one or more classemes in common (Greimas 1966: 53), or b. an inventory of sememes characterized by the presence of a certain classeme (Greimas 1966: 120). Objectively speaking, an isotopy can vary in dimension from a syntagm through a sentence to an entire text (Greimas 1966: 71–72, 127, 147); several isotopies can exist in unspecified relations to one another (Greimas 1966: 88–89, 96–97), as primary and secondary isotopies (Greimas 1966: 120–121) relating hyperotactically or hypotactically to one another (Greimas 1966: 162), and in relations specified as positive, negative, neutral, or complex (Greimas 1966: 97, 99–100, 134–135). Methodologically speaking, the discovery of an isotopy can be difficult (Greimas 1966: 90–91, 98–99), requires a textual sample of adequate size (Greimas 1966: 92–93), and involves selection or elimination (Greimas 1966: 145–146). Examples of isotopies are "cosmological", "noological", "animate", "inanimate", etc. One might add that the principle of isotopy has not really been weakened by Derrida. This writer has seriously questioned the assumption of primary and secondary thematicisms in texts — conceived as emphases upon fundamental signifieds — as being incompatible with the differential nature of language itself (Derrida 1972^2: 279–294). Yet it is neither the implied sameness of Greimas' isotopy nor the *soi-disant* otherness of Derrida's dissemination, but the interaction of sameness and otherness in family resemblances which ultimately reveals the process of discourse.
259. This argument is elaborated by Eco 1976: 131–133, 1979: 24–27, 1984: 189–201.
260. "Semantic features" are units of the semantic field when these are considered in isolation. They correspond roughly with Hjelmslev's "substance" on the content-plane of language. See n. 932. Semantic features contrast with "semantic relations". See n. 263
261. An encyclopaedic competence is an enormous concatenation of sememes which is only partially describable. The need for such a concept in semiotic research has been stressed by Eco 1984: 68–86.
262. Nevertheless, the relations between all these pairs are determined by those envisioned between three pre-eminent pairs. For future reference, a graphic presentation may be added (see figure N6). That a pair of semes is the minimal unit of any semantic system is noted by Greimas 1966: 108–109.

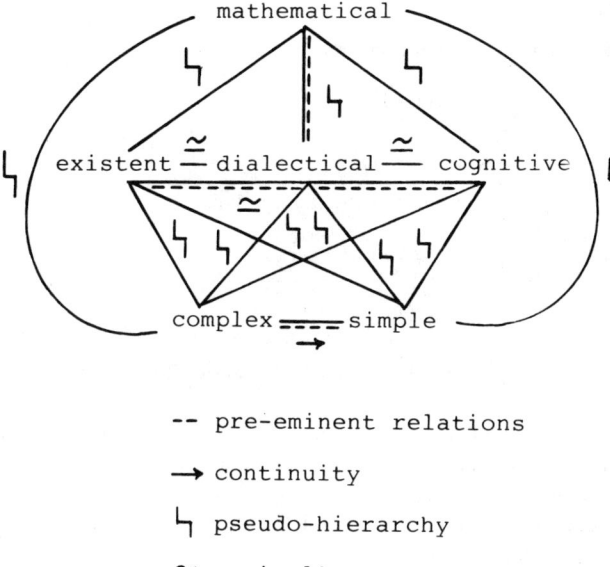

Figure N6. Semantic features

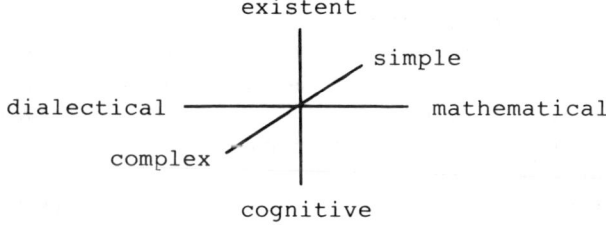

Figure N7. Semantic relations

263. "Semantic relations" are units of the semantic field when these are considered in combination. They correspond roughly with Hjelmslev's "form" on the content-plane of language. See n. 932. Semantic relations contrast with "semantic features". See n. 260.
264. On the reasons for visualizing these relations of continuity, pseudo-hierarchy, and equivalence as geometrical axes see n. 279. For future reference, a graphic presentation may be appended (figure N7).
265. See nn. 543, 552.
266. It is noteworthy that Eriugena begins by examining a term and not a thing. Since this term — "nature" — is explicitly said to comprehend the non-

294   *Notes*

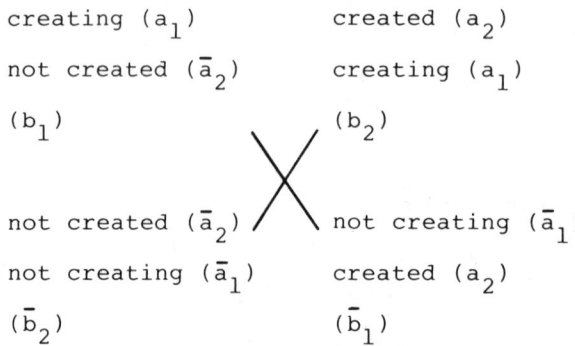

Figure N8. Eriugena's metaphysical analysis as a semiotic square

existent and the existent, the zero-degree of Eriugena's discussion is semantic and not ontological. See Cristiani 1981; d'Onofrio 1986.
267. Eriugena: *Pe.* I. 441 A – 442 A.
268. Eriugena's metaphysical analysis — and the diagram to which he later alludes — can be identified with a Greimasian semantic projection of n. 112 as shown above (figure N8). Greimas himself suggests analysis if not of "creating" "created" at least of "causant"-"causé" in this manner. See Greimas 1966: 80 ff.
269. A sememe corresponds to one "sense" (produced by a combination of actualized semes) within a lexeme. See n. 81.
270. Eriugena apparently treats contrariety and contradiction as synonymous. On Eriugena's fourfold analysis see further Schrimpf 1989, d'Onofrio 1990.
271. The shift from semantic to ontological is *for Eriugena*. Naturally, the discussion is entirely semantic from our viewpoint.
272. Eriugena: *Pe.* II. 523 D – 528 A.
273. The wording indicates that Eriugena envisages a graphic representation of the square of opposition as in n. 268.
274. Cf. Eriugena: *Pe.* III. 621 A – 622 A, III. 688 D – 689 A, V. 1019 A – 1020 A.
275. Eriugena: *Pe.* III. 630 A – 631 B.
276. Eriugena: *Pe.* III. 623 C – D.
277. Eriugena: *Pe.* III. 695 A – 696 A.
278. See p. 70.
279. It will be convenient to label the three groups X = "existent" + "cognitive", Y = "dialectical" + "mathematical", Z = "complex" + "simple", where the alphabetical order of the letter-codes reflects increasing logical complexity. Application of the square of opposition to these semantic features differs from Greimas' procedure in two ways. First, the Greimasian analysis applies primarily to single semantic categories each of which has an internal fourfold articulation, whereas our proposal applies mainly to pairs of semantic

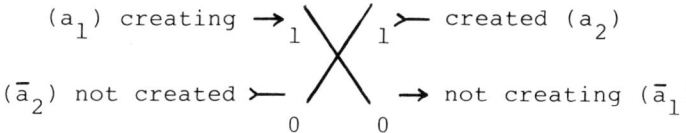

Figure N9. Semiotic square of "creation"

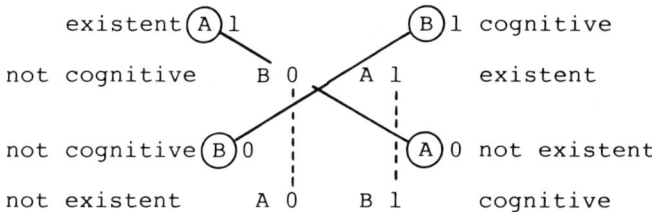

Figure N10. Semiotic square of "existent-cognitive"

categories each of which has an internal twofold articulation. Greimas' analysis may be illustrated by constructing a square for the single semantic category "creation". Since there is one category which can be articulated by two oppositions: positive (1) vs. negative (0) and active (→) vs. passive (⊁−), we obtain the square (figure N9). Such a square cannot be constructed for the single semantic categories "existence", "dialecticity", "mathematicity", "complexity", "simplicity" which can be articulated into positive vs. negative but not into active vs. passive. Our proposal may be illustrated by constructing a square for the pair of semantic categories "existence" + "cognition", Since there are two categories which can be articulated by one opposition: positive (1) vs. negative (0), we obtain the square (figure N10). Such a square can be constructed for the pairs of semantic categories "dialecticity" + "mathematicity", "complexity" + "simplicity" which can be articulated into positive vs. negative. The change between Greimas' analysis and our proposal is important since it makes the square applicable a. not only to amalgamations of semes between sememes but also to combinations of semes within a sememe; b. not only to a restricted group of semantic features but to the entire range of such features. Secondly, the Greimasian analysis speaks of "axes" between the four single terms into which the single semantic categories are articulated, whereas our proposal speaks of axes between two or more pairs of terms into which the pairs of semantic categories are articulated. Greimas' analysis may be illustrated by unfolding the square into a line and marking all possible interrelations of two terms (figure N11). He calls 1, 2, 3, 4, 5, 6 axes but not 7 nor the combinations 1 + 2, 1 + 2 + 3, etc. Our proposal may be similarly illustrated by unfolding the square into a line and marking all possible interrelations

296   Notes

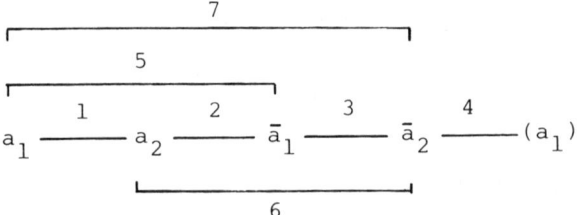

Figure N11. Unfolding of the semiotic square according to Greimas' analysis

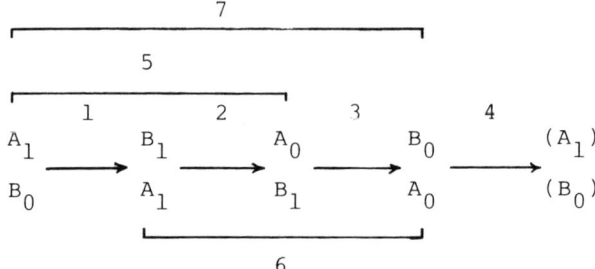

Figure N12. Unfolding of the semiotic square according to the present analysis

$$(b_2) \quad \begin{matrix} B_1 \\ A_1 \end{matrix} \qquad (\bar{b}_2) \quad \begin{matrix} B_0 \\ A_0 \end{matrix}$$

Figure N13. The axis of equivalence

$$(b_2) \quad \begin{matrix} B_1 \\ A_1 \end{matrix} \quad (\bar{b}_1) \quad \begin{matrix} A_0 \\ B_1 \end{matrix} \quad (\bar{b}_2) \quad \begin{matrix} B_0 \\ A_0 \end{matrix}$$

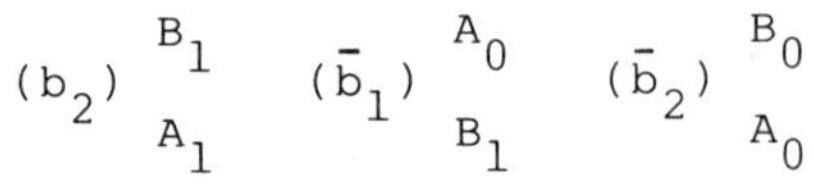

Figure N14. The axis of pseudo-hierarchy

of two terms (figure N12). We call 1, 2, 3, 4, 5, 6 axes and also 7, and the combinations 1 + 2, 1 + 2 + 3, etc. Greimas' comparatively restricted use of the term "axis" is more logical when the terms are arranged in a square than when they are arranged in a line. However, it is unnecessary from the viewpoint of a semantics liberated from dependence on a single graphic image.

280. See n. 261.
281. The axis of equivalence would appear as shown above (figure N13).

$$(b_1) \begin{matrix} A_1 \\ B_0 \end{matrix} \quad (b_2) \begin{matrix} B_1 \\ A_1 \end{matrix} \quad (\bar{b}_1) \begin{matrix} A_0 \\ B_1 \end{matrix} \quad (\bar{b}_2) \begin{matrix} B_0 \\ A_0 \end{matrix}$$

Figure N15. The axis of continuity

282. The axis of pseudo-hierarchy would appear as shown above (figure N14). This arrangement is hierarchical in that the relation between components is similar to that between genus and species in the *Arbor Porphyriana*. However, it is "pseudo-" hierarchical because the subordinate component unlike Porphyry's species extends beyond the superordinate one. That there are also pseudo-hierarchical elements in the *Arbor Porphyriana* itself has been demonstrated by Eco 1984: 58–68.
283. The axis of continuity would appear as shown above (figure N15).
284. The complete list is:

Table N1. The 24 clusters of semantic features

X	(b_2)	Y	(b_2)	Z	(b_1)
X	(b_2)	Y	(b_2)	Z	(b_2)
X	(b_2)	Y	(b_2)	Z	$(\bar{b}_1)$
X	(b_2)	Y	(b_2)	Z	$(\bar{b}_2)$
X	(b_2)	Y	$(\bar{b}_1)$	Z	(b_1)
X	(b_2)	Y	$(\bar{b}_1)$	Z	(b_2)
X	(b_2)	Y	$(\bar{b}_1)$	Z	$(\bar{b}_1)$
X	(b_2)	Y	$(\bar{b}_1)$	Z	$(\bar{b}_2)$
X	(b_2)	Y	$(\bar{b}_2)$	Z	(b_1)
X	(b_2)	Y	$(\bar{b}_2)$	Z	(b_2)
X	(b_2)	Y	$(\bar{b}_2)$	Z	$(\bar{b}_1)$
X	(b_2)	Y	$(\bar{b}_2)$	Z	$(\bar{b}_2)$
X	$(\bar{b}_2)$	Y	(b_2)	Z	(b_1)
X	$(\bar{b}_2)$	Y	(b_2)	Z	(b_2)
X	$(\bar{b}_2)$	Y	(b_2)	Z	$(\bar{b}_1)$
X	$(\bar{b}_2)$	Y	(b_2)	Z	$(\bar{b}_2)$
X	$(\bar{b}_2)$	Y	$(\bar{b}_1)$	Z	(b_1)
X	$(\bar{b}_2)$	Y	$(\bar{b}_1)$	Z	(b_2)
X	$(\bar{b}_2)$	Y	$(\bar{b}_1)$	Z	$(\bar{b}_1)$
X	$(\bar{b}_2)$	Y	$(\bar{b}_1)$	Z	$(\bar{b}_2)$
X	$(\bar{b}_2)$	Y	$(\bar{b}_2)$	Z	(b_1)
X	$(\bar{b}_2)$	Y	$(\bar{b}_2)$	Z	(b_2)
X	$(\bar{b}_2)$	Y	$(\bar{b}_2)$	Z	$(\bar{b}_1)$
X	$(\bar{b}_2)$	Y	$(\bar{b}_2)$	Z	$(\bar{b}_2)$

285. Arguably, the sememes "relation" and "internality" — owing to the prevailing metaphysical monism — have semiotic identity.
286. An "isotopy of transcendence" — which will be needed in chapters three and four — may also be mentioned here. The semantic feature "transcendent" forms an axis of pseudo-hierarchy with the semantic feature "immanent".
287. The origins and transmission of the ps.-Augustinian treatise are discussed by Pfligersdorffer 1950–1951; Minio-Paluello 1961: lxxvii–xcvi.
288. ps.-Augustine: *CD* 9. 135. 13–17, 26. 139. 7–8, 31. 140. 10, 38. 142. 1–2, 50. 144. 12 gives the signifying/signified distinction. The two overlapping sections will therefore be a. Signifying: *CD* 9. 135. 13–26. 139. 8+50. 144. 12–55. 145. 22; b. Signified: *CD* 27. 139. 9–49. 144. 11. In antiquity, the main controversy surrounding the interpretation of Aristotle's *Categories* was whether the categories signified words, concepts, things, or combinations thereof. See Evangeliou 1988: 17–34; Vollrath 1969: 1–5.
289. ps.-Augustine: *CD* 20. 137. 20–23.
290. Cf. ps.-Augustine: *CD* 2. 133. 9 ff.
291. A/B = ps.-Augustine: *CD* 9. 135. 15–17; A1 = *CD* 10. 135. 18–136. 9; A2 = *CD* 12. 136. 5–9; A3 = *CD* 22. 138. 8–15; B1 = *CD* 14. 136. 16–19; B2 = *CD* 15. 136. 19–23; A1 a/b = *CD* 17. 136. 26–30; A1 b α–β = *CD* 18. 136. 30–137. 12. The discussion concerning types of words — especially concerning synonymy and homonymy — indicates a shift from the logical to the semantic sphere. From the standpoint of modern linguistic theory which, in associating words with meanings rather than things, is philosophically non-realist: a. synonyms are expressions materially (phonically or graphically) different but having similar meanings — where resemblance is between "signifieds" —; b. homonyms are expressions materially (phonically or graphically) similar but having different meanings — where resemblance is between "signifiers" —; the existence of such phenomena being interpreted by generative grammarians as testimony to the contrast between surface and deep structures of language. Within the ancient and medieval Platonic traditions, the problem of synonymy is rarely discussed and that of homonymy deliberately evaded — as presenting a peculiar challenge to their realist assumptions.
292. ps.-Augustine: *CD* 26. 139. 5–8. Cf. 51. 144. 15–21, 55. 145. 7–22.
293. ps.-Augustine: *CD* 31. 140. 10–34. 141. 9. Cf. 29. 139. 28–30. 140. 9, 51. 144. 19–21.
294. ps.-Augustine: *CD* 42. 142. 32–143. 22. Cf. 47. 143. 23–144. 11.
295. ps.-Augustine: *CD* 52. 144. 21–145. 6.
296. ps.-Augustine: *CD* 95. 154. 17–18. On the problem of relation in late antiquity see Conti 1983.
297. ps.-Augustine: *CD* 96. 154. 21–27.
298. ps.-Augustine: *CD* 98. 155. 10–11.

299. ps.-Augustine: *CD* 98. 155. 13–14.
300. ps.-Augustine: *CD* 99. 155. 21–31.
301. ps.-Augustine: *CD* 102. 156. 15–28.
302. ps.-Augustine: *CD* 102. 156. 28–29.
303. ps.-Augustine: *CD* 104. 157. 6–9.
304. ps.-Augustine: *CD* 104. 157. 11–17.
305. ps.-Augustine: *CD* 108. 158. 9–15.
306. ps.-Augustine: *CD* 110. 158. 23–29.
307. On Eriugena's use of ps.-Augustine: *Categoriae decem* see Stock 1980; Courtine 1980; Marenbon 1980, 1981; d'Onofrio 1986.
308. At *Pe.* I. 463B, Eriugena cites Augustine's *De Trinitate* as source for the doctrine of categories. Cf. Augustine: *dTr.* V. 1. 2. However, since that text concerns the application of the categories to God rather than the nature of the categories themselves, the material derived from it will not be further explored here. Eriugena would also have known the parallel discussion in Boethius: *dTr.* 4.
309. "Pseudo-logic" is a necessary consequence of "pseudo-definitions". See pp. 13–14.
310. Eriugena: *Pe.* I. 464C–474B.
311. Eriugena's doctrine of relation is discussed by Flasch 1971.
312. Since the text is arranged as a dialogue between *N[utritor]* "teacher" and *A[lumnus]* "pupil", this distinction of speakers has been retained in our translation. In general, the pupil reports the standard doctrine of categories stated by ps.-Augustine, whereas the teacher adds commentary and explanation found in Greek patristic sources. The dialogic structure of *Periphyseon* is discussed by Liebeschütz 1958; Desrosiers-Bonin 1986.
313. Section 2.3 will be concerned primarily with dialectical and section 2.5 mainly with mathematical relation. Thus, sections 2.3 and 2.5 will be correlated with the two poles of the axis of dialecticity and mathematicity.
314. See Gersh 1978: 217–225.
315. See Gersh 1978: 253 ff.
316. On the geometrical image see pp. 70, 73.
317. On lexemes and sememes see n. 81. Relevant portions of Eriugena's lexematic inventory have been studied by Desrosiers-Bonin 1986; Touchette 1986. For the lexicon associated with geometry see Desrosiers-Bonin 1986, and for that associated with relation Coallier 1986.
318. On the axes X, Y, Z see p. 72 ff.
319. Sememes interact with axis Y because a, b, c, d are linked with dialectics and d with mathematics. Lexemes interact with axis Z because *relatio* is linked with complexity and *habitus* with simplicity.
320. The distribution of sememes among lexemes might be summarized (figure N16). The text supplies an additional correlation which will be discussed in

	sememes				
	a	b	c	d	e
	substance+ substance	opposition	genus+ species	ratio	substance+ accident
lexemes					
1. <u>relatio</u>	+		+	+	
2. <u>habitus</u>		+	+	+	+
3. <u>proportio</u>				+	

Figure N16. Distribution of sememes (relation)

	f
	presence+ absence
lexemes	
1. <u>relatio</u>	
2. <u>habitus</u>	+
3. <u>proportio</u>	+

Figure N17. Additional distribution of sememe (relation)

chapter four (figure N17). Eriugena also employs the lexemes *ad aliquid* and *habitudo* as synonyms of *relatio* and *habitus* respectively.
321. In sections 2.3 ff. Relation (with capital R) will correspond to the English lexeme "relation", and relation (with lower-case r) to the Latin lexeme *relatio*.
322. The fullest analysis of interrelations between lexemes and sememes occurs in Greimas 1966. From this viewpoint, each lexeme contains various semes as its meaning-effects, and each sememe several semes. The relations between sememes themselves are extremely complicated since i. each sememe consists of a semic nucleus and contextual semes, ii. contextual semes may be shared by the nuclei of different sememes — such contextual semes being here called "classemes", iii. contextual semes of one sememe may comprise the nucleus of another sememe. For an analysis similar to that applied to Eriugena see Greimas 1966: 44–53.
323. On equivalence, pseudo-hierarchy, and continuity see pp. 72–73.
324. The axes will be studied in the order X, Z, Y for exegetical convenience only. Movement along each axis corresponds roughly to the dynamic junction between different levels of signification described by Barthes. According to this author, a particular structure of signification in which a primary signified functions as a secondary signifier underlies "myth". This signified-signifier is both full and empty — the secondary level distorts rather than suppresses the first — and can be compared with a moving turnstile. See Barthes 1957: 224–235.
325. Cognitivity here implies correlation of a knower and the known. Existence and cognitivity can be identified with objectivity and subjectivity understood as a *non*-exclusive opposition.
326. There is nowhere else in the text anything existent which is not knowable.
327. In chapter four, complexity will be associated with the ternary and simplicity with the binary.
328. Paragraph 2.2.
329. Paragraph 4.2.2.2. At this point, the isotopy of "internal relation" is activated. See p. 73.
330. Paragraph 2.2.
331. Paragraph 4.2.2.3. At this point, the isotopy of "internal relation" is activated. See p. 73.
332. Paragraph 2.2.
333. Paragraphs 4.2.2.2 and 4.2.2.3.
334. Mathematicity here implies the possibility of quantification.
335. There is elsewhere in the text something mathematical which is not dialectical: the monad. One need not assume that the whole discussion of semantic properties in terms of structuring and geometrical analogies is necessarily inconsistent with the notion of "dissémination" advocated by Derrida. This envisages an interrelation of semantic properties using many

"structural" analogies: for example, of the angle (Derrida 1972²: 31 ff.), of reversal (Derrida 1972²: 11–12, 49), of the square (Derrida 1972²: 31 ff.), and of chiasmus (Derrida 1972²: 41–42, 52–53, 145–146). However, in accordance with its anti-ontological — which it equates with anti-structural (Derrida 1972²: 31 ff.) — intent, it modifies the analogies slightly: the angle is a skew (Derrida 1972²: 285–286), the reversal asymmetrical (Derrida 1967²: 399, 1972²: 10, 1972¹: vii, x), the square splayed (Derrida 1972²: 31 ff.), the chiasmus uneven (Derrida 1972²: 41 ff.), etc. Since Derrida's concept of dissemination seems to utilize such images primarily in order to counteract the circularity implicit in Hegelian metaphysics (Derrida 1967¹: 39, 1972¹: i–ii, 20–21, 88–89), and to modify them primarily in order to explain the irreducible openness of semiotic analysis (Derrida 1967¹: 25–26, 100, 1972²: 33), it conflicts with Eriugena's own perspective on the first point but not on the second, and with our perspective on Eriugena neither on the first point nor on the second.

336. On Boethius' mathematical writings see Obertello 1974; Caldwell 1981; Chadwick 1981: 69–107. On his arithmetic see Batschelet-Massini 1979; Regali 1983; di Mieri 1984. The Pythagorean teachings underlying these treatises have been discussed by Robbins and Karpinski in d'Ooge 1926; van der Waerden 1947–1949; Michel 1950, and the philosophical developments from such Pythagorean doctrines by D. O'Meara 1989. On the medieval influence of Boethius' mathematical writings see Obertello 1971; White 1981. On the medieval influence of his arithmetic see Masi 1981; Illmer 1984; Bernhard 1988.

337. Boethius: *dIA* I. 1, 7. 26–8. 15.

338. Boethius: *dIA* I. 1, 8. 15–23.

339. Boethius: *dIA* I. 1, 8. 23–29.

340. Boethius: *dIA* I. 1, 8. 29–9. 1.

341. Boethius: *dIA* I. 1, 9. 1–10. 1.

342. Boethius: *dIA* I. 1, 10. 1 ff.

343. Boethius: *dIA* I. 1, 10. 10–11. 10.

344. Boethius: *dIA* I. 1, 11. 10–22.

345. Boethius: *dIA* I. 21, 45. 11 ff. The change of terminology is demanded by Boethius' unsatisfactory abridgement of the beginning of Nicomachus' text. At *IA* I. 2, 4. 13 ff. Nicomachus had distinguished *megethos* [magnitude] and *plēthos* [multitude] but, since their infinity renders them unknowable, science must rather study *to pēlikon* [size] and *to poson* [quantity]. It is the latter which are next divided into static and mobile and into absolute and relative respectively, and thereby provide objects of the four mathematical disciplines. Boethius omits the reasoning about infinity and unknowability, bases his fourfold division on magnitude and multitude themselves, and finds himself with no explanation of the terminological change at *IA* I. 17, 44. 8 ff.

Notes   303

346. Boethius: *dIA* I. 21, 45. 13–25.
347. Boethius: *dIA* I. 21, 45. 26–46. 4.
348. Boethius: *dIA* I. 22, 46. 6–9. The multiple is discussed at *dIA* I. 23, 46. 19–49. 12.
349. Discussed at Boethius: *dIA* I. 24, 49. 15 ff.
350. Discussed at Boethius: *dIA* I. 28, 57. 8–60. 18.
351. Discussed at Boethius: *dIA* I. 29, 60. 20–I. 30, 64. 24.
352. Discussed at Boethius: *dIA* I. 31, 65. 2–66. 2.
353. Boethius: *dIA* I. 22, 46. 9–17, etc.
354. Boethius: *dIA* II. 1, 77. 15–17. Cf. I. 32, 66. 8 ff.
355. Boethius: *dIA* I. 32, 66. 8–15.
356. Boethius: *dIA* I. 32, 66. 15–18.
357. Boethius: *dIA* I. 32, 66. 18–22.
358. On Eriugena's use of Boethius in general see d'Onofrio 1980^1, 1981^1, 1981^2. On his use of the Boethian arithmetic see d'Onofrio 1980^2: 707–708, 721 ff.
359. See p. 97 ff.
360. See Sheldon-Williams 1967: 457–472; Gersh 1978: 217–225. Jeauneau 1990 has also noted the influence of Maximus the Confessor.
361. In what follows, "Ratio" corresponds to mathematical relation as "Relation" corresponded to dialectical relation in section 2.3. It is natural to depict "Ratio" as shifted along the axes of existent-cognitive and of unitary-binary. It is also possible to conceive "Ratio" as shifted along the axis of dialectical-mathematical itself.
362. The absence of a consistent element makes it particularly difficult to find stable English equivalents for the various Latin lexemes unfolded in this section.
363. For the geometrical image see pp. 70, 73; for lexemes and sememes n. 81; and for the axes X, Y, Z p. 72 ff.
364. To distinguish denotative and connotative sememes is to contrast units of signification within a lexeme which are more or less prominent in a given discourse. On denotation and connotation see p. 187.
365. The distribution of sememes among lexemes might be diagrammed (figure N18).
366. For statistical analysis of the term *numerus* in Eriugena's vocabulary see Coallier 1986: 353.
367. Cognitivity here implies necessary correlation between a knowing subject and a known object.
368. *intellectuales*. See Eriugena: *Pe.* III. 651 B–D, 656B, 658A, etc. On Eriugena's theory of number see Jeauneau 1990; D. O'Meara 1990.
369. Eriugena: *Pe.* IV. 769B–770A. Cf. *iDdCH* 6. 165–198.
370. Eriugena: *Pe.* V. 1012A–1013C.
371. Eriugena: *Pe.* III. 657B–659A. Such arithmological speculation has reemerged in the semiotic literature of recent years. On the question of

MOTION 1

	sememes		
	a	b	c
	ratio	relation	number
lexemes			
1. <u>inaequalitas</u>	+		
2. <u>proportio</u>	+	+	
3. <u>habitus</u>	+	+	
4. <u>numerus</u>	+	+	+

MOTION 2

lexeme	<u>numerus</u>	
sememes (denotative)	ratio ◇	number
sememe (connotative)	unfolded reason	

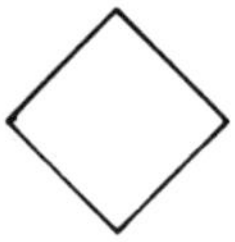

Figure N18. Distribution of sememes (ratio)

    the dyad and difference see Derrida 1972[2]: 31 ff., Kristeva 1969: 150–153, 183, 185.
372. *vis, potestas, actus, operatio*
373. Eriugena: *Pe.* III. 658A.
374. *in notionem*
375. Eriugena: *Pe.* III. 658B.
376. *intra se*
377. Eriugena: *Pe.* III. 658C.
378. *ipsius intellectus actu*
379. Eriugena: *Pe.* III. 658C–D.

380. On local and global actualization of semes see pp. 83–84.
381. On equivalence, pseudo-hierarchy, and continuity see pp. 72–73.
382. To use "Ratio" in a dialectical sense seems peculiar in English. However, Eriugena clearly employs the corresponding Latin terms *proportio* and *habitus* in this way.
383. *genera, species/formae*. See Eriugena: *Pe.* III. 657B.
384. *numeri*. See Eriugena: *Pe.* II. 546CD, etc.
385. *ratio*
386. Eriugena: *Pe.* V. 881C–882A.
387. *singulares rationes*
388. *propriae rationes*
389. See Eriugena: *Pe.* V. 965C–966A where not only the monad but the numbers and ratios derived from it are located in the ineffable i.e. supra-dialectical realm.
390. The axis of simple and complex functions as an axis of unitary and binary throughout this chapter. Cf. p. 84.
391. *inaequalitas ad aequalitatem*. Eriugena: *Pe.* III. 655B.
392. Eriugena: *Pe.* III. 657C.
393. Eriugena: *Pe.* III. 654C–655A.
394. Eriugena: *iEI* VI. 4, 343C–D.
395. *intra terminos duodenarii*
396. See Boethius: *dIA* II. 49, 158. 16–160. 4.
397. Eriugena: *Pe.* III. 655B–656A.
398. *in unitate numerorum*
399. Eriugena: *iDdCH* 6. 179–194.
400. See p. 149 ff.
401. *in perfectissimis senarii numeri rationibus*
402. On the notion of "quasi-temporality" see p. 99 ff. Eriugena does not consider the distinctions between atemporality and temporality and between non-spatiality and spatiality to be rigid. See Cristiani 1973[1], 1973[2]; Courtine 1980.
403. See p. 90.
404. See p. 73.
405. Eriugena: *Pe.* III. 730C ff. For Augustine's theory of number see P. Hadot 1967; Cilleruelo 1968. The corresponding Plotinian theory is discussed by Saget 1982: 93–185.
406. Eriugena: *Pe.* III. 731B–C.
407. Eriugena: *Pe.* III. 732A. On the numerical doctrine of Augustine: *De Musica* VI see Guitton 1959: 149–160; Nowak 1975; Pizzani 1978[1]. On the medieval influence of the doctrine see le Boeuf 1986.
408. See Augustine: *dMu*. VI. 6. 16.
409. See Gregory of Nyssa: *dHO* 8. 148C ff. and Eriugena: *VOG* 9, 218. 20–10, 220. 3.

410. Eriugena: *Pe.* III. 731 C – D.
411. Eriugena's theory is more schematic in listing eight levels as such. Augustine distinguishes five levels at *dMu.* VI. 6. 16: the *sonantes* [sounding], *occursores* [encountering], *progressores* [progressive], *recordabiles* [recalling], and *iudiciales* [judging]. At *dMu.* VI. 9. 24 he renames the sounding *corporales* [corporeal] and the judging *sensuales* [sensual], and at *dMu.* VI. 11. 31 adds a sixth level: the † *rationis* [rational]. Eriugena's eight levels are therefore obtained by dividing Augustine's lowest and highest levels each into two.
412. Eriugena: *Pe.* III. 732 A.
413. Eriugena's interpretative combination of Augustine and Gregory is also made plausible by the latter's references to *susceptio* [reception] of external impressions, to *stili* [recorders] of those impressions, etc. Of course, the doctrinal affinities between Augustine and Gregory are not imagined by Eriugena but stem from their use of the same Neoplatonic sources: Plotinus and Porphyry. For the latter see Moutsopoulos 1971; Gersh 1992.
414. See Augustine: *dMu.* VI. 7. 18 – 12. 36. Cf. VI. 17. 57.
415. Eriugena: *Pe.* IV. 786 C ff.
416. Eriugena: *Pe.* IV. 787 B – C.
417. For example, Alumnus assigns to the progressive the function of introducing and to the recalling that of commending.
418. Cf. Eriugena: *Pe.* IV. 790 A – 791 A, etc.
419. Eriugena: *Pe.* I. 474 B ff.
420. Eriugena is assumed to be referring to another passage in Augustine's *De musica* — namely *dMu.* VI. 17. 58 — although he is clearly paraphrasing rather than quoting at this point.
421. Eriugena: *Pe.* I. 482 B – C.
422. Numbers in corporeal objects and in sensory organs' phantasies are not really psychic. Soul is present to them but does not contain them.
423. Eriugena: *Pe.* III. 730 C. From Augustine: *dMu.* VI. 5. 10.
424. Eriugena: *Pe.* III. 659 B – C. From Augustine: *dMu.* VI. 11. 32. Cf. Eriugena: *Pe.* II. 573 C.
425. See pp. 91, 95.
426. Eriugena: *Pe.* V. 871 D. From Augustine: *dMu.* VI. 13. 40.
427. Eriugena: *iMCdNPM(P)* 78. 11 – 13.
428. See p. 149 ff.
429. Eriugena: *iDdCH* 3. 157, 3. 370. Cf. *iDdCH* 1. 623, 4. 432, 4. 435, 9. 343, 10. 67, 13. 229 – 230.
430. See le Boeuf 1987.
431. Anonymous: *IAdMu.* VI. 251 – 256, 319 – 326, 444 – 455. Cf. *iAdMu.* VI. 133–142. For the terminology see Augustine: *dMu.* VI. 6. 16, etc.
432. Anonymous: *iAdMu.* VI. 332 – 347 (on Augustine: *dMu.* VI. 9. 24).

433. The glossator extensively pursues the question which numbers begin and end simultaneously with physical sound — obviously the sounding and the progressive — and in the course of this discussion lists the grades of numbers. Cf. Anonymous: *iAdMu.* VI. 59–108.
434. See pp. 97–99.
435. Anonymous: *iAdMu.* VI. 60–61, 91–108.
436. See pp. 97–99.
437. Anonymous: *iAdMu.* VI. 142–151, 206–210.
438. Anonymous: *iAdMu.* VI. 155, 340–343.
439. Anonymous: *iAdMu.* VI. 156–159. The progressive numbers are here called the † *actuale* [actual]. The whole scheme is made more complex by the additional distinction between *extra animam* [outside the soul] and *in anima* [in the soul] which produces two categories within that of the made.
440. Anonymous: *iAdMu.* VI. 12–20.
441. Anonymous: *iAdMu.* VI. 235–256 (on Augustine: *dMu.* VI. 7. 19). Cf. *iAdMu.* VI. 398–405, 458–461.
442. Anonymous: *iAdMu.* VI. 327–331 (on Augustine: *dMu.* VI. 9. 23 with the reading *quanta spatia).*
443. See p. 99.
444. Anonymous: *iAdMu.* VI. 160–168.
445. Anonymous: *iAdMu.* VI. 411–419.
446. Anonymous: *iAdMu.* VI. 422–424 (on Augustine: *dMu.* VI. 14. 44).
447. Anonymous: *iAdMu.* VI. 424–434 (on Augustine: *dMu.* VI. 14. 45).
448. Augustine: *dMu.* VI. 14. 45–46.
449. Anonymous: *iAdMu.* VI. 444–454.
450. The emphasis on ternarity in certain medieval texts can usefully be compared with a similar preoccupation in Peirce's philosophical writings. Moreover, since the American philosopher believed that ternary relations are inherently signifying, the hypothesis that medieval writers also drew this conclusion should at least be entertained. Peirce reiterates the fundamental character of ternary relations — they are a. irreducible to binary relations although b. n-tuple relations are reducible to them (Peirce 1931–1958, 1: ss. 345–347) — and to their mode of being which has a necessary reference to two other terms or division into three terms he applies a label: "thirdness". The ideas in which thirdness is predominant are more complicated than those containing firstness or secondness "and mostly require careful analysis to be clearly apprehended" (Peirce 1931–1958, 1: ss. 337–340). Consequently, Peirce gives various examples of thirdness rather than a single definition. A sign is an instance of thirdness — it involves reference to an object and to an idea — as are the associated notions of meaning and manifestation. A middle exemplifies thirdness — in contrast with the firstness of a beginning and the secondness of an end — and likewise the fork in a road. Acceleration instances thirdness — contrasting with

the firstness of position and the secondness of velocity — as do continuity, diffusion, and growth. Law as order exemplifies thirdness — in contrast with the secondness of law as force — and likewise sympathy. The syllogistic conclusion instances thirdness — contrasting with the firstness of the major and secondness of the minor premiss — as does intelligence. Conduct exemplifies thirdness — in contrast with the firstness of action — and likewise moderation (Peirce 1931–1958, 1: ss. 337–340, 345–347). That Peirce should hold thirdness to be fundamental apparently follows from his assumptions a. that the semiotic process is basic, and b. that the semiotic process is ternary. However, he clearly moves beyond a position i. that semiosis is essentially ternary to a thesis ii. that ternarity is essentially semiotic. In fact, he writes: "Every genuine triadic relation involves meaning, as meaning is obviously a triadic relation... every triadic relation involves meaning... you will convince yourself thoroughly that every genuine triadic relation involves thought or meaning" (Peirce 1931–1958, 1: ss. 345–347). A passage where Peirce distinguishes genuine from spurious ternarity indicates the underlying argument. Here, he contrasts the situation of *A* giving *B* to *C* — which is a single ternary relation — with that of *A* throwing *B* away and hitting *C* by accident — which constitutes two binary relations — by saying that the former situation involves the transfer of property-rights enshrined within a legal system (Peirce 1931–1958, 1: ss. 345–347). In other words, for Peirce the transformation of binary into ternary relation involves the *revelation by the latter of some hidden semantic complexity in the former*. This idea has important consequences. First, it distinguishes the genuine ternarity from the relation between two species and their genus in formal logic — Russell's quotation of the ancient Chinese saying that if two particulars and their class made three things, the dun cow and the bay horse would be three (Russell 1956: 260) reveals the spurious ternarity of the latter — and brings that genuine ternarity closer to the relation between the two abstract moments and their concrete Notion in Hegelianism. Secondly, Peirce's idea dissociates the genuine ternarity from closure of meaning. When Derrida argues that only the dyad not preceded by the monad or completed by the triad — as *différance*, dissemination, or trace — is productive of meaning (Derrida 1967[1]: 19–20, 91–92, 1972[2]: 11–13, 33ff., 234), this rejection of ternarity because of its association with closure of meaning stems from an understanding of that ternarity in the spurious rather than the genuine Peircian sense. Discussions of thirdness in Peirce can be found in Dewey 1946; Oehler 1979; Freeman 1983.
451. On Thierry of Chartres in general see Häring 1955; Maccagnolo 1976, 1981; Evans 1982; Gersh 1982; Dronke 1988. On his educational programme see Jeauneau 1954; Evans 1983.
452. See Burnett 1982: 347–348.

453. See Häring 1971: 19–52; Bataillon 1977.
454. Thierry: *iBdTr (CV)* 81, 498. 42–44. Cf. *iBdTr (C)* 2. 37, 80. 62–66, *iBdTr (L)* 7. 5, 224. 43–45, *iBdTr (G)* 5. 17, 297. 37–40, *iBdTr (T)* 12, 306. 97–99. On Thierry's mathematical ideas see Jeauneau 1963; Brunner 1966.
455. Cf. Augustine: *dDC* I. 5. 5.
456. See Thierry: *dSDO* 41, 572. 99, *iBdTr (L)* 7. 5, 224. 46–48, *iBdTr (G)* 5. 18, 297. 41–42.
457. Thierry: *iBdTr (C)* 2. 39–40, 81. 86–94.
458. Thierry: *dSDO* 38, 571. 66–71, 43, 573. 37–39, *iBdTr (L)* 7. 7, 225. 71–72, *iBdTr (CV)* 87, 499. 94–95.
459. Thierry: *dSDO* 37–38, 570. 52–571. 71, *iBdTr (C)* 2. 30, 77. 92–78. 3, *iBdTr (L)* 7. 6, 225. 54–58, *iBdTr (G)* 5. 18, 297. 42–45, *iBdTr (T)* 13, 306. 10–14, *iBdTr (CV)* 82, 498. 56–83, 499. 72.
460. Otloh of St. Emmeram: *dTQ* 35, 106C–D.
461. Thierry: *dSDO* 42, 572. 9–11. Identifications with the biblical *verbum* and *sapientia* occur at *dSDO* 46, 574. 66–70, *iBdTr (C)* 2. 32, 78. 10–12, 2. 35, 79. 43.
462. See Gersh 1986, 2: 457ff., 535–538.
463. Thierry: *dSDO* 45–46, 574. 58–65.
464. Thierry: *dSDO* 2, 555. 18–19, 43, 573. 30–34, 44, 574. 49–50, 45, 574. 55–57, *iBdTr (C)* 2. 39, 81. 84, 2. 40, 81. 95–99, 2. 46, 82. 45–83. 49, *iBdTr (L)* 2. 38, 167. 33–34, *iBdTr (CV)* 86, 499. 83–86, 87, 499. 91.
465. Thierry: *dSDO* 29, 568. 75–76, 41, 572. 6–8, 43, 573. 26–28, 44, 573. 40–574. 1, 45, 574. 57, 47, 575. 73–74.
466. Thierry: *iBdTr (L)* 7. 7, 225. 71–72.
467. Thierry: *iBdTr* (C) 2. 37, 80. 56–2. 38, 80. 71, *iBdTr (T)* 13, 306. 7–8, 16, 307. 36–41, *iBdTr (CV)* 84–85, 499. 73–82. The doctrine is mentioned but not discussed where Thierry's text breaks off at *dSDO* 47, 575. 79–80.
468. Thierry: *iBdTr (CV)* 84, 499. 73–77.
469. Thierry: *dSDO* 27, 566. 44–567. 52.
470. See Gersh 1986, 2:474–479, 551 ff.
471. Thierry: *dSDO* 26, 566. 32–43, *iBdTr (C)* 2. 39, 81. 84–85.
472. See Gersh 1986, 1:361–363.
473. Thierry: *iBdTr (L)* 2. 10, 157. 8–10.
474. See Gersh 1986, 2:474–479, 707ff.
475. Thierry: *dSDO* 22, 564. 79–81, 25, 566. 29–31, 28, 567. 53–57, *iBdTr (C)* 2. 43, 82. 18ff., *iBdTr (L)* 2. 9, 157. 86–90, 2. 11, 158. 17–19, *iBdH (AM)* 40, 412. 39–40.
476. Thierry: *iBdTr (L)* 7. 7, 225. 71–72.
477. See p. 116.
478. See p. 86ff.
479. See pp. 354–357. On Thierry's notion of otherness see Evans 1975–1976.

480. Thierry: *iBdTr (CV)* 87, 499. 94–88, 499. 3. Cf. *dSDO* 43, 573. 37–44, 574. 48, *iBdTr (C)* 2. 36, 79. 47–51.
481. See pp. 45 ff., 73, etc.
482. Thierry: *iBdTr (L)* 7. 2, 224. 17–23, 7. 8, 225. 74–78, 7. 21, 229. 90–91. The peculiarities of relation in the Trinity are discussed further at *iBdTr (C)* 6. 7, 114. 54–58, *iBdTr (L)* 7. 10, 226. 98–5.
483. Thierry: *iBdTr (C)* 2. 17, 74. 83–84, 4. 7, 97. 75–8. 97. 90.
484. For the influence of Augustine see n. 455. There is no explicit citation of *De musica* in the Thierrian commentaries, although it is possible that Augustine's discussion of the multiplication of 1×1 in the context of metrics — see *dMu.* V. 7. 13–14, V. 8. 16–9. 17 — influenced the speculation about Trinitarian generation. For the acknowledged debt to Boethius see p. 117. The relation between music and philosophy in Augustine and Boethius is discussed by Montico 1938, and the notion of music as liberal art in Augustine and Boethius by Dehnert 1969; Frova 1985.
485. Augustine: *dMu.* V. 7. 13. On Augustine's musical theory see Huré 1924; Amerio 1954; Perl 1955. On the treatise *De musica* see Edelstein 1929.
486. Augustine: *dMu.* V. 7. 15.
487. Augustine: *dMu.* II. 10. 18–19. Augustine arranges ratios in a hierarchy of value at *dMu.* I. 9. 15–10. 17. Arguing for the priority of multiple and superparticular ratios (but with different terminology), he comes to the same conclusion about duration values as does Nicomachus concerning pitch ratios. A hierarchy of ratios based on different principles occurs at *dMu.* II. 10. 19, V. 5. 9.
488. Augustine: *dMu.* II. 9. 16, II. 11. 20, V. 4. 7, V. 4. 8.
489. Augustine: *dMu.* V. 4. 8. Cf. V. 3. 3, V. 3. 4, V. 4. 7, V. 5. 9, V. 7. 14.
490. Augustine: *dMu.* V. 7. 15 – V. 8. 16.
491. Augustine: *dMu.* V. 2. 2.
492. Augustine: *dMu.* V. 9. 19. Cf. III. 1. 1, V. 3. 4, V. 8. 16.
493. Boethius: *dIM* II. 20, 253. 9–25. Cf. I. 3, 191. 3–4, IV. 1, 301. 25–302. 5. On Boethius' musical theory see Potiron n.d.; von Lepel 1958; Massera 1976; Pizzani 1978[2]. Its sources are examined by Bragard 1945; Pizzani 1965; Bower 1978. Its relation to philosophy is discussed by Schrade 1930, 1932, 1947; Obertello 1967. Its medieval influence is examined by Heller 1939. The tradition of glossing *De institutione musica* is discussed by Pizzani 1957; Masi 1971; Pizzani 1980; Bower 1988; Bernhard 1988. On Boethius' musical vocabulary see Bernhard 1979.
494. Boethius: *dIM* I. 3, 191. 3–4, I. 28, 220. 3–7, I. 31, 221. 22–25, II. 18, 249. 22–25.
495. Boethius: *dIM* I. 29, 221. 3–5.
496. Boethius: *dIM* II. 20, 253. 9–25.
497. Boethius: *dIM* I. 31, 221. 22–25.

498. Boethius: *dIM* I. 3, 191. 3–4, I. 31, 221. 22–25, II. 20, 253. 9–25. Distinction between aural *consonantia* [consonance] and metaphysical *concordia* [concord] underlying it occurs at *dIM* I. 3, 191. 3–4, I. 31, 221. 22–25. However, Boethius' clearest references to non-aural concord are *dIM* II. 16, 247. 6–248. 15, V. 3, 355. 7–12. Cf. *dIA* I. 1, 10. 10–17.
499. Boethius: *dIM* II. 18, 250. 2–3.
500. Boethius: *dIM* I. 32, 222. 14–27, II. 18, 249. 25–29.
501. Boethius: *dIM* II. 18, 249. 18–250. 25. Cf. *dIM* II. 20, 251. 16ff., V. 7, 357. 13ff.
502. Boethius: *dIM* V. 8, 358. 13–10, 360. 26.
503. For Boethius see *dIM* I. 3, 191. 3–4, for Censorinus: *dDN* 10. 4–6. Our concern is strictly with the *logical* properties identified by the traditional definitions. Those definitions also identify *sensory* aspects — sweetness of the sound, etc. — which are less relevant here. See Boethius: *dIM* I. 8, 195. 6–8, I. 28, 220. 3–7, V. 7, 357. 13–14, V. 11, 361. 10–12.
504. For example, see Eriugena: *iMCdNPM (P)* 19. 4–5 (*harmonia*), Anonymous: *ME* 10, 23. 5–6 (*symphonia*), Remigius of Auxerre: *iMCdNPM* VII. 185, 22–23 (*harmonia*), Regino of Prüm: *dHI* 10.237 (*consonantia*), Otloh of St. Emmeram: *dTQ* 43, 119D–120A (*consonantia*), Hugh of St. Victor: *Di.* II. 15 (*concordia*), William of Conches: *iPTi.* 153. 257 (*harmonia*).
505. See p. 118.
506. See p. 123ff.
507. See p. 130ff. For Boethius see *dIM* II. 12, 241. 14ff. The geometrical progression particularly exhibits these features.
508. See pp. 130ff., 142ff. The arithmetical progression particularly exhibits these features.
509. The structure underlying concord discussed here is a mathematical version of the structure underlying signification in certain semiotic theories. There is broad equivalence between the function of inequality and equality in the former and those of difference and sameness in the latter. See n. 517.
510. See Augustine: *dTr.* V. 6. 7ff. During the remainder of this chapter the three geometrical axes which figured in the earlier discussion will play a different role. On the one hand, their application *to* texts will diminish. The axis of equivalence between existent and cognitive will reappear both as static structure and dynamic analysis, that of pseudo-hierarchy between dialectical and mathematical as static structure but not as dynamic analysis, and that of continuity between simple and complex neither as static structure nor as dynamic analysis. On the other hand, their justification *by* texts will increase. Henceforth, an explicitly formulated axis — that of continuity between good and evil or between their various synonyms — will determine the expository order within primary sources.
511. Augustine: *Co.* IV. 16.
512. Aristotle: *Ca.* 7, 6^b 28, 7, 7^a 23.

513. Aristotle: *Ca.* 7, 7^b 15, 13, 14^b 24. The terms "existent" and "cognitive" are not Aristotelian.
514. Aristotle: *Ca.* 7, 6^a 36–37, 7, 8^b 13–15, 10, 11^b 17–18. Relation to perception is indicated by the verb *legetai* [is said].
515. Aristotle: *Ca.* 5, 4^a 11, 6, 6^a 2, 10, 11^b 18, 11, 13^b 36 ff. On Aristotle's theory of contrariety see Anton 1957.
516. Aristotle: *Ca.* 7, 6^b 38–39, 7, 8^a 16, 7, 8^b 15–18.
517. That these contraries are treated by Augustine as excluding a middle term (cf. Aristotle: *Ca.* 10, 11^b 15 ff., *APo.* I. 3, 72^a 12 ff.) might suggest the notation $s_1 \rightarrow \bar{s}_1$. However, it is better to retain $s_1 \rightarrow s_2$ as reflecting a. the logical inexplicitness and b. the combination of contrary and part in the texts. It is in applying these ideas that Augustine comes closest to articulating the geometrical axis of our metalinguistic discourse and the modern notion of "structure" in general. A summary of the latter — as formulated particularly by Greimas — might run as follows. A. Theory. 1. "Structure" is relational; 2. Structure is ternary; 3. A first term is connected to a second term by a relation which can itself be treated as a further first term connected to a further second term by a further relation, and so forth; 4. The first and second terms are called "termes-objets", the relation an "axe" (or "relation" or "catégorie") (Greimas 1966: 18–29); 5. The object-terms constitute an element of "non-identité" in the structure (Greimas 1966: 19–20) — this non-identity being sometimes that between presence and absence of a semantic property (s vs. -s), and sometimes that between alternations of semantic properties (s vs. non-s) (Greimas 1966: 23–25) — while the relation constitutes an element of "identité" in that structure (Greimas 1966: 19–20); 6. The first term, second term, and relation correspond to individual semes or groups of semes according to the level of analysis. B. Practice. /b/ and /p/ are object-terms (s and -s) and voicing their axis, boy and girl are object-terms (s and non-s) and sex their axis, large and small are object-terms and measure of matter their axis, black and white are object-terms and absence of colour their axis (Greimas 1966: 20–23). Other examples show transition between levels of analysis. Dimensionality and non-dimensionality are object-terms and spatiality their axis, vertical and horizontal are object-terms and dimensionality their axis (Greimas 1966: 31–34). This summary makes it obvious that "existent", "cognitive", and "complex" in the metalinguistic discourse and "good", "evil", and "created" in the Augustinian material would correspond to object-terms and axes within Greimas' formulation.
518. The process of assimilation could be represented graphically (figure N19). The notions of whole and parts as well as those of contrary and contrary in Augustine's theory correspond to elements in the modern theory of structure, since the whole performs the function of an axis and the parts that of the two object-terms. Officially Greimas is circumspect about such a

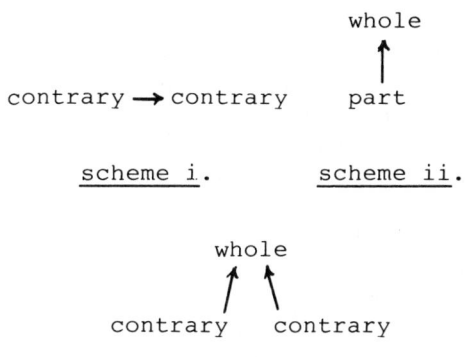

Figure N19. The Augustinian oppositions

correspondence — criticizing Hjelmslev's liberal recourse to it (Greimas 1966: 28–29) — although he re-establishes it in different terminology — saying that the axis has a "relation hyperonymique" to the object-terms (Greimas 1966: 29, 105–106). His hesitancy is justifiable given that the relation between axis and object-term is not that of logical class to particulars but a genuine ternarity in Peirce's sense. See n. 450.
519. On this treatise see Cress 1976.
520. Augustine: *Ep.* 138. 5.
521. Augustine: *Co.* IV. 13. Augustine's aesthetic theories are discussed by Svoboda 1933; Müller 1956; Beierwaltes 1975; O'Connell 1978, and their Plotinian background by de Keyser 1955; Schoendorf 1974.
522. The terms "existent" and "cognitive" have the meanings noted in n. 325. However, Augustine's idealism is less complete.
523. Scheme i. + existent.
524. Augustine: *dLA* III. 13. 36–38. Cf. *dLA* III. 5. 12–17, III. 15. 42–44, *dCD* XII. 1.
525. Relationality is suggested by the use of the genitive case *eius rei*. Cf. Aristotle: *Ca.* 7, 6^a 37. In addition, virtue and vice were traditional examples of relatives. Cf. Aristotle: *Ca.* 7, 6^b 15–16.
526. Augustine: *dVR* 34. 63.
527. Scheme ii. + existent.
528. Augustine: *dLA* III. 9. 25. Cf. *dCD* XVI. 8 ff.
529. Relationality is suggested by the verb *referri*. Cf. Aristotle: *Ca.* 7, 8^a 35–37, 10, 11^b 24–31.
530. Scheme iii. + existent.
531. Augustine: *cFM* XXI. 5.

532. Relationality is suggested by the preposition *ad.* Cf. Aristotle: *Ca.* 7, 6^a 37.
533. Augustine: *dCD* XI. 18. Cf. *En.* 96. It is evident that Augustine is really deriving ontology from rhetoric throughout these arguments. Thus, the ontological relations of contrary to contrary (scheme i.) and of part to whole (scheme ii.) correspond to the rhetorical figures of antithesis and synecdoche respectively. Augustine's method is perhaps further evidence for the "semantic" character of ternary relations in general. On antithesis and synecdoche see Lausberg 1960, 1:295–298, 390–391, 453–454. On the semantic question cf. nn. 450, 517–518, 543, 552.
534. Our remarks should be compared with those on "participation" in n. 89.
535. It is Aristotle's fundamental teaching that substances cannot admit contrary properties at the same time: for example, the same colour cannot be white and black, the same action good and bad, the same person sick and healthy. Cf. *Ca.* 5, 4^a 10, 6, 6^a 1. But substances can admit contrasting relative properties at the same time: for example, the same mountain can be great and small depending on the external standard of comparison. Cf. *Ca.* 6, 5^b 11–6^a 11. The problem of disentangling contraries and relatives had been bequeathed to Aristotle by Plato. See Kirwan 1974.
536. Augustine: *En.* 14.
537. Augustine has further discussions of the relation between good and evil at *dCD* XII. 3, XIV. 11, etc.
538. In Greek Neoplatonism, all relations characterizing the level of *nous* [intellect] are treated as internal in character. However for Augustine, only relations between certain fundamental moral and ontological contraries are similarly handled.
539. Scheme i. + cognitive.
540. Augustine: *dNB* 14.
541. Relationality is indicated by the use of the phrase *in...comparatione.* Cf. Aristotle: *Ca.* 6, 5^b 16–20.
542. Augustine: *dNB* 15. Cf. *dNB* 23, *dGaL* XI. 11. 14.
543. The notion that contrary terms can only be defined through one another is the ontological counterpart of an idea in modern linguistics: the thesis of Saussure 1967–1974: 264–272 that a linguistic sign is defined only by its difference from other signs. This idea has of course exercised enormous influence both within and outside linguistics. See Hjelmslev 1961: 63–65; Barthes 1985^1: 63 ff.; Greimas 1966: 102–104.
544. Augustine: *dGaL* VIII. 15. 33–16. 35.
545. Scheme ii. + cognitive.
546. Augustine: *dMu.* VI. 11. 30. Cf. *dMu.* VI. 10. 28–11. 29, *dOr.* I. 1. 1–2. 4.
547. Relationality is implied by the parallelism between scheme ii. + cognitive and scheme ii. + existent. See pp. 123–124.
548. Scheme iii. + cognitive.
549. Augustine: *dGcM* I. 16. 26.

Notes 315

550. Relationality is implied by the parallelism between scheme iii. + cognitive and scheme iii. + existent. See pp. 124–125.
551. Augustine: *dGcM* I. 16. 25.
552. The notion that partial terms can only be defined through the whole is the ontological counterpart of Saussure's thesis — see n. 543 — that a linguistic sign is defined only by its difference from other signs.
553. Augustine: *dCD* XII. 4. Cf. *dGcM* I. 21. 32.
554. See pp. 122–123.
555. Augustine: *dNB* 8.
556. Augustine: *dGcM* I. 21. 32. *Convenientia* is synonymous with *concordia*. See *Ep.* 166. 13.
557. See p. 21 ff.
558. See pp. 121–122.
559. On the notion of encyclopaedia see pp. 70, 72–73, n. 261. On the axis of mathematical and dialectical see pp. 72–73.
560. On Calcidius' teachings in general see Gersh 1986, 2: 421 ff.
561. According to the *Timaeus,* the physical and psychic worlds are both to be understood in harmonic terms. Calcidius agrees with this viewpoint, although he tends to discuss the components of harmonic theory separately — proportions, proportionalities, mediators, etc. — rather than harmonic theory as a unified whole. See however Calcidius: *iPTi.* 50. 99, 24–100. 2, 73. 120. 11–13, 267. 272. 11–273. 4, 304. 305. 21–306. 2.
562. See pp. 72–73.
563. *congrua mensura*
564. *quae...eadem...quae...haec*
565. Calcidius: *VPTi.* 24. 5–25. 10 (= Plato: *Ti.* 31b–32c).
566. Calcidius: *iPTi.* 16. 67. 17–68. 17. References to *analogia* in late ancient philosophical literature are studied by Dörrie 1981.
567. Calcidius: *iPTi.* 21. 71. 24–22. 73. 4.
568. Cf. Calcidius: *iPTi.* 14. 65. 20–66. 11.
569. *contrariae*
570. *ex ipsa contrarietate*
571. *adversum*
572. *iuxta*
573. *iuxta*
574. *adversus*
575. *adversum*
576. *adversum*
577. *iuxta*
578. *adversum*
579. *adversum*
580. *adversus*
581. *duae virtutes*

582. *una...vero*
583. *duae virtutes*
584. *una...vero*. On the medieval theory of the four elements see Boll 1913; Vossen 1950; Duhem 1954, 3:44–62; Kilbansky — Panofsky — Saxl 1964: 4ff.; Viarre 1975; Viret 1983. The use of the four elements as a basis of literary imagery has been studied by Bachelard 1961.
585. *medietates*
586. Calcidius: *VPTi*. 27. 1–28. 13 (= Plato: *Ti*. 34b–36c).
587. Calcidius: *iPTi*. 33. 82. 9–15.
588. *cuius duplum linea*
589. *lineae duplum superficies*
590. *cuius duplum cubus*
591. Calcidius: *iPTi*. 33. 82. 15–83. 19.
592. Calcidius; *iPTi*. 92. 144. 19–145. 4.
593.

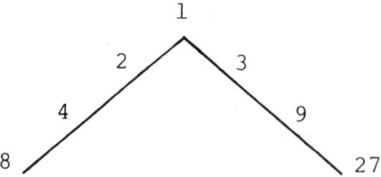

Figure N20. The Platonic lambda-diagram

594. See Handschin 1950; Moutsopoulos 1959: 363 – 375; Arnoux 1960.
595. Calcidius: *iPTi*. 35. 84. 1– 37. 87. 5.
596. Another discussion of means occurs at Boethius: *dIA* II. 40, 137. 1 ff.
597. See p. 122.
598. Eriugena: *Pe*. I. 466B. Eriugena does indicate that condition is a more generic notion than proportion. However, he maintains this distinction on the grounds that the former needs one term but the latter two, and not that the former is dialectical but the latter mathematical in meaning.
599. Eriugena: *Pe*. I. 466A – C. Cf. *Pe*. III. 686Aff.
600. Eriugena: *Pe*. I. 466C. Eriugena also gives the illustration of high, low, and middle in the category of place.
601. Eriugena: *Pe* I. 466B.
602. For the theory of axes see pp. 72–73.
603. Examples of similar semiotic entanglements between mathematical-dialectical and binary-ternary are quoted at Lévi-Strauss 1958: 51–55, 248–249, 1964: 317–318. On semiotic entanglement in general see Greimas 1966: 168–170.

604. Terms in the squares of opposition will be arranged in a standard format — irrespective of their order of presentation in the primary sources — i.e. that of Eriugena. See p. 71.
605. Porphyry: *iACa.* 78. 34 ff. As Hadot 1954, 1968: 148 ff; de Libéra 1976 have shown, elements of the scheme can be traced beyond Porphyry to Aristotle and even Plato. On Apuleius' application of the scheme to propositions see n. 611 and pp. 167–168.
606. Marius Victorinus: *aCa.* 8. 1–21, 11. 1–11, 13. 1 ff. Victorinus' scheme is similar to one in Proclus: *iPTi.* I. 233. 1–4, scholium on Proclus: *iPTi.* I. 469. 18. The latter provides a diagram (figure N21).

Here, the original semes are placed in the centre of the diagram, and the lexemes — soul, intellect, matter, sensible — corresponding to the sememes $b_1, b_2, \bar{b}_1, \bar{b}_2$ on the horizontal and diagonal axes.
607. Boethius: *iACa.* I. 169B ff. — perhaps after Ammonius: *iACa.* 25. 12. At *iACa.* I. 175B–C Boethius gives a diagram (figure N22). Here, the lexemes — universal substance, universal accident, particular accident, particular substance — corresponding to the sememes $b_1, b_2, \bar{b}_1, \bar{b}_2$ are placed on the vertical and diagonal axes, and the original semes in the corner of the

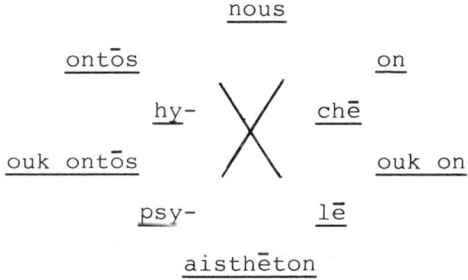

Figure N21. Procline square of opposition

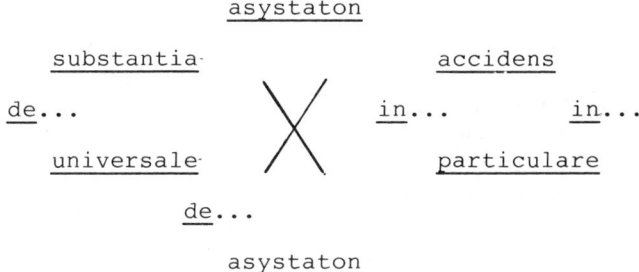

Figure N22. Boethian square of opposition

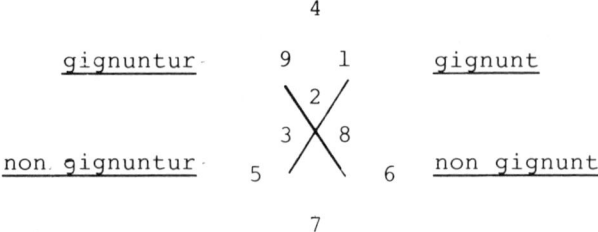

Figure N23. Macrobian square of opposition

       diagram. Boethius uses a fourfold scheme based on other terms at *dDT* I. 1180D.
608. See Philo Iudaeus: *dOM* 33, 99–100, Theo Smyrnaeus *ERM* 103. 1–16.
609. Macrobius: *iCSS* I. 5. 16, Martianus Capella: *dNPM* VII. 738. No arithmological text has preserved a diagram although one can easily be constructed following the pattern in the Proclus scholium (see figure N23).
610. Augustine: *dCD* V. 9 making but not made, both made and making, made but not making; Claudianus Mamertus: *dSA* II. 2, 103. 5–9 judging but not judged, both judged and judging, judged but not judging (= God, soul, body respectively).
611. Eriugena: *iMCdNPM (P)* 36. 22–37. 6. Eriugena may also have been influenced by the traditional application of the fourfold scheme to propositions — see Apuleius: *Pe.* 5. 86–88, Martianus Capella: *dNPM* IV. 400–401, Boethius: *VAdI* 9. 11–13 — which he reports at *dPr.* 14, 83. 68–81. On Eriugena's use of the square of opposition in general see Stock 1980; D. O'Meara 1981; Piemonte 1986; d'Onofrio 1986, 1990.
612. Eriugena was also preoccupied with the symbolic properties of the number 4 itself which dominates the square. See Eriugena: *dPr.* 1, 1–27, *Pe.* III. 705B, *HiPI* 14, 291B–C, *iDdCH* 4. 137–152. On the Pythagorean reverence for the number 4 see Delatte 1915; Kucharski 1927; Burkert 1972: 72–73, 186ff.
613. At *Pe.* I. 466D he uses the term *diametrum* [diameter] to indicate the proportional condition between contraries in the category of situation. Since he employs the same term at *Pe* II. 525B to indicate opposition within the fourfold scheme, he probably understands the analyses of the categories and of the square of opposition as embodying identical principles.
614. Eriugena: *Pe.* III. 688C–D.
615. Eriugena: *Pe.* I. 441A–B, II. 523D–524A, III. 621B–D, V. 1019C–1020A.
616. At *Pe.* III. 689A–B, V. 1019C Eriugena reduces the four terms to three by uniting the second and third. At *Pe.* III. 623C, III. 630Aff., III. 695A–C he

reduces the four terms to three by omitting the fourth. Eriugena's concern with such reductions suggests that he views fourfold relations as ultimately threefold in nature.
617. The principle of infinite semiosis was established — with a formulation unsurpassed to ths day — by Peirce. See p. 16. Cf. n. 450.
618. Eriugena: *Pe.* I. 476C–D, III. 735C. Cf. *Pe.* III. 728A.
619. Eriugena: *Pe.* III. 732D. Cf. Eriugena: *iMCdNPM (P)* 67. 26.
620. Eriugena: *iMCdNPM (P)* 10. 16–24, 22. 20–27. For Calcidius' influence over Eriugena see Mathon 1960; Huglo 1990.
621. This notion was defined in connection with Calcidius on p. 129.
622. Eriugena: *iDdCH* 4. 86 ff.
623. *congruens sibi propriae substitutionis modus*
624. Eriugena: *iDdCH* 1. 76–117.
625. *analogia...numerus...pondus*
626. See p. 129.
627. See pp. 24–25.
628. Eriugena: *Pe.* I. 477B–C. Cf. Gregory of Nyssa: *dHO* 128C ff. On Eriugena's knowledge of Gregory's writings in general see Levine 1958; Jeauneau 1983.
629. Eriugena: *Pe.* III. 714A–B.
630. Eriugena: *Pe.* III. 706C–D + 711D–712A. Cf. Ambrose *iHe.* 4. 40C–D. On Eriugena's knowledge of Ambrose's writings in general see Madec 1976.
631. Eriugena: *Pe.* III. 712B–D.
632. *contrariae extremitates/extremitates...e contrario*
633. *in medio/media/medietas*
634. *aequali lance librare...ponderata*
635. *proportionalis*
636. *in medio*. Erigena's theory of elements is discussed by Schrimpf 1990.
637. *librabat*
638. Eriugena: *Pe.* III. 695A ff.
639. Eriugena: *Pe.* III. 714A.
640. *synodus*
641. Eriugena: *Pe.* III. 706D.
642. *contradicere*
643. Eriugena: *Pe.* I. 477B.
644. *proportionale moderamen inter gravitatem et levitatem*
645. Eriugena: *Pe.* III. 706D.
646. *misceri*. Transcendence and immanence are closely associated with the "isotopy of time-space" discussed in chapter one. See p. 34.
647. Eriugena: *Pe.* III. 706C, III. 712A.
648. *ubique universaliter diffusa*
649. *pura et a se invicem segregata/per se purissima*
650. Eriugena: *Pe* III. 714A.

320 Notes

651. *synodus...una eademque uniformiter commensurabilis*
652. *quaedam...plus...quaedam...minus*
653. Eriugena: *Pe.* III. 706 D.
654. *contradicere*
655. *misceri*
656. Eriugena: *Pe.* III. 713 A.
657. Eriugena: *Pe.* III. 712 B.
658. *qualitatibus sibi invicem proportionaliter copulatis*
659. Calcidius: *iPTi.* 304, 305. 17–306. 10.
660. See p. 130 ff.
661. See section 5.4.
662. Boethius: *dIA* II. 40, 137. 2 ff.
663. See p. 142. On Eriugena's concept of mediation see Allard 1990. Similar ideas are exploited in the semiotic context by Lévi-Strauss 1958: 277 ff.; Greimas 1966: 212–213.
664. *generalis...anima*
665. Eriugena: *iMCdNPM (P)* 10. 19.
666. Eriugena: *iMCdNPM (P)* 10. 16–22. Cf. *iMCdNPM (P)* 202. 26–30 — a text which is Eriugenian if not by Eriugena himself.
667. Eriugena: *iMCdNPM (P)* 202. 26–30. See n. 666.
668. Eriugena: *iMCdNPM (P)* 10. 19–21.
669. *universalissima anima/generalis anima*
670. Eriugena: *Pe.* III. 729 A, III. 734 B.
671. *generalis vita/generalissima vita*
672. Eriugena: *Pe.* III. 728 A, III. 728 D–729 A. Cf. Eriugena: *iDdCH* 13. 144 ff.
673. Eriugena: *Pe.* III. 732 B–C.
674. Eriugena: *Pe.* III. 732 C.
675. Eriugena: *Pe.* III. 729 A–B.
676. *mesotēs, analogia, harmonia*
677. Eriugena: *iDdCH* 6. 167–198. Eriugena's notion of angelic hierarchies is discussed by Dondaine 1950; d'Alverny 1965: 85–108; Häring 1973; de Gandillac 1977.
678. Eriugena: *iDdCH* 9. 81–146.
679. Eriugena: *iDdCH* 11. 124–134.
680. Eriugena: *iDdCH* 10. 60–172.
681. *primae et mediae et ultimae virtutes*
682. *superessentialis harmonia*
683. *proportio*
684. *analogia*
685. *primus...ultimus*
686. *medius*
687. *medietatis proportio/proportionalis medietas*
688. *participatio*

689. *illuminatio*
690. *reductio/anagoga*
691. *longitudo...latitudo...*
692. *condita*
693. See p. 130ff.
694. See Gersh 1973: 83–90.
695. *telesiourgein, phōtizein, kathairein*
696. See ps.-Dionysius: *dCH* 165B–C, 205C–D, 240B, 272D, etc. Eriugena interprets this doctrine at *iDdCH* 3. 204ff.
697. On Eriugena's use of Augustine in general see Madec 1980^1, 1980^2.
698. See p. 122.
699. See p. 122. D'Onofrio 1990 has shown that Eriugena's discussion also combines two traditional types of logical *divisio:* i. of genus into species, ii. of whole into parts. See Cicero: *To.* 2. 9, 5. 26–8. 34, Martianus Capella: *dNPM* IV. 350–354, V. 475–480, Boethius: *iCTo.* I. 1058Dff., *dDi.* 877B–878D, etc.
700. This doctrine will show that Eriugena assimilates the negative-affirmative disjunction to both opposition and relation. Yet Aristotle had included the negative-affirmative disjunction within the class of oppositions but distinguished it from relation. See Aristotle: *Ca.* 10, 11^b 15–23.
701. See n. 522.
702. This doctrine could perhaps encourage us to create an axis of transcendence and immanence as supplement to the three axes employed in earlier analyses. See n. 286.
703. Eriugena: *Pe.* III. 681A, III. 683A–B. Cf. *Pe.* III. 633A–B.
704. Eriugena: *Pe.* III. 681B–C, III. 683A–B.
705. The Latin verb *respicere* indicates relationality in Eriugena's usage.
706. See pp. 158–162. The distinction between the negation of transcendence and other types of negation required by the argument here is occasionally ignored by Eriugena.
707. Eriugena: *Pe.* I. 459B–C.
708. Eriugena: *Pe.* I. 459C–D.
709. Eriugena: *Pe.* I. 459D–460D.
710. Eriugena: *Pe.* I. 462B–D.
711. Eriugena: *Pe.* I. 462C.
712. The term "super-affirmative" is not Eriugenian.
713. See p. 162ff.
714. See pp. 158, 160.
715. Scheme ii. + existent = cognitive
716. On finality of the cosmic process see p. 163.
717. Relationality is suggested by the terms *collatio* and *comparatio*. Cf. n. 541.
718. The verbs *existimari,* etc. reveal the cognitive aspect.
719. Eriugena: *Pe.* V. 953C–954C. Cf. *Pe.* III. 684B–C.

720. Eriugena: *Pe.* V. 967A–C.
721. Eriugena: *Pe.* II. 523D–524D. Cf. *Pe.* III. 621A–B.
722. See n. 716.
723. In distinction from Augustine's practice, Eriugena clearly uses the terms "part" and "whole" as equivalent to logical particularity and universality. Cf. n. 699.
724. On the interplay of these two dialectics cf. p. 163.
725. Eriugena: *Pe.* II. 617B–C, III. 621D–622A, III. 645B. Eriugena explicitly links this theory with ps.-Dionysius.
726. Scheme i. + existent = cognitive.
727. See Eriugena: *Pe.* I. 458D–459D.
728. This theory is discussed by Gersh 1978: 152–190.
729. Eriugena: *Pe.* II. 525C–526A.
730. Eriugena: *Pe.* III. 637B–638A. The end of the passage contains a striking simile of *organicum melos* [instrumental melody].
731. Eriugena: *Pe.* III. 637C.
732. Eriugena: *Pe.* V. 982C–D. The passage here refers to the final state. See n. 716.
733. Scheme iii. + existent = cognitive.
734. On finality of the cosmic process see p. 163.
735. The verbs *putari*, etc. reveal the cognitive aspect.
736. Relationality is suggested by the terms *collatio* and *comparatio*. Cf. n. 541.
737. Eriugena: *Pe.* V. 953C–954C. The argument is interwoven with that concerning part and whole.
738. Eriugena: *Pe.* V. 965A–B.
739. Eriugena: *Pe.* I. 510D–511A + 517C. Cf. *Pe.* III. 637B–D.
740. See n. 716.
741. In distinction from Augustine's practice, Eriugena clearly treats God as unifier of contraries, opposites, and dissimilars.
742. On the interplay of these two dialectics see p. 163.
743. Eriugena: *Pe.* I. 511A–B. Eriugena specifically refers to his discussion in *Periphyseon* V.
744. See p. 158.
745. Eriugena: *Pe.* I. 460D.
746. See pp. 192–193.
747. See p. 187.
748. See p. 29 ff.
749. Eriugena: *Pe.* II. 560A–B.
750. Eriugena: *Pe.* II. 550C. A similar harmony occurs among numbers which are sometimes treated as coinciding with the primordial causes. Cf. *Pe.* II. 602B–C, II. 618C, III. 630C–631A, III. 658A.
751. Eriugena: *Pe.* III. 637D–638A. Cf. *Pe.* I. 501A–B.
752. Eriugena: *Pe.* III. 695C. Cf. *Pe.* I. 494D, II. 545D–546A, III. 706D.

753. Eriugena: *Pe.* V. 966B–C. Cf. *Pe.* V. 915C, V. 954B–C, V. 965B–C, V. 973A, V. 987B.
754. Eriugena: *Pe.* V. 965D–966A.
755. On the final resolution see pp. 158, 160–161, n. 732.
756. Cf. Eriugena: *Pe.* IV. 855B–C. On the doctrine of return in Eriugena see also Gersh 1990.
757. Cf. p. 156.
758. See p. 157.
759. See pp. 157, 159, 161–162, n. 725.
760. See pp. 158, 160–161.
761. pp. 121–138.
762. On this variant of the square of opposition see n. 112.
763. This was represented schematically by three intersecting lines:
764. On the contrast between sememe and lexeme see n. 81.
765. On the schemata of equivalence, pseudo-hierarchy, and continuity see pp. 72–73.
766. This could be represented schematically by three connected lines:
767. On the substitution of sememes for semes see n. 94.
768. These schemata govern the structure of *Concord in Discourse* as a whole.
769. See section 4.3. Eriugena applies a square of opposition explicitly to signification at *Pe.* III. 623C–D (three terms only). For a similar classification of signifiers see Jakobson 1973: 94 ff., 100.
770. See p. 185 ff. Strictly speaking, it is the sememes which are so analyzed.
771. Eriugena: *Pe.* I. 457D. Since Eriugena has a conception of the signifying process and a classification of signs which are ontological in character, it will be better to analyze him from an ontologically neutral position than with a different ontological bias. Nevertheless, comparison with the most extensive discussion of signs in modern philosophical literature is hard to avoid. Thus, Peirce's second triad of signs — classified according to their relation to objects — would contain the main Eriugenian types: a. the "icon" which so relates "by virtue of characters of its own" and includes visual images; b. the "index" which so relates "by virtue of being really affected by that object" and includes certain physical forces; c. the "symbol" which so relates "by virtue of a law" and includes linguistic signs (Peirce 1931–1958, 2: s. 243 ff.). However, the "qualisign" (first member of first triad) and the "rheme" (first member of third triad) distinguished by Peirce have no real counterparts in Eriugena. Finally, of Peirce's ten classes of signs — derived by combining various triadic properties — one would represent the primary Eriugenian type: the "dicent sinsign" which "is any object of direct experience, in so far as it is a sign, and, as such, affords information concerning its object. This it can only do by being really affected by its object; so that it is necessarily an index. The only information it can afford is of actual fact" (Peirce 1931–1958, 2: s. 254 ff.).

772. Eriugena: *Pe.* I. 458A–C.
773. Eriugena: *Pe.* I. 458C.
774. Eriugena: *Pe.* I. 458C–460B.
775. Eriugena: *Pe.* I. 460C–461A. Eriugena's attitude to metaphor is considered by Lopez Silonis 1967²; Trouillard 1976; Beierwaltes 1976. Comparison of the Eriugenian, Aristotelian, and modern interpretations of metaphor is useful here. According to Aristotle: *Po.* 21, 1457^b 7ff., metaphor is the transferring to one thing of a name belonging to something else, this transfer being either from genus to species, or from species to genus, or from species to species, or through analogy. Each of the main ideas in this description has generated controversy in modern times: i. The notion of linguistic normality versus deviation. Some modern theorists reject the implied contrast between the natural or non-metaphorical and the artificial or metaphorical functions of language. For example, Derrida stresses the impossibility of deciding whether various terms employed by traditional philosophy — *eidos, logos, metaphora* itself — are non-metaphorical or metaphorical (Derrida 1972¹: 261–262, 266–267, 301–302). ii. The notion of transferring the name of one thing to something else. Some modern theorists have viewed metaphor not as that unilateral process constituting the transfer of object A's name to object B but as the bilateral one representing the transfer of object A's name to object B and the transfer of object B's name to object A simultaneously. This twofold process is described by Richards: "When we use a metaphor we have two thoughts of different things active together and supported by a single word, or phrase, whose meaning is a resultant of their interaction" (Richards 1936: 93). iii. The notion of genus-species logic. Some modern theorists find the logical structure of genus and species too rigid to account for the various semantic displacements. For example, Eco replaces this with general encyclopaedic competence within which the diverse relations among terms — identities, similarities, differences, oppositions — represent metonymic substitutions (Eco 1979: 67–89, 1984: 87–129). Eriugena's handling of metaphor can be articulated clearly against a background of such issues and debates. As we shall see, he is enabled to combine the Aristotelian notion of linguistic normality and deviation with the modern concept of bilateral transference and the Aristotelian notion of genus-species logic through his metaphysical theory that God is simultaneously transcendent of and immanent in created things. Cf. p. 185 ff.
776. Eriugena: *Pe.* I. 461A.
777. Eriugena: *Pe.* I. 461A–462D.
778. Eriugena: *Pe.* I. 463A–C.
779. Eriugena: *Pe.* I. 508C–D.
780. Eriugena: *Pe.* I. 508D–509B.
781. Eriugena: *Pe.* I. 509B–512B.
782. Eriugena: *Pe.* I. 512B–513A.

783. See p. 7 ff.
784. The theory described here is Hjelmslev's — updated by Eco. See Eco 1976: 4, 48 ff.
785. Eco 1976: pp. 91–93, 105–110.
786. Eco 1976: p. 93.
787. The theory described here is Peirce's — again updated by Eco. See Eco 1979: 180–184.
788. Eco 1976: 68–69, 122–125.
789. Eco 1979: 180–181, 1984: 115–118, 127–129.
790. Eco 1979: 183–184.
791. Eco 1979: 178 ff.
792. Eco 1976: 69–71.
793. Eco 1976: 127–128, 1984: 113, 123–124, 127–129.
794. Eco 1976: 279–283, 1979: 68 ff., 76–77, 1984: 114–115.
795. Eco 1976: 109, 279–283, 1979: 68 ff., 78 ff., 1984: 96, 113–114, 118 ff.
796. Eco 1976: 69–71, 1979: 197, 1984: 113.
797. In the description to follow, Eriugena's paradigm of the signifying process will be translated first into the abstract schema and secondly into the two concrete models. The first translation will provide a general format and the second specific details of interpretation.
798. These relations can be diagrammed:

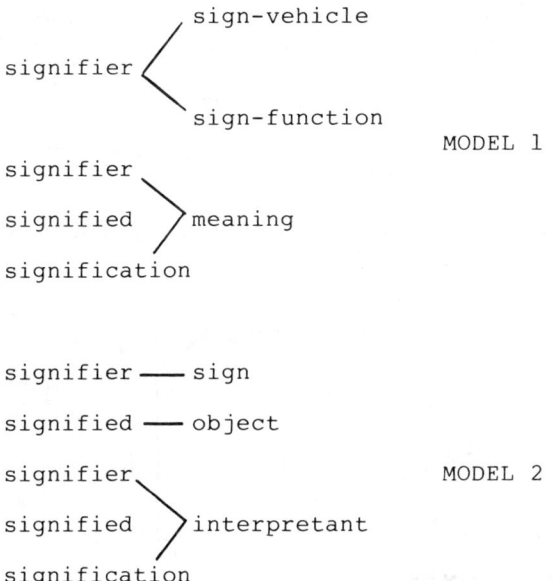

Figure N24. Interpretation of Eriugena's theory of signification

799. According to Platonic realism — which Eriugena endorses — the signified has priority.
800. Further signifieds are implied: namely, the various members of the class "creature".
801. These are elsewhere called "semes".
802. Such sememes are called "actants" by Greimas. See Greimas 1966: 121 ff.; Greimas — Courtés 1979: 3–4.
803. Such sememes are called "prédicats" by Greimas. See Greimas 1966: 12 ff.; Greimas — Courtés 1979: 289–290.
804. This signifier sometimes occurs with substantival or verbal syntactic markers.
805. This signifier sometimes occurs with substantival or verbal syntactic markers.
806. A "family resemblance" is constituted here.
807. Further significations are implied: namely, the activation and de-activation of individual semes.
808. See p. 182.
809. The distinction between denotation and connotation is a convenient way of contrasting levels of semes within a sememe. In a referential semantic theory like that of Frege, a denotation is a seme to which a sign-vehicle corresponds without mediation, and a connotation a seme to which it corresponds with mediation. See Eco 1976: 84–86. However, in the intentional semantic theory endorsed by us, what is non-mediate or mediate can only be defined in terms of a certain isotopy. Cf. Eco 1976: 54–57, 91–93, 105 ff., 12 ff.
810. For this variant of the square of opposition see n. 279.
811. For the semes see p. 182 ff.
812. See n. 809.
813. For the sememe see pp. 182–183.
814. These semes are never correlated with individual lexemes in Eriugena's text.
815. The process can be illustrated:

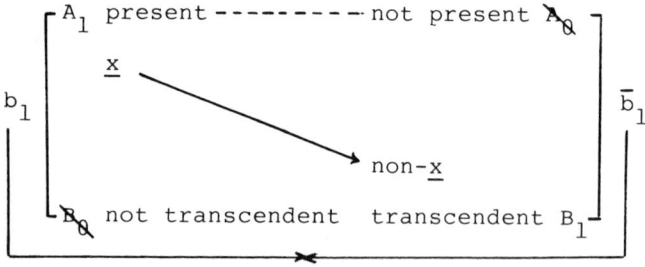

Figure N25. Analysis of super-affirmative predicate

816. The origins and transmission of Martianus Capella's treatise have been extensively discussed. See Lutz 1971; Stahl — Johnson — Burge 1971–1977; Lenaz 1975; Gersh 1986, 2: 597ff., Shanzer 1986 for Martianus Capella in general; Leonardi 1959, 1960 for the diffusion of his treatise; Nuchelmans 1957 for the influence of its allegory. The contribution of *De nuptiis* to medieval theories of signification has not been studied hitherto.
817. See n. 833.
818. Martianus Capella: *dNPM* I. 6–7.
819. Martianus Capella: *dNPM* I. 7, 5. 7–9.
820. Martianus Capella: *dNPM* I. 8.
821. Martianus Capella: *dNPM* I. 21–23.
822. Martianus Capella: *dNPM* I. 26–30.
823. Martianus Capella: *dNPM* I. 37.
824. Martianus Capella: *dNPM* I. 92, 26. 13–I. 93, 27. 6.
825. Martianus Capella: *dNPM* II. 99–100.
826. Martianus Capella: *dNPM* II. 101–109.
827. Martianus Capella: *dNPM* II. 111–133.
828. Martianus Capella: *dNPM* II. 126, 40. 14–17.
829. Martianus Capella: *dNPM* II. 134–140.
830. Martianus Capella: *dNPM* II. 138, 43. 1–2.
831. Martianus Capella: *dNPM* II. 143–199.
832. Martianus Capella: *dNPM* II. 208–218.
833. The term "symbol" is here used in the sense current among late ancient and medieval Platonists. See p. 201 ff. and nn. 951, 954.
834. Martianus Capella: *dNPM* II. 101–109.
835. Martianus Capella: *dNPM* II. 101, 29. 8–10. Martianus' thinking was undoubtedly influenced by Plato's doctrine of the "nuptial number" transmitted to him by Aristides Quintilianus. On this doctrine see Vincent and Martin 1865; Zanoncelli 1977. Aristides' influence over Martianus was first detected (à propos book IX) by Deiters 1881.
836. Martianus Capella: *dNPM* II. 102, 29, 10–104, 30. 3.
837. Martianus Capella: *dNPM* II. 104, 30. 2.
838. Martianus Capella: *dNPM* II. 105, 30. 3–10.
839. Martianus Capella: *dNPM* II. 105, 30. 7.
840. Martianus Capella: *dNPM* II. 106, 30. 10–15.
841. Martianus Capella: *dNPM* II. 107, 30. 15–24.
842. Martianus Capella: *dNPM* II. 107, 30. 24–108, 31. 4.
843. Martianus Capella: *dNPM* II. 108, 31. 4–10.
844. Martianus Capella: *dNPM* II. 109, 31. 10. On Martianus' musical theories — stated primarily in *De nuptiis* IX — see Cristante 1974–1975, 1987.
845. Martianus Capella: *dNPM* I. 1, 1. 4–2. 4.
846 Martianus Capella: *dNPM* I. 1, 1. 6–8.

847. Martianus Capella: *dNPM* I. 1, 1. 9–10.
848. Martianus Capella: *dNPM* IX. 922, 354. 2–6.
849. Martianus Capella: *dNPM* IX. 921, 353. 18–24.
850. Martianus Capella: *dNPM* IX. 899, 342. 14 ff. For Martianus, the placing of a musical discussion at the *end* of an encyclopaedia of liberal arts was perfectly logical. The point was missed by I. Hadot 1984: 149.
851. Cf. Martianus Capella: *dNPM* I. 36, I. 92, II. 118–121, II. 138, II. 169 ff. on the two protagonists.
852. The notion of a harmony between signifier and signified had occurred in the Stoic tradition. See Augustine: *dDi.* 6. 9, 20–6. 10, 11, 6. 11, 18–19, 6. 12, 8–10. Cf. n. 869.
853. On Eriugena's use of Martianus Capella: *De nuptiis Philologiae et Mercurii* see Schrimpf 1973; Jeauneau 1978; Schrimpf 1980; Schrimpf 1982; Leonardi 1980; Herren 1986.
854. For non-signifying relation see pp. 45–53. Such a relation may consist of three terms. However, it will not possess the special "ternarity" described in n. 861.
855. For signifying relation see pp. 4–9 — where it is identified with the modern notion of "structure" — and pp. 185–187.
856. This feature is shown by Eriugena's treatment of proportional condition. See p. 139.
857. On internal relation see pp. 51–55.
858. See pp. 4–5. Cf. pp. 118–121 where equality and inequality are the mathematical counterparts of sameness and difference.
859. This feature is shown in Eriugena's treatment of super-affirmative names. See p. 187.
860. On self-contradictory relation see pp. 125, 147.
861. The ternarity of the signifying relation corresponds to Peirce's notion of "thirdness". See n. 450. Yet *pace* Peirce this relation has a semiotic but not a logical value.
862. See pp. 72–73.
863. See n. 884 and p. 212.
864. Interaction of axes and categories might be represented below (figure N26). Regarding the procedure to be adopted during this chapter one should note i. the presence of four signifying categories, and — as a result of Eriugena's ontological priorities — ii. the order of discussing these categories.
865. Simplicity vs. complexity here = absence vs. presence of interpreter.
866. See p. 157. On Eriugena's theory of signification see D. O'Meara 1983; Beierwaltes 1986; d'Onofrio 1986.
867. Eriugena: *Pe.* III. 632B. Cf. *iDdCH* 7. 264–275, 8. 15–20, etc. On medieval notions of grammatical realism see Jolivet 1966.
868. Eriugena: *Pe.* I. 512B–C.

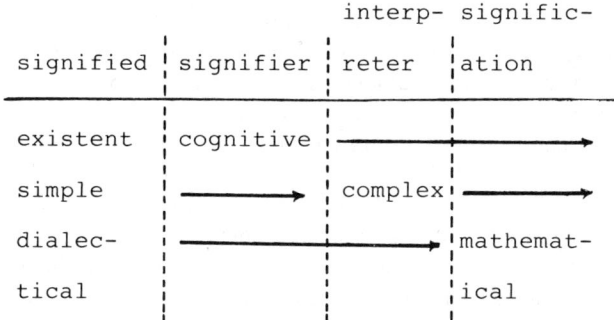

Figure N26. Axes and signifying categories

869. Eriugena: *HiPI* 6. 286B. Other deductions by Eriugena from the meanings of tenses can be found at *Pe.* IV. 808C–809A and *iEI* I. 23, 298C. The ontological aspect of Eriugena's theory of signification testifies to the non-influence of Stoic linguistic doctrine in the early Middle Ages. Some fragmentary remains allow us to conclude that the Stoics had distinguished in language a *sēmainon* [signifier] and a *sēmainomenon* [signified], corresponding to linguistic expression and content respectively in Hjelmslev's sense. The mode of conceiving the signifieds is clearly the most important part of their teaching. By identifying these with the *asōmata* [incorporeals] (Sextus: *aMa.* 8. 12) — including the class of *lekta* [utterances] which may be complete as propositions or incomplete as elements of propositions — the Stoics indicate that they cannot be i. external things or ii. psychic images which are for them equally corporeal. In other words, the signifieds are strictly linguistic or semantic objects. See Pohlenz 1939; Frede 1978; Graeser 1978. Remnants of this teaching are transmitted to the Latin Middle Ages particularly by certain early works of Augustine. See *dMa.* 2. 4 (explanation of syncategorematic term *ex*) and *dDi.* 5. 7, 7ff. (notion of *dicibile* [the utterable]). However, neither the mature Augustine nor later medieval writers develop these ideas further. On the consequences of Eriugena's linguistic realism see also pp. 212–213.
870. Eriugena: *Pe.* I. 454B–C.
871. "Quasi-temporal" because the emanative process is neither atemporal nor temporal in the strict sense. Rather, it begins from atemporality and evolves into temporality.
872. Eriugena: *Pe.* II. 551C–D. Sheldon-Williams makes a muddle of the text and commentary. For Eriugena's notion of *phantasia* see Foussard 1977.
873. Eriugena: *Pe.* II. 573A–B.
874. It is useful to locate Eriugena's theory of signification in relation to the important philosophical controversies in the history of linguistics 1. whether language imitates thought or is identical with thought, 2. whether language

is primarily representational or communicative in character. On the first question, Aristotle: *dIn.* 1, 16ᵃ 3–4 definitely understood language as an external manifestation of inner thought. This viewpoint reappeared in the Grammar of Port-Royal and implies a. that language is expression but not content, b. that language has a motivated relation to thought. However, Wittgenstein 1953: s. 329, 1958: 6, 113 rejected the notion of inner thought manifested externally in language. He implicitly agreed with Saussure who argued a. that language is both expression and content, b. that language has an arbitrary relation to that content. On the second question, the Grammar of Port-Royal indicated that the representational and communicative functions of language are interconnected so that neither can operate to the detriment of the other. However, the comparative philologists maintained that these two functions of language are independent to the extent that the communicative can operate to the detriment of the representational. The Eriugenian texts under discussion suggest an author who hesitates between the two solutions of question 1 but inclines towards the first, and who is equally ambivalent concerning the two solutions of question 2 but inclines towards the second. His position is therefore quite close to that of Hegel's *Enzyklopädie*.

875. Eriugena: *Pe.* III. 633B–C.
876. This simultaneity must be understood in terms of the quasi-temporality of the whole process. See n. 871.
877. Eriugena: *Pe.* III. 633C–D. Sheldon-Williams gives a confused translation.
878. Eriugena: *iMCdNPM (P)* 9. 15–10. 3.
879. Eriugena has more to say on the question of interpretation. At *Pe.* IV. 757D–758A, *iDdCH* 2. 517–535 he discusses the extent to which meaning may be transmitted; at *Pe.* I. 518C, III. 693B he explains that signification is adapted to the level of the receiver; and at *iEI* I. 30, 308A–B, VI. 2, 341B he speaks of the extent to which meaning may be received. Eriugena's entire explanation of signification could therefore be summarized as follows:

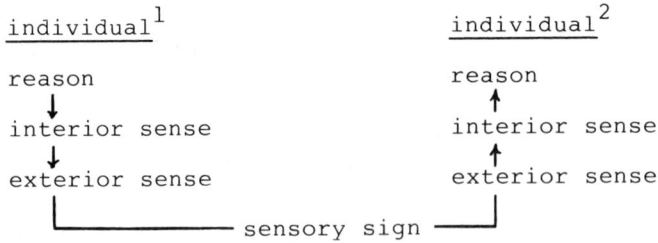

Figure N27. Eriugena's theory of signification

880. See n. 865.
881. See p. 91.
882. Eriugena: *iDdCH* 2, 334–344. Cf. *iDdCH* 2, 730–737.
883. See pp. 214–216.
884. On the notion of "mediated signification" see n. 898.
885. The historical situation is actually more complicated than these comments might suggest. In particular, 1. The signification of spiritual truths by natural objects rather than by biblical texts was generally assumed. This approach is illustrated by Isidore of Seville's *De natura rerum*. 2. Pagan texts signifying natural objects or imaginary objects were often assumed to signify not spiritual truths but other natural objects. This approach is exemplified by Eriugena, Remigius of Auxerre, and others. On 1. see further n. 954.
886. On ps.-Dionysius in general see Völker 1958; Louth 1981. The doctrine of divine names is discussed by Corsini 1962, and the doctrine of hierarchy by Roques 1954. On ps.-Dionysius' background in Greek philosophy see Sheldon-Williams 1967; Gersh 1978.
887. Cf. p. 149 ff.
888. Cf. p. 196 ff.
889. Eriugena: *VOD (dCH)* 1. 1073C–1039B (= ps.-Dionysius: *dCH* 120B–124A). In the remainder of this section, ps.-Dionysian texts will be cited primarily in the Latin translation of Eriugena.
890. Eriugena: *VOD (dCH)* 1. 1037C–D.
891. Eriugena: *VOD (dCH)* 1. 1037D–1038C.
892. Eriugena: *VOD (dCH)* 1. 1038C–D.
893. Eriugena: *VOD (dCH)* 1. 1038D–1039A.
894. Eriugena: *VOD (dCH)* 1. 1039A–B.
895. Eriugena: *VOD (dCH)* 1. 1039B.
896. On Eriugena's use of ps.-Dionysius in general see Faes de Mottoni 1977: 35–37; Gersh 1978; Jeauneau 1983. On his methods of translating the ps.-Dionysian corpus see Théry 1931; Roques 1969–1970, 1973; Pépin 1986.
897. Eriugena: *iDdCH* 2. 86–1253. The numbering of the text follows that of the ps.-Dionysian lemmata in the previous summary.
898. We shall employ these terms in order to clarify certain arguments where Eriugena envisages a sign's relation simultaneously to *two* objects. From i. a general semantic viewpoint: a. the signifier is a lexeme, b. the unmediated signified a denotative meaning, and c. the mediated signified a connotative meaning. From ii. Eriugena's ontological viewpoint: a. the signifier is a word, psychic image, etc., b. the unmediated signified an immanent (sensible, etc.) object or something in a psychic image corresponding to the latter, and c. the mediated signified a transcendent (intelligible, etc.) object or something in a psychic image corresponding to the latter. In squares of opposition, i. b and ii. b will occur in position b_1 or more usually $\bar{b}_2$, while

i. c and ii. c will occur in position b_2. Our employment of these terms also seems justified by Eriugena's own text. In gloss 19 he speaks of ii. b as a *medietas* [mediator] — the Latin word having an active sense — through which we may come to know ii. c. On the theory of "symbolism" implied by all this see nn. 951, 954.

899. Strictly speaking, all signification is ternary and therefore mediated. However, one may provisionally distinguish a binary or unmediated variety. This is because the ternarity or medation may be expressed to varying degrees. In general, three ternary structures of signification can be envisaged: i. signified, signifier, signification; ii. mediated signified, unmediated signified, signifier; iii. signified, signifier, interpreter. However, since in i. and iii. the third term is frequently unexpressed whereas in ii. it is always expressed, it is possible to characterize i. and iii. as binary or unmediated and ii. as ternary or mediated. One should note that the three structures are inseparable in a thorough semantic analysis. This is because signification always involves the activation and deactivation of semes (mediated vs./= unmediated signified) by an interpreter.

900. Interaction of axes and categories might be represented as in n. 864.

901. Cf. n. 865. Simplicity vs. complexity here = absence vs. presence of interpreter.

902. Eriugena speaks explicitly of all components of the signifying relation in these glosses. Thus, the signifier is indicated by *significare, significantius* in gloss 49; the signified by *significanda* in glosses 30, 42 and by *significari* in gloss 49; and the signification by *significatio* in glosses 30, 49.

903. Gloss 44. Cf. gloss 30.

904. *res* (glosses 6, 30, 37), *essentia* (gloss 6), *substantia* (glosses 23, 33, 52), *intellectus* (gloss 19).

905. *immaterialis* (glosses 38, 44), *intelligibilis* (glosses 6, 23, 37, 38, 44), *intellectualis* (gloss 44), *rationabilis* (gloss 49).

906. Gloss 44.

907. *creatura* (gloss 49), *natura* (gloss 38), *materia* (glosses 38, 44).

908. *naturalis* (glosses 23, 30), *materialis* (glosses 37, 38, 44, 49), *corporalis* (gloss 49).

909. See n. 898.

910. See n. 904. In gloss 52 *intellectus* possibly has both senses.

911. See n. 902.

912. *imaginatio* (glosses 9, 23, 30, 33, 44, 49), *formatio* (glosses 19, 30, 52), *figuratio* (gloss 49).

913. *imago* (glosses 18, 19, 23, 30), *symbolum* (glosses 6, 9, 49, 52), *forma* (gloss 23), *figura* (gloss 49). For *similitudo* see n. 945.

914. Glosses 6, 9.

915. Glosses 9, 20, 23, 52.

916. Of course, Eriugena considers the phonic substance elsewhere. See pp. 185, 196, 198.
917. It will be noted that semantic properties are here attributed to the signifier. This occurs for two reasons: i. The signifier already contains a signified within itself. Cf. pp. 185–186, ii. Realist ontology requires the division of such properties between signifier and signified. See p. 214.
918. See n. 901.
919. See nn. 899, 902.
920. Gloss 6.
921. Glosses 6, 9, 30, 35, 42, 49.
922. Glosses 6, 49, 52.
923. *cogitatio* (gloss 6), *arbitrari* (gloss 9), *existimare* (gloss 33), *putare* (gloss 49).
924. *contemplatio* (glosses 6, 19, 38), *cognitio* (glosses 19, 20, 37).
925. See p. 215.
926. See n. 902.
927. See glosses 23, 30 for examples of human forms combined with the bovine, leonine, aquiline, and of a winged man, etc.
928. In the present set of glosses, Eriugena adopts a realist viewpoint in which a mental image is opposed to a real object rather than his usual idealist position whereby a mental image is co-extensive with a real object. In other words, the existent-cognitive axis becomes one of opposition (or pseudo-hierarchy) instead of one of equivalence. This emphasis stems more from the need to comment on a pseudo-Dionysian text than from a fundamental revision of his philosophical perspective. Contrast Eriugena's more idealistic treatment of signification in section 4.3.
929. See n. 898.
930. Glosses 30, 44, 49. Eriugena considers the negative/affirmative disjunction to be the ontological basis of "dissimilar" images. However, to some degree this explanation must apply to the origin of all types. Cf. n. 946.
931. The harmonic aspect is particularly stressed in glosses 44, 49 where images are termed *resonantiae* [resonances] or *resultationes/apēchēmata* [reverberations]. On the harmony constituted by negative and affirmative divine names see p. 162 ff.
932. The "form" and "content" of signification mentioned here — our terms — correspond roughly to the form and substance of content in Hjemslevian linguistics. See Hjelmslev 1961: pp. 47–60.
933. Gloss 18.
934. Gloss 23.
935. For the distinction of levels see especially gloss 44, and for shifting between levels especially glosses 30, 49. One of the characteristics of "dissimilar" images is their tendency to promote this shifting. See glosses 44, 49.

334 Notes

936. On combination, transference, and transference-combination see also pp. 185–187.
937. See n. 932.
938. Gloss 23 *absolutae imaginationes* (1a), *formarum confusio* (1b), *humana* (2a), *bestiarum* (2b), *spiritualium substantiarum intelligibiliumque virtutum* (3a). 3b has been extrapolated from 2b.
939. The minimum requirement of a semantic operation is two semes. Sometimes there is an apparent monosemic situation e.g. regarding the image "irrationality" in gloss 44. However, the surrounding context suggests a semantic analysis similar to that applied to a divine name. See p. 187 and n. 815. One actually begins with the sememe "rational" and articulates it into four semes: present, transcendent, not present, and not transcendent. Hence, the use of the image "irrationality" exhibits a hidden semantic complexity.
940. This can be analyzed semantically by i. positing a semantic value x; ii. establishing a square of opposition within this value based on two generations of terms with A_1 and A_0 explicit but B_1 and B_0 implicit in the text; iii. establishing two sememes b_2 ($=B_1 + A_1$) and $\bar{b}_2$ ($=B_0 + A_0$); iv. understanding the image as a relation along the diagonal axis b_2–$\bar{b}_2$ (see figure N28).
941. Gloss 44. This can be analyzed semantically in the same manner as before (see figure N29).
942. Thus, applying the square in n. 940 (see figure N30).
943. Thus, applying the square in n. 940 (see figure N31).
944. Glosses 6, 30, 38, 42, 44, 49, 52 *dissimiles*. Cf. gloss 35.
945. The substitution of *similitudo* for *imago* as the term for the image in glosses 38, 42, 44 is important. Given that the word *similitudo* in Latin means not only something embodying similarity but also the property of similarity as

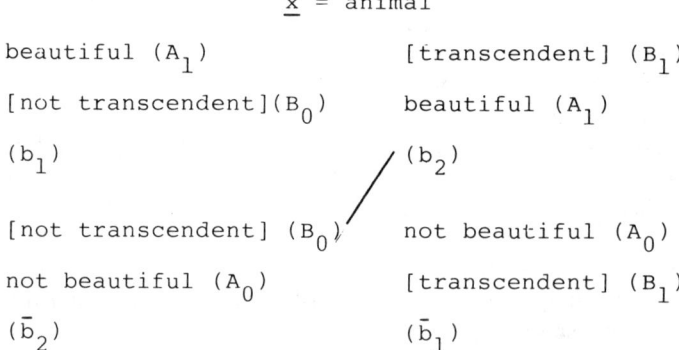

Figure N28. Semantic analysis of the Dionysian image "animal"

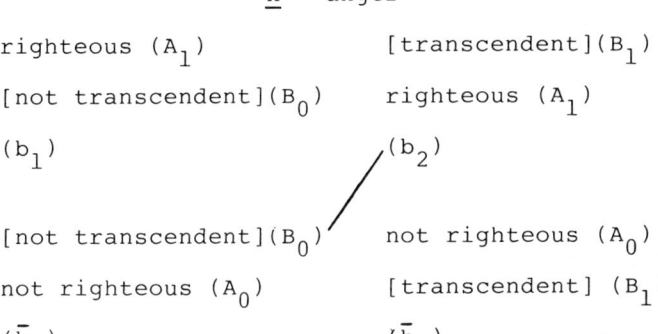

Figure N29. Semantic analysis of the Dionysian image "anger"

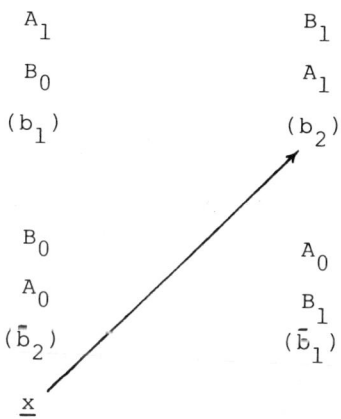

Figure N30. Semantic analysis of "animal" (continued)

such, its employment here together with *dissimilis* both reinforces the idea of similarity and emphasizes the aspect of contradictoriness.
946. This interpretation of Eriugena's reasoning brings out what his text shows if not what it says. Regarding dissimilar images he actually states the following: A. Their dissimilarity occurs 1. between the imagined form and the natural form (gloss 30), 2. between the transcendent object and the immanent object (glosses 44, 49), and 3. between the imagined form and the transcendent object (gloss 49); B. The preference for dissimilarity results from 1. the priority of negativity as such (glosses 18, 30, 44, 49) and 2. the possibility of concealment from the unworthy (glosses 20, 49).

```
┌─────────────────────────┐
│  A₁            B₁       │
│  B₀            A₁       │
│  (b₁)          (b₂)     │
│                         │
│                         │
│  B₀            A₀       │
│  A₀            B₁       │
│  (b̄₂)          (b̄₁)    │
└─────────────────────────┘
            x̲
```

Figure N31. Semantic analysis of "anger" (continued)

947. See p. 214.
948. Glosses 9, 20, 30, 49.
949. Cf. n. 941 where the seme "righteous" could conceivably be replaced by several others.
950. See pp. 191—192.
951. In Eriugena there is an important relation between "symbol" and "allegory." See n. 954.
952. Cf. n. 899.
953. Eriugena's *transitus* corresponds to *transitio* and his *recapitulatio* to *enumeratio* in classical rhetorical theory. Some metaphysical aspects of his handling of the two ideas are discussed by Jeauneau 1971; Allard 1977; Jeauneau 1978: 84–87; Beierwaltes 1986.
954. We shall not consider Eriugena's understanding of allegory in detail here since it is mostly quite conventional. However, it is worth noting that his *allegoria* is related to yet different from his *symbolum* — a single signifier having both unmediated and mediated signifieds — in that it may entail i. a smaller group of such signifiers (see *Pe.* IV. 816B, IV. 818B, V. 990C), ii. a larger group of such signifiers where at least one signifier has a verbal syntactic maker (see *Pe.* III. 723B, V. 996A) — cf. pp. 185–186 —, iii. the reading of such signifiers in general (see *Pe.* III. 693C, III, 700B, III. 705B–706A, III. 707B). A good example of senses ii. + iii. occurs in the *Commentarius in Evangelium Iohannis*. Here, he interprets the Gospel narrative of Christ's journey from Judaea through Samaria to Galilee as signifying on a higher level human nature's development from subjection to carnal law through life according to natural law to governance by eternal law *(iEI* IV. 1. 330D–332A). He then interprets Jesus' transfiguration on the

mountain and teaching of eight beatitudes as signifying on the higher level humanity's recapturing of the blessed state and the numerical perfection of that state respectively *(iEI* IV. 1, 332B). There are perhaps two innovations in Eriugena's theory of allegory. First he distinguishes more clearly than do other writers between factual allegory — where the signifiers are independent forms capable of subsisting externally to human consciousness — and linguistic allegory — where the signifiers are dependent forms incapable of subsisting externally to human consciousness. See *iEI* VI. 5, 344D–345C. Secondly, he goes beyond other writers when he presents allegorical theory itself through an allegory. See pp. 219–220. On Eriugena's treatment of allegory see also Pépin 1973; Dronke 1977; Rigoni 1978.

955. The distinction between syntagm and paradigm — if not the actual terminology — goes back to Saussure. He indicated by this the contrast between a linear and irreversible sequence of units in speech and a non-linear and reversible association of those units in memory. For the general theory see Barthes 1985[1]: 53 ff. For its specific application to ancient rhetorical doctrine see Barthes 1985[2]: 92, 155–158, etc. The application of this distinction to be developed below has some explicit justification in ancient texts. In particular, the contrast between sequence in speech and association in memory is apparently utilized in establishing that between figures of diction and figures of thought. See Anonymous: *aHe.* IV. 13, 18.

956. Eriugena: *Pe.* I. 477D. See n. 953. In ancient rhetorical theory, *transitio* [transition] is one of the *verborum exornationes* [figures of diction]. It recalls what has been said and then anticipates what is to come. See Anonymous: *aHe.* IV. 26, 35. For discussion see Lausberg 1960, 1:188–190; Lanham 1991: 99.

957. Eriugena: *Pe.* IV. 746C. Cf. *Pe.* V. 951B.
958. Eriugena: *Pe.* V. 1008B–1009D, V. 1011A–1012C.
959. Eriugena: *Pe* V. 1014D–1015A.
960. Eriugena: *Pe.* V. 1010A.
961. Eriugena: *Pe.* V. 101C–D.
962. Eriugena: *Pe.* V. 890D. Cf. *Pe.* V. 993A–B.
963. Eriugena: *Pe.* V. 933D–934B (forms, qualities, quantities, etc.)
964. Eriugena: *Pe.* II. 544A (sensible to intelligible); *Pe.* V. 876C–D, V. 879A–B, V. 1015C (bodies to souls to minds to causes to God); *Pe.* V. 1020D (mind to knowledge to inner contemplation); *Pe.* V. 897B, V. 906B, V. 926B–C (saints to God).
965. Eriugena: *Pe.* V. 987B–C.
966. For example, the discussion might pass from another question to that regarding the nature of transition itself.
967. Barthes considers this arrangement the basis of metalinguistic discourse. See Barthes 1985[1]: 76–80 where Hjelmslev's theory is developed.
968. Cf. n. 955.

969. Eriugena: *Pe.* II. 554C ff. See n. 953. In ancient rhetorical theory *enumeratio* [recapitulation] forms part of the *dispositio* [arrangement] of a speech. See Anonymous: *aHe.* II. 30, 47. For discussion see Lausberg 1960, 1:337–340; Lanham 1991: 55–56.
970. Eriugena: *Pe.* III. 688A ff. The passage also signals a shift to a more paradigmatic sense of recapitulation.
971. Eriugena: *Pe.* IV. 829B ff.
972. Eriugena: *Pe.* V. 895C ff. Cf. n. 970. The verb *recapitulare* (but not the noun *recapitulatio*) occurs at Eriugena: *Pe.* II. 588B where the repeated material comprises the ten Aristotelian categories.
973. Maximus' term *anakephalaiōsis* has a number of meanings. Among other things, it means both a rhetorical device of enumerating points in a discourse i.e. a relatively static collection of properties (cf. our "constituent part of") and a metaphysical notion of restoring multiplicity to unity i.e. a relatively dynamic transformation of properties (cf. our "principle of unifying"). Eriugena's development of Maximus exploits this polysemy.
974. Eriugena: *Pe.* II. 529D–531A — Eriugena had himself translated the *Ambigua*. Cf. *Pe.* III. 641B–C. On the fivefold division in Maximus' anthropology and Christology see von Balthasar 1961: 132 ff.; Thunberg 1965: 52 ff. The influence on Eriugena is studied by Trouillard 1956; Olivieri 1963; Stock 1967; Sheldon-Williams 1967; Roques 1967[1]; Bertin 1977; Moran 1986; Steel 1986.
975. The actual reference to harmony occurs only in Eriugena's gloss, although it implies no distortion of the Maximian theory. That is: that man is the mediator between (e.g.) intelligible and sensible which are extremes because he contains something of each of them within himself. Ontologically speaking, man exemplifies that relation combining the features of mathematical proportion and dialectical condition which was discussed on p. 139.
976. Eriugena: *Pe.* II. 534B. It is with regard to Maximus' doctrine particularly that Eriugena associates man's cognitive function with his proportional status. See pp. 198–199.
977. Eriugena: *Pe.* II. 535B. Presumably, the unification of earth with heaven is to be understood similarly.
978. At *Pe.* II. 535D Eriugena apparently refers to his later discussion which will draw out these implications.
979. Eriugena: *Pe.* IV. 768C–769C. According to *Pe.* IV. 768B man is himself *notio quaedam intellectualis in mente divina* [a certain intellectual concept in the divine mind].
980. Eriugena: *Pe.* II. 529C–D. On the semantic foundation of this theory see pp. 71–72.
981. See pp. 198–199, 201 ff.
982. Eriugena: *Pe.* V. 895C–896A — Eriugena had also translated the *Quaestiones ad Thalassium*. The geometrical allegory here is fairly unusual.

A more commonplace illustration of the same method is Eriugena's interpretation of Noah's Ark at *Pe*. III. 724B–C.
983. This would represent a combination of metalanguage with connotation according to Barthes' Hjelmslevian analysis. Cf. n. 967.
984. Eriugena: *iEI* I. 29, 306C–307B.
985. Eriugena: *iEI* VI. 3, 342C.
986. Eriugena: *iEI* VI. 3, 342D–343A.
987. Eriugena: *iEI* VI. 4, 343A–344A (with reference to harmony).
988. Eriugena: *iEI* VI. 6, 345C–346A. Cf. *iEI* I. 27, 303D–305A, IV. 1, 331D–332B, VI. 2, 341C–D.
989. Eriugena: *HiPI* 14, 291B–C.
990. For the notions of isotopy and encyclopaedia see pp. 69–70.
991. The following table shows the distribution of terminology in the selected passages:

Table N2. The terminology of consonance

5.1	A	*consonantia*	
	B	*consonantia, (harmonicus)*	+ *dissonantia*
	C	*consonantia, convenientia, harmonia*	
	D	*concordia, consonantia, harmonia*	
5.2	A	*convenientia*	
	B	*concordia, consonantia, consensus*	+ *dissonans*
	C	–	
	D	–	
	E	*consonantia*	
	F	*consonare, harmonia*	
5.3	A	*concordia, consonus*	
	B	–	
	C	–	
	D	*concordia, concorditer*	
	E	–	
	F	*concordia*	
	G	*concorditer, consonantia*	
	H	–	
	I	*concorditer, consonantia*	
	J	*concordia, harmonia*	
5.4	A	*concordare, convenire*	
	B	–	+ *dissonus*
	C	*consensus, convenire*	+ *discors*
	D	–	
	E	*concors*	

Table N2 (continued)

5.4	F	*convenire*	+ *discordare*
	G	*convenientia, convenire, convenienter*	
	H	*concordare*	
5.5	A	*concentus, harmonia*	
	B	*symphonia*	
	C	*concentus*	
	D	*consonus, harmonia, symphonia*	
	E	*consonare, symphonia*	
	F	*symphonia*	
	G	*consonare, harmonia*	
	H	*concordia, concentus, harmonia*	
	I	*consonantia*	
	J	*concordia, concentus*	
5.6	A	*concordia, concors, harmonia*	
	B	*consonantia, consonans*	
5.7	A	*symphonia*	
	B	–	
5.8	A	*concordia, consonus, consonare*	
	B	–	

992. For the axes of opposition, continuity, and equivalence see pp. 72–73, n. 928.
993. In much semiotic literature, "code" is treated as a synonym for "sign-system" in general. However, I shall exploit the narrower definition of code as "correlation of two systems as signifier and signified" employed by certain authors. See Prieto 1966: 43–45, Eco 1976: 36ff., 1984: 164ff. Various typologies of such correlational codes have been suggested. See Guiraud 1971: 45ff.; Fabbri 1976.
994. Eco 1976: 231ff. speaks of a "second articulation" of distinctive but meaningless "figurae", a "first articulation" of distinctive and meaningful "signs", and so forth.

Bibliographies

Abbreviations

AHDLMA	*Archives d'histoire doctrinale et littéraire du moyen âge*
AL	*Aristoteles Latinus*
BGPM	*Beiträge zur Geschichte der Philosophie des Mittelalters*
CAG	*Commentaria in Aristotelem Graeca*
CCCM	*Corpus Christianorum, Continuatio Mediaevalis*
CCSL	*Corpus Christianorum, Series Latina*
CSEL	*Corpus Scriptorum Ecclesiasticorum Latinorum*
MGH	*Monumenta Germaniae Historica*
MS	*Mediaeval Studies*
NEMBI	*Notices et extraits des manuscrits de la Bibliothèque Impériale*
PG	*Patrologia Graeca*
PL	*Patrologia Latina*
RE	*Recherches augustiniennes*
RTAM	*Recherches de théologie ancienne et médiévale*
SC	*Sources chrétiennes*
SE	*Sacris Erudiri*
SEMSP	*Scriptores Ecclesiastici de Musica Sacra potissimum*
SM	*Studi Medievali*

Bibliography I: Primary sources

Abbo of Fleury	QG	Quaestiones grammaticales, ed. Anita Guerreau-Jalabert, Paris: Les Belles Lettres 1982.
Adalbold of Utrecht	Mu.	Musica, ed. Joseph Smits van Waesberghe, Buren: Knuf 1981.
Adelard of Bath	dED	De eodem et diverso, ed. Hans Willner, BGPM 4, Münster: Aschendorff 1903.
Alan of Lille	An.	Anticlaudianus, ed. Robert Bossuat, Paris: Vrin 1955.
	dPN	De planctu Naturae, ed. Nikolaus M. Häring (SM 19, 1978: 797–879).
	EPdA	Expositio Prosae de angelis, cd. Marie-Thérèse d'Alverny (Alain de Lille, Textes inédits), Paris: Vrin 1965.
	Hi.	Hierarchia, ed. Marie-Thérèse d'Alverny (Alain de Lille, Textes inédits).
Ambrose	iHe.	In Hexaemeron, ed. Karl Schenkl, CSEL 32/1, Wien: Tempsky 1897.
Ammonius	iACa.	In Aristotelis Categorias, ed. Adolf Busse, CAG 4/4, Berlin: Reimer 1885.
Anonymous	aHe.	Ad Herennium, ed. Harry Caplan, Cambridge/ MA: Harvard University Press 1954.
Anonymous	dPP	De philosophia et partibus eius, ed. Gilbert Dahan (AHDLMA 49, 1982: 155–193).
Anonymous	EpB	Epistula ad B., ed. Ernst Dümmler, MGH, Epist. Karol. Aev. VI, Berlin: Weidmann 1925: 197–201.
Anonymous	iAdMu.	Expositiunculae in Augustini De musica, ed. Patrick le Boeuf (RE 22, 1987: 243–316).
Anonymous	ME	Musica enchiriadis, ed. Hans Schmid, München: Verlag der Bayerischen Akademie der Wissenschaften/Beck 1981.
Apuleius	Pe.	Perihermeneias, ed. David Londey, Carmen Johanson (The Logic of Apuleius), Leiden: Brill 1987.
Aristotle	APo.	Analytica posteriora, ed. W. David Ross, Oxford: Oxford University Press 1949.
	Ca.	Categoriae, ed. Lorenzo Minio-Paluello, Oxford: Oxford University Press 1949.

	dIn.	*De interpretatione*, ed. Lorenzo Minio-Paluello, Oxford: Oxford University Press 1949.
	Me.	*Metaphysica*, ed. W. David Ross, Oxford: Oxford University Press 1924.
	Po.	*Poetica*, ed. Rudolf Kassel, Oxford: Oxford University Press 1965.
Augustine	cA	*Contra Academicos*, ed. William M. Green, CCSL 29, Turnhout: Brepols 1970.
	cALP	*Contra adversarium Legis et Prophetarum*, ed. Klaus D. Daur, CCSL 49, Turnhout: Brepols 1985.
	cEMF	*Contra Epistulam Manichaei quam vocant Fundamenti*, ed. Joseph Zycha, CSEL 25/1, Wien: Tempsky 1891.
	cFM	*Contra Faustum Manichaeum*, ed. Joseph Zycha, CSEL 25/1, Wien: Tempsky 1891.
	Co.	*Confessiones,* ed. Martin Skutella, Leipzig: Teubner 1934.
	cSM	*Contra Secundinum Manichaeum*, ed. Joseph Zycha, CSEL 25/2, Wien: Tempsky 1892.
	dCD	*De civitate Dei*, ed. Bernhard Dombart, Alfons Kalb, CCSL 47–48, Turnhout: Brepols 1955.
	dDC	*De doctrina Christiana*, ed. Joseph Martin, CCSL 32, Turnhout: Brepols 1962.
	dDi.	*De dialectica*, ed. B. Darrell Jackson, Dordrecht: Reidel 1975.
	dGaL	*De Genesi ad litteram*, ed. Joseph Zycha, CSEL 28/1, Wien: Tempsky 1894.
	dGcM	*De Genesi contra Manichaeos*, PL 34, Paris 1841.
	dGLI	*De Genesi ad litteram imperfectus liber*, ed. Joseph Zycha, CSEL 28/1, Wien: Tempsky 1894.
	dLA	*De libero arbitrio*, ed. William M. Green, CCSL 29, Turnhout: Brepols 1970.
	dMa.	*De magistro*, ed. William M. Green, CCSL 29, Turnhout: Brepols 1970.
	dMECdMM	*De moribus Ecclesiae Catholicae et de moribus Manichaeorum*, PL 32, Paris 1841.
	dMu.	*De musica*, PL 32, Paris 1841.

	dNB	*De natura boni*, ed. Joseph Zycha, CSEL 25/2, Wien: Tempsky 1892.
	dOr.	*De ordine,* ed. William M. Green, CCSL 29, Turnhout: Brepols 1970.
	dQA	*De quantitate animae,* PL 32, Paris 1841.
	dTr.	*De Trinitate,* ed. William J. Mountain, François Glorie, CCSL 50/50A, Turnhout: Brepols 1968.
	dVR	*De vera religione,* ed. Klaus D. Daur, CCSL 32, Turnhout: Brepols 1962.
	En.	*Enchiridion,* ed. E. Evans, CCSL 46, Turnhout: Brepols 1969.
	Ep.	*Epistulae,* ed. Alois Goldbacher, CSEL 34/1, 34/2, 44, 57, 58, Wien: Tempsky 1895–1923.
ps.-Augustine	CD	*Categoriae decem,* ed. Lorenzo Minio-Paluello, AL I, 1–5, Bruges — Paris: Desclée de Brouwer 1961.
Aurelian of Réôme	MD	*Musica disciplina,* ed. Lawrence Gushee, n. p.: American Institute of Musicology 1975.
Basil	iHe.	*In Hexaemeron,* ed. Stanislas Giet, SC 26 bis, Paris: Cerf 1968.
Bede	iGe.	*In Genesim,* ed. Charles W. Jones, CCSL 118A, Turnhout: Brepols 1967.
Bernard Silvestris	Co.	*Cosmographia,* ed. Peter Dronke, Leiden: Brill 1978.
	iMCdNPM	*Commentum in Martianum,* ed. Haijo J. Westra, Toronto: Pontifical Institute of Mediaeval Studies 1986.
Berno of Reichenau	PiT	*Prologus in Tonarium,* ed. Martin Gerbert, SEMSP 2, repr. Hildesheim: Olms 1963.
Boethius	dCP	*De consolatione philosophiae,* ed. Hugh F. Stewart, Edward K. Rand (Boethius, *The Theological Tractates...*), Cambridge/MA.: Harvard University Press 1918.
	dDi.	*De divisione,* PL 64, Paris 1847.
	dDT	*De differentiis topicis,* PL 64, Paris 1847.
	dIA	*De institutione arithmetica,* ed. Gottfried Friedlein, Leipzig: Teubner 1867.
	dIM	*De institutione musica,* ed. Gottfried Friedlein, Leipzig: Teubner 1867.

Bibliography I: Primary sources 345

	dTr.	*De Trinitate*, ed. Hugh F. Stewart, Edward K. Rand (Boethius, *The Theological Tractates*...), Cambridge/MA.: Harvard University Press 1918.
	iACa.	*In Categorias Aristotelis*, PL 64, Paris 1847.
	iCTo.	*In Ciceronis Topica*, ed. Johann C. Orelli, Johann G. Baiter (*Ciceronis Opera Omnia*), Zürich: Tauchnitz 1833.
	iIsPep.	*In Isagogen Porphyrii commenta*, ed. Georg Schepss and Samuel Brandt, CSEL 48, Wien: Tempsky 1906.
	VAdI	*Versio Aristotelis De interpretatione*, ed. Lorenzo Minio-Paluello, AL II. 1–2, Bruges — Paris: Desclée de Brouwer 1965.
Bovo of Corvey	iBdCP	*In Boethii Consolationem*, ed. Robert B.C. Huygens (SE 6, 1954: 373–427).
Calcidius	iPTi.	*In Platonis Timaeum*, ed. Jan H. Waszink (*Timaeus a Calcidio translatus*...), London — Leiden: Brill 1962.
	VPTi.	*Versio Platonis Timaei*, ed. Jan H. Waszink (*Timaeus a Calcidio translatus*...), London — Leiden: Brill 1962.
Cassiodorus	In.	*Institutiones*, ed. Roger A. B. Mynors, 2nd ed., Oxford: Oxford University Press 1961.
Censorinus	dDN	*De die natali*, ed. Nicolaus Sallmann, Leipzig: Teubner 1983.
Cicero	dND	*De natura deorum*, ed. Martin van den Bruwaene, Bruxelles: Latomus 1970–1986.
	dRe.	*De republica*, ed. Konrat Ziegler, Leipzig: Teubner 1915.
	TD	*Tusculanae disputationes*, ed. Max Pohlenz, Leipzig: Teubner 1912.
	Ti.	*Timaeus*, ed. Wilhelm Ax, Stuttgart: Teubner 1977.
	To.	*Topica*, ed. Augustus S. Wilkins, Oxford: Oxford University Press 1903.
Claudianus Mamertus	dSA	*De statu animae*, ed. August Engelbrecht, CSEL 11, Wien: Tempsky 1885.
Clement of Alexandria	Pr.	*Protrepticus*, ed. Otto Stählin, Leipzig: Hinrichs 1936.
ps.-Dionysius the Areopagite	dCH	*De caelesti hierarchia*, eds. René Roques. Gunther Heil, Maurice de Gandillac, SC 58 bis, 2 ed., Paris: Cerf 1970.

Eriugena	dPr.	*De divina praedestinatione*, ed. Goulven Madec, CCCM 50, Turnhout: Brepols 1978.
	HiPI	*Homelia in prologum Iohannis*, ed. Édouard Jeauneau, SC 151, Paris: Cerf 1969.
	iDdCH	*Expositiones in Ierarchiam coelestem*, ed. Jeanne Barbet, CCCM 31, Turnhout: Brepols 1975.
	iEI	*Commentarius in Evangelium Iohannis*, ed. Édouard Jeauneau, SC 180, Paris: Cerf
	iMCdNPM (O)	*Glosae Martiani*, ed. Édouard Jeauneau (*Quatre thèmes érigéniens*), Montréal — Paris: Institut d'Études Médiévales Albert-le-Grand — Vrin 1978.
	iMCdNPM (P)	*Annotationes in Marcianum*, ed. Cora E. Lutz, Cambridge/MA.: Mediaeval Academy of America 1939.
	Pe.	*Periphyseon* I–III, ed. Inglis P. Sheldon-Williams, Dublin: Dublin Institute for Advanced Studies 1968–1981.
		Periphyseon IV–V, PL 122, Paris 1853.
	VOD (dCH)	*Versio Dionysii De caelesti hierarchia*, PL 122, Paris 1853.
	VOG	*Versio Gregorii*, ed. Maïeul Cappuyns (RTAM 32, 1965: 205–262).
Favonius Eulogius	DdSS	*Disputatio de Somnio Scipionis*, ed. Roger E. van Weddingen, Bruxelles: Latomus 1957.
Gerbert of Aurillac	dRRU	*De rationali et ratione uti*, ed. Alexandre Olleris, Clermont-Ferrand — Paris: Thibaut, Dumoulin 1867.
Gregory of Nyssa	dHO	*De hominis opificio*, PG 44, Paris 1863.
ps.-Hermes Trismegistus	dSP	*De sex rerum principiis*, ed. Theodore Silverstein (AHDLMA 22, 1955: 217–302).
Honorius Augustodunensis	dIM	*De imagine mundi*, ed. Valerie Flint (AHDLMA 49, 1982: 7–153).
Hrotsvitha	Pa.	*Pafnutius*, ed. Helene Homeyer, München — Paderborn — Wien: Schöningh 1970.
Hugh of St. Victor	Di.	*Didascalicon*, ed. Charles H. Buttimer, Washington DC: Catholic University of America Press 1939.
	iDdCH	*In Hierarchiam coelestem*, PL 175, Paris 1879.
Irenaeus	aHa.	*Adversus Haereses*, PG 7, Paris 1882.

Isidore of Seville	*Et.*	*Etymologiae*, ed. Wallace M. Lindsay, Oxford: Oxford University Press 1911.
Macrobius	*iCSS*	*Commentarii in Somnium Scipionis*, ed. James Willis, Leipzig: Teubner 1970.
Marius Victorinus	*aCa.*	*Ad Candidum*, eds. Paul Henry, Pierre Hadot, SC 68, Paris: Cerf 1960.
Martianus Capella	*dNPM*	*De nuptiis Philologiae et Mercurii*, ed. James Willis, Leipzig: Teubner 1983.
Nicomachus of Gerasa	*IA*	*Institutio arithmetica*, ed. Richard Hoche Leipzig: Teubner 1866.
Origen	*dPr.*	*De principiis*, ed. Henri Crouzel, Manlio Simonetti, SC 252, 253, 268, 269, Paris: Cerf 1978–1980.
Otloh of St. Emmeram	*dTQ*	*De tribus quaestionibus*, PL 146, Paris 1884.
Philo Iudaeus	*dOM*	*De opificio mundi* ed. Leopold Cohn, Paul Wendland (*Philonis Alexandrini Opera I*), Berlin: Reimer 1896.
	dSo.	*De somniis*, ed. Leopold Cohn, Paul Wendland (*Philonis Alexandrini Opera III*), Berlin: Reimer 1898.
Plato	*Ti.*	*Timaeus*, ed. John Burnet, Oxford: Oxford University Press 1902.
Pliny the Elder	*NH*	*Naturalis historia*, ed. Karl Mayhoff, Leipzig: Teubner 1865–1898.
Plotinus	*En.*	*Enneades*, eds. Paul Henry, Hans-Rudolph Schwyzer, Paris — Bruxelles — Leiden: Desclée de Brouwer — Brill 1951–1973.
Porphyry	*iACa.*	*In Aristotelis Categorias*, ed. Adolf Busse, CAG 4/1, Berlin: Reimer 1887.
Proclus	*iPTi.*	*In Platonis Timaeum*, ed. Ernst Diehl, Leipzig: Teubner 1903–1906.
Regino of Prüm	*dHI*	*De harmonica institutione*, ed. Martin Gerbert, SEMSP I, repr. Hildesheim: Olms 1963.
Remigius of Auxerre	*iBdCP*	*In Boethii Consolationem*, ed. Hugh F. Stewart (JTS 17, 1915–1916: 22–42).
	iMCdNPM	*Commentum in Martianum Capellam*, ed. Cora E. Lutz, Leiden: Brill 1962–1965.
Sextus Empiricus	*aMa.*	*Adversus mathematicos*, ed. Hermann Mutschmann, Leipzig: Teubner 1914.
Simplicius	*iACa.*	*In Aristotelis Categorias*, ed. Carl Kalbfleisch, CAG 8, Berlin: Reimer 1907.

Theo Smyrnaeus	*ERM*	*Expositio rerum mathematicarum ad legendum Platonem utilium*, ed. Eduard Hiller, Leipzig: Teubner 1878.
Thierry of Chartres	*dSDO*	*De sex dierum operibus*, ed. Nikolaus M. Häring (*Commentaries on Boethius by Thierry of Chartres and his School*), Toronto: Pontifical Institute of Mediaeval Studies 1971.
	He.	*Heptateuchon*, prologue ed. Édouard Jeauneau (MS 16, 1954: 171–175).
	iBdH(AM)	*In Boethii De hebdomadibus* (*Abbrevatio Monacensis*), ed. Nikolaus M. Häring, *Commentaries*.
	iBdTr (C)	*In Boethii De Trinitate* (*Commentum*), ed. Nikolaus M. Häring, *Commentaries*.
	iBdTr(CV)	*In Boethii De Trinitate* (*Commentarius Victorinus*), ed. Nikolaus M. Häring, *Commentaries*.
	iBdTr (G)	*In Boethii De Trinitate* (*Glosa*), ed. Nikolaus M. Häring, *Commentaries*.
	iBdTr (L)	*In Boethii De Trinitate* (*Lectiones*), ed. Nikolaus M. Häring, *Commentaries*.
	iBdTr (T)	*Tractatus de Trinitate*, ed. Nikolaus M. Häring, *Commentaries*.
Vitruvius	*dAr.*	*De architectura*, ed. Frank Granger, Cambridge/MA: Harvard University Press 1931–1934.
William of Aubérive	*Re.*	*Regulae*, ed. H. Lange (*Les données mathématiques des traités du XIIe siècle sur la symbolique des nombres*), Copenhague 1979.
William of Conches	*iBdCP*	*Glosae super Boethium*, ed. Charles Jourdain (NEMBI 20, 1862: 40–82).
	iMiCSS	*Glosae super Macrobium*, ed. Helen Rodnite (*The Doctrine of the Trinity in Guillaume de Conches' Glosses on Macrobius*), Diss. Columbia University 1972.
	iPTi.	*Glosae super Platonem*, ed. Édouard Jeauneau, Paris: Vrin 1965.

Bibliography II: Secondary works

Ackrill, John L.
1963 *Aristotle's "Categories" and "De Interpretatione"*. Translated with Notes. Oxford: Oxford University Press.
Allard, Guy-H.
1977 "Quelques remarques sur la 'disputationis series' du 'De Divisione Naturae'", in: René Roques (ed.), *Jean Scot Érigène et l'histoire de la philosophie*. Paris: Centre National de la Recherche Scientifique, 211–224.
1983 (ed.) *Johannis Scoti Eriugenae Periphyseon Indices Generales*. Montréal — Paris: Institut d'Études Médiévales — Vrin.
1990 "'Medietas' chez Jean Scot", in: Werner Beierwaltes (ed.), *Begriff und Metapher, Sprachform des Denkens bei Eriugena*. Heidelberg: Winter, 95–107.
Alverny, Marie-Thérèse d'
1965 *Alain de Lille, textes inédits*. Paris: Vrin.
Amerio, Franco
1954 "S. Agostino e la musica", *Humanitas* 9:1050–1058.
Andrews, Robert
1986 "Boethius on Relation in 'De Trinitate'", in: Monika Asztalos (ed.), *The Editing of Theological and Philosophical Texts from the Middle Ages*. Stockholm: Almqvist and Wiksell International, 281–289.
Anscombe, Gertrude E.M. and Geach, Peter T.
1961 *Three Philosophers*. Oxford: Blackwell.
Anton, John P.
1957 *Aristotle's Theory of Contrariety*. London: Routledge.
Ard, Josh
1983 "The Semiotics of Mathematical Symbolism", *Kodikas/Code* 6: 3–14.
Arnoux, Georges
1960 *Musique platonicienne. Âme du monde*. Paris: Dervy.
Avalle, d'Arco S.
1973 *L'ontologia del segno in Saussure*. Torino: Giappichelli.
Ayer, Alfred J.
1938 *Language, Truth and Logic*. London: Gollancz.
Bach, Emmon and Harms, Robert (eds.)
1968 *Universals in Linguistic Theory*. New York: Holt, Rinehart and Winston.
Bachelard, Gaston
1961 *La poétique de l'espace*. Paris: Presses Universitaires de France.

Balthasar, Hans Urs
1961 *Kosmische Liturgie. Das Weltbild Maximus' des Bekenners*, 2. Auflage. Einsiedeln: Johannes.
Bambrough, Renford
1976 "Universals and Family Resemblances", in: Michael J. Loux (ed.), *Universals and Particulars. Readings in Ontology*. Notre Dame/IN: Notre Dame University Press, 106–124.
Barthes, Roland
1957 *Mythologies*. Paris: Seuil.
1970 *S/Z*. Paris: Seuil.
1985[1] "Éléments de sémiologie", *L'aventure sémiologique*. Paris: Seuil, 17–84.
1985[2] "L'ancienne rhétorique", *L'aventure sémiologique*. Paris: Seuil, 85–165.
Bataillon, Louis-J.
1977 "Sur quelques éditions de textes platoniciens médiévaux", *Revue des sciences philosophiques et théologiques* 61:243–261.
Batschelet-Massini, W.
1979 "Zur kosmologischen Arithmetik des Boethius", in: Karin Figala and Ernst H. Berninger (eds.), *Arithmos-Arrithmos* = Festschrift Joachim Fleckenstein. München: Minerva, 9–28.
Beierwaltes, Werner
1969 "Augustins Interpretation von 'Sapientia' 11.21", *Revue des études augustiniennes* 15:51–61.
1971 "Zu Augustins Metaphysik der Sprache", *Augustinian Studies* 2: 179–195.
1975 "'Aequalitas numerosa'. Zu Augustins Begriff des Schönen", *Wissenschaft und Weisheit* 38:140–157.
1976 "Negati affirmatio. Welt als Metapher. Zur Grundlegung einer mittelalterlichen Ästhetik durch Johannes Scotus Eriugena", *Philosophisches Jahrbuch* 83:237–265.
1986 "Language and Object. Reflections on Eriugena's Valuation of the Function and Capacities of Language", in: Guy-H. Allard (ed.), *Jean Scot écrivain*. Montréal — Paris: Bellarmin — Vrin, 209–228.
Bernhard, Michael
1979 *Wortkonkordanz zu Anicius Manlius Severinus Boethius, De institutione musica*. München: Verlag der Bayerischen Akademie der Wissenschaften/Beck.
1988 "Glossen zur Arithmetik des Boethius", in: Sigrid Krämer and Michael Bernhard (eds.), *Scire Litteras*. München: Verlag der Bayerischen Akademie der Wissenschaften/Beck, 23–34.

Bertin, Francis
1977 "Les origines de l'homme chez Jean Scot", in: René Roques (ed.), *Jean Scot Érigène et l'histoire de la philosophie*. Paris: Centre National de la Recherche Scientifique, 307–314.

Black, Max
1949 "Vagueness. An Exercise in Logical Analysis", *Language and Philosophy*, Studies in Method. Ithaca/NY: Cornell University Press, 23–58.
1962 *Models and Metaphors*. Studies in Language and Philosophy. Ithaca/NY: Cornell University Press.

Blanché, Robert
1966 *Structures intellectuelles*. Essai sur l'organisation systématique des concepts. Paris: Vrin.

Böhner, Philotheus
1952 *Medieval Logic*. Manchester: Manchester University Press.

Boeuf, Patrick le
1986 *La tradition manuscrite du "De Musica" de Saint Augustin et son influence sur la pensée et l'esthétique médiévales*. Diss. Paris.
1987 "Un commentaire d'inspiration érigénienne du 'De musica' de saint Augustin", *Recherches augustiniennes* 22:243–316.

Boll, Franz
1913 "Die Lebensalter", *Neue Jahrbücher für das klassiche Altertum* 31:101–120.

Bonnardière, Anne-Marie la
1970 *Biblia Augustiniana, Le Livre de la Sagesse*. Paris: Études augustiniennes.

Bower, Calvin
1978 "Boethius and Nicomachus. An Essay Concerning the Sources of 'De Institutione Musica'", *Vivarium* 16:1–45.
1988 "Boethius' 'De Institutione Musica'. A Handlist of Manuscripts", *Scriptorium* 42:205–251.

Bragard, R.
1945 "Boethiana. Études sur le 'De Institutione Musica' de Boèce", in: Suzanne Clercx and A. van der Linden (eds.), *Hommage Charles van den Borren*. Anvers: De nederlandsche Boekhandel, 84–139.

Brøndal, Viggo
1943 *Essais de linguistique générale*, Copenhague.

Brownlee, Marina, Brownlee, Kevin, and Nichols, Stephen (eds.)
1991 *The New Medievalism*. Baltimore: Johns Hopkins University Press.

Brunner, Fernand
1966 "Creatio numerorum rerum est creatio", in: Pierre Gallais and Yves J. Riou (eds.), *Mélanges René Crozet II*. Poitiers: Société d'Études Médiévales, 719–725.

Bruyne, Édgar de
  1946   Études d'esthétique médiévale I: De Boèce à Jean Scot Érigène. Bruges: De Tempel.
Burkert, Walter
  1972   Lore and Science in Ancient Pythagoreanism. Translated by Edwin L. Minar. Cambridge/MA: Harvard University Press.
Burnett, Charles.
  1982   Hermann of Carinthia, De Essentiis. A Critical Edition with Translation and Commentary. Leiden: Brill.
Burrow, John A.
  1986   The Ages of Man. A Study in Medieval Writing and Thought. Oxford: Oxford University Press.
Buyssens, Eric
  1967   La communication et l'articulation linguistique. Bruxelles — Paris.
Caldwell, John
  1981   "The 'De Institutione Arithmetica' and the 'De Institutione Musica'", in: Margaret Gibson (ed.), Boethius. His Life, Thought and Influence. Oxford: Blackwell, 135–154.
California, University of
  1928   Studies in the Problem of Relations. Berkeley/CA: University of California Press.
Callaghan, William J.
  1986   "Charles Sanders Peirce. His General Theory of Signs", Semiotica 61:123–161.
Cassirer, Ernst
  1955 – The Philosophy of Symbolic Forms. Translated by Ralph Manheim.
  1957   3 volumes. Newhaven/CT: Yale University Press.
Catalogus
  1976+   Catalogus verborum quae in operibus sancti Augustini inveniuntur. Eindhoven: Augustijnendreef 15 — Thesaurus Linguae Augustinianae.
Chadwick, Henry
  1981   Boethius. The Consolations of Music, Logic, Theology, and Philosophy. Oxford: Oxford University Press.
Chamberlain, David S.
  1969   "Anticlaudianus III, 412–445 and Boethius' 'De Musica'", Manuscripta 13:167–169.
  1970   "Philosophy of Music in the 'Consolatio' of Boethius", Speculum 45:80–97.
  1980   "Musical Learning and Dramatic Action in Hrotsvit's 'Pafnutius'", Studies in Philology 77:319–343.
Châtillon, Jean
  1977   "Hugues de Saint-Victor critique de Jean Scot", in: René

Roques (ed.), *Jean Scot Érigène et l'historie de la philosophie*. Paris: Centre National de la Recherche Scientifique, 415–431.

Chydenius, Johan
1960   *The Theory of Medieval Symbolism*. Helsingfors: Centraltryckeriet.

Cilleruelo, P. L.
1968   "Numerus et sapientia", *Estudio agustiniano* 3:109–121.

Coallier, Christine
1986   "Le vocabulaire des arts libéraux dans le 'Periphyseon'", in: Guy-H. Allard (ed.), *Jean Scot écrivain*. Montréal — Paris: Bellarmin — Vrin, 343–360.

Colish, Marcia
1985   *The Stoic Tradition from Antiquity to the Early Middle Ages*. 2 volumes. Leiden: Brill.

Collart, Jean
1962   "Analogie et anomalie", *Fondation Hardt, Entretiens sur l'Antiquité classique* 9:117–132.

Comeau, Marie
1930   *Saint Augustin exégète du quatrième Évangile*. Paris: Beauchesne.

Conti, Alessandro D.
1983   "La teoria della relazione nei commentatori neoplatonici delle 'Categorie' di Aristotele", *Rivista critica di storia della filosofia* 38:259–283.

Corbin, Solange
1962   "Musica spéculative et cantus pratique. Le rôle de saint Augustin dans la transmission des sciences musicales", *Cahiers de civilisation médiévale* 5:1–12.

Corsini, Eugenio
1962   *Il trattato "De Divinis Nominibus" dello Pseudo-Dionigi e i commenti neoplatonici al Parmenide*. Torino: Giappichelli.

Coseriu, Eugenio
1975   *Die Geschichte der Sprachphilosophie von der Antike bis zur Gegenwart. Eine Übersicht*. Tübingen.

Courcelle, Pierre
1969   *Late Latin Writers and their Greek Sources*. Translated by Harry E. Wedeck. Cambridge/MA: Harvard University Press.

Courtine, Jean-François
1980   "La dimension spatio-temporelle dans la problématique catégoriale du 'De Divisione Naturae' de Jean Scot Érigène", *Les études philosophiques* 3:343–367.

Cress, Donald A.
1976   "Hierius and St. Augustine's Account of the Lost 'De Pulchro et Apto'. Confessions IV, 13–15", *Augustinian Studies* 7:153–163.

Cristante, Lucio
1974 – "Musica e grammatica nella enciclopedia di Marziano Capella e
1975 nelle tradizione anteriore", *Atti e Memorie dell'Accademia Patavina di Scienze, Lettere ed Arti* III, 87:353–379.
1987 *Marziano Capella, De Nuptiis Philologiae et Mercurii Liber IX*. Introduzione, traduzione e commento. Padova: Liviana.

Cristiani, Marta
1973[1] "Lo spazio e il tempo nell'opera dell'Eriugena", *Studi medievali* 3ª serie 14:39–136.
1973[2] "Le problème du lieu et du temps dans le livre Ier du 'Periphyseon'", in: John J. O'Meara and Ludwig Bieler (eds.), *The Mind of Eriugena*. Dublin: Irish University Press, 41–48.
1981 "Nature-essence et nature-langage. Notes sur l'emploi du terme 'natura' dans le 'Periphyseon' de Jean Érigène", *Miscellanea Mediaevalia* 13/2:707–717.

Dehnert, Edmund J.
1969 "Music as Liberal in Augustine and Boethius", *Arts libéraux et philosophie au moyen âge*. Montréal — Paris: Institut d'Études Médiévales — Vrin, 987–991.

Deiters, Hermann
1881 *Studien zu den griechischen Musikern. Über das Verhältnis des Martianus Capella zu Aristides Quintilianus*. Programm des Marien-Gymnasiums, Posen.

Delatte, Armand
1915 *Études sur la littérature pythagoricienne*. Paris: Champion.

Derossi, Giorgio
1965 *Segno e struttura linguistica nel pensiero di Ferdinand de Saussure*. Udine: Del Bianco.

Derrida, Jacques
1967[1] *De la Grammatologie*. Paris: Minuit.
1967[2] *L'écriture et la différence*. Paris: Seuil.
1972[1] *Marges de la philosophie*. Paris: Minuit.
1972[2] *La dissémination*. Paris: Seuil.
1972[3] *Positions*. Paris: Minuit.

Desrosiers-Bonin, Diane
1986 "Étude des radicaux et de leur répartition dans le dialogue du 'Periphyseon'", in: Guy-H. Allard (ed.), *Jean Scot écrivain*. Montréal — Paris: Bellarmin — Vrin, 311–315.

Deusen, Nancy van (ed.)
1990 *Paradigms in Medieval Thought. Applications in Medieval Disciplines*. Lewiston/NY: Mellen.

Dewey, John
1946 "Peirce's Theory of Linguistic Signs, Thought and Meaning", *Journal of Philosophy* 43:85–95.

Dillon, John
1976 "Image, Symbol and Analogy. Three Basic Concepts of Neoplatonic Allegorical Exegesis", in: R. Baine Harris (ed.), *The Significance of Neoplatonism*. Albany/NY: State University New York Press, 247–262.

Dörrie, Heinrich
1977 "Der Begriff 'Pronoia' in Stoa und Platonismus", *Freiburger Zeitschrift für Philosophie und Theologie* 24:60–87.
1981 "'Formula analogiae'. An Exploration of a Theme in Hellenistic and Imperial Platonism", in: Henry J. Blumenthal and Robert A. Markus (eds.), *Neoplatonism and Early Christian Thought*. London: Variorum, 33–49.

Dondaine, Hyacinthe
1950 "Cinq citations de Jean Scot chez Simon de Tournal", *Recherches de théologie ancienne et médiévale* 17:303–311.

Dronke, Peter
1977 "'Theologia veluti quaedam poetria'. Quelques observations sur la fonction des images poétiques chez Jean Scot", in: René Roques (ed.), *Jean Scot Érigène et l'histoire de la philosophie*. Paris: Centre National de la Recherche Scientifique, 243–252.
1988 "Thierry of Chartres", in: Peter Dronke (ed.), *A History of Twelfth-Century Western Philosophy*. Cambridge: Cambridge University Press, 358–385.

Duchez, Marie-Elisabeth
1980 "Jean Scot Érigène premier lecteur du 'De Institutione Musica' de Boèce", in: Werner Beierwaltes (ed.), *Eriugena, Studien zu seinen Quellen*. Heidelberg: Winter, 165–187.

Duchrow, Ulrich
1965 *Sprachverständnis und biblisches Hören bei Augustin*. Tübingen: Mohr.

Duclow, Donald F.
1977 "Nature as Speech and Book in John Scotus Eriugena", *Mediaevalia* 3:131–140.

Duhem, Pierre
1954 *Le système du monde. Histoire des doctrines cosmologiques de Platon à Copernic*, volume 3. Paris: Hermann, 44–62.

Dummett, Michael
1973 *Frege, Philosophy of Language*. New York: Harper and Row.

Dutton, Paul E. and Jeauneau, Édouard
    1983   "The Verses of the 'Codex Aureus' of Saint Emmeram", *Studi Medievali* 3ª serie 24:75–120.

Eco, Umberto
- 1962   *Opera aperta*. Milano: Bompiani.
- 1968   *La struttura assente*. Milano: Bompiani.
- 1976   *A Theory of Semiotics*. Bloomington/IN: Indiana University Press.
- 1979   *The Role of the Reader*. Explorations in the Semiotics of Texts. Bloomington/IN: Indiana University Press.
- 1984   *Semiotics and the Philosophy of Language*. London: Macmillan.
- 1986   *Art and Beauty in the Middle Ages*. Translated by Hugh Bredin. New Haven/CT: Yale University Press.
- 1990   *The Limits of Interpretation*. Bloomington/IN: Indiana University Press.

Eco, Umberto and Marmo, Constantino (eds.)
    1989   *On the Medieval Theory of Signs*. Amsterdam: Benjamins.

Edelstein, Heinz
    1929   *Die Musikanschauung Augustins nach seiner Schrift "De Musica"*. Freiburg i. Br: Eschenhagen.

Evangeliou, Christos
    1988   *Aristotle's Categories and Porphyry*. Leiden: Brill.

Evans, Gillian R.
- 1975–1976   "'Alteritas'. Sources of the Notion of Otherness in Twelfth-Century Commentaries on Boethius' 'Opuscula Sacra'", *Archivum Latinitatis Medii Aevi* 40:103–113.
- 1977   "'Studium Discendi': Otloh of St. Emmeram and the Seven Liberal Arts", *Recherches de théologie ancienne et médiévale* 44:29–54.
- 1978[1]   "A Commentary on Boethius's 'Arithmetica' of the Twelfth or Thirteenth Century", *Annals of Science* 35:131–141.
- 1978[2]   "Introduction to Boethius's 'Arithmetica' of the Tenth to the Fourteenth Century", *History of Science* 16:22–41.
- 1982   "Thierry of Chartres and the Unity of Boethius' Thought", Studia Patristica 17:440–445.
- 1983   "The Uncompleted 'Heptateuch' of Thierry of Chartres", *History of Universities* 3:1–13.

Ewing, Alfred
    1933   *Idealism, A Critical Survey*. New York: Humanities Press.

Fabbri, Paolo etc.
    1976   "Rassegna critica sulla nozione di codice", *Intorno al "Codice"* = Atti del III Convegno della Associazione Italiana di Studi Semiotici. Firenze.

Faes de Mottoni, Barbara
1977 *Il "Corpus Dionysianum" nel Medioevo*. Rassegna di studi 1900 — 1972. Bologna: Il mulino.

Fine, Gail
1983 "Relational Entities", *Archiv für Geschichte der Philosophie* 65: 225–249.

Firth, Raymond
1973 *Symbols Public and Private*. Ithaca/NY: Cornell University Press.

Fisch, Max H.
1978 "Peirce's General Theory of Signs", in: Thomas A. Sebeok (ed.), *Sight, Sound and Sense*. Bloomington/IN: Indiana University Press, 31–70.

Flasch, Kurt
1974 "Zur Rehabilitierung der Relation. Die Theorie der Beziehung bei Johannes Eriugena", in: Wilhelm F. Niebel and Dieter Leisegang (eds.), *Philosophie als Beziehungswissenschaft* = Festschrift Julius Schaaf. Frankfurt: Heiderhoff, 1–25.

Foucault, Michel
1966 *Les mots et les choses. Une archéologie des sciences humaines*. Paris: Gallimard.

Foussard, Jean-Claude
1971 "'Aulae sidereae'. Vers de Jean Scot au roi Charles. Introduction, texte, traduction et notes", *Cahiers archéologiques* 21: 79–88.
1977 "Apparence et apparition. La notion de 'phantasia' chez Jean Scot", in: René Roques (ed.), *Jean Scot Érigène et l'histoire de la philosophie*. Paris: Centre National de la Recherche Scientifique, 337–348.

Frede, Michael
1978 "Principles of Stoic Grammar", in: John M. Rist (ed.), *The Stoics*. Berkeley/CA: University of California Press, 27–75.

Freeman, Eugene (ed.)
1983 *The Relevance of Charles Peirce*. La Salle/IL: Hegler Institute.

Frege, Gottlob
1892 "Über Sinn und Bedeutung", *Zeitschrift für Philosophie und philosophische Kritik* 100:25–50.

Frova, Carla
1985 "Gerberto 'philosophus'. Il 'De rationali et ratione uti'", *Gerberto. Scienza, storia e mito* = Atti del Gerberti Symposium, Bobbio (Piacenza): Archivi Storici Bobiensi, 351–377.
1985 "La musica nell'insegnamento delle arti liberali. I trattati di Sant' Agostino e di Boezio", *Benedictina* 32:377–388.

Früchtel, Edgar
- 1970 *Weltentwurf und Logos. Zur Metaphysik Plotins.* Frankfurt: Klostermann.

Gallacher Patrick and Damico, Helen (eds.)
- 1989 *Hermeneutics and Medieval Culture.* Albany/NY: State University New York Press.

Gallop, David
- 1976 "Relations in the 'Phaedo'", in: Roger A. Shiner and John King-Farlow (eds.), *New Essays on Plato and the Presocratics.* Guelph: Canadian Association for Publishing in Philosophy, 149–163.

Gandillac, Maurice de
- 1977 "Anges et hommes dans le Commentaire de Jean Scot sur la 'Hiérarchie céleste'", in: René Roques (ed.), *Jean Scot Érigène et l'histoire de la philosophie.* Paris: Centre National de la Recherche Scientifique, 393–403.

Gandillac, Maurice de, Goldmann, Lucien, and Piaget, Jean (eds.)
- 1965 *Entretiens sur les notions de genèse et de structure.* Paris: Mouton.

Gellrich, Jesse M.
- 1985 *The Idea of the Book in the Middle Ages.* Language Theory, Mythology and Fiction. Ithaca/NY: Cornell University Press.

Gérold, Théodore
- 1931 *Les Pères de l'Église et la musique.* Paris: Alcan.

Gersh, Stephen
- 1973 *Kinesis Akinetos.* A Study of Spiritual Motion in the Philosophy of Proclus. Leiden: Brill.
- 1978 *From Iamblichus to Eriugena.* An Investigation of the Prehistory and Evolution of the Pseudo-Dionysian Tradition. Leiden: Brill.
- 1980 "Omnipresence in Eriugena. Some Reflections on Augustino-Maximian Elements in 'Periphyseon'", in: Werner Beierwaltes (ed.), *Eriugena, Studien zu seinen Quellen.* Heidelberg: Winter, 55–74.
- 1982 "Platonism, Neoplatonism, Aristotelianism. A Twelfth-Century Metaphysical System and its Sources", in: Robert L. Benson and Giles Constable (eds.), *Renaissance and Renewal in the Twelfth Century.* Cambridge/MA: Harvard University Press, 512–534.
- 1986 *Middle Platonism and Neoplatonism.* The Latin Tradition. 2 volumes. Notre Dame/IN: Notre Dame University Press.
- 1987 "Honorius Augustodunensis and Eriugena. Remarks on the Method and Content of the 'Clavis Physicae'", in: Werner Beierwaltes (ed.), *Eriugena Redivivus.* Heidelberg: Winter, 162–173.
- 1990 "The Structure of the Return in Eriugena's 'Periphyseon'", in: Werner Beierwaltes (ed.), *Begriff und Metapher.* Sprachform des Denkens bei Eriugena. Heidelberg: Winter, 108–125.

1992 "Porphyry's Commentary on the 'Harmonics' of Ptolemy and Neoplatonic Musical Theory", in: Stephen Gersh and Charles Kannengiesser (eds.), *Platonism in Late Antiquity*. Notre Dame/IN: Notre Dame University Press, 141–155.
1992 "Pseudo(?)-Bernard Silvestris and the Revival of Neoplatonic Virgilian Exegesis", *Sophiēs Maiētores — Chercheurs de sagesse* = Mélanges Jean Pépin, Paris: Institut des études augustiniennes, 573–593.

Ghyka, Matila C.
1931 *Le nombre d'or*. Paris: Gallimard.

Godwin, Joscelyn
1987 *Harmonies of Heaven and Earth*. The Spiritual Dimension of Music from Antiquity to the Avant-Garde. Rochester/VT: Inner Traditions International.
1986 *Music, Mysticism and Magic*. A Sourcebook, New York — London: Routledge.

Gogacz, Mieczyslaw
1985 "Problème des relations dans la philosophie médiévale", *Journal philosophique* 1–5:201–217.

Graeser, Andreas
1978 "The Stoic Theory of Meaning," in: John M. Rist (ed.), *The Stoics*. Berkeley/CA: University of California Press, 77–100.

Greenberg, Joseph H.
1966 *Universals of Language*. 2nd Edition. Cambridge/MA: Massachusetts Institute of Technology Press.

Greenlee, Douglas
1973 *Peirce's Concept of Sign*. The Hague: Mouton.

Greimas, Algirdas J.
1966 *Sémantique structurale*. Recherche de méthode. Paris: Presses Universitaires de France.
1970, *Du sens*. Essais sémiotiques, 2 volumes. Paris: Seuil.
1983

Greimas, Algirdas J. and Courtés, Joseph
1979, *Sémiotique*. Dictionnaire raisonné de la théorie du langage.
1986 2 volumes. Paris: Hachette.

Groupe μ.
1970 *Rhétorique générale*. Paris: Seuil.

Guiraud, Pierre
1971 *La sémiologie*. Paris: Presses Universitaires de France.

Guitton, Jean
1959 *Le temps et l'éternité chez Plotin et saint Augustin*. Paris: Vrin.

Hadot, Pierre
- 1954 "'Cancellatus respectus'. L'usage du chiasme en logique", *Archivum Latinitatis Medii Aevi* 24:277–282.
- 1967 "'Numerus intelligibilis infinite crescit'. Augustin, Epistula 3. 2", *Miscellanea A. Combes*. Rome, 181–191.
- 1968 *Porphyre et Victorinus*. Paris: Études augustiniennes.

Hadot, Ilsetraut.
- 1984 *Arts libéraux et philosophie dans la pensée antique*. Paris: Études augustiniennes.

Häring, Nikolaus M.
- 1955 "The Creation and Creator of the World according to Thierry of Chartres and Clarenbaldus of Arras", *Archives d'histoire doctrinale et littéraire du moyen âge* 22:137–216.
- 1971 *Commentaries on Boethius by Thierry of Chartres and his School*. Toronto: Pontifical Institute of Mediaeval Studies.
- 1973 "John Scottus in Twelfth-Century Angelology", in: John J. O'Meara and Ludwig Bieler (eds.), *The Mind of Eriugena*. Dublin: Irish University Press, 158–169.

Hammerstein, Reinhold
- 1962 *Die Musik der Engel*. Untersuchungen zur Musikanschauung des Mittelalters. Bern — München: Francke.

Handschin, Jacques
- 1927 "Die Musikanschauung des Johannes Scotus (Erigena)", *Deutsche Vierteljahrsschrift für Literaturwissenschaft und Geistesgeschichte* 5:316–341.
- 1950 "The 'Timaeus' Scale", *Musica Disciplina* 4:3–42.

Hegel, Georg W. F.
- 1934 *Wissenschaft der Logik*, ed. G. Lasson. 2 volumes. Hamburg: Meiner.

Heller, B.
- 1939 *Boethius im Lichte der frühmittelalterlichen Musiktheorie*. Diss. Wien.

Hellgardt, Ernst
- 1973 *Zum Problem symbolbestimmter und formalästhetischer Zahlenkomposition in mittelalterlicher Literatur*. München: Beck.

Herren, Michael
- 1986 "The Commentary on Martianus Attributed to John Scottus. Its Hiberno-Latin Background", in: Guy-H. Allard (ed.), *Jean Scot écrivain*. Montréal — Paris: Bellarmin — Vrin, 265–286.

Hjelmslev, Louis
- 1935, "La catégorie des cas", *Acta Jutlandica* 7, 9.
- 1937

1961   *Prolegomena to a Theory of Language*. Translated by Francis J. Whitfield. Madison/WI: University Wisconsin Press.
1971   *Essais linguistiques*. Paris: Minuit.

Höffding, Harald
1922   *Der Relationsbegriff. Eine erkenntnistheoretische Untersuchung*. Leipzig.

Hübner, W.
1987   "Der 'ordo' der Realien in Augustins Frühdialog 'De ordine'", *Revue des études augustiniennes* 33:23–48.

Hüschen, Heinrich
1954   "Eriugena", *Die Musik in Geschichte und Gegenwart*, volume 3, Kassel — Basel 1492–1496.

Hüttig, Albrecht
1990   *Macrobius im Mittelalter*. Ein Beitrag zur Rezeptionsgeschichte der "Commentarii in Somnium Scipionis". Frankfurt: Lang.

Huglo, Michel
1990   "La réception de Calcidius et des 'Commentarii' de Macrobe à l'époque carolingienne", *Scriptorium* 44:3–20.

Huré, Jean
1924   *Saint Augustin, musicien*. Paris: Senart.

Illmer, D.
1984   "Arithmetik in der gelehrten Arbeitsweise des frühen Mittelalters", in: L. Fenske, etc. (eds.), *Institutionen, Kultur und Gesellschaft = Festschrift Josef Fleckenstein*. Sigmaringen: Thorbecke 35–58.

Jackson, B. Darrell
1972   "The Theory of Signs in St. Augustine's 'De Doctrina Christiana'", in: Robert Markus (ed.), *Augustine*. Garden City/NY, 92–147.

Jacquart, Danielle
1984   "De 'crasis' à 'complexio': note sur le vocabulaire du tempérament en latin médiéval", *Mémoires* 5, *Textes medicaux latins antiques*, St.-Étienne, 71–75.

Jakobson, Roman
1932   "Musikwissenschaft und Linguistik", *Prager Presse*. December 7.
1973   "Le langage en relation avec les autres systèmes de communication", *Essais de linguistique générale*. Paris: Minuit, 91–103.
1971   "Two Aspects of Language and Two Types of Aphasic Disturbances", in: Roman Jakobson and Morris Halle, *Fundamentals of Language*. The Hague: Mouton, 67–96.
1980   *The Framework of Language*. Ann Arbor/MI: Graduate School, University of Michigan.

Jeauneau, Édouard
1954   "Le 'Prologus in Eptatheucon' de Thierry de Chartres", *Medieval Studies* 16:171–175.

1957 "L'usage de la notion d''integumentum' à travers les gloses de Guillaume de Conches", *Archives d'histoire doctrinale et littéraire du moyen âge* 24:35–100.

1963 "Mathématiques et Trinité chez Thierry de Chartres", *Miscellanea Mediaevalia* 2, Berlin, 289–295.

1971 "Le symbolisme de la mer chez Jean Scot Érigène", *Le Néoplatonisme* = Colloque du Centre National de la Recherche Scientifique. Paris: Centre National de la Recherche Scientifique, 385–394.

1978 *Quatre thèmes érigéniens*, Montréal — Paris: Institut d'Études Médiévales Albert-le-Grand — Vrin.

1982 "Jean l'Erigène et les 'Ambigua ad Iohannem' de Maxime le Confesseur", in: Felix Heinzer and Christoph von Schönborn (eds.), *Maximus Confessor* = Actes du Symposium sur Maxime le Confesseur. Fribourg: Éditions universitaires, 343–364.

1983 "Pseudo-Dionysius, Gregory of Nyssa, and Maximus the Confessor in the Works of John Scottus Eriugena", in: Uta-Renate Blumenthal (ed.), *Carolingian Essays*. Washington D.C.: Catholic University of America Press, 138–149.

1987 "Le renouveau érigénien du XIIe siècle", in: Werner Beierwaltes (ed.), *Eriugena Redivivus*. Heidelberg: Winter, 26–46.

1990 "Jean Scot et la métaphysique des nombres", in: Werner Beierwaltes (ed.), *Begriff und Metapher*. Sprachform des Denkens bei Eriugena. Heidelberg: Winter, 126–141.

Jolivet, Jean
1966 "Quelques cas de 'platonisme grammatical' du VIIe au XIIe siècle", in: Pierre Gallais and Yves J. Riou (eds.), *Mélanges René Crozet I*. Poitiers: Société d'études médiévales, 93–99.

Jones, Percy
1957 *The Glosses "De Musica" of John Scottus Eriugena in the MS. Lat. 12960 of the Bibliothèque Nationale, Paris*. Diss. Rome.

Kassler, Jamie C.
1982 "Music as a Model in Early Science", *History of Science* 20: 103–139.

Katz, Jerrold J. and Ford, Jerry A.
1963 "The Structure of a Semantic Theory", *Language* 39:170–210.
1964 *The Structure of Language*. Readings in the Philosophy of Language. Englewood Cliffs/NJ: Prentice-Hall.

Kerbrat-Orecchioni, Catherine
1976 "Problématique de l'isotopie", *Linguistique et sémiologie* 1: 11–34.
1977 *La connotation*. Lyon: Presses universitaires de Lyon.

Keyser, Édouard de
1955 *La signification de l'art dans les "Ennéades" de Plotin*. Louvain: Bibliothèque de l'université.

Kirwan, Christopher
 1974 "Plato and Relativity", *Phronesis* 19:112–129.
Klibansky, Raymond, Panofsky, Erwin, and Saxl, Fritz
 1964 *Saturn and Melancholy*. London: Nelson.
Knappitsch, Anton
 1905 *Sankt Augustins Zahlensymbolik*. Graz.
Koerner, E. F. Konrad
 1973 *Ferdinand de Saussure. Origin and Development of his Linguistic Theory in Western Studies of Language*. Braunschweig: Vieweg.
Kretzmann, Norman
 1967 "Semantics, History of", in: Paul Edwards (ed.), *The Encyclopedia of Philosophy*, volume 7. New York: Macmillan, 358–406.
 1974 "Aristotle on Spoken Sound Significant by Convention", in: John Corcoran (ed.), *Ancient Logic and its Modern Interpretations*. Dordrecht: Reidel, 3–21.
Kristeva, Julia
 1969 *Sēmeiōtikē. Recherches pour une sémanalyse*. Paris: Seuil.
Kucharski, Paul
 1927 *Étude sur la doctrine pythagoricienne de la tetrade*. Paris.
Lacan, Jacques
 1966 *Écrits*. Paris: Seuil.
Lakoff, George
 1973 "Hedges. A Study in Meaning Criteria and the Logic of Fuzzy Concepts", *Journal of Philosophical Logic* 2:458–508.
Lamizet, Bernard
 1983 "Sémiotique du nombre", in: T. Borbé (ed.), *Semiotics Unfolding*, volume 3. Berlin: Mouton de Gruyter, 1483–1491.
Lanham, Richard A.
 1991 *A Handlist of Rhetorical Terms*, 2nd edition. Berkeley — Los Angeles: University of California Press.
Lausberg, Heinrich
 1960 *Handbuch der literarischen Rhetorik*, 2 volumes. München: Hueber.
Lenaz, Luciano
 1975 *Martiani Capellae De Nuptiis Philologiae et Mercurii Liber Secundus. Introduzione, traduzione e commento*. Padova: Liviana.
Leonardi, Claudio
 1960 "I codici di Marziano Capella", *Aevum* 33:443–489; 34:1–99 and 411–524.
 1977 "Glosse eriugeniane a Marziano Capella in un codice leidense", in: René Roques (ed.), *Jean Scot Érigène et l'histoire de la philosophie*. Paris: Centre National de la Recherche Scientifique, 171–182.

1980	"Martianus Capella et Jean Scot. Nouvelle présentation d'un vieux problème", in: Guy-H. Allard (ed.), *Jean Scot écrivain*. Montréal — Paris: Bellarmin — Vrin, 187–207.

Lepel, F. von
1958 *Die antike Musiktheorie im Lichte des Boethius*. Berlin.

Levine, P.
1958 "Two Early Latin Versions of St. Gregory of Nyssa's 'Peri Kataskeuēs anthrōpou'", *Harvard Studies in Classical Philology* 63:473–492.

Lévi-Strauss, Claude
1958 *Anthropologie structurale*. Paris: Plon.
1962 *La pensée sauvage*. Paris: Plon.
1964 *Mythologiques I: Le cru et le cuit*. Paris: Plon.

Lévy-Bruhl, Lucien
1922 *Les fonctions mentales dans les sociétés inférieures*. Paris: Alcan.

Libéra, Alain de
1976 "La sémiotique d'Aristote", in: Frédéric Nef (ed.), *Structures élémentaires de la signification*. Bruxelles, 28–55.

Lieb, Hans H.
1981 "Das 'Semiotische Dreieck' bei Ogden und Richards. Eine Neuformulierung des Zeichenmodells von Aristoteles", in: Jürgen Trabant (ed.), *Logos Semantikos* = Festschrift Eugenio Coseriu I. Berlin: De Gruyter, 137–156.

Liebeschütz, Hans
1958 "Texterklärung und Weltdeutung bei Johannes Eriugena", *Archiv für Kulturgeschichte* 40:66–96.

Linsky, Leonard
1967 *Referring*. New York: Routledge — Humanities Press.

Londey, David and Johanson, Carmen
1987 *The Logic of Apuleius*. Leiden: Brill.

Lopez Silonis, R.
1967[1] "Paradojas del conocimiento de Dios en Escoto Erígena", *Pensamiento* 23:21–49.
1967[2] "Sentido y valor del conocimiento de Dios en Escoto Erígena", *Pensamiento* 23:131–165.

Louth, Andrew
1981 *The Origins of the Christian Mystical Tradition from Plato to Denys*. Oxford: Oxford University Press.

Lubac, Henri de
1959– *Exégèse médiévale. Les quatre sens de l'Écriture*. Paris: Aubier.
1964

Lucentini, Paolo
1976 "La nuova edizione del 'Periphyseon' dell'Eriugena", *Studi Medievali* 3ª serie 17:393–414.

Lutz, Cora
1971 "Martianus Capella", in: Paul O. Kristeller and F. Edward Cranz (eds.), *Catalogus Translationum et Commentariorum… Annotated Lists and Guides*. Washington D.C.: Catholic University of America Press, 367–381.

Lyons, John
1963 *Structural Semantics. An Analysis of Part of the Vocabulary of Plato*. Oxford: Blackwell.

Maccagnolo, Enzo
1976 *Rerum Universitas. Saggio sulla filosofia di Teodorico di Chartres*. Firenze: Le Monnier.

McGinn, Bernard
1975 "Negative Theology in John the Scot", *Studia Patristica* 13: 232–238.

Madec, Goulven
1976 "Jean Scot et les Pères latins: Hilaire, Ambroise, Jérôme et Grégoire le Grand", *Revue des études augustiniennes* 22:134–142.
1980[1] "Le dossier augustinien du 'Periphyseon' de Jean Scot (Livres I–II)", *Recherches augustiniennes* 15:241–264.
1980[2] "Observations sur le dossier augustinien du 'Periphyseon'", in: Werner Beierwaltes (ed.), *Eriugena, Studien zu seinen Quellen*. Heidelberg: Winter, 75–84.
1986 "Jean Scot et ses auteurs", in: Guy-H. Allard (ed.), *Jean Scot écrivain*. Montréal — Paris: Bellarmin — Vrin, 143–186.

Magee, John
1989 *Boethius on Signification and Mind*. Leiden: Brill.

Marenbon, John
1980 "John Scottus and the 'Categoriae Decem'", in: Werner Beierwaltes (ed.), *Eriugena, Studien zu seinen Quellen*. Heidelberg: Winter, 117–134.
1981 *From the Circle of Alcuin to the School of Auxerre. Logic, Theology and Philosophy in the Early Middle Ages*. Cambridge: Cambridge University Press.

Markus, Robert A.
1957 "St. Augustine on Signs", *Phronesis* 2:60–83.

Marrou, Henri-Irénée
1956 *A History of Education in Antiquity*. Translated by G. Lamb. New York: Sheed and Ward.

Martinet, Andre
1946 "Au sujet des fondements de la théorie linguistique de L. Hjelmslev", *Bulletin de la Société de Linguistique* 43:19–42.
Martinet, Jeanne
1974 "La sémiologie du numero", *La linguistique* 10:47–61.
Masi, Michael
1971 "MSS containing the De Musica of Boethius", *Manuscripta* 15: 89–95.
1981 "Boethius' 'De Institutione Arithmetica' in the Context of Medieval Mathematics", in: Luca Obertello (ed.), *Congresso Internazionale di Studi Boeziani, Atti*. Roma: Herder, 263–272.
Massera, Giuseppe
1976 *Severino Boezio e la scienza armonica tra l'antichità e il medio evo*. Parma: Studium Parmense.
Mathiesen, Thomas J.
1976 "Problems of Terminology in Ancient Greek Theory", in: Burton L. Karson (ed.), *Harmonia. Festival Essays for Pauline Alderman*. Provo/UT: Brigham Young University Press, 3–17.
Mathon, Gérard
1960 "Jean Scot Érigène, Chalcidius et le problème de l'âme universelle", *L'homme et son destin d'après les penseurs du moyen âge*. Louvain — Paris, 361–375.
Mauro, Tullio de
1987 *Ludwig Wittgenstein. His Place in the Development of Semantics*. Dordrecht: Reidel.
Mayer, Cornelius P.
1969– *Die Zeichen in der geistigen Entwicklung und in der Theologie*
1974 *des jungen Augustinus*, 2 volumes. Würzburg: Augustinus-Verlag.
Merguet, Hugo
1961 *Lexikon zu den philosophischen Schriften Ciceros*. Hildesheim: Olms.
Mertz, Elizabeth and Parmentier, Richard J. (eds.)
1985 *Semiotic Mediation*. Orlando/FL: Academic Press.
Metz, Christian
1967 "Remarque sur le mot et sur le chiffre. À propos des conceptions sémiologiques de L. J. Prieto", *La linguistique* 2:41–56.
Meyer, Bonaventura
1932 *Harmonia. Bedeutungsgeschichte des Wortes von Homer bis Aristoteles*. Diss. Zürich.
Meyer, Heinz
1975 *Die Zahlenallegorese im Mittelalter. Methode und Gebrauch*. München.

Meyer, Heinz and Suntrup, Rudolf
  1977   "Zum Lexicon der Zahlenbedeutungen im Mittelalter. Einführung in die Methode und Probeartikel. Die Zahl 7", *Frühmittelalterliche Studien* 11:1–73.
Michel, Paul-Henri
  1950   *De Pythagore à Euclide*. Contribution à l'histoire des mathématiques préeuclidiennes. Paris: Belles Lettres.
Mieri, F. di
  1984   "Il 'De Institutione Arithmetica' di Severino Boezio", *Sapienza* 37:179–202.
Miller, James
  1986   *Measures of Wisdom*. The Cosmic Dance in Classical and Christian Antiquity. Toronto: University Toronto Press.
Minio-Paluello, Lorenzo
  1961   *Aristoteles Latinus I. 1–5. Categoriae vel praedicamenta*. Bruges — Paris: Desclée de Brouwer.
  1971   "Nuovi impulsi allo studio della logica. La seconda fase della riscoperta di Aristotele e di Boezio", *Centro Italiano di Studi sull'alto Medioevo, Settimane* 19:743–766.
  1972   *Opuscula. The Latin Aristotle*. Amsterdam: Hakkert.
Minnis, Alastair J.
  1988   *Medieval Literary Theory and Criticism, c. 1100-c. 1375*. The Commentary-Tradition. Oxford: Oxford University Press.
Molino, Jean
  1971   "La connotation", *La linguistique* 7:5–30.
Montico, M. G.
  1938   "Il valore psicagogico della musica nel pensiero di S. Agostino e di altri filosofi cristiani (Boezio, Cassiodoro e S. Bonaventura)", *Miscellanea Francescana* 38:389–410.
Mooij, Jan J. A.
  1975   "Tenor, Vehicle and Reference", *Poetics* 4:257–272.
Moore, George E.
  1922   "External and Internal Relations", *Philosophical Studies*. London — New York: Kegan Paul, Trench, Trubner, 276–309.
Moran, Dermot
  1986   "'Officina omnium' or 'Notio quaedam intellectualis in mente divina aeternaliter facta'...", in: Christian Wenin (ed.), *L'homme et son univers au moyen âge I*. Louvain-la-Neuve: Institut Supérieur de Philosophie, 195–204.
Mortley, Raoul
  1986   *From Word to Silence*. 2 volumes. Bonn: Hanstein.
  1988   *Désir et différence dans la tradition platonicienne*. Paris: Vrin.

Mounin, Georges
- 1962 "Les analyses sémantiques", *Cahiers de l'Institut de Science Économique Appliquée* 123.

Moutsopoulos, Evangelos
- 1959 *La musique dans l'oeuvre de Platon*. Paris: Presses Universitaires de France.
- 1971 "Sur la 'participation' musicale chez Plotin", *Philosophia* 1:379–389.

Müller, A.
- 1956 *Ars divina. Eine Interpretation der Artifex-Deus-Lehre des heiligen Augustinus.* München.

Münxelhaus, Barbara
- 1976 *Pythagoras musicus. Zur Rezeption der pythagoreischen Musiktheorie als quadrivialer Wissenschaft im lateinischen Mittelalter.* Bonn — Bad Godesberg: Verlag für systematische Musikwissenschaft.
- 1977 "Aspekte der 'musica disciplina' bei Eriugena", in: René Roques (ed.), *Jean Scot Érigène et l'histoire de la philosophie*. Paris: Centre National de la Recherche Scientifique, 253–262.

Nattiez, Jean-Jacques
- 1975 *Fondements d'une sémiologie de la musique.* Paris: Union générale d'éditions.
- 1987 *Musicologie générale et sémiologie.* Paris: Bourgeois

Nebois, Josef
- 1940 *Entwicklungsgeschichtliche Darstellung des Wortes "Harmonia" und sein Ausklang bei Boethius.* Diss. Wien.

Nichols, Stephen
- 1991 "An Intellectual Anthropology of Marriage in the Middle Ages", in: Marina S. Brownlee, etc. (eds.), *The New Medievalism*. Baltimore/MD: Johns Hopkins University Press, 70–95.

Nowak, A.
- 1975 "Die 'numeri judiciales' des Augustinus und ihre musiktheoretische Bedeutung", *Archiv für Musikwissenschaft* 32:196–207.

Nuchelmans, Gabriel
- 1957 "Philologia et son mariage avec Mercure jusqu'à la fin du XIIe siècle", *Latomus* 16:84–107.

Obertello, Luca
- 1967 "Motivi dell'estetica di Boezio", *Rivista di estetica* 12:360–387.
- 1971 "Boezio, le scienze del quadrivio e la cultura medievale", *Atti dell'Accademia Ligure di Scienze e Lettere* 28:152–170.
- 1974 *Severino Boezio.* 2 volumes. Genova: Accademia Ligure di scienze e lettere.

O'Connell, Robert J.
1978   *Art and the Christian Intelligence in St. Augustine.* Oxford: Blackwell.
O'Daly, Gerard J.P.
1991   *The Poetry of Boethius.* Studies in the "Consolation of Philosophy". Chapel Hill/NC: University of North Carolina Press.
Oehler, Klaus
1979   "Peirce's Foundation of a Semiotic Theory of Cognition", *Studies in Peirce's Semiotics.* Lubbock/TX.
Olivieri, F. J.
1963   "La concepción del hombre en 'De Divisione Naturae' de Escoto Eriugena", *Cuadernos filosóficos* 4:61–74.
O'Meara, Dominic J.
1981   "The Concept of 'Natura' in John Scottus Eriugena ('De Divisione Naturae', Book I)", *Vivarium* 19:126–142.
1983   "The Problem of Speaking about God in John Scottus Eriugena", in: Uta-Renate Blumenthal (ed.), *Carolingian Essays.* Washington D.C.: Catholic University of America Press, 151–167.
1989   *Pythagoras Revived. Mathematics and Philosophy in Late Antiquity.* Oxford: Oxford University Press.
1990   "The Metaphysical Use of Mathematical Concepts in Eriugena", in: Werner Beierwaltes (ed.), *Begriff und Metapher. Sprachform des Denkens bei Eriugena.* Heidelberg: Winter, 142–148.
Onofrio, Giulio d'
1980[1]   "A proposito del 'magnificus Boetius' ...", in: Werner Beierwaltes (ed.), *Eriugena, Studien zu seinen Quellen.* Heidelberg: Winter, 189–200.
1980[2]   "Giovanni Scoto e Boezio. Tracce degli 'Opuscula Sacra' e della 'Consolatio' nell'opera eriugeniana", *Studi Medievali* 3ª serie 21:707–752.
1981[1]   "Giovanni Scoto e Remigio di Auxerre. A proposito di alcuni commenti altomedievali a Boezio", *Studi Medievali* 3ª serie 22: 587–693.
1981[2]   "Agli inizi della diffusione della 'Consolatio' e degli 'Opuscula Sacra' nella scuola tardo-carolingia...", in: Luca Obertello (ed.), *Congresso Internazionale di Studi Boeziani, Atti.* Roma: Herder, 343–354.
1986   "'Disputandi disciplina'. Procédés dialectiques et 'logica vetus' dans le langage philosophique de Jean Scot", in: Guy-H. Allard (ed.), *Jean Scot écrivain.* Montréal — Paris: Bellarmin — Vrin, 229–263.
1990   "Über die Natur der Einteilung. Die dialektische Entfaltung von Eriugenas Denken", in: Werner Beierwaltes (ed.), *Begriff und*

Metapher. Sprachform des Denkens bei Eriugena. Heidelberg: Winter, 17–38.

Ooge, Martin L. d'
1926 *Nicomachus of Gerasa, Introduction to Arithmetic, Translated into English... With Studies on Greek Arithmetic* by Frank E. Robbins and Louis C. Karpinski. New York: Macmillan.

Otten, Willemien
1991 *The Anthropology of Johannes Scottus Eriugena.* Leiden: Brill.

Owen, Gwilym E. L.
1957 "A Proof in the 'Peri Ideōn'", *Journal of Hellenic Studies* 77: 103–111.

Parma, Christian
1971 *Pronoia und Providentia. Der Vorsehungsbegriff Plotins und Augustins.* Leiden: Brill.

Parmentier, Richard
1985 "'Signs' Place in medias res. Peirce's Concept of Semiotic Mediation", in: Elizabeth Mertz and Robert J. Parmentier (eds.), *Semiotic Mediation.* Orlando/FL, 23–48.

Parodi, Massimo
1984 "Misura, numero e peso. Un'analogia nel XII secolo", *La storia della filosofia come sapere critico* = Studia Mario dal Pra. Milano, 52–71.

Peirce, Charles S.
1931– *Collected Papers.* 8 volumes, eds. Charles Hartshorne, Paul Weiss,
1935, and Arthur W. Burks. Cambridge/MA: Harvard University Press.
1958

Pépin, Jean
1973 "'Mysteria' et 'Symbola' dans le commentaire de Jean Scot sur l'Évangile de saint Jean", in: John J. O'Meara and Ludwig Bieler (eds.), *The Mind of Eriugena.* Dublin: Irish University Press, 16–30.
1976 "Aspects théoriques du symbolisme dans la tradition dionysienne. Antécédents et nouveautés", *Centro Italiano di Studi sull'Alto Medioevo, Settimane* 35:33–66.
1986 "Jean Scot, traducteur de Denys. L'exemple de la 'Lettre IX'", in: Guy-H. Allard (ed.), *Jean Scot écrivain.* Montréal — Paris: Bellarmin — Vrin, 129–141.

Peri, I.
1983 "'Omnia mensura et numero et pondere disposuisti'. Die Auslegung von Weis. 11. 20 in der lateinischen Patristik", *Miscellanea Mediaevalia* 16/1, Berlin, 1–21.

Perl, Carl J.
1955 "Augustine and Music", *The Musical Quarterly* 41:496–510.

Pfligersdorffer, Georg
- 1950– "Zur Frage nach dem Verfasser der pseudo-augustinischen
- 1951 'Categoriae decem'", *Wiener Studien* 65:131–137.

Phillips, Nancy and Huglo, Michel
- 1985 "Le 'De Musica' de saint Augustin et l'organisation de la durée musicale du IXe au XIIe siècles", *Recherches augustiniennes* 20:117–131.

Piaget, Jean
- 1968 *Le structuralisme*. Paris: Presses Universitaires de France.

Piemonte, Gustavo
- 1985 "Las realidades que superan toda inteligencia. Observaciones sobre el capítulo I de la 'Vox Spiritualis' de Eriúgena (segunda parte)", *Patristica et Mediaevalia* 6:19–41.
- 1986 "L'expression 'quae sunt et quae non sunt'. Jean Scot et Marius Victorinus", in: Guy-H. Allard (ed.), *Jean Scot écrivain*. Montréal — Paris: Bellarmin — Vrin, 81–113.
- 1988 *"Vita in omnia pervenit". El vitalismo eriugeniano y la influencia de Mario Victorino*. Buenos Aires: Ediciones Patristica et Mediaevalia.

Pietzsch, Gerhard W.
- 1929 *Die Klassifikation der Musik von Boetius bis Ugolino von Orvieto*. Halle: Niemeyer.

Pinborg, Jan
- 1967 *Die Entwicklung der Sprachtheorie im Mittelalter*. Münster — Copenhagen: Aschendorff — Frost-Hansen.
- 1972 *Logik und Semantik im Mittelalter*. Ein Überlick. Stuttgart — Bad Canstatt: Fromann-Holzboog.
- 1976 "Konnotation", in: Joachim Ritter, Karlfried Gründer (eds.), *Historisches Wörterbuch der Philosophie* 4. Darmstadt: Wissenschaftliche Buchgesellschaft, 975–977.

Pizzani, Ubaldo
- 1957 "Uno pseudo-trattato dello pseudo-Beda", *Maia* 9:36–48.
- 1965 "Studi sulle fonti del 'De Institutione Musica' di Boezio", *Sacris Erudiri* 16:5–164.
- 1978[1] "Spunti escatologici nel 'De musica' di S. Agostino", *Augustinianum* 18:209–218.
- 1978[2] "Boezio 'consulente tecnico' al servizio dei re barbarici", *Romanobarbarica* 3:189–242.
- 1980 "(Bedae presbyteri) musica theoretica sive scholia in Boethii de institutione musica libros quinque", *Romanobarbarica* 5:299–361.

Pogorzelski, H. A. and Ryan, W.J.
- 1982 *Foundations of Semiological Theory of Numbers*. Orono/ME: University of Maine Press.

Pohlenz, Max
1939 "Die Begründung der abendländischen Sprachlehre durch die Stoa", *Gesellschaft der Wissenschaft zu Göttingen, Nachrichten*, phil.-hist. klasse 1, 3–6, Göttingen.
Potestà, Gian Luca
1983 "Teologia e rivelazione nell''Omelia' di Giovanni Scoto", *Cristianesimo nella storia* 4:293–333.
Potiron, Henri
n. d. *Boèce, théoricien de la musique grecque*, Paris: Bloud et Gay.
Prantl, Carl
1855 *Geschichte der Logik im Abendlande*, volume 1. Leipzig: Hirzel.
Prieto, Luis
1966 *Messages et signaux*. Paris: Presses universitaires de France.
1968 "La sémiologie", *Le Langage* (Encyclopédie de la Pléiade). Paris, 93–144.
1975 *Études de linguistique et de sémiologie générales*. Genève: Droz.
Putnam, Hilary
1975 *Mind, Language and Reality*. Cambridge: Cambridge University Press.
Quillian, Ross
1968 "Semantic Memory", in: Marvin Minsky (ed.), *Semantic Information Processing*. Cambridge/MA: M. I. T. Press, 227–270.
Quine, Willard V.O.
1951 "Two Dogmas of Empiricism", *Philosophical Review* 60:20–43.
Regali, Mario
1983 "Intenti programmatici nel 'De Institutione Arithmetica' di Boezio", *Studi classici e orientali* 33:193–204.
Richards, Ivor A.
1936 *The Philosophy of Rhetoric*. New York: Oxford University Press.
Richardson, H.
1984 "Number and Symbol in Early Christian Irish Art", *Journal of the Royal Society of Antiquaries of Ireland* 114:28–47.
Rief, Josef
1962 *Der Ordobegriff des jungen Augustinus*. Paderborn: Schöningh.
Rigoni, M.
1978 "La lettera e la tomba. Nota su 'Allegoria' e 'Simbolo' nel pensiero di Giovanni Scoto Eriugena", *Conoscenza religiosa* 3:267–285.
Rössler, Gerda
1979 *Konnotationen. Untersuchung zum Problem der Mit- und Nebenbedeutung*. Wiesbaden: Steiner.
Roques, René
1954 *L'univers dionysien. Structure hiérarchique du monde selon le Pseudo-Denys*. Paris: Aubier.

1962	*Structures théologiques de la Gnose à Richard de Saint-Victor.* Paris: Presses Universitaires de France.
1967¹	"Remarques sur la signification de Jean Scot Érigène", *Miscellanea A. Combès.* Roma — Paris: Lateran — Vrin, 245–329.
1967²	"Tératologie et théologie chez Jean Scot Érigène", *Mélanges Marie-Dominique Chenu*, Paris, 419–437.
1969 - 1970	"'Valde artificialiter'. Le sens d'un contresens", *Annuaire de l'École Pratique des Hautes Études V^e section.* Paris, 31–72.
1973	"Traduction ou interprétation? Brèves remarques sur Jean Scot traducteur de Denys", in: John J. O'Meara and Ludwig Bieler (eds.), *The Mind of Eriugena.* Dublin: Irish University Press, 59–77.

Roy, Olivier du
1966   *L'intelligence de la foi en la Trinité selon saint Augustin.* Paris: Études augustiniennes.

Ruef, Hans
1981   *Augustin über Semiotik und Sprache.* Bern: Wyss Erben.

Russell, Bertrand
1910   "The Monistic Theory of Truth", *Philosophical Essays.* London: Longmans, Green.
1919   *Introduction to Mathematical Philosophy.* London: Allen and Unwin.
1926   *Our Knowledge of the External World*, Revised Edition. London: Allen and Unwin.
1935   *Principia Mathematica* I, Second Edition. Cambridge: Cambridge University Press.
1938   *The Principles of Mathematics*, Second Edition. London: Allen and Unwin.
1956¹   "The Philosophy of Logical Atomism", in: Robert C. Marsh (ed.), *Logic and Knowledge.* Essays 1901–1950. London: Allen and Unwin, 175–281.
1956²   "Logical Atomism", *Logic and Knowledge*, 323–343.
1959   *My Philosophical Development.* London: Allen and Unwin.

Rutten, Christian
1961   *Les catégories du monde sensible dans les "Ennéades" de Plotin.* Paris: Belles Lettres.

Ruwet, Nicolas
1972   *Langage, musique, poésie.* Paris: Seuil.

Saget, Annick Charles
1982   *L'architecture du divin.* Mathématique et philosophie chez Plotin et Proclus. Paris: Belles Lettres.

Saussure, Ferdinand de
1967– *Cours de linguistique générale.* Édition critique par E. Engler.
1974 Wiesbaden: Harrassowitz.

Schaaf, Julius
1984 "Aristoteles 'Erste Wissenschaft' als Relationstheorie Betrachter", *Perspektiven der Philosophie* 10:325–334.

Schmitt, A.
1930 "Mathematik und Zahlenmystik", in: Martin Grabmann and Joseph Mausbach (eds.), *Aurelius Augustinus.* Köln, 353–366.

Schoendorf, Hildegard
1974 *Plotins Umformung der platonischen Lehre vom Schönen.* Bonn: Habelt.

Scholz, Gunther
1969 "'Struktur' in der mittelalterlichen Hermeneutik", *Archiv für Begriffsgeschichte* 13:73–75.

Schrade, Leo
1930 "Das propaedeutische Ethos in der Musikausschauung des Boethius", *Zeitschrift für Geschichte der Erziehung und des Unterricht* 20:179–215.
1932 "Die Stellung der Musik in der Philosophie des Boethius als Grundlage der ontologischen Musikerziehung", *Archiv für Geschichte der Philosophie* 41:368–400.
1947 "Music in the Philosophy of Boethius", *Musical Quarterly* 33:188–200.

Schrimpf, Gangolf
1973 "Zur Frage der Authentizität unserer Texte von Johannes Scottus' 'Annotationes in Martianum'", in: John J. O'Meara and Ludwig Bieler (eds.), *The Mind of Eriugena.* Dublin: Irish University Press, 125–139.
1980 "Johannes Scottus Eriugena und die Rezeption des Martianus Capella im karolingischen Bildungswesen", in: Werner Beierwaltes (ed.), *Eriugena, Studien zu seinen Quellen.* Heidelberg: Winter, 135–148.
1982 *Das Werk des Johannes Scottus Eriugena im Rahmen des Wissenschaftsverständnisses seiner Zeit.* Münster: Aschendorff.
1989 "Die systematische Bedeutung der beiden logischen Einteilungen (divisiones) zu Beginn von 'Periphyseon'", *Giovanni Scoto nel suo tempo.* Spoleto, 113–151.
1990 "Der Begriff des Elements in 'Periphyseon' III", in: Werner Beierwaltes (ed.), *Begriff und Metapher. Sprachform des Denkens bei Eriugena.* Heidelberg: Winter, 65–79.

Schubert, Venanz
1968 *Pronoia und Logos*. Die Rechtfertigung der Weltordnung bei Plotin. Salzburg: Pustet.
Sebeok, Thomas A. (ed.)
1960 *Style in Language*. Cambridge/MA: MIT Press.
Shanzer, Danuta
1986 *A Philosophical and Literary Commentary on Martianus Capella's "De Nuptiis Philologiae et Mercurii", Book I*. Berkeley — Los Angeles: University California Press.
Sheldon-Williams, Inglis P.
1961 "The Title of Eriugena's 'Periphyseon'", *Studia Patristica* 3/1: 297–302.
1967 "The Greek Christian Platonist Tradition from the Cappadocians to Maximus and Eriugena", in: A. Hilary Armstrong (ed.), *Cambridge History of Later Greek and Early Medieval Philosophy*. Cambridge: Cambridge University Press, 421–533.
Simone, Raffaele
1972 "Sémiologie augustinienne", *Semiotica* 6:1–31.
Spitzer, Leo
1963 *Classical and Christian Ideas of World Harmony*. Baltimore/MD: Johns Hopkins University Press.
Stahl, William H., Johnson, Richard, and Burge, E. L.
1971– *Martianus Capella and the Seven Liberal Arts*. 2 volumes. New
1977 York: Columbia University Press.
Starobinski, Jean
1971 *Les mots sous les mots*. Les anagrammes de Ferdinand de Saussure. Paris: Gallimard.
Steel, Carlos
1986 "La création de l'univers dans l'homme selon Jean Scot Érigène", in: Christian Wenin (ed.), *L'homme et son univers au moyen âge I*. Louvain-la-Neuve: Institut Supérieur de Philosophie, 205–210.
Stock, Brian
1967 "The Philosophical Anthropology of Johannes Scottus Eriugena", *Studi Medievali*, 3ª serie 8:1–57.
1972 *Myth and Science in the Twelfth Century*. A Study of Bernard Silvester. Princeton: Princeton University Press.
1980 "In Search of Eriugena's Augustine", in: Werner Beierwaltes (ed.), *Eriugena, Studien zu seinen Quellen*. Heidelberg: Winter, 85–104.
Strawson, P. F.
1950 "On Referring", *Mind* 59:320–344.
Stump, Eleonore
1978 *Boethius's "De Topicis Differentiis"*. Translated with Notes and Essays on the Text. Ithaca/NY: Cornell University Press.

Svoboda, Karel
    1933   *L'esthétique de saint Augustin et ses sources*. Diss. Brno.
Taeger, Burkhard
    1970   *Zahlensymbolik bei Hraban, bei Hincmar und im "Heliand"*. Studien zur Zahlensymbolik im Mittelalter. München: Beck.
"Tel Quel"
    1968   *Théorie d'ensemble*. Paris: Seuil.
Théry, Gabriel
    1931   "Scot Érigène traducteur de Denys", *Archivum Latinitatis Medii Aevi* 6, 2:185–278.
Thom, René and Marcus, Solomon
    1986   "Mathematics and Semiotics", in: Thomas A. Sebeok (ed.), *Encyclopedic Dictionary of Semiotics I*. Berlin: Mouton-De Gruyter, 487–497.
Thomson, Rodney M.
    1980   "The Reception of Censorinus, 'De Die Natali' in Pre-Renaissance Europe", *Antichthon* 14:177–185.
Thunberg, Lars
    1965   *Microcosm and Mediator*. The Theological Anthropology of Maximus the Confessor. Lund: Gleerup.
Todorov, Tsvetan
    1967[1]   *Littérature et signification*. Paris.
    1967[2]   "Connaissance de la parole", *Word* 23:500–518.
    1977   *Théories du symbole*. Paris: Seuil.
Togeby, Knud
    1965   *Structure immanente de la langue française*, 2nd edition. Paris.
Touchette, Gilles
    1986   "L'affixation dans le 'Periphyseon'. Analyse générale et étude d'un cas-type", in: Guy-H. Allard (ed.), *Jean Scot écrivain*. Montréal — Paris: Bellarmin — Vrin, 327–341.
Trouillard, Jean
    1956   "L'unité humaine selon Jean Scot Érigène", *L'homme et son prochain*: Actes du VIIIe Congrès des Sociétés de philosophie de langue française. Paris, 298–301.
    1976   "La notion de 'théophanie' chez Érigène", in: Stanislas Breton (ed.), *Manifestation et révélation*. Paris: Beauchesne, 15–39.
Trubetzkoy, Nikolai S.
    1969   *Principles of Phonology*. Translated by Christiane Baltaxe. Berkeley/Los Angeles: University California Press.
Turlot, F.
    1985   "Le logos chez Plotin", *Les études philosophiques* 4:517–528.

Ushida, N.
1984 "Le concept de relation chez Aristote", *Reports of the Keio Institute of Cultural and Linguistic Studies* 16:47–65.
Vance, Eugene
1986 *Mervelous Signals. Poetics and Sign Theory in the Middle Ages*. Lincoln/NB: University of Nebraska Press.
1987 *From Topic to Tale. Logic and Narrativity in the Middle Ages*. Minneapolis/MN: University of Minnesota Press.
Vance, Eugene and Brind' Amour, Lucie (eds.)
1983 *Archéologie du signe*. Toronto: Pontifical Institute of Mediaeval Studies.
Van Helden, Albert
1985 *Measuring the Universe. Cosmic Dimensions from Aristarchus to Halley*. Chicago: University of Chicago Press.
Vecchi, Giuseppe ed.
1950 *Praecepta artis musicae collecta ex libris sex Augustini "De Musica"*, Bologna.
Viarre, Simone
1975 "Cosmologie antique et commentaire de la création du monde", *Centro Italiano di Studi sull'alto Medioevo, Settimane* 22:541–573.
Vincent, Alexandre J. and Martin, Thomas H.
1865 *Passage du traité de la musique d'Aristide Quintilien rélatif au nombre nuptial de Platon*, Rome.
Viret, J.
1980 "Harmonie musicale et harmonie naturelle à l'époque carolingienne", in: Danielle Buschinger and André Crépin (eds.), *Musique, littérature et société au moyen âge*. Paris, 85–98.
1983 "Le quaternaire des éléments et l'harmonie cosmique selon Isidore de Séville", in: Danielle Buschinger and Andre Crépin (eds.), *Les quatre éléments dans la culture médiévale*. Göppingen: Kümmerle, 7–26.
Völker, Walther
1958 *Kontemplation und Ekstase bei Pseudo-Dionysius Areopagita*. Wiesbaden: Steiner.
Vollrath, Ernst
1969 *Studien zur Kategorienlehre des Aristoteles*. Ratingen: Henn.
Vossen, Peter
1950 "Über die Elementen-Syzygien", in: Bernhard Bischoff and Suso Brechter (eds.), *Liber Floridus* = Festschrift Paul Lehmann. St. Ottilien: Eos Verlag der Erzabtei, 33–46.
Vyver, André van de
1929 "Les étapes du développement philosophique du haut moyen âge", *Revue Belge de philologie et d'histoire* 8:425–452.

Waeltner, Ernst L.
1977 *"Organicum melos". Zur Musikanschauung des Iohannes Scottus (Eriugena)*. München: Verlag der Bayerischen Akademie der Wissenschaften/ Beck.

Waerden, Bartel L. van der
1949 "Die Arithmetik der Pythagoreer I", *Mathematische Annalen* 120: 127–153.

Weisweiler, Heinrich.
1952 "Die Ps.-Dionysiuskommentare 'In Coelestem Hierarchiam' des Skotus Eriugena und Hugos von St. Viktor", *Recherches de théologie ancienne et médiévale* 19:26–47.

Wetherbee, Winthrop
1972 *Platonism and Poetry in the Twelfth Century*, The Literary Influence of the School of Chartres. Princeton/NJ: Princeton University Press.

White, Alison
1981 "Boethius and the Medieval Quadrivium", in: Margaret Gibson (ed.), *Boethius. His Life, Thought and Influence*. Oxford: Blackwell, 162–205.

Wille, Gunther
1967 *Musica romana. Die Bedeutung der Musik im Leben der Römer*. Amsterdam: Schippers.

Wiora, Walter
1971 "Das vermeintliche Zeugnis des Johannes Eriugena für die Anfänge der abendländischen Mehrstimmigkeit", *Acta Musicologica* 43:33–43.

Witt, Rex E.
1938 "The Plotinian Logos and its Stoic Basis", *Classical Quarterly* 32:190–196.

Wittgenstein, Ludwig
1953 *Philosophische Untersuchungen (Philosophical Investigations)*. Translated by Gertrude E. M. Anscombe. Oxford: Blackwell.
1958 *Preliminary Studies for the "Philosophical Investigations". Generally known as the Blue and Brown Books*. Oxford: Blackwell.

Wunderli, Peter
1972 *Ferdinand de Saussure und die Anagramme*. Linguistik und Literatur. Tübingen: Niemeyer.
1981 "Saussure und die 'signification'", in: Jürgen Trabant (ed.), *Logos Semantikos* = Festschrift Eugenio Coseriu, I. Berlin: De Gruyter, 267–284.

Zanoncelli, Luisa
1977 "La filosofia musicale di Aristide Quintiliano", *Quaderni Urbinati di cultura classica* 24:51–93.

Zeman, J. Jay
 1977 "Peirce's Theory of Signs", in: Thomas A. Seboek (ed.), *A Perfusion of Signs*. Bloomington/IN: Indiana University Press, 22–39.
Ziolkowski, Jan
 1985 *Alan of Lille's Grammar of Sex. The Meaning of Grammar to a Twelfth-Century Intellectual*. Cambridge/MA: Medieval Academy of America.

Addenda to bibliography (1995)

The following items were published (or became known to the author) after *Concord in Discourse* was completed.

Beierwaltes, Werner
 1994 *Eriugena. Grundzüge seines Denkens*. Frankfurt a. M.: Klostermann.
Bernhard, Michael and Bower, Calvin (eds.)
 1993+ *Glossa maior in institutionem musicam Boethii*. München: Verlag der Bayerischen Akademie der Wissenschaften/Beck. (2 volumes so far published).
Martello, Concetto
 1990 *Analogia e fisica in Giovanni Scoto*. Firenze: La nuova Italia.

Index

Abbo of Fleury, 170–172
   n. 151
Absolute, 15; *see also* Relative
Accident, *see* Substance
Actant (Greimas), n. 256
Actualization of semes, 83–85, 92, 94, 97, 139, 187, 192, 214, 231
   nn. 269, 380, 807
Adalbold of Utrecht, 231, 265–268
   n. 151
Adelard of Bath, 58, 63
Aesthetics, n. 521
Affirmation, 157–158, 162, 182–184, 186, 203
   nn. 700, 706, 930–931
Alan of Lille, 56–58, 65–66, 167, 169–170, 224–227
   n. 182
Alcuin, 129
Allard, G.-H., nn. 163, 663, 953
Allegory, 188 ff.
   nn. 951, 954, 982
Alverny, M.-T. d', n. 677
Ambrose, 148, 217
   n. 146
Amerio, F., n. 485
Ammonius, nn. 224, 230, 607
Anagrammes, n. 17
Analogia, 130–132, 142, 148–149, 151, 154–155, 199
   nn. 566, 755; *see also* Proportionality
Angels, 150 ff., 199–201, 233–236,
   n. 677
Anonymous (1C BC), n. 955
Anonymous (9C), 231, 255, 260–261

Anonymous (11C), nn. 431–433, 435, 437–442, 444–447, 449
Anonymous (12C), n. 189
Antithesis, n. 533; *see also* Contraries
Apuleius, 167–169
   nn. 605, 611
Arbor Porphyriana, 15
   nn. 126, 282
Archimedes, 258, 264
Aristides Quintilianus, n. 835
Aristotle, 47–51, 74–75, 122, 125, 167, 182–184
   nn. 67, 77, 222–223, 288, 512–517, 525, 529, 532, 535, 541, 605, 700, 775, 972
Arnoux, G., n. 594
Articulation, first or second, n. 994
Arts, *see* Sciences
Aspects, astrological, 265
Asymmetrical relations, *see* Symmetrical relations
Atomism, logical, 52
Augustine, 21–28, 32–34, 35–40, 44–45, 89, 98, 100–103, 116–118, 120–128, 138, 142, 148, 156–158, 163, 183, 188, 191, 199
   nn. 80, 140–152, 166–174, 179, 308, 405, 407–408, 411, 413–414, 420, 423–424, 426, 431–432, 441–442, 446–447, 448, 484–492, 510–511, 518, 520–522, 524, 526, 528, 531, 533, 536–538, 540, 542, 544, 546, 549, 551, 553, 555–556, 610, 723, 741, 852, 869

Augustine, ps.-, 73–76, 83, 100
    nn. 288–307, 312
Aurelian of Réôme, 58, 60
    n. 185
Axis, 19–20, 70, 72–73, 83–86,
    89 ff., 141, 186, 192 ff., 212–214,
    232
    nn. 111, 264, 279, 319, 324, 390,
    510, 517–518, 559, 602, 606, 702,
    864, 900, 940, 992

Bach, E., n. 82
Bachelard, G., n. 584
Balthasar, H. U. von, n. 974
Bambrough, R., n. 99
Barthes, R., nn. 79, 85–86, 120–122,
    127, 131, 133, 139, 234, 324, 543,
    955, 967, 983
Basil, 148
    n. 146
Bataillon, L.-J., n. 453
Batschelet-Massini, W., n. 336
Beauty, 21, 40, 123
Bede, n. 151
Bedeutung (Frege), n. 95
Beierwaltes, W., nn. 147, 163, 521,
    775, 866, 953
Being, 117, 182, 185
Berkeley, G., n. 245
Bernard Silvestris, 58, 64–65,
    221–223, 231, 248, 252–253,
    271–273
    n. 185
Bernhard, M., nn. 165, 336, 493
Berno of Reichenau, n. 188
Bertin, F., n. 974
Bible, 18, 38, 149, 199–201, 213,
    219, 233
Binary, 15, 18–19, 69 ff., 139–141,
    212; *see also* Ternary, Unitary
Black, M., n. 82
Blanché, R., n. 89
Blowing up (Eco), n. 211

Body, 44, 58, 272
Boethius, 40–45, 58–60, 74, 86–89,
    95–96, 104–107, 115–120, 140,
    149, 167
    nn. 157, 179–180, 189, 192, 195,
    224, 253, 336 - 358, 396, 484,
    493–503, 507, 596, 607, 611, 662,
    699
Boeuf, P. le, n. 407
Boll, F., n. 584
Bonnardière, A. M. la, n. 147
Bovo of Corvey, 231, 248–251
Bower, C., n. 493
Bradley, F. H., n. 237
Brøndal, V., nn. 89, 110
Brunner, F., n. 454
Bruyne, E. de, n. 184
Burge, E. L., n. 816
Burkert, W., n. 612
Burnett, C., n. 452

Calcidius, 116–117, 120, 128–139,
    142, 148–149, 154, 164
    nn. 560–561, 565–568, 586–587,
    591–592, 595, 620–621, 659
Caldwell, J., n. 336
Cantineau, n. 131
Cassiodorus, n. 151
Cassirer, E., n. 89
Categories, Aristotelian, 75–78,
    83–84, 100, 122, 139, 186
    n. 308
Celestial world, 265–268
Censorinus, 111–112, 119, 231, 255,
    257–258
    n. 503
Chadwick, H., n. 336
Chamberlain, D. S., n. 180
Christ, 171, 217
Cicero, 249
    nn. 75, 144, 164, 699
Cilleruello, P. L., n. 405
Classemes, n. 257

Claudianus Mamertus, 140 n. 151
Clement of Alexandria, n. 146
Clusters, 73
Coallier, C., nn. 163, 317, 366
Code, 5, 231–232 ff. n. 993
Cognitive, *see* Existent
Complex, *see* Simple
Concept, 15, 213
Connotation, 90, 185, 187 nn. 120, 364, 809, 983
Constant, *see* Function
Content, of image, *see* Form of image
Contextual selection, 48–49 n. 213
Conti, A. D., n. 296
Continuity, axis of, 73, 181, 192 nn. 264, 283, 323, 381, 510, 765, 928, 992
Contradiction, law of, 5, 89
Contraries, 24, 123–128, 133, 139, 156–164, 250–251 nn. 515, 518, 533, 535, 543, 741
Converse domain, *see* Domain
Conversion, *see* Procession
Corsini, E., n. 886
Courtés, J., nn. 3, 9, 81, 110, 137, 257–258
Courtine, J.-F., nn. 307, 402
Creation, 21–24, 26–28, 32–34, 39, 71, 123, 156, 163
Cress, D. A., n. 519
Cristante, L., n. 844
Cristiani, M., nn. 266, 402

Decoder, *see* Encoder
Deconstruction, 17
Dehnert, E. J., n. 484
Deiters, H., n. 835
Delatte, A., n. 612
Denotation, *see* Connotation

Derrida, J., 5 nn. 10, 34, 51, 70, 85–86, 119, 123, 258, 335, 371, 450, 775
Descent, *see* Procession
Desrosiers-Bonin, D., nn. 312, 317
Dewey, J., n. 450
Dialectical, 15, 70, 72, 83–86, 89–90, 92–94, 139–141, 142, 212–214, 232
Dialogism, n. 312
Dictionary (Eco), n. 97
Différance (Derrida), 5 nn. 10, 34, 51, 371, 450
Different, *see* Same
Differential, signifying (Kristeva), 6–7
Dionysius, ps.-, 83, 89, 96, 142, 150 ff., 182–184, 191, 199–204 nn. 696, 725, 886, 896, 928
Dissemination (Derrida), nn. 335, 450
Dissimilar, *see* Similar
Dissimilar image, 214–216 nn. 930, 935, 946
Division, n. 699
Dörrie, H., n. 566
Domain, 46
Dondaine, H., n. 677
Dronke, P., n. 451
Duchez, M.-E., n. 163
Duhem, P., n. 584
Dyadic relations, *see* Monadic relations

Eco, U., 5, 8–9 nn. 3, 11, 79, 83, 86, 95, 97, 101, 106, 108–109, 121, 126, 211, 213, 259, 261, 282, 775, 784–796, 809, 993–994
Edelstein, H., n. 485
Elements, 26, 29–34, 117, 144 ff., 248–249, 271–273 nn. 584, 636
Emanation, 73, n. 871

Encoder, 198
Encyclopaedia (Eco), 72–73, 231
  nn. 97, 261, 559, 775, 990
Entanglement, semiotic, n. 603
Equal, 14, 24, 27, 32–33, 46, 50,
  88–90, 94–95, 116–121, 133, 233
Equivalence, axis of, 72–73, 83, 181,
  192, 232
  nn. 264, 281, 323, 381, 510, 765,
  928, 992
Equivalence, semiotic, n. 89
Eratosthenes, 257, 263
Eriugena, 28–34, 69–73, 77–86,
  89–103, 120, 129, 139–164,
  181–187, 191–199, 210ff., 231,
  255, 261–264
  nn. 92, 151, 154–156, 158–161,
  163, 185, 266, 267–268, 270–277,
  307–308, 310–311, 317, 322, 335,
  358, 366, 368–371, 373, 375, 377,
  379, 382–384, 386, 389, 391–394,
  397, 399, 402, 405–407, 410–413,
  415–416, 418–421, 423–424,
  426–427, 429, 504, 599–601, 604,
  611–616, 617–620, 622, 624,
  628–631, 636, 638–639, 641, 643,
  645, 647, 650, 653, 656–657, 663,
  665 668, 670, 671–675,
  677–680, 696–697, 703–712,
  719–721, 723, 725, 727, 729–732,
  737–739, 741, 743, 745, 749–756,
  769, 771–782, 797, 799, 859,
  866–870, 872–875, 877–879, 882,
  885, 889–896, 898, 902, 916, 946,
  954, 956–965, 969–980,
  981–989
Etymology, 116, 193
Evangeliou, C., n. 288
Evans, G.R., nn. 451, 479
Even, 87
Evil, 117, 122, 125, 128, 156, 158
Existent, 15, 70, 72, 84, 89–92,
  212–214

External relations, *see* Internal
  relations
Extreme, 130–141, 146, 150, 154,
  164–166; *see also* Mediator

Fabbri, P., n. 993
Faes de Mottoni, B., n. 896
Family resemblances, 16–17
  nn. 81, 98, 100, 116, 126, 257, 806
Fate, 117
Favonius Eulogius, 231, 255,
  258–259
Figure, 188–191, 200–201, 213, 216
  nn. 75, 956
Firstness (Peirce), nn. 102–104, 450
Flasch, K., n. 311
Floss, H.J., n. 154
Fodor, J., n. 126
Form of content (Hjelmslev), 8
  nn. 58, 263, 932
Form of expression (Hjelmslev), 8
  n. 58
Form of images, 215
Forms, Platonic, 29, 32, 116–117
Foussard, J.-C., n. 872
Frede, M., n. 869
Freeman, E., n. 450
Frege, G., nn. 61, 95, 809
Frova, C., n. 484
Function, n. 204
Function, propositional, n. 212

Gandillac, M. de, nn. 1, 677
Geno-text (Kristeva), 7
  n. 34
Genus, 14–15, 85, 91, 93, 139, 149
  nn. 215, 282, 699, 775
Geometrical analogy, 19
Gerbert, 172–175
Gérold, T., n. 179
Gersh, S., nn. 314–315, 360, 413,
  451, 462, 470, 472, 474, 560, 694,
  728, 756, 816, 886, 896

God, 23–26, 39, 72, 78, 83, 89, 103, 156 ff., 182–186, 216–218
Goldmann, L., n. 1
Goodness, 89, 117, 125, 212
Graeser, A., n. 869
Gram (Derrida), nn. 10, 21–24
Grammar, 162, 188
Greenberg, J. H., n. 82
Gregory of Nyssa, 98–99, 101, 142, 148, 217
nn. 409, 413, 628
Greimas, A. J., nn. 3, 5, 9, 38, 81, 83, 110, 112–113, 126, 137, 213, 234, 256–258, 262, 279, 322, 517–518, 543, 663, 802–803
Ground, 16, n. 105
Guiraud, P., n. 993
Guitton, J., n. 407

Hadot, I., n. 850
Hadot, P., nn. 405, 605
Häring, N. M., nn. 451, 453, 677
Handschin, J., nn. 163, 594
Harmonic, 13–15, 18–19, 113 ff.; *see also* Logical, Semiotic
Harms, R., n. 82
Hegel, G. W. F., 53–55, nn. 235, 335, 450, 874
Heller, B., n. 493
Hermes Trismegistus, ps.-, 231, 248, 253–254
Herren, M., n. 853
Hjelmslev, L., 8
nn. 7, 9, 58–60, 62–63, 65, 86, 204, 260, 543, 784, 932, 967, 983
Homonymy, 74,
n. 291
Honorius Augustodunensis, 231, 255, 264–265
Hrotsvitha, 58, 61–63
Hüschen, H., n. 163

Hugh of St. Victor, 58, 64, 224–225, 231, 268–271
nn. 187, 191, 504
Huglo, M., n. 620
Hume, D., n. 245
Humours, 272–273
Huré, J., n. 485
Hyle, *see* Matter

Iamblichus, n. 254
Icon (Peirce), n. 771
Idealism, nn. 522, 928
Ideas, Platonic, n. 67; *see also* Forms, Platonic
Identity, semiotic, 15
n. 285
Illmer, D., n. 336
Illumination, 153–155, 200
Image, 201, 208 ff., 212–216
nn. 930–931, 935, 939–940, 945
Immanence, see Transcendence
Incarnation, 170
Incorporeals, Stoic, n. 869
Index (Peirce), n. 771
Ineffable, n. 389
Infinite semiosis, 215–216
nn. 86, 617
Integument, 240, 243, 246
Intellect, 97, 100, 102, 193 ff., 213
n. 538
Intensional semantics, 15
nn. 95, 809
Internal relations, 51–53
nn. 237, 329, 331, 857
Interpretant (Peirce), 8, 16, 184–185
nn. 102–103, 107, 115
Interpretation, 17–18, 21
Interpreter, 192, 196
nn. 64, 899, 901
Intertexte, n. 122
Intransitive relations, *see* Transitive relations

Irenaeus, n. 146
Isidore of Seville, 188
   nn. 151, 885
Isomorphism, 13
Isotopy, 27–28, 34, 40, 69, 71, 73, 125, 147, 231
   nn. 153, 258, 286, 809, 990
Jakobson, R., 5
   nn. 11, 78, 110, 133–134, 769
Jeauneau, E., nn. 360, 368, 451, 454, 853, 896, 953
Johnson, R., n. 816
Jolivet, J., n. 867
Jones, P., n. 163
Judgment, 101
Justice, 236–237

Karpinski, L.C., n. 336
Katz, J.J., n. 126
Keyser, E. de, n. 521
Kirwan, C., n. 535
Klibansky, R., n. 584
Kristeva, J., 6–7
   nn. 14–18, 20–47, 49–51, 69–70, 371
Kucharski, P., n. 612

Labdoma, 136
   n. 593
Lacan, J., 2–4, 7
   n. 86
Lakoff, G., n. 82
Lanham, R.A., n. 969
Lausberg, H., nn. 533, 956, 969
Lenaz, L., n. 816
Leonardi, C., nn. 163, 816, 853
Lepel, F. von, n. 493
Levine, P., n. 628
Lévi-Strauss, C., nn. 5, 7, 9, 79, 133, 603, 663
Lévy-Bruhl, L., n. 89
Lexeme, 13, 15–16, 18–19, 27, 34, 45, 48–49, 51, 69, 83–85, 90, 92, 94, 139, 181, 186, 192, 212, 215, 231
   nn. 81, 234, 256, 317, 319–322, 362, 365, 606–607, 764, 814, 898
Lexicalization, n. 256
Libéra, A. de, n. 605
Liebeschütz, H., n. 312
Lisible (Barthes), n. 121
Literal, 219–220
   n. 954
Logical, 18–19, 67 ff.; *see also* Harmonic, Semiotic
Logos, 50, 141, 143–144, 152; *see also* Reason
Lopez Silonis, R., n. 775
Louth, A., n. 886
Lucentini, P., n. 154
Lutz, C., n. 816

Maccagnolo, E., n. 451
Macrobius, 116, 140, 199, 227–228, 231, 240, 242–245, 249, 255, 258, 265, 267–269
   n. 609
Macrocosm, *see* Microcosm
Madec, G., nn. 154, 630
Man, 271–273
   nn. 975, 979
Manichaeans, 22–24, 28, 40, 45
Marenbon, J., n. 307
Marius Victorinus, 140
   n. 606
Marmo, C., n. 95
Martianus Capella, 1–2, 86, 107–109, 140, 149, 188–191, 197, 221, 231, 255, 259–260
   nn. 609, 611, 699, 816, 818–832, 834–851, 853, 856, 859, 864
Martin, T.H., n. 835
Masi, M., nn. 336, 493
Massera, G., n. 493
Mathematical, *see* Dialectical

Mathematics, 28, 30, 86, 104, 128
  nn. 25, 334–336, 345, 454
Mathiesen, T.J., nn. 140, 181
Mathon, G., n. 620
Matter, 24, 117, 212
Maximus the Confessor, 83, 194, 218–219
  nn. 360, 973–976
Meaning, 184–185
Means, 134–138, 248–251
  n. 596; *see also* Mediator
Measure, 24–25, 33, 40
  nn. 146–147, 149, 151
Mediator, 128 ff., 248–251
  nn. 561, 663, 809
Memory, 98–99, 188–189
Merguet, H., n. 164
Metaphor, 85, 159, 182–185, 269
  nn. 91, 775
Meyer, B., n. 140
Michel, P.-H., n. 336
Microcosm, 56, 58–60, 271
Mieri, F. di, n. 336
Minio-Paluello, L., n. 287
Mode, musical, 257, 260
Model, 6–7, 16–17
  nn. 17, 20, 51, 69
Model Q (Eco), n. 126
Monad, 73, 91–96, 117
  n. 389
Monadic, n. 240
Montico, M.G., n. 484
Moran, D., n. 974
Moutsopoulos, E., nn. 413, 594
Müller, A., n. 521
Münxelhaus, B., n. 163
Myth, 245–246
  n. 324

Names, divine, 158, 160, 182
  nn. 886, 939
Nature, 71, 160, 167, 212, 253
Nebois, J., n. 140

Negation, *see* Affirmation
Neoplatonism, 22, 25–28, 97, 116, 200
  n. 91
Neopythagoreanism, 86, 139, 148, 154
Nicomachus, 86, 118–119, 136
  nn. 345, 487
Nothing, 29
Nowak, A., n. 407
Nuchelmans, G., n. 816
Numbers, 24, 27, 32, 39, 87, 90 ff., 97 ff., 117, 171, 190, 198, 200, 219, 227, 233–235, 238, 240–248, 268–271
  nn. 368, 389, 405, 407, 422, 433, 439, 750
Nuptial number, n. 835

Obertello, L., nn. 336, 493
O'Connell, R.J., n. 521
Odd, *see* Even
Oehler, K., n. 450
Olivieri, F.J., n. 974
O'Meara, D., nn. 336, 368, 611, 866
One-many relations, 46
One-one relations, *see* One-many relations
Onofrio, G. d', nn. 266, 270, 307, 358, 611, 699, 866
Ontological, 69 ff., 115 ff.
Ooge, d', M.L., n. 336
Opposition, 4, 6, 19, 32–33, 56, 70–72, 76, 83, 121 ff., 140–141, 232
  nn. 127, 700
Order, 21, 23–25, 27–34, 38, 40, 42, 126, 150 ff.
Origen, 199, 231, 236–240
  n. 146
Other, *see* Same
Otloh of St. Emmeram, 116, 231, 233–236
  nn. 460, 504

Panofsky, E., n. 584
Paradigmatic, 19–20, 216 ff.
  nn. 955, 970
Paragram (Kristeva), *see* Model
Parodi, M., n. 151
Paronymy, *see* Homonymy
Part, 122–128, 138, 156, 158 ff.
  nn. 89, 518, 533, 552, 699, 723, 737
Participation, mythological, n. 89
Participation, Platonic, 29–32, 154–156, 193
Particulars, *see* Universals
Peirce, C. S., 8, 16
  nn. 66, 101–107, 450, 518, 617, 771, 787, 861
Pépin, J., n. 896
Peri, I., n. 146
Perl, C. J., n. 485
Pfligersdorffer, G., n. 287
Phano-text (Kristeva), 7
Phantasies, 97–99, 101
Philo, nn. 146, 608
Phonemes, 6, 182, 198
Physis, 272–273
Piaget, J, n. 1
Piemonte, G., n. 611
Pietzsch, G., n. 184
Pizzani, U., nn. 189, 407, 493
Planets, 255–265
Plato, 129, 141–142, 242–247, 249, 260, 265
  nn. 67, 245, 535, 565, 586, 605, 835
Platonism, 25, 29, 44, 49, 212, 265
  nn. 215, 291
Pliny 231, 255–257
Plotinus, 23, 25, 50, 122, 125
  nn. 141, 143–145, 152, 216–217, 219, 226–228, 232, 413, 521
Pohlenz, M., n. 869
Polysemy, 5, 200
  n. 973

Porphyry, 23, 50, 54, 74, 122, 140, 258
  nn. 216–217, 224, 232, 282, 605
Potiron, H., n. 493
Prédicats, *see* Actants
Prieto, L., n. 993
Primordial Causes, 29, 32, 72, 146
Privation, 125–126
Procession, 23–24, 71, 89, 93, 163, 200–201
Proclus, 154
  nn. 606, 609
Proportion, *see* Ratio
Proportionality, 34, 91, 117, 145–146, 148–149, 153, 199, 201, 224, 232;
  see also Analogia
Proposition, 167
  nn. 605, 611, 809
Providence, 24, 116, 126, 127, 128, 252
Ps.-Hierarchy, axis of, 72–73, 86, 139, 181, 192
  nn. 264, 282, 323, 381, 510, 928, 992
Pseudo-logic, 77
  n. 309
Psychology, 128 ff., 156, 164, 191
Ptolemy, 118–119, 266
Putnam, H., n. 82
Pythagoras, 256–257, 259, 262–263
Pythagoreanism, 25, 43, 54

Quadrivium, *see* Trivium
Qualisign (Peirce), n. 771
Quillian, R., n. 126
Quine, W. V. O., n. 82

Ratio, 43, 78 ff., 107, 111, 116, 118–119, 149, 232
Realism, nn. 799, 917, 928
Realism, grammatical, nn. 867, 869
Reason, faculty of, 102, 183
Reason, 93–94, 194; *see also* Logos

Recapitulation, 217–219
  nn. 953, 969, 972–973
Referent, 7–8, 45–46, 191–192
Regali, M., n. 336
Regino of Prüm, nn. 183, 504
Relation, 4–9, 14–21, 45–55, 69 ff., 115 ff., 181 ff.; *see also* Absolute
Remigius of Auxerre, 231, 271–272
  nn. 185, 504, 885
Representamen (Peirce), 8
  nn. 102, 104
Return, n. 756
Reversion, *see* Procession
Rheme, (Peirce), n. 771
Rhythm, 118 ff.
Richards, I. A., nn. 91, 775
Robbins, F. E., n. 336
Roques, R., nn. 886, 896, 974
Roy, O. du, n. 147
Russell, B., 51–53
  nn. 135, 197–204, 212, 237–251

Saget, A. C., n. 405
Saints, 233–236
Salvation, 32, 235
Same, 5, 16–17, 27, 32–33, 116–117
Saussure, F. de, 6–8, 14
  nn. 7, 13, 17, 86, 95, 543, 955
Saxl, F., n. 584
Scale, musical, 43, 96, 118, 255–256
Schoendorf, H., n. 521
Schrade, L., n. 493
Schrimpf, G., nn. 270, 853
Sciences, 30, 40, 86–87
S-code (Eco), n. 11
Scriptible (Barthes), *see* Lisible
Scripture, *see* Bible
Sedulius, 272
Self-contradiction, 192, n. 860
Sémanalyse (Kristeva), n. 16
Semantic, 14; *see also* Ontological

Semantics, intensional, 15
Semantic categories, 212 ff.
  nn. 125, 279
Semantic elements, 84
Semantic features, 70, 72–73
  nn. 260, 263, 279, 286
Semantic field, 15, 46, 48–51, 85
  nn. 97, 260
Semantic markers, 184
Semantic objects, *see* Semantic properties
Semantic process, 214
Semantic properties, 14–17, 193, 213
  nn. 126, 517
Semantic relation, 70
  nn. 260, 262–264
Semantic spectrum, 187
Seme, 13, 15–19, 27, 34, 45, 48–49, 51, 69–73, 85, 92, 94, 97, 140–141, 167, 170–172, 181, 185–187, 192, 212, 214–215
  nn. 81–82, 92–93, 256–258, 517, 606–607, 767, 801, 807, 809, 811, 814, 939–949
Sememe, 16–17, 71–72, 83, 90, 140–141, 167, 170–173, 181, 185–187, 214–215
  nn. 81, 257–258, 261, 269, 283, 285, 317, 319 - 320, 322, 363–365, 606–607, 764, 767, 770, 802–803, 809, 813, 939
Semiotic, 4–7, 14–15, 18–20, 27–28, 34, 139, 141, 179 ff., 195; *see also* Logical, Harmonic
Sense, 97–101
Sensible World, 22, 97–98
Sextus, n. 869
Shanzer, D., n. 816
Shaumyan, S. K., n. 28
Sheldon-Williams, I. P., nn. 154, 360, 872, 877, 974
Siger of Courtrai, n. 96

Sign, 6–7, 14, 16, 198
   nn. 552, 771
Sign-emitter, 197–198, 200
Sign-function, 8, 184–185
   n. 58
Significatio, medieval, nn. 95, 816, 869
Signification, *see* Signifier
Signified, *see* Signifier
Signified, mediated, 212–214, 216
   nn. 324, 884–885, 898–899
Signified, unmediated, *see* Signified, mediated
Signifier, 4–6, 8, 14–15, 181–187, 191 ff., 200, 232
   nn. 64, 71, 84, 86, 95, 288, 291, 450, 771, 797, 804–805, 852, 855, 866, 869, 874, 879, 898–899, 917, 993
Signifying category, nn. 864, 900
Signifying relation, 4–9, 191–192
   nn. 855, 861, 902
Sign-receiver, 197–198, 200
Sign-vehicle, 184
   n. 809
Silva, 252–253; *see also* Matter
Similar, 24, 27, 33, 44, 46, 50, 71–72, 124, 133, 160–161
Simple, 15, 70, 72, 84, 89–90, 139–141, 212–214
Simplicius, 49–50
   nn. 220–221, 224–225, 229–230, 232–233, 252–254
Sin, 102–103, 123, 127, 162
Sinn (Frege), n. 95
Soul, human, 44, 58, 97–103, 194, 198, 237–238, 264, 268–271
Space, *see* Time
Species, *see* Genus
Spirit, 116–117
Spirit, Holy, 217, 240, 242, 246
Spiritual, *see* Literal
Square of opposition, *see* Square, semiotic

Square, semiotic, 16–17, 20–21, 71–73, 139–141, 160, 167, 170–174, 181, 218–219
   nn. 112–116, 137, 270, 273, 279, 604, 611–613, 762, 769, 810, 940, 942–943
Stahl, W.H., n. 816
Starobinski, J., n. 17
Steel, C., n. 974
Stock, B., nn. 307, 611, 974
Strawson, P.F., n. 95
Structure, 4–9, 232
   nn. 7, 11, 20, 71, 74–75, 126, 164–165, 335, 509, 517, 855
Substance, 75, 163
   n. 535
Substance, graphic, 213
   n. 81
Substance of content (Hjelmslev), 8
   n. 58, 260, 932
Substance of expression (Hjelmslev), 8
   n. 58
Substance, phonic, 213
   nn. 81, 916
Substantive, 74, 182, 186
Super-affirmative, 158, 186–187
   nn. 712, 859
Suppositio, medieval, n. 95
Svoboda, K., n. 521
Symbol (Peirce), n. 771
Symbolism, 199 ff.
   nn. 833, 898, 951, 954
Symmetrical relations, 46–48
Syncategorematic terms, n. 869
Synecdoche, n. 533
Synonymy, *see* Homonymy
Syntactic markers, 184
   nn. 804–805
Syntagmatic, *see* Paradigmatic

Tenses, n. 869
Ternary, 14–19, 25, 69, 115 ff., 181 ff.;
   see also Binary

Tetractys, 111
Texts, 6–7, 18, 38
Themistius, 74
Theo Smyrnaeus, n. 608
Théry, G., n. 896
Thierry of Chartres, 115–118, 172–177, 221–222
  nn. 151, 451, 454, 456–459, 461, 463–469, 471, 473, 475–476, 479–480, 481–483
Thomas of Hereford, n. 96
Thunberg, L., n. 974
Timaeus, the, 129, 132, 141, 242, 245, 258, 265
Time, 22–24, 28, 31–32, 40, 71–72, 97, 99–103
Togeby, K., n. 89
Topics, 69
Touchette, G., n. 317
Trace (Derrida), n. 10
Transcendence, 146–148, 157–159, 161–164, 187, 194, 196–198, 212, 214
  nn. 286, 646, 706, 946
Transference, semic, 214–215
Transition, 216–217
  nn. 953, 956
Transitive relations, 46–48
Triads, 16; *see also* Ternary
Trinity, 24–27, 85, 116–117, 142, 170–171, 234
  n. 484
Trivium, 115, 221
Trouillard, J., nn. 775, 974
Trubetzkoy, N. S., n. 131
Truth, 182

Unequal, *see* Equal
Unitary, 94–97, 116, 120, 124; *see also* Binary

Universals, 13–14, 155–157
  nn. 82, 723

Vagueness, n. 82
Valeur (Saussure), nn. 7, 543
Variable, *see* Function
Varro, 188
Verb, 74, 182, 184, 186
Viarre, S., n. 584
Vincent, A., n. 835
Viret, J., nn. 163, 584
Virgil, 242, 246–247
Vitruvius, 227–228
Voelker. W., n. 886
Vollrath, E., n. 288
Vossen, D., n. 584

Waeltner, E. L., n. 163
Waerden, B. van der, n. 336
White, A., n. 336
Whole, *see* Part
Wille, G., n. 179
William of Aubérive, 107, 109–111
William of Conches, 231, 240–248, 255, 264–265
  n. 504
Wiora, W., n. 163
Wittgenstein, L., nn. 98, 100, 248
Words, 15, 74, 182
World body, 129–134, 143
World soul, 58, 116, 134–138, 149, 240–248
Writing, 17–18
Wunderli, P., n. 17

Zanoncelli, L., n. 835
Zigzag, 84
Zodiac, signs of, 253–254